ENERGETICS
OF
PERSONALITY

ARISTOS PSYCHOLOGY TRILOGY
VOLUME I

John G. Geier
Dorothy E. Downey

Aristos Publishing House
Minneapolis, Minnesota

First published March, 1989.

ISBN: 0-927634-03-1

Printed in the United States of America.
Library of Congress Catalog Card Number 88-83729

Editor, Kathleen Jesme
Text and Graphic Design, Ginger McCauley
Typesetting Coordination, Shirley Heyer

Published by Aristos Publishing House

CONTENTS

Book I: Workshops

Book II: Interpretation

Introduction

Defining a Self

O ver a lifetime we encounter many forces that have the power to influence us. Some are human; we can see and touch them. Other forces have only a token human face; we are confronted with the power of the anonymous "they."

Many of these forces conflict with one another. Breeding guilt and anxiety within us, they create pain. When individuals are overwhelmed by these forces, they are defined by the needs of others. Becoming an extension, they fulfill another's purpose, abide by another's conviction—even live out another's life.

Parents are the first major force. When we are young, parents are omnipotent figures who spell out right and wrong. Using the potent tools of acceptance and rejection, they shape us according to their perception of the world. They help to flesh out the "bare bones" of our temperament with behavior and character.

Other significant individuals make their appearance as we move through life. They influence our behavior because of their proximity or because we desire their approval. We are shaped by our interactions with siblings, playmates, school friends, confidantes, and work associates. Through all these relationships, we play out variations of the joy in being chosen first and the anguish of being last.

Our loved ones also have great defining power. A spouse or intimate friend plumbs depths that others cannot reach, holding the keys to our innermost self. They touch us through their closeness, affection, sexual satisfaction, or intellectual stimulation. Even our children have defining power. Representing our immortality here on earth, children arouse our protectiveness and our sense of responsibility. They shape us even as we shape them.

However influential these forces are, they do have names and faces. Identifying the force is half of the struggle in defining ourselves. It is possible to stand up to an individual. It is much more difficult to contend with the power of an essentially faceless entity.

Less than 10 percent of the population are self-employed and, thus, exempt from the defining force of the work organization. The majority of people are influenced during most of their lives by job accountabilities that define and often limit. Policies and procedures are often issued by an anonymous "they." As personal responsibilities grow, many allow the power of the work organization over them to increase. Seeking a sense of security, they console themselves with the remuneration.

Finally, there are the compelling forces that seek to connect what we do in this life with what we can expect in the next. In exchange for ascribing to certain beliefs or adhering to specified standards, many are accepted into a spiritual fellowship with others. They are comforted by the presence of a covenant for the next life. Ultimately, they are influenced by their *hope* for inclusion and by their *fear* of exclusion from the next world.

Defining of self does not take place in a vacuum. It occurs against the backdrop of people and events of a certain time. These forces are often essential to the individual. Religion, for example, may infuse the individual with hope and strength. Many of these forces represent greater knowledge, experience, concern—even wisdom.

Still, we must be willing to try our wings—to find our unique path in life. To test any of these forces is to risk rejection, disapproval, error, ostracism, isolation. And yet, risk we must. It is the only way to define ourselves and to come to terms with the conflicting forces. We have the freedom of choice and the power of will. The alternative is to be blown hither and yon by the opposing winds of life.

Amidst these conflicting forces, the central human problem becomes obscured. Submerged under layer after layer of expectations, we have difficulty identifying the basic problem in the multiplicity of answers.

**We all share the same human problem—
the push toward a shared existence and
the pull toward a separate existence.**

The three possible answers to this push-pull dilemma are depicted in the following illustration.

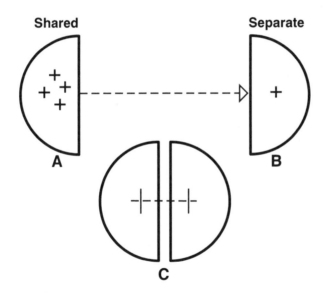

An overemphasis on the pole of shared existence (A) may result in the failure to develop individual potential. The *psychology of adjustment* promotes a shared existence. A predominant mode in the past, this approach assumed that all emotional difficulties were primarily a failure to adjust to the group. However, adjustment to negative conditions is ill-advised. Such an approach can result in negative relationships, stagnant organizations, and a static society.

An overemphasis on the pole of separate existence (B) may result in losing contact with the common reality that makes it possible to live and work together. The *psychology of growth* inclines toward a separate existence. Coming to the forefront in the last two decades, this approach has stressed self-actualization along specified need levels. However, the levels assumed a sameness in individuals. This approach cited the needs as physiological, safety and security, love and belongingness, self-esteem and self-actualization. It failed to consider freedom, justice, and order as basic rather than higher needs. Unchecked, a drive toward self-actualization can result in a "me first" mentality. An undue accent on separateness can breed a dangerous isolation.

An imbalance on either pole of existence—separate or shared—results in a weak tie between the two realities.

Aristos Psychology enables us to complete the *connection* between our separate and shared existence (C). It goes beyond the adjustment mode and the growth mode. Aristos Psychology is the *psychology of responsibility.* Making the vital connection between the two realities, we enrich and temper both of them. We are able to develop our individual potential while renewing the relationship, the organization, or the society. *In defining ourselves, we help to redefine the forces surrounding us.*

Energetics of Personality is the first in a trilogy of books that focus on the major tenets of Aristos Psychology. Through the *Behavior Indicator,* you will be able to identify the three components of your personality—temperament, behavior, and character. The Behavior Indicator is a psychological instrument that is self-administering, self-developing, and self-interpreting.

Users of our educational material will recognize it as a quantum leap from our previous works. One of the stimuli for these innovations was the work of D. Havice (1977), who challenged psychologists to build a bridge between psychology and philosophy.

Some of the major differences between the Behavior Indicator and existing instruments are:

- Earlier instruments focused only on behavior. The Behavior Indicator identifies and describes not only *behavior*—but *temperament* and *character* as well.

- Earlier instruments were descriptive only. The Behavior Indicator describes and *evaluates*—a critical factor in defining of self.

In addition, *Energetics of Personality* contains a series of personal workshops that present key concepts and relevant personal interpretations that individualize learning. These are some of the objectives that you can expect to accomplish:

- Create a climate of compatibility in your work and social environment.

- Use newly discovered knowledge to tap another's private logic.

- Effect change in yourself and others through an analysis of conscious intention.

- Learn about the power of unconscious evaluation.

- Persuade others through quality action.

- Use behavior dynamics in change, conflict, control, and choice.

- Identify your character strength and limitation in relating to others.

Energetics of Personality is more than a ray of light piercing the darkness. It is a powerful searchlight that illuminates your pathway from survival to success. It enables you to take charge of your life and direct your energy toward those choices that influence your destiny.

Chapter I

Emotions: Psychic Energy

Personal energy is our most precious resource. It determines what we can and cannot do.

Energy is most often associated with a proper diet, sufficient exercise, and good physical health. Few make an automatic connection between emotions and energy. Yet our affective nature—feeling, emotion, and passion—has the power to energize or to stifle our actions.

A High Price

A recent study suggests the high price that we are paying for not understanding the connection between emotions and energy. In a study of 1,159 adults without observable illnesses, K. Kroenke (1988) discovered that 24 percent of the study population identified fatigue as a *major* problem.

Even those who do not cite fatigue as a major problem often experience a lack of energy without a physical cause. Unfortunately, this can become the "normal" state. We can forget what it is like to feel vital and bursting with energy.

Thinking vs. Feeling

In western society, thinking has been overvalued. Consequently, feelings and emotions have been undervalued. Persons who express their feelings and emotions are often viewed as subjective, weak, or unstable. The very source of our psychic energy has been devalued, ignored, and often suppressed.

Historically, emotions were a part of philosophical discourse. About 100 years ago, psychology separated from philosophy. For the first time, emotions became the direct focus of study in the empirical laboratories of such early giants as Wundt (1893) and Titchner (1912).

Attention was also directed to the study of emotions by W. James (1890) and C. Lange (1922). Observing the excitation factor of emotions, they tried to interpret the bodily changes that occurred. They confirmed in the laboratory what great novelists had always known: emotions are activating.

Above all, it was S. Freud (1920) who forced the realization that feelings, emotions, and passions are central to our lives. Freud emerged from a biomedical background to pursue the study of emotions with rigor and discipline.

Freud worked with patients in the sexually repressed society of the Victorian era. Therefore, it is not surprising that his theory of energy within the personality focused on sexuality. He was dealing with the results of repressed sexual energy.

Over 50 years later, the richness of his theoretical work still provides hypotheses for research. The importance of sexuality as a source of energy has been replaced by other formulations.

From Freud's work and those who followed—Carl Jung, Alfred Adler, Harry Stack Sullivan, Erich Fromm, and many others—this principle stands the test of time:

**Behavior is energized by emotions. Emotions are
purposive, dynamic, and meaningful.**

The implication of this principle becomes clear if we try to visualize a person without feelings and emotions. The person's thinking may have contributed to setting a goal and even to devising a plan of action. But, without emotions, the person would have great trouble in taking a stance, acting with force, or showing conviction. Complete objectivity is not conducive to action.

Emotions and Energy

Emotions are vital to the integration of our personalities. They energize our actions. Rudolf Dreikurs (1953), a disciple of Adler, wrote that "[emotions] provide the fuel, the steam so to speak for our actions, the driving force without which we would be impotent."

Emotions make these specific functions possible:

- Facilitate forceful action.
- Provide energy for implementing decisions.
- Enable us to develop attitudes, form convictions, and take a stance.
- Create a basis for personal relationships.
- Permit us to appreciate and devaluate, accept and reject.
- Allow us to enjoy and dislike.

Tending to associate logic only with our thinking processes, we view ourselves primarily as thinking beings. We lack understanding and appreciation of the power of the logic that stems from our emotions.

Separate from one another, we are not always sure what we do feel. Concerned that the expression of our emotions will result in our being labeled irrational, we tend to suppress them. But suppression of emotions can lead to more than fatigue.

Wilhelm Reich (1949) contended that "attitudes and emotional experiences can give rise to certain muscular patterns that block the flow of energy." Evidence has accumulated to support that view. Less than 40 years later, F. Capra (1982) could review the literature and make this conclusion: "Non-constructive emotions block the free flow of energy."

One of the studies that documented the energy stifling process was a study by L. LeShan (1977) with 500 cancer patients. He identified significant events in the life history of patients which led to a blocking of vital energy. This history is consistent with the general mode of major illnesses involving negative emotions that stifle or block psychic energy.

A state of imbalance occurs under the prolonged stress of negative emotions. When negative emotions interfere with the flow of psychic energy, the immune system breaks down. The imbalance is channeled through a particular personality configuration and gives rise to a specific disorder.

A Preventive Approach

Physicians C. and S. Simonton (1978) devised a therapy for releasing the stifled psychic energy. They help patients to travel back along the same path used in developing the illness in order to identify the blockage and release the energy.

The therapy involves a listing of the major stresses that occurred prior to the onset of the illness. It encourages a continual examination of the patient's belief system and environment. Support and encouragement are provided while the patient develops a new set of attitudes.

Once feelings of hope and emotions of desire are generated, the patient's body translates that psychic energy into biological processes that begin to restore balance. The immune system is revitalized and improvement begins.

Identifying emotions and evaluating the embedded beliefs are critical steps in treating illness. But they are of even greater importance in preventing illness and optimizing one's potential for a healthy and satisfying life.

A periodic appraisal of our personality that includes an assessment of emotions allows us to bring emotions to the conscious level. Rather than being driven by unconscious forces, we come to understand the *intelligence* of our emotions. And, occasionally, we can show them the possibility of another way of doing things.

Control of Psychic Energy

Authorities within a society are always concerned about the expression of emotion and the direction of the individual's psychic energy. Moralists have been fearful of the power of psychic energy. They have often come down on the side of suppressing emotion—unless they point the way.

However, a society can be harmed by the ill health of its members as much as it can be harmed by the expression of emotions in destructive ways. Learning to identify and express emotions in a constructive way is a very high priority.

Sidney Jourard (1963) felt that the critical factor was to develop the capacity to choose between the alternatives of suppression and expression. His definition of a healthy personality is a thoughtful one:

The healthy personality displays neither immediate expression nor chronic suppression of emotions.

Chapter II
Character: The Energetics of Personality

U ntil very recently, character was an infrequently used term. Crowded out by newer concepts, character seemed to have retreated into personality.

However, recent scandals have involved high public figures in every area—governmental, educational, financial, and even the religious sector. Interest has been rekindled in the concept of character.

The Importance of Character

The development of character has usually been of vital interest to society. The desired character depended upon the beliefs of the time. In ancient Greece, there was a distinct difference in the training of the young in the city state of warlike Sparta as opposed to that in peaceful Athens.

We also see the difference in the Bible. The Old Testament contains an admonition about sparing the rod and spoiling the child. The New Testament strikes a gentler tone. Still another difference in child rearing is found in the literature of Charles

Dickens. Character training in 19th century England incorporated a belief that adversity strengthened the child's character.
This belief permitted, and even condoned, a shocking abuse
of children that proved lethal to many.

The Horatio Alger stories of a few generations ago give us
some idea of the character that was desired in the United States.
The stories reflected the belief that hard work would pay off
in fame and fortune.

Character is usually shaped according to what is desired in
that society. Sometimes, this shaping process deteriorates into
what is good for the authority doing the shaping. The results
may or may not be good for the child.

Character: What Is It?

Erich Fromm (1973) made a striking analogy between the
character of humans and the instinctive apparatus in animals.
The similarity and difference are instructive.

**Instinct in animals is *innate;* it ensures
survival but only minimal adaptation.
Character in humans is *learned;* it ensures
survival and maximum adaptation.**

The fact that character is learned permits greater ability to
adapt to many different environments. While most people associate the instinct in animals with survival, they do not often
associate character in humans with the ongoing survival process.

To ensure survival, character begins to develop very early in
life. Exquisitely sensitive, infants learn by how they are touched
and held. Later, they learn through what they see, hear, taste,
touch, and smell. All this *information is processed as feelings and
emotions.*

Through thousands of interactions with parents and siblings,
young children learn what behavior will help them survive *and*
succeed. They also learn what works against their survival.

By the age of reason, a feeling pattern has been deeply im-
pressed on the child's psyche. It is our character structure and
our ability to learn through our feelings and emotions that have

ensured our survival in the early years. What, then, is character?

**Character is how we have learned to survive
and succeed. Character is the largely *unconscious*
channeling of psychic energy into a pattern
that will meet our personal needs.**

Some are reluctant to accept the thought that their early experiences have such a profound influence, resisting the implication of being predetermined before they had the ability to decide.

This is a reflection of a world view that has placed such emphasis on rational thinking for the past 250 years. As a society, we have not yet learned to understand and appreciate the *intelligence* of our feelings and emotions.

Even into adulthood, the emotional roots of our character structure serve the functions of survival and success. Not all situations allow the time for a mediated response; character enables us to act instantly when necessary. Our character gives our behavior a predictability; our actions are true to our character. If our actions were based solely on thinking, our functioning would be so inconsistent as to imperil life.

Even though our character serves a vital purpose, there are some drawbacks.

**Not everything we learned about survival and success
in our early years is appropriate to other settings.**

Thus, the question can be raised: Can character be altered?

Can Character Change?

Belief in the permanency of character can be seen as far back as Thomas Aquinas in the 13th century: Give me the child and I will give you the man. No one doubts the tremendous influence of those early years. But opportunities for change were rare in that day.

The group was predominant; the concept of the individual, as we know it, was still several centuries in the future. An individual was born into and died in the same station of life. Serfs were largely illiterate and tied to the soil. Only the clergy and some of the aristocracy were educated. Travel was difficult; outside influences were minimal.

Even 50 years ago, the Freudians believed that character structure was relatively permanent and could be changed only with great difficulty. Analysis might take years. The highly structured society emerging from the Victorian era fought against individual change. In addition, the patients had the complication of neurosis, which impeded change.

In more recent years, the psychoanalysts who have worked most consistently with character strike a more optimistic note. Fromm felt that character change does take place in response to life experiences.

Remarkably little is known about how much or how little character changes in the normal population. Certainly, we are different people at 2 or 10 than we are at 20, 40, or 80. The character of some persons seems to interact with life experiences and evolve into wisdom and integrity. The character of others does not.

Our experience with a normal population has been that persons can and do make significant changes if they see that it is to their benefit. The process occurs in this way:

**Character changes as old beliefs become conscious
and are replaced by new formulations
of what will bring satisfaction.**

In contrast to animals, who are governed by instinct, we are governed by character—and character is learned. You *can* teach "old dogs" new tricks.

Energetics of Personality

In the past, we have not had the means to identify character other than by lengthy analysis. This was neither desirable nor practical for a normal population.

Energetics of Personality provides us with the means to identify and describe character. This systematic method enables us to examine feelings, emotions, and unconscious beliefs at a conscious level. We are able to make first-hand acquaintance with our character—the *controller* of our psychic energy.

However, character is not an entity that can be understood in isolation. Like the biologist, we cannot understand the forest by studying a single tree. A systematic approach is necessary to understand the forest or the personality—to identify the systems and their interrelationships.

Personality is studied because character is embedded within. Above all, we need to understand the *Living Mind System*—the directing force of the personality. For this purpose, we turn now to the *Aristos Psychology Model*.

Chapter III
The Aristos
Psychology Model

The *Aristos Psychology Model* has been formulated to help you consciously work with the systems that generate and direct your psychic energy.

Aristos

Aristos is a Greek word that is roughly translated as "toward the best." It should not be interpreted as a static perfection; "toward" implies continual movement. In a systems approach, *aristos,* or toward the best, means finding a dynamic balance.

The Aristos Psychology Model is presented in figure 1. Note the arrows that indicate the flow of psychic energy. The psychic energy originates in the Energy System (A), and is expressed through the Orientation System (B), in life experiences. Continuing through the Self-Affirmation System (C), the psychic energy is evident in the life plan. If all goes well, some psychic energy is returned to the Energy System. The individual gains momentum through a validating process.

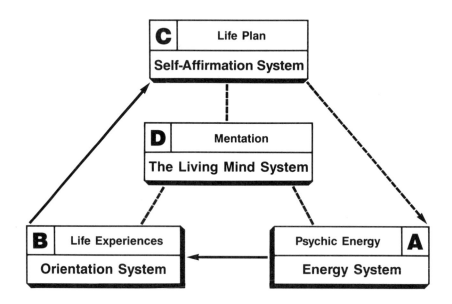

Figure 1. Aristos Psychology Model

In the center of figure 1 is the Living Mind System (D), or mentation. The guiding force of this system is depicted by the dotted lines radiating outward to the other systems. Understanding how the Living Mind System functions is helpful.

The Living Mind System

Mind is the essence of being alive. From a systems point of view, mind is not simply an entity interacting with a single object. Rather, mind is the pattern of organization.

To understand the nature of the Living Mind System, it is helpful to suspend the usual association we make between thinking, reasoning, and the mind. The Living Mind System, or mentation, is a broader concept.

Mentation describes the way in which we respond—both within ourselves and within our environment. It can be summed up in this way:

Mentation is all our mental activity; it organizes all our functions. As a process, the Living Mind System is viewed (1) within the body, and (2) in the pathways and messages outside the body.

---

1) *Within the body,* mentation is involved with the other systems in these ways.

   Energy System: Mentation provides a sense of direction.

   Orientation System: Mentation poses thought and intention and triggers action.

   Self-Affirmation System: Mentation contributes significantly to the formation of a personal identity.

2) *Outside the body,* mentation represents all three systems with the outside world, other humans in the form of friends, family, community, society—and all of nature.*

---

*See Doris Lessing's 1980 novel, *The Marriages Between Zones Three, Four and Five,* for a vivid portrayal of mentation in three different cultures and the dynamic effect upon relationships.

The Scope of Mentation

When encountering other humans, we experience a form of mentation similar to our own. However, mentation is not confined solely to us or, for that matter, to animals. Why is this important?

Our attitude toward nature begins to change when we realize that our environment is not only alive—but *mindful*. Mentation replaces the view of the universe as a machine, a view that has led to exploitation.

Mentation, in different forms, involves every living organism in two different tendencies—self-assertive and integrative. *Our commonality with all of nature is that we have a push toward a separate existence and a pull toward a shared existence.*

The Human Brain

Our version of mentation exists in the human brain. Paul Maclean's model (1973) represented in figure 2 consists of three structurally different parts. The parts are the "old brain" or the brain stem, the limbic, and the neocortex.

Although the three parts of the brain are intimately linked, the activities of each can be contradictory and difficult to integrate. Ambivalence and conflict are only a few of the possible results. The significant principle concerning the three parts of the brain is as follows:

Each area of the brain controls a different part of our total functioning. Each part operates with a different *intelligence* and *subjectivity*.

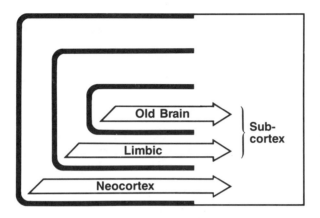

Figure 2. Maclean's Model of the Triune Brain

The function of the neocortex—thinking—is highly valued in western society. Consequently, we know much less about working with the other two areas of the brain on a practical level. However, gaining knowledge about the kind of behavior each part of the brain controls can help us generate and direct our psychic energy.

Old Brain

The innermost part of the brain is called the "old brain." It is responsible for keeping our body functioning automatically. We don't have to consciously keep our heart beating or remember to take a breath.

This part of the brain is also concerned with instinctive behavior patterns. Even though character has largely replaced the mechanism of instinct in humans, we still do have some instinctual or organic drives. These include irresistible drives and impulses such as the drive for food or sex.

More important to our understanding of personality, and the behavior controlled by the "old brain," is the place of *temperament*.

Temperament is associated with reactive patterns and compulsive behavior; it is viewed as part of the "old brain."

Our bodily functions and reactive patterns associated with this area of the brain have usually been regarded as permanent and not subject to conscious control. Since temperament is associated with reactive patterns, the question of change in temperament can be posed.

Can Temperament Be Changed?

The study of temperament has a long and questionable association with body types or physiques. It has also been regarded as a relatively permanent part of our behavior, an assessment with which we agree, in general. But we hasten to point out that temperament constitutes only a small portion of the total personality. Unfortunately, there has been great confusion in this area. Some have broadened the concept of temperament to include all behavior and have insisted that individuals cannot change. This idea is misleading, and it ignores the learning capacity of humans.

While we accept the relative permanency of behavior controlled by the "old brain," other information should be recognized. In the area of bodily functions, such as blood pressure and pulse, outstanding feats of conscious control have been demonstrated. This has even included the control of bleeding. In our own society, biofeedback has been used successfully to lower blood pressure. However, it should be noted that dramatic alterations of bodily functions have been performed by relatively few people.

It can be argued that temperament may be altered in the same way that bodily functions are modified. At this point in our knowledge, however, it seems more appropriate to begin with behavior that has a greater potential for change.

Limbic Area of the Brain

The middle part of the brain is known as the limbic area. It surrounds the "old brain" or the brain stem. Interesting research findings are expanding knowledge of the limbic area. Nobel Prize winner R. Guillemin (Brain/Mind Bulletin, 1977) has contributed to an understanding of how this part of the brain affects behavior. His research into the production and circulation of endorphins establishes a system and suggests a link between brain function and behavior.

The limbic area of the brain processes information in such a way that it is experienced as feelings and emotions. The majority of our psychic energy originates in this area of the brain and is regulated by the private logic of our character.

The limbic area of the brain directs our private logic that makes "sense" of our affective nature—feelings, emotions, and passions.

Limbic Area and Change

Change in behavior directed by the limbic area of the brain can and does occur. This behavior is associated with our character traits—and character is learned. However, change does not come easily. A critical step is to bring the feelings and emotions in which our beliefs are embedded to a conscious level. At that point, evaluation can occur. New formulations can replace the old and bring greater satisfaction.

Neocortex Area of The Brain

The outermost part of the brain is called the neocortex. Erich Jantsch (1980) states that the "neocortex is the location at which information is processed in the ways that are characteristic of the self-reflexive mind."

This area of the brain facilitates abstract functions such as thought and language. This is the start of the creative process and the transformation of the outer world. The transformation occurs in this way:

Our response to events arouses specific behavior traits and activates *intentions* in the neocortex area of the brain.

Most of the behavior emanating from the neocortex area of the brain occurs on a conscious level, although later we will see that it is influenced by unconscious forces from the limbic area of the brain.

The Neocortex and Change

Behavior directed by the neocortex area of the brain is the easiest to change precisely because it is conscious. However, if the desired changes are to last longer than most New Year's resolutions, it is necessary to involve the limbic as well as the neocortex. The limbic area directs the character—the regulator of the psychic energy needed to fuel the intentions.

The *Behavior Indicator*

The instrument contained in this book, the Behavior Indicator, identifies and describes the behavior that is controlled by the three different areas of the brain.

The Behavior Indicator measures the pattern and intensity of:
- **temperament directed by the "old brain,"**
- **character directed by the limbic area, and**
- **behavior intentions directed by the neocortex.**

Combined with the conscious and unconscious realms, this totality of the mind makes up the psyche.

We turn now to the Behavior Indicator. Your responses to the indicator will provide the basis for the in-depth interpretations of the various systems of your personality.

Chapter IV
Using the
Behavior Indicator

T he *Behavior Indicator* is designed to be self-administered, self-developed, and self-interpreted. Repeated usage of the indicator in changing life situations is a vital key—enabling you to witness and understand the complexity of your unfolding personality. Following this easy step-by-step procedure will ensure optimal results:

1 Responding: *Part I and II*

2 Counting and Recording: *Steps One, Two, and Three*

3 Transferring, Plotting, and Graphing

4 Preparing for Your Interpretation: *Finding Your Entry Numbers*

5 Selecting Your Workshops

① Responding

Part I	What Are You The Most?

Procedure:

- Note the first group of words* on panel A, row 1 (opposite page).

- Write an "M" in the symbol after *one* word that is *most* descriptive of your general behavior (see Example A).

- Follow the same procedure for each group of words on panels A, B, and C (pages 29, 30, and 31).

Response Time:
5-6 minutes

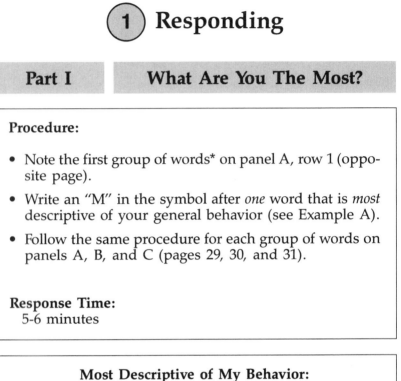

Most Descriptive of My Behavior:

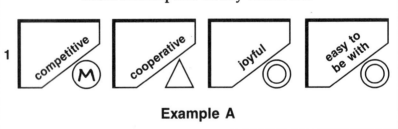

Example A

---

*See Appendix A, Glossary of Response Words/Phrases, for definitions. Complete your selections in those groups in which the meanings of the words are clear. Then return to those groups in which you need clarification.

Descriptive root words for Part I are adapted from *Varieties of Temperament,* by W. H. Sheldon, *Emotions of Normal People,* by W.M. Marston, and *Man for Himself* by E. Fromm.

PANEL A

Most Descriptive of My Behavior:

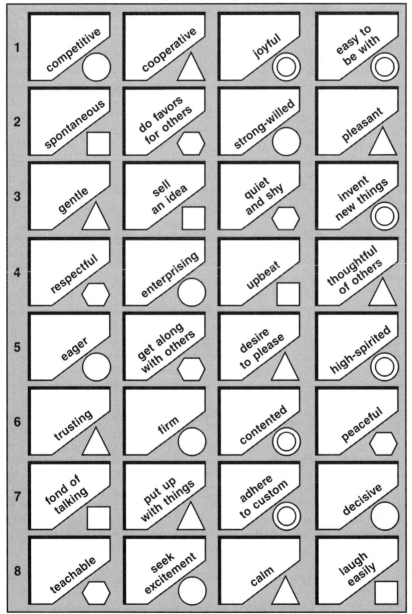

PANEL B

Most Descriptive of My Behavior:

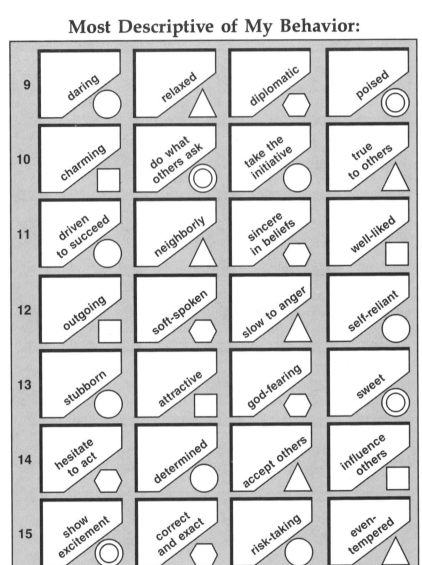

PANEL C

Most Descriptive of My Behavior:

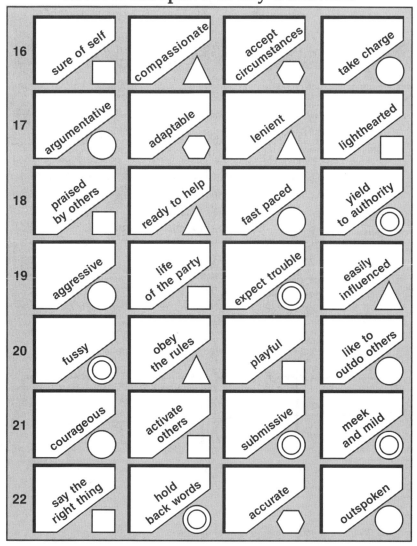

Responding (Con't.)

Procedure:

- Note the first group of words on panel D, row 1 (opposite page).

- Write an "L" in the symbol after *one* word that is *least* descriptive of how you *feel* (see Example B).

- Follow the same procedure for each group of words on panels D, E, and F (pages 33, 34, and 35).

Response Time:
5-6 minutes

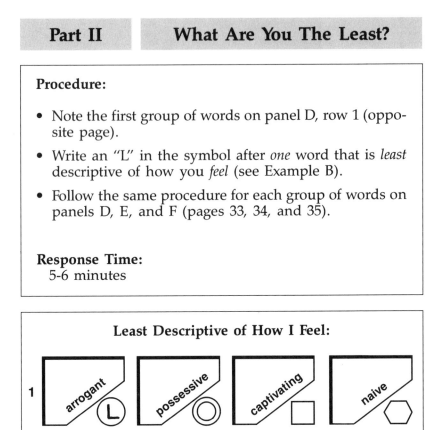

Least Descriptive of How I Feel:

1   arrogant Ⓛ   possessive ◎   captivating ☐   naive ⬡

Example B

Descriptive root words for Part II adapted from *Man for Himself* by E. Fromm and *Emotions of Normal People* by W.M. Marston.

PANEL D

Least Descriptive of How I Feel:

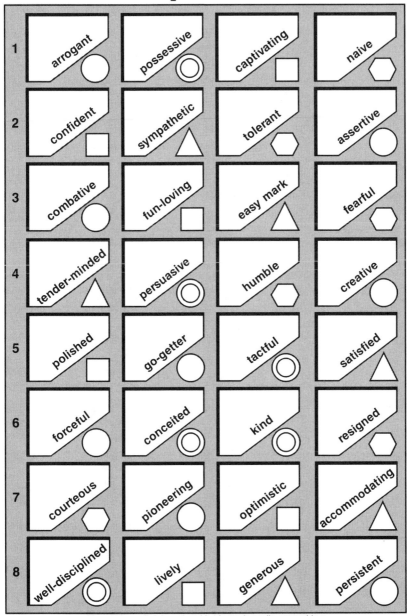

PANEL E

Least Descriptive of How I Feel:

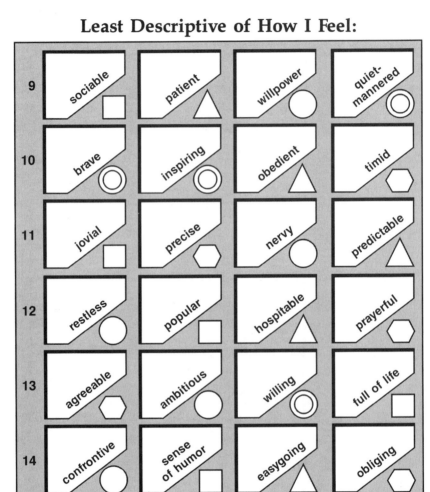

PANEL F

Least Descriptive of How I Feel:

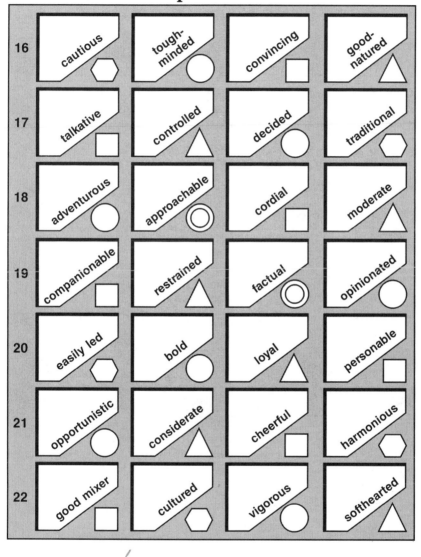

(2) Counting and. . . .

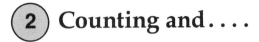

Step I	**Count the Most**
Refer to Part I, panels A, B, C **Pages 29, 30, 31**	• Count the number of M's in the circles. • Record the total in the circle, *Most* row on the opposite page. • Follow the procedure for the remaining symbols. **RECORD THE MOST** ➡

Step II	**Count the Least**
Refer to Part II, panels D, E, F **Pages 33, 34, 35**	• Count the number of L's in the circles. • Record the total in the circle, *Least* row on the opposite page. • Follow the procedure for the remaining symbols. **RECORD THE LEAST** ➡

Step III	**Determine the Difference**

Most
(4)
 	
Least
(7)
 	
Difference
(-3)
 	
Example
	• Find the difference between the numbers in the Most and Least circles on the opposite page.
	• Record the number in the difference row.
	• Follow the procedure for the remaining symbols.
	• Add a plus (+) or minus (−). See Example.
	If Most symbol is greater than Least = +
	   Most symbol is less than Least = −
	   Most symbol is same as Least = 0
	
	RECORD THE DIFFERENCE ➡

....Recording

The Tally Page

Most: *Graph I*, page 40

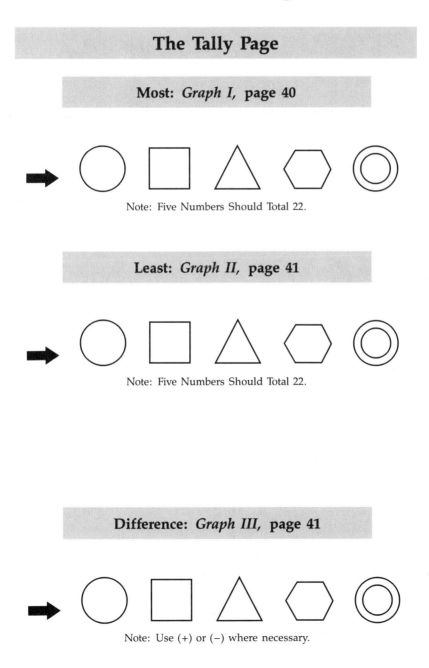

Note: Five Numbers Should Total 22.

Least: *Graph II*, page 41

Note: Five Numbers Should Total 22.

Difference: *Graph III*, page 41

Note: Use (+) or (−) where necessary.

③ Transferring. . . .

Transferring Numbers to Graphs

- Transfer the numbers in the symbols from the Tally page (37) to the symbols above each of the three graphs on pages 40 and 41.

  Note the example below:

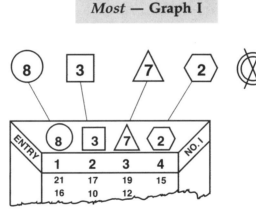

- Transfer:

  Most to Graph I

  Least to Graph II

  Difference to Graph III

Note: The ○'s numbers are *not* transferred.

....Plotting and Graphing

Plotting: Use X's

- Begin with Graph I, page 40.

- Locate and place an X over the number in each column of the graph that corresponds to the number in the symbol.

  Note the example below.

- Estimate the X if the precise number is not shown.

- Plot Graphs II and III on page 41.

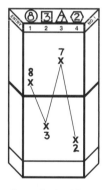

Graph I *Most*

Graphing: Connect the X's

- Begin with Graph I, page 40.

- Draw a line connecting the X's. See example above.

- Complete Graphs II and III on page 41.

(4) Preparing....

Finding Your Entry Numbers

- Note the entry *bar* at the top of Graph I.

- Circle number 1 if the X in that column is above the midline (see Example below).

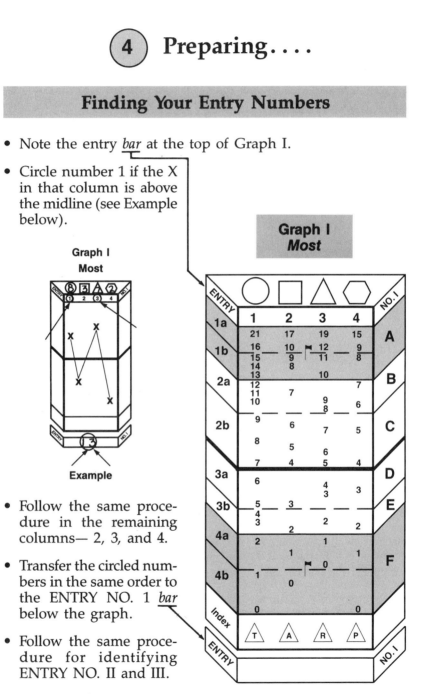

Graph I
Most

Example

- Follow the same procedure in the remaining columns— 2, 3, and 4.

- Transfer the circled numbers in the same order to the ENTRY NO. 1 *bar* below the graph.

- Follow the same procedure for identifying ENTRY NO. II and III.

....for Your Interpretation

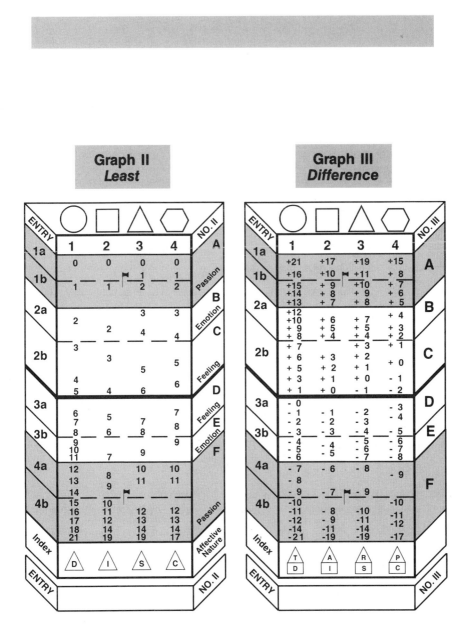

Graph II
Least

Graph III
Difference

Selecting Your Workshops

Workshops: *An Overview*

Approaching Change: All eight of the workshops contain content and application that has an interdisciplinary basis—psychology, sociology, and philosophy.

The potential for personal change is underscored in the material. The approach to change can be summarized in this manner:

There are four ways to bring about change.

1) **Change the situation.**

2) **Change your perception of the situation.**

3) **Leave the situation.**

4) **Change yourself.**

It is obvious that you do have choices. As you take each workshop, new understanding and opportunities will open up for you. You may decide to make major moves or engage in a slight course correction. Given the nature of the personal workshops, you will find it difficult to remain the same.

At this point, you have a psychological menu from which to make a selection. A more specific reference to the workshops will assist you in your choice.

Personal Workshops

Purpose: Your interpretations are presented in the form of six personal workshops. This approach enables you to master the vital Energetics of Personality while applying it to your personal behavior. Your personality is viewed in terms of the energy you direct toward intended activity.

Objectives. *You will be able to:*

1) Identify the ways you respond to life's problems.

2) Evaluate your action in moving from a survival mode to a success mode.

3) Determine possible change, if needed and if desired.

While we suggest that you begin with workshop I and follow the logical order, you can take them in a sequence based on your personal preference. Refer to table 1 on the next page.

Professional Workshops

Purpose: There are two workshops for the professional or the interested student of personality. They provide basic information related to Aristos Psychology and to the design of the Behavior Indicator.

Objectives.

1) To help you make distinctions in regard to personal choices that directly assist you.

2) To select appropriate ways to influence behavior and situations. Refer to table 1 on the next page.

Table 1

Index of Workshops

Personal Workshop	No.	Page
Personality Analysis	I	47
Behavior Dynamics	II	61
The Danger Zone: *Extended Pattern Analysis*	III	87
The Compatibility Factor	IV	99
Persuasion as a Quality Action	V	117
Energetics of Leadership	VI	139

Professional Workshop	No.	Page
Understanding Your Graphs*	I	161
Understanding Aristos Personality Theory	II	185

*Do You Have An Unusual Pattern?

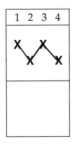

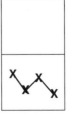

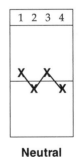

Overdrive	**Underdrive**	**Neutral**
All plotting points above the midline	All plotting points below the midline	All plotting points clustered around the midline

Book I
Workshops

Personal Workshop I
Personality Analysis

Step One:	**Orientation System:** *Intended Behavior*
Step Two:	**Energy System:** *Concealed Behavior*
Step Three:	**Self-Affirmation System:** *Predicted Behavior*
Step Four:	**Shared Behavior:** *An Exercise*

The first three steps of this workshop will provide personal interpretations for the three systems of your personality—Orientation, Energy, and Self-Affirmation. In the fourth step, you will be guided to the patterns of those with whom you would be most compatible in the work and social setting.

Step One
Orientation System: *Intended Behavior*

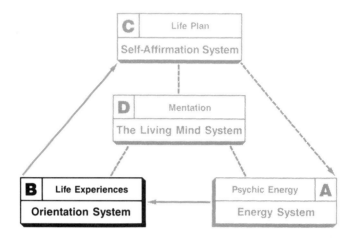

The behavior described in this interpretation is primarily directed by the neocortex area of the brain. Although there is some influence from the unconscious, behavior is largely on a conscious level.

What is the implication of this information for you? First, you will recognize most of the interpretation. Second, much of the behavior is under your conscious control. Third, the behavior in the Orientation System of your personality is where you begin if you want to make changes.

Your Orientation System deals with the changes that you encounter through your life experiences. The interpretation gives you a look at your "proving ground." It reflects how you are coming to grips with two forces that are often conflicting:

Expectations
of Others  Your Desires
and Needs

Struggle occurs when there is a conflict between what you want to do and what others expect of you. The outcome is your intentions and sometimes your actions.

Your intentions are couched in four orientations of behavior adapted from E. Fromm (1947). The orientation factors describe your direction. They are:

t   taking   ☐

a   attracting   ☐

r   responding   ☐

p   preserving   ☐

Note the box after each orientation factor. Take a few moments to rank them according to the direction in which you think you are moving at this time. Use 1 as the highest rank and 4 as the lowest.

Each orientation factor—taking, attracting, responding, and preserving—indicates a way of interacting with others and a way of developing productiveness in work. Your direction, or orientation, is inherent in your intentions.

**To Obtain
Your Interpretation**

- Refer to your Entry No. I. (Bottom of Graph I, page 40.)

- Locate the page number in table 2.

- Study the interpretation of your intentions.

- Proceed to Step Two of the workshop.

**Table 2.
Interpretation Patterns:
Intended Behavior**

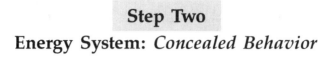

Step Two
Energy System: *Concealed Behavior*

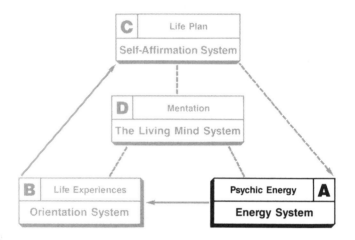

The interpretation for the Energy System of your personality will describe your affective nature—the source of your psychic energy.

Your affective nature is directed by the limbic area of the brain. This part of the brain processes information as feelings, emotions, and passions. For the most part, this occurs in the unconscious realm.

What is the significance of information processing in the limbic area of the brain? First, you can expect the interpretation of your affective nature to be less familiar than the description of your intentions. The interpretation deals with feelings, emotions, and passions that are concealed not only from others, but often from yourself. Sometimes, during stress periods, these emotions thrust themselves into your consciousness, startling both you and others. You may wonder: Now where did that come from?

Second, emotions are not as easy to change as intentions. They exist primarily in the unconscious and are not as accessible as intentions. Arising from the limbic area without conscious volition, they flicker along the nervous system and dissipate. Nevertheless, there is a process that will give you greater access and control over your affective nature. It will be discussed in Personal Workshop II.

Third, the interpretation that describes your affective nature will provide the first glimpse of your character structure. The beliefs that undergird your character are deeply enmeshed in your emotions. And character is the regulator of your psychic energy.

As your character structure developed, your beliefs merged into strong convictions. These convictions are the basis for the *private logic* of your character. The function of private logic can be stated in this way:

**The private logic of your character structure
evaluates what you intend to do. It
energizes some actions and *rejects* others.**

Your interpretation reflects your selection of character traits in Part II of the Behavior Indicator. The flow of your psychic energy is reflected in the placement of four energy points on Graph II:

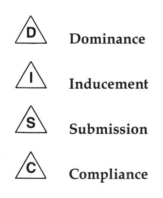

△D   **Dominance**

△I   **Inducement**

△S   **Submission**

△C   **Compliance**

How Orientation Relates to Energy Points

Note the four letters at the bottom of Graph I—

△ t   △ a   △ r   △ p

They represent the four orientations—taking, attracting, responding, and preserving. The placement of the plotting points on Graph I indicated your specific intentions.

The success of the intentions depends on the energy that is directed from and through the character structure as reflected in Graph II. This dynamic is observed in the following combinations.

Orientation		*Energy*
taking	←	Dominance
attracting	←	Inducement
responding	←	Submission
preserving	←	Compliance

The highest or preferred intention in Graph I will falter without the corresponding energy in Graph II that is needed to ensure success. Example A in Figure 3 indicates a potentially successful alignment of the *taking* orientation with the *Dominance* source of energy.

Example B reveals a less successful alignment. Again, the individual has a preferred orientation of taking, but lacks the psychic energy of the Dominance source of energy. The result is disappointing. It is not unusual for the person to be both physically and emotionally drained. Complaints of fatigue are common.

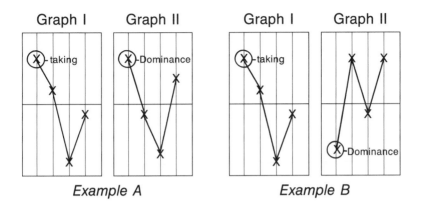

Figure 3. Examples of Alignment Between
Orientation and Energy

To Obtain
Your Interpretation

- Refer to your Entry No. II.

- Locate the page number in table 3.

- Study the interpretation of your concealed behavior.

- Proceed to Step Three of the workshop.

Table 3.
Interpretation Patterns:
Concealed Behavior

Self-Affirmation System: *Predicted Behavior*

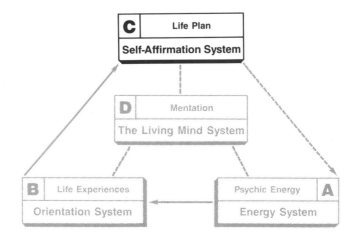

The third step in exploring your personality focuses on the Self-Affirmation System. The interpretation, or *central pattern,* will describe your predicted behavior. That is the outcome when some of your intentions are empowered by your psychic energy. There are two parts to the interpretation of your predicted behavior—social and work patterns. Together, these patterns reflect your *life plan.*

We all have a life plan; we only vary in how we fulfill it. Our life plan contains both our conscious and unconscious attempts to affirm who we are and what we do. The life plan emanates from our character and takes on some of the qualities surrounding our character.

Our life plan
begins on an unconscious level,
reflects our private logic,
tends to be evaluative,
implies energy direction.

Like our character, the life plan is dynamic. It unfolds and evolves over a lifetime. Much of the life plan lies in the unconscious, functioning like a blueprint for a cathedral. The interpretation will give you an aerial view of the edifice you are erecting. It will provide insight into the pattern of your daily life; this insight allows you to become a conscious architect of your life plan. You can use the blueprint for direction and modify it to fit the requirements of the situation.

The life plan is concerned with solving *the* human problem—the need to be separate and the need to be together. We see the answers in two ways:

Our life plan reflects our search for:
- **a sense of importance**
- **a sense of productive meaning**

A Sense of Importance

The family setting was the first environment in which we sought a sense of importance. Attempting to cope with the natural feeling of inferiority that goes with a child's immaturity, we developed a pattern of relating to our siblings. Later, we strengthened or modified our way of seeking importance in other settings.

The power of the life plan—in terms of achieving a sense of self-importance—is evident when young people marry. They attempt to mesh their unconscious life plans and to identify ways of seeking self-importance that will not be harmful to each other.

A Sense of Productive Meaning

Our efforts to achieve productive meaning is most often concerned with our work. The concept of work should not be equated with a job or monetary reward. A job may provide a niche in a work organization and the necessary remuneration. But it is only *work* that can bring productive meaning. Work is that which allows us to develop our individual potential and creativity. But work only for ourselves ultimately falls short. To bring a sense of productive meaning, work must not only develop our individual potential, it must also contribute to the common good.

Your life plan is consciously or unconsciously reflected in the interpretation of your predicted behavior—social and work.

Social. The interpretation for your social or home environment will provide information on what you can expect from others and what they can hope to receive from you. These are a few of the questions that will be answered in the interpretation: What is your potential for an effective relationship with your mate? How do you respond to opposition? How do you tend to communicate?

Work. The interpretation for the work situation will identify your ideal work. Here are a few of the questions that will be answered: Do you use a unique approach to problem solving? How do you view and use time intensity? What kind of person can best assist you in the work environment? What kind of balance are you demonstrating?

To Obtain
Your Central Pattern
Interpretation

- Refer to your Entry No. III.
- Locate the page number in table 4.
- Study the two parts of the interpretation—work and social—of your predicted behavior.
- Proceed to Step Four of the workshop.

Table 4.
Interpretation Patterns:
Predicted Behavior

Entry No. III	Page
one	240
two	243
three	246
four	249
twelve	252
thirteen	255
fourteen	258
twenty-three	261
twenty-four	264
thirty-four	267
one twenty-three	270
one twenty-four	273
one thirty-four	276
two thirty-four	279

Step Four
Shared Behavior: *An Exercise*

The fourth step considers your shared behavior in the present situation. You are encouraged to become familiar with the personalities that tend to be most compatible with yours— in both the work and social situation.

A theoretical basis for individual and group compatibility is combined with practical application in Personal Workshop IV. This step lays the basis for that workshop in acquainting you with the interpretations of your compatibility persons.

To Prepare for Your Compatibility Exercise

Social Compatibility

- Refer to your Central Pattern interpretation for predicted social behavior (Entry No. III).

- Record the patterns and pages of your social compatibility persons located at the end of the social interpretation.

  Natural Choice _____ Recommended _____

        page _____   page _____

- Read and study the interpretation of the natural pattern. (You will study the recommended choice in Personal Workshop IV.)

In the social situation, regarding your compatibility person...

1. What can you do for the person that he/she would find difficult to do for himself/herself?

   _____

   _____

   _____

2. What common limitations do you observe in the other person and in yourself?

_____

_____

_____

3. Is there an aspect of the other person's personality that would negate an ongoing linkage?

_____

_____

_____

Work Compatibility

- Refer to your Central Pattern interpretation for predicted work behavior.
- Record the patterns and pages of your work compatibility persons located at the end of the interpretation.

    1st Choice _____   2nd Choice _____

        page _____   page _____

- Read and study the interpretation for the first choice of work compatibility persons. (You will study the second choice in Personal Workshop IV.)

In the work situation, regarding your compatibility person...

1. What can you do for the person that he/she would find difficult to do for himself/herself?

_____

_____

_____

2. What common limitations do you observe in the other person and in yourself?

_____

_____

_____

3. Is there an aspect of the other person's personality that would negate an ongoing linkage?

_____

_____

_____

Compatibility Review

Respond to these items by using your own behavior interpretation and the interpretation patterns for your work and social
compatibility persons.

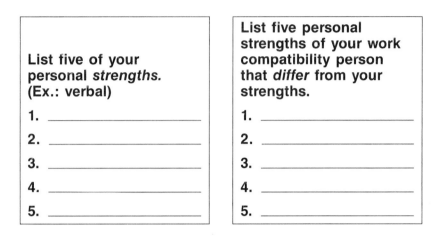

List five of your
personal *strengths.*
(Ex.: verbal)

1. _____
2. _____
3. _____
4. _____
5. _____

List five personal
strengths of your work
compatibility person
that *differ* from your
strengths.

1. _____
2. _____
3. _____
4. _____
5. _____

List five of your
personal *limitations.*
(Ex.: disorganized)

1. _____
2. _____
3. _____
4. _____
5. _____

List five personal
strengths of your social
compatibility person
that are *similar* to your
strengths.

1. _____
2. _____
3. _____
4. _____
5. _____

Personal Workshop II
Behavior Dynamics

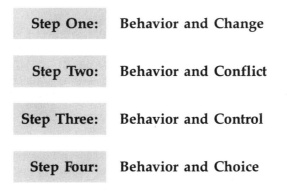

Step One: Behavior and Change

Step Two: Behavior and Conflict

Step Three: Behavior and Control

Step Four: Behavior and Choice

This workshop is designed for those who want to expand their choices and exert greater control over the direction of their lives. Each step in the workshop focuses on an element of behavior dynamics. Instruction and interpretation of your behavior are combined at each step to facilitate application to your personal or work situation. Behavior Dynamics can be understood in this way:

**Behavior Dynamics is the energy we exert
in dealing with four elements of life—
change, conflict, control, and choice—in the
shaping and reshaping of our behavior.**

From Survival to Success

Many meaningful responses are possible when dealing with the four elements of change, conflict, control, and choice. However, they are diminished if they lack an overall focus. For every change, the question can be posed: Toward what purpose? Screening our responses through the success mode provides that overall direction.

**The success mode acknowledges the human
condition—the push toward a separate existence
and the pull toward a shared existence.**

The survival mode is focused primarily on self. The success mode emphasizes both self and others. The balance of these two factors in the success mode is never static. It is dependent upon circumstances. But the concept of an overall balance between self and others is critical. It incorporates the ability to stand alone and to embrace the thought and action that we are all bound together in intricate ways.

Table 5 provides a differentiation of the modes of survival and success. The first column identifies the Orientation System. The second column depicts the Energy System.

Table 5. Moving from Survival to Success

I Orientation of		II Energized by		III Surviving with		IV Succeeding through
taking	+	Dominance	=	controlling	*or*	creating
attracting	+	Inducement	=	seducing	*or*	leading
responding	+	Submission	=	depending	*or*	providing
preserving	+	Compliance	=	protecting	*or*	organizing

The third column identifies the limitations of the survival mode, while the fourth column depicts the potential of the succeeding mode. For example, the taking orientation can be taken beyond the survival mode of controlling into the succeeding mode of creating. The success mode has a broader focus; it consciously acknowledges the needs of self and the needs of others.

Step One
Behavior and Change

This step begins with an opportunity to assess your perception of change. Use an X to denote your responses to the list of 28 items. For example, if you believe that it is impossible to change the color of your eyes, place an X in the column *Impossible to Change* opposite that item.

What Can Individuals Change about Themselves?

Items	Impossible to Change	Possible to Change Partially	Possible to Change Substantially
1. color of eyes			
2. ability to verbalize			
3. shyness			
4. body weight			
5. laziness			
6. manual dexterity			
7. reliability			
8. feeling of inferiority			
9. skin color			
10. tone of voice			
11. tendency to lie			
12. response to authority			
13. habit of daydreaming			
14. perfectionism			
15. body coordination			
16. concern for others			
17. tendency to blame others			
18. color perception			
19. sexual attractiveness			
20. superstitiousness			
21. artistic ability			
22. like or dislike of others			
23. tendency to gossip			
24. fear of machinery			
25. meanness			
26. temper			
27. sloppiness			
28. intellectual capacities			

After completing your responses, check your answers with those in Appendix B.

With an understanding of what we can and cannot change about ourselves, we consider a question that is asked frequently—consciously or unconsciously—in regard to change:

Can we change another person?

This question is asked in both the personal and work situation. When men and women choose each other in marriage, they assume that the other person has the potential for change in response to life events. Employers and employees attempt to size up one another in regard to the present "fit" and the potential for accommodation to growth. Salesperson and client gauge the distance between them and ponder a change in position.

When we ask the question "Can we change another person?" we often fail to recognize that the person is constantly changing. The rate of change is such that it is easy to lose sight of that very basic fact. Subtle as it may be, change is always taking place.

In fact, we alter the person by posing the possibility of change. Our presence changes the dynamic even in the absence of an intent to change the other person. But less frequently recognized is that, with or without the intention to change the other person, we are ourselves changed by our proximity.

Thus, we can and do change the other person just as the other person changes us. It may not be in the desired direction nor at the desired rate, but there is a very definite influence.

Our perception of change—within ourselves and within the other person—is a critical variable in the actual outcome. Let us examine the results of underestimating and overestimating the potential for change.

Underestimating the Potential for Change

More than a few people believe that the behavior of another is fixed, unyielding, and immutable. They do not believe that anything will change the behavior of the other person. As a consequence, they develop a fixed mode of relating to the other. Their belief becomes a self-fulfilling prophecy; there is less change that can be traced to their influence.

The importance of beliefs cannot be overstated in regard to the change that can be effected. Some individuals believe that people are "just no damn good." They think that no matter what is done, others will remain untrustworthy, dishonest, selfish, lustful, and everything else that is considered bad and evil.

Many marriages have been terminated or endured with resignation because one spouse has incorrectly diagnosed the changeability of his or her partner. Many spouses, following a divorce, have been astounded at the change in the other person. A stodgy, rigid, unimaginative husband may metamorphose into a dapper, flexible, attentive man. A demanding, unresponsive wife may evolve into a charming, thoughtful woman after the marriage has terminated.

Obviously, the persons were capable of change. But it is also evident that they did not want to change for each other. And *neither knew how to behave so that the other would want to change.*

Overestimating the Potential for Change

While behavior is subject to change, there are also powerful forces that militate against change. These forces include such factors as the need to feel safe, protect self-esteem, or maintain a sense of identity.

In theory it is possible to arrange conditions so that a person will change his or her response pattern. But even skilled professionals do not attempt to create a facilitating environment in the absence of a person's desire for change. There are two reasons. First, meaningful change will not occur unless the person desires to change. Second, the ethical therapist does not set the direction of the other person's life.

Thus, it is good advice to choose employees, friends, associates, or spouses on the basis of who they are, and not on the condition that they change. The major consequences of overestimating the potential for change in the other person are disappointment, failure, and resentment.

It is quite enough to deal with the "small" changes that are necessary if two fairly compatible persons are to work or live together successfully. This is not to say that far-reaching changes are impossible; they can and do occur. But, in general, the changes we make seem large to us and small to the other person.

How To Change the Other Person

The most effective and healthy way to produce change is to behave toward the other person so that he or she will want to change. People have voluntary control over their response pattern to a surprising extent. People can act, within limits, as they want to act. If the other person's behavior is unsatisfactory, that person can modify it so that it becomes satisfactory.

The precise means of achieving this goal—creating a desire for different behavior in the other person—will vary with the desired change. However, this general proposition can be stated:

The most effective means of inducing change in the other person is to behave toward him or her in ways that will satisfy basic needs.

At first blush, it would appear as if the person wanting the changes in the other person's behavior is "bribing" that person with satisfactions. In a sense, this is true. But there is a difference between a cold, calculated attempt to bribe another person into conforming with one's wishes and a spontaneous wish that the other person, who is loved, will change.

In the former instance, the one being bribed will eventually discover the manipulation and resent it. In the latter, the relationship is more likely to be one of mutual requests to change and mutual compliance with the other's wish.

For example, diet and exercise are prime topics of change as the link with health grows ever stronger. We can make changes in these habits easier for the other person by changing our own eating and exercising patterns.

In much the same way, many work organizations have recognized the relationship between productivity and good health. Providing facilities for exercise and clinics for nonsmoking have been helpful in reducing illness and absences from work.

Still another example is the sedentary child who watches too much television. Many parents nag their children to go outside and play in the fresh air. But the parent who is intent upon change goes outside with the child and organizes activities until the change is well-established and the child has developed other interests besides television. In this case, the basic need is the parent's involvement and approval.

In summary, behavior change occurs when one desires to respond differently to life's situations. Before turning to your interpretation to discover possible changes in your own behavior, respond to the following three items.

1. **Use an X to determine the degree of change you believe is occurring in your behavior.**

Degree of Change Occurring in Your Behavior		
Little	Some	Much
1.0 2.0	3.0 4.0	5.0

2. **Write the name of one, two, or three persons who may have influenced your behavior change at this time.**

_____

_____

_____

3. **Record one, two, or three events that may be contributing to your behavior change.**

_____

_____

_____

You are now ready to read the *first* of four parts in the Behavior Dynamics Interpretation. The four parts correspond to the four steps of the workshop: (1) Behavior and Change, (2) Behavior and Conflict, (3) Behavior and Control, and (4) Behavior and Choice.

Procedure for Obtaining Interpretation

☐ Write in your Entry No. in the appropriate spaces:

Entry No. I _____ Entry No. II _____

☐ Refer to the Key for Identifying Behavior Dynamics Interpretation on the next page.

☐ Circle your Entry No. I in the bar lying horizontally across the top. See Example A.

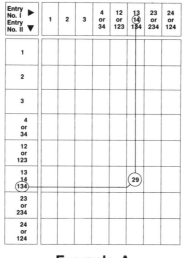

Example A

☐ Circle your Entry No. II in the bar to the left.

☐ Extend the two circled points so that they intersect. In Example A, the key number at the intersecting point is 29.

☐ Locate your key number in table 6 (page 71), Behavior Dynamic Interpretations, and turn to the page number indicated.

☐ Read Part I of the interpretation and then proceed to Step Two of the workshop.

Key for Identifying Behavior Dynamics Interpretation

Entry No. I ▶ / Entry No. II ▼	1	2	3	4 or 34	12 or 123	13 14 134	23 or 234	24 or 124
1	57	50	28	32	46	48	18	44
2	37	30	49	55	36	63	22	13
3	61	38	58	54	19	60	41	10
4 or 34	42	21	17	51	24	3	27	25
12 or 123	20	35	45	16	2	8	23	12
13 14 134	59	64	47	40	7	29	4	6
23 or 234	53	56	31	62	15	39	52	33
24 or 124	9	14	43	34	11	5	26	1

Table 6.
Behavior Dynamics Interpretations

Key No.	Page	Key No.	Page	Key No.	Page	Key No.	Page
1	284	17	316	33	348	49	380
2	286	18	318	34	350	50	382
3	288	19	320	35	352	51	384
4	290	20	322	36	354	52	386
5	292	21	324	37	356	53	388
6	294	22	326	38	358	54	390
7	296	23	328	39	360	55	392
8	298	24	330	40	362	56	394
9	300	25	332	41	364	57	396
10	302	26	334	42	366	58	398
11	304	27	336	43	368	59	400
12	306	28	338	44	370	60	402
13	308	29	340	45	372	61	404
14	310	30	342	46	374	62	406
15	312	31	344	47	376	63	408
16	314	32	346	48	378	64	410

Step Two
Behavior and Conflict

Of the four elements of Behavior Dynamics, conflict is perhaps the least understood. We begin the process of learning to respond constructively to conflict by defining the term.

Conflict exists when each of our choices has positive values and negative implications associated with it.

Conflict arouses opposing emotions that absorb our psychic energy. Even thrusting through the conflicting forces into action, we have a wavering sense of direction and reduced energy. For example, a person wishes to take a business risk, but has an equal desire for security. Choosing to risk, the person pays a high price in terms of worry over results, apprehension over failure, and a general anxiety.

It is entirely possible for an individual to hang suspended between conflicting forces for a considerable period of time. For example, many people dislike their jobs, but they have an equal liking for the money it brings. Never resolving the conflict, they stay in the same job for months and even years. They pay a high price in terms of anger, hostility, and frustration.

Two key questions can be posed about conflict:

Why do some people have more conflict than others?
How can we resolve conflict?

The answers to these questions begin with the identification of the basis of conflict—conditioning. You probably remember Pavlov's classical conditioning experiment in which he paired a neutral stimulus—a bell—with an effective stimulus—food. Eventually, the dog was conditioned to salivate at the sound of the bell.

As a laboratory process, conditioning has been used by scientists to study brain function and to discover the principles of learning. For example, infants and young children learn through the pairing of stimuli. To young infants, mothers are often paired with food and comfort. It is a powerful conditioning that can last a lifetime.

Throughout childhood we have learned to speak, to smile—or to cry and whine—to have good manners—or to be aggressive and rude—in response to certain stimuli.

Conditioning is a part of the socializing process that shapes our behavior through social and environmental influences. We are products of a specific family, a specific group, and a specific society.

As a result of the conditioning process, we are *bound* to certain ideas, practices, aspirations, expectations—and people. It is the process of being *attached*. It is half of the human equation—the pull toward a shared existence.

We are not normally aware that we are bound by conditioning other than in a general sense. We are aware only that we suffer conflict. These statements are links in a chain to understanding why some people have more conflict than others and how we can resolve that conflict:

1) Conditioning binds our behavior to certain stimuli.

2) Conditioning leads to attachments such as work, tradition, property, ideas, or people.

3) Detachment causes conflict.

We vary in our awareness of this conditioning/socializing process that binds us in the form of attachments. This lack of awareness can create conflict at an international level, between social groups, between families, between individuals, and within the person. It can prevent us from developing the other half of the human equation—the push toward a separate existence.

Our attachment to country, to work, to spouse, to family, to ideas, to tradition is a part of our identity. However, it is not the same as an individual identity. That is achieved only at the price of separateness.

Conflict is the price we pay for achieving a separate existence and an individual identity.

Ongoing conflict is inevitable unless we recognize the conditioning process. If the attachment reaches an addictive level, we are using it as an escape from ourselves—into work, ideology, or another person.

Conflict provides the opportunity to identify the conditioning and to evaluate the attachment. In the process, we become our own person and resolve the conflict.

Conditioning has value in that we can repeat productive and meaningful actions. But not all conditioned behavior is constructive. A very wise psychiatrist of our personal acquaintance said that we spend the adult portion of our lives "getting rid of our parents." In this most basic of human attachments, we are required to move through many different phases, and each phase is accompanied by conflict—and the potential for expanding our individual identity and developing a different and more satisfying relationship.

Northrup Frye, professor of literature at the University of Toronto, made an interesting comment in regard to conditioning. In a televised interview on Bill Moyers' World of Ideas (1988), he estimated that we have to unlearn approximately nine-tenths of what we have learned. He cited the challenge of disengaging from the information while avoiding withdrawing from the people.

Identifying the Nature of Your Conflict

- **Turn to Part II of your Behavior Dynamics Interpretation— Behavior and Conflict.**
- **Study the Analysis.**
- **Complete the Attachment Survey that follows.**

ATTACHMENT SURVEY

Directions: Circle **one** answer for **each** question.	Almost Never	Sometimes	Moderately Often	Often	Very Often
(1) To what extent do you observe the behavior described in the interpretation section, "Your behavior when under pressure"?	AN	S	MO	O	VO
(2) Are you consciously aware of the internal conflict described in the interpretation section, "Your internal conflict"?	AN	S	MO	O	VO
(3) Do you identify as **attachment** relationships those individuals who tend to condition your behavior?	AN	S	MO	O	VO
(4) Do you identify as **attachment** places or events those places or events that tend to condition your behavior?	AN	S	MO	O	VO
(5) Are you free to make choices regarding your activities and your associates?	AN	S	MO	O	VO

Step Three
Behavior and Control

When we are unaware that many of our behavior patterns are conditioned, we tend to respond with the same conditioned action—even in new situations. Like automatons and machines, we repeat the same responses over and over. To a certain degree, we are programmed.

English philosopher and novelist Colin Wilson described this conditioned aspect of the human personality as that part which is like a robot—a nonhuman. He pointed out the usefulness of his robot, the conditioned part of himself. For example, he does not have to think about walking, driving a car, or typing. The response patterns for these behaviors are programmed into the nervous system. His robot allows him to do those things more or less automatically. Extra energy is available for creative activities.

However, the more pervasive the conditioning, the more intrusive is our robot. These are some of the dangers of conditioning:

1) Conditioning shapes our perception; it may hinder an accurate perception of reality in a rapidly changing situation.

2) Attachments are often the result of conditioning, and they can become addictive.

3) Conditioned responses inhibit spontaneous feeling and original thinking.

4) Conditioning sets the stage for manipulation.

For example, our robot may insist on getting into the act when we see a dramatic production, read an essay, listen to a piece of music, relate to our spouse, or talk to our manager. Consequently, we see what we have been programmed to see. We continue to think, do, and say the same things—and fall back on the same cliches.

This step in the workshop focuses on the third element of Behavior Dynamics—control. We will answer these questions:

- **How do we regain some control over our "robot" in critical areas?**
- **How do we exert a conscious influence over our vital interests?**

Awareness of our conditioning is the first step; it often comes with the occurrence of conflict. Recognition of an attachment to persons or events that may be addictive and against our interests can bring a sense of freedom. We need not be determined by our early behavior conditioning. We function on this principle:

Human beings *learn* by their own conscious energetic interactions with the environment.

We may not be total masters of our fate, but we can be partners in actively identifying and embracing our destiny. We can consciously play the cards that fate has handed us. We can learn to "operate" our environment—to respond rather than to react.

B. F. Skinner formulated principles of operant conditioning through a series of laboratory experiments with rats in a Skinner box. He demonstrated that random actions on the part of the rat could be strengthened or extinguished through a process of rewards or punishments. These principles are widely used by parents, teachers, and employers.

Unlike the experimental animal, we do not have to wait for others to reward or punish certain behaviors. Sometimes, the very goal of our learning is the reward: thinking creatively, or becoming spontaneous. Because we have a human mind, we can try our new behaviors and tolerate the immediate discomfort of conflict or the effort that is required.

At this point, you have the opportunity to use operant behavior—that is, to exert control and determine how purposeful your future actions will be. You are exploring and testing the parameters of your "skinner" box.

Two specific exercises will enable you to review self-assumptions, correct them, if necessary, and determine possible new courses of action.

Exercise I: Self-Assumption

Begin this section by choosing a response (X) for each of the following assumptions you make about yourself.

	true	somewhat true	not true
1. cooperativeness			
2. independence			
3. above average intelligence			
4. personal charm			
5. self-confidence			
6. coolness under stress			
7. cope well with uncertainty			
8. good appearance			
9. efficiency			
10. energy			
Score			

Grand total _____

Scoring

- **Assign a value to every response.**

> true—10 points
> somewhat true— 5 points
> not true— 0 points

- **Add each column and find the grand total.**
- **Locate your score in this scale.**

> 90 - 100 Excellent opinion
> 80 - 89   Very good opinion
> 70 - 79   Good opinion
> 60 - 69   Average
> 50 - 59   Low Average
> 40 - 49   Poor
> 0 - 39   Very Poor

Your score on the Self-Assumption Inventory gives you some idea of the positive or negative opinion you have of yourself. Many people refer to themselves in broad generalities such as "dumb" or "inadequate." They allow a feeling of inadequacy in one area to stand for their whole behavior. Too often, they perceive it as impossible to change. They have been conditioned.

The first step in changing your self-programming is to become aware of the assumptions you have made about yourself. Exercise I enabled you to begin the process of how and sometimes why you limit yourself by the assumptions you make. Exercise II provides an opportunity for you to appraise and possibly correct some of those assumptions.

Exercise II: Self-Appraisal

- Turn again to your Behavior Dynamics Interpretation.

- Read and study Part III: Behavior and Control.

- Read and study Part IV: Behavior and Predictive Action.

- Note the +1 in Part IV.

- Circle the (+1) for any of the eleven entries if you rate your ability higher than the numbers that are circled.

- See Example A.

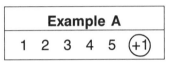

- Count the number of (+1) that you have circled. Place the total on line 2 of the calculation section.

- Find the subtotal by adding line *1* and line *2*. Place on line *3*.

- Refer to your Graphs I, II, and III on pages 40 and 41.

- Count the number of plotting points in the shaded areas on all three graphs. Place the total on line *4*.

- Find the grand total by subtracting line *4* from line *3*. Place on line *5*.

- Refer to the following scoring for your rating.

Scoring Scale for Self-Appraisal
90 - 110 Superior
84 - 89 Excellent
78 - 83 Very Good
72 - 77 Good
66 - 71 Fair
60 - 65 Poor
21 - 59 Very Low

Step Four
Behavior and Choice

Understanding the components of the *behavior act* is helpful in making choices—for managing change, conflict, and control. The behavior act is the means for redirecting our energy from conditioned responses.

**The behavior act has four components:
(1) acting, (2) thinking, (3) feeling,
and (4) the underlying bodily functions.**

Each of us varies in how and to what degree we have developed and integrated the four components of the behavior act.

There has been a marked tendency in our culture to value thinking more than feeling. In addition, the component of thinking has been emphasized in the socialization of males and the component of feeling in the socialization of females.

Before considering the important aspect of integration of the components of the behavior act, let us first consider this question:

**How much choice—and control—do we have over
the components of the behavior act?**

---

(1) Acting

At first glance, we seem to have total choice and control over what we do. We can get out of bed, take a walk, call a friend, find a job, ask for a raise. However, our actions are not random; they are purposeful. They are usually consistent with our character structure.

Based in our feelings, emotions, and passions, the private logic of our character structure influences the course of many of our actions. We feel conflict when we depart too far from our beliefs—our truth. Thus, we can conclude that, while we have some control over our actions, it is not as complete as we might have thought.

(2) Thinking

In managing change, conflict, and control, we rely upon our ability to "think our way through." Without doubt, the degree of our ability to reason marks us as distinctly human. We have the power to focus our thoughts, and to bring our reason to bear on problems.*

On the other hand, we can do so for only a certain amount of time before we tire and our thoughts begin to wander. And our character structure usually directs our thoughts along in a predictable pattern. Moreover, we cannot exert the kind of choice over our thinking that allows us to not think. Our minds are still busy even as we sleep or meditate. We have less choice over our thinking than we have over our actions.

(3) Feelings, Emotions, and Passions

We have already seen that our character structure, which is deeply embedded in our affective nature, has an impact on our actions and our thinking. How much choice and control do we have over the feeling component of the behavior act?

Most of us have experienced the power of our emotions and our passions. When experiencing anger, we know the difficulty of maintaining control. Choosing not to be angry in the midst of the emotion would be difficult, if not impossible. Conversely, we know that it is hard to pretend what we do not feel.

Our feelings, emotions, and passions come unbidden and sometimes unwanted. Even though we may deny what we feel, we eventually must claim the feelings as our own. But overall, we can conclude that we often lack direct control over our affective nature.

(4) Bodily Functions

We have the least amount of choice—and control—over the physiological component of the behavior act. For example, it is very hard to control the heartbeat when we see a test question

---

*The third book of the Aristos Psychology trilogy is devoted to the processes of thinking and reasoning. It is due for publication in early 1990.

for which we do not have an immediate answer. When our fear subsides and we can think more clearly, we drum up a possible answer and our heartbeat returns to normal.

We have some control over our actions, less control over our thinking, and even less over our affective state—feelings, emotions, and passions. The bodily functions which underlie behavior acts are almost entirely automatic.

That may not seem like an entirely bright picture to someone who has been brought up on "you can do anything you want" or "being a self-made person." However, we do have choice and we do have control.

The answer does not lie in one or the other components, but in an integrated approach that results in choice and control.

We choose our behavior by learning to orchestrate acting, thinking, and feeling together.

Even though we are not totally free agents, we do have significant areas of choice and change—if we understand how to bring it about. That is, we can consciously choose to integrate the components of our behavior which war with each other.

Integrating the Components of Behavior

Anyone who has tried to carry out an intention to go on a diet, or stop smoking or drinking, experiences the difficulty of handling change, conflict, and control by thought alone. Our intentions, however well-meaning, are not always charged with psychic energy. But that is where it starts—intentions. It is the first step in a three-step process.

1) Choosing to redirect intentions.

2) Choosing to make the unconscious conscious.

3) Choosing to practice the action.

Step 1: Choosing to Redirect Intentions

You may or may not have liked what you read concerning your behavior in the Behavior Dynamics Interpretation. You may wish to change or to modify some part of how you are responding to change or conflict. We begin with intentions.

- **Refer to the interpretation for Entry No. I that you received in Personal Workshop I (table 2, page 49). This is referred to as Intended Behavior.**

- **Note the box before each intention.**

- **Write "Y" for Yes, if you desire to continue the intention.**

- **Write "N" for No, if you desire to discontinue the intention.**

- **Add to the list additional intentions that are essential in your new behavior direction.**

Remember that change is a series of approximations rather than one huge leap. New intentions are easier if they tap the psychic energy that is implicit in Graph II. Rethinking your intentions gives a new direction to your Orientation System.

Step 2. Choosing to Make the Unconscious Conscious*

The energy to implement your new intentions comes primarily from your affective nature—your feelings, emotions, and passions. These coalesce into beliefs. Becoming familiar with your affective nature is the key to your beliefs. Careful study of the interpretation of your affective nature sensitizes you to this aspect of your behavior that is often hidden from yourself as well as from others.

- **Refer to the interpretation for Entry No. II that you received in Personal Workshop I (table 3, page 53). This is referred to as Concealed Behavior.**

- **Note the box before each description of your affective nature.**

- **Write "Y" for Yes, if you feel this description is helpful to your intention.**

---

*The second book of the trilogy on Aristos Psychology is devoted to the process of recognizing and working with the feelings, emotions, and passions of our affective nature. It is due for publication in the latter part of 1989.

- Write "N" for No, if you feel that this description is not helpful to your new intentions.

As you begin to recognize how you demonstrate your affective nature in everyday life, you are making the unconscious conscious. Gradually, you can turn that psychic energy in a new direction.

This step is as critical as redirecting your intentions. Matching your emotions and beliefs with your intentions empowers your actions.

Step 3: Choosing to Practice the Action

Redirected intentions and greater consciousness of your emotions set the stage for positive change. Positive change can be small or large. It may involve a major step such as moving from a survival mode to a success mode. It may involve learning to say yes or no at appropriate times.

People vary a great deal in their approach to taking new actions. Some see it as exciting; others see it as dangerous. But most of us feel threatened when taking actions that are a departure from our "truth." When making significant changes, we are often questioning what we have learned or what we have been taught. To some, it is an earthshaking experience to move to an individual identity.

Choosing to integrate the components of the behavior act—thinking, feeling, and acting—is critical in managing change, conflict, and control. New actions tend to be weak and inconsistent; they require effort.

As the action is repeated, some of our doubt fades and the action becomes stronger. Our own behavior becomes the reward as we begin to see the results. Very slowly, our belief system becomes engaged and turns in a new direction, releasing the psychic energy that is needed. Actions become easier and grow in strength.

Responding to the Behavior Indicator at periodic intervals of three to four weeks will enable you to obtain a fresh fix and to make course corrections.

Change and conflict present an opportunity for the unfolding of your character in a new situation—an opportunity that permits you to realign yourself with a new reality in constructive ways.

Personal Workshop III
The Danger Zone...
Extended Pattern Analysis

Step One:	The Danger Zone
Step Two:	Red-Flagged Intentions: *Graph I*
Step Three:	Red-Flagged Passions: *Graph II*
Step Four:	Red-Flagged Behavior: *Graph III*

This workshop will identify the effect of intense or changing forces within you or your environment on the three systems of your personality—Orientation, Energy, and Self-Affirmation.

Step One

The Danger Zone

Plotting points in the flagged or shaded areas on any one of the three graphs result in an extended pattern. Plotting points in those areas are a warning: You are in the danger zone.

In figure 4 there are two flagged plotting points in the shaded area of the sample graph. The plotting point in column 1 on the t (taking) factor is in the shaded area at the *top* of the graph. Identified by the capital letter to the right, this area is designated as area *A*.

The plotting point in column 3 on the r (responding) factor is in the shaded area at the *bottom* of the graph. Identified by the capital letter to the right, this area is designated as area *F.*

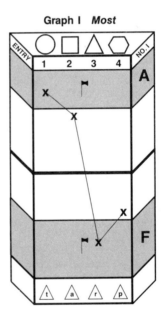

Graph I *Most*

Figure 4. Red-Flagged Plotting Points on Graph I

The treatment of flagged plotting points will vary for the three graphs. If you have flagged plotting points in Graph I or II, you will receive a general explanation for their occurrence and what measures you can take. If you have flagged plotting points in Graph III, you will receive an analysis of your extended pattern.

Step Two
Red-Flagged Intentions: *Graph I*

Examine your Graph I and respond to these questions.

- **Do you have any flagged plotting points in the shaded *A* area at the top of the graph?**

  yes _____   no _____

- **Do you have any flagged plotting points in the shaded *F* area at the bottom of the graph?**

  yes _____   no _____

- **If you have one or more yes responses, read the following material. (You will find it helpful to study the material even if you do not have plotting points in the flagged or shaded areas.)**

When Red-Flagged Plotting Points Occur in Graph I

Extreme plotting points are not unusual in Graph I. Despite their frequency, they do indicate the presence of some anxiety, a tilt toward distress. In some situations, the distress can be severe.

Graph I reflects your adaptive behavior. As the situation changes, you reconsider your intentions and respond accordingly. It is not unusual to overreach or to fall short when faced with different circumstances. New behavior often follows this principle.

**We use extreme positions to gain momentum
for the adaptive effort. When adaptation is
complete, we return to a moderate position.**

This change syndrome can have lasting effects. It is not unlike a rubber band that has been expanded. Depending upon
how long and how much it has stretched, there will be a difference in circumference when it is again relaxed.

Graph I often reflects this stretching phenomenom, resulting
in such things as unrealistic judgments and trial and error learning. Sometimes the extreme position that is taken on intentions
reflects negative influences in the environment.

Teenagers, with their tendency to make unrealistic judgments,
are a good example of trial and error learning. They frequently
have flagged plotting points in Graph I. Approximately 350
young people were included in our research population and a
high percentage demonstrated a flagged plotting point in Graph
I. Struggling to cope with many new experiences, teenagers often
careen between the extremes of behavior.

Flagged plotting points in Graph I may also result from negative influences in the environment. Faced with such life experiences as an alcoholic spouse, an unfair employer, or a dictatorial
parent, many persons engage in red-flagged intentions. They
are attempting to balance the extreme behavior of the other
person.

On the other hand, a red-flagged plotting point may not arise
out of new experiences, or out of a reaction to changes in the
environment. It may be the person's usual direction or orientation to life situations.

Intervention is sometimes necessary in the sense of rethinking your intentions or altering your environment. (The means
of doing so was discussed in Personal Workshop II.) What began
as a slight tilt toward distress can become entrenched and may
lead to a wild toboggan ride down an increasingly steep slope.

Step Three
Red-Flagged Passions: *Graph II*

Examine your Graph II and respond to these questions.

• **Do you have any flagged plotting points in the shaded *A* area at the top of the graph?**

yes _____   no _____

• **Do you have any flagged plotting points in the shaded *F* area at the bottom of the graph?**

yes _____   no _____

• **If you have one or more *yes* response, read the following material. (Even if you do not have plotting points in the flagged or shaded areas, you will find it helpful to study the material.)**

When Red-Flagged Plotting Points Occur in Graph II

Figure 5 depicts a sample of Graph II. Note the components of the affective nature—feeling, emotion, and passion in relationship to the flagged or shaded areas of the graph.

Feeling is the part of our affective nature that contains the least psychic energy. It is represented in areas *C* and *D*—the graph's inner ranges. In general, this is a comfortable zone. The exception occurs in the case of suppressed emotion. When that occurs, we may experience long-term negative feelings in coping with our inner conflict.

Emotion has a higher intensity of psychic energy than feeling. This is depicted in areas *B* and *E*. Emotions are largely identified with our survival mode but they are also evident in our struggle to succeed.

Graph II *Least*

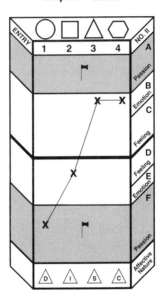

Figure 5.   Red-Flagged Plotting Points on Graph II

Passion, as you might expect, is the most intense in terms of psychic energy. It is found in the extremes of the graph—the shaded and flagged areas *A* and *F.* Passion is often the most enduring element of our affective nature. *Passions underlie our deepest beliefs and our strongest convictions.*

When flagged plotting points occur in Graph II, an excess of psychic energy has been released from your passions. That creates a climate of discomfort and often danger—for yourself or for others. Your behavior is in the extreme range. You are acting in response or in opposition—moving toward or away from people and events with great energy.

Table 7 depicts some of the potential behavior that occurs at the extremes on the energy points of D, I, S, and C.

Table 7. Passions Associated with Red-Flagged Behavior in Graph II

Flagged Area A (passion)	Energy Points	Flagged Area F (passion)
overcoming	D or Dominance	fear
captivating	I or Inducement	distrust
surrendering	S or Submission	overactive
hostility	C or Compliance	unyielding

In the example in figure 5, the person has a flagged energy point on D or Dominance in area F. The person has a passion of *fear* and uses the intensity of the psychic energy to perceive and avoid all kinds of danger. There is a marked resistance to accepting responsibility for people or events.

Examine your Graph II to identify what energy points are in the shaded or flagged areas *A* or *F*. Indicate by checking (✔) the energy point in either the *A* or *F* column.

A	Energy Point	F
_____ ( )	Dominance	( ) _____
_____ ( )	Inducement	( ) _____
_____ ( )	Submission	( ) _____
_____ ( )	Compliance	( ) _____

Fill in the appropriate word for your (✔) energy point by referring to table 7.

Obviously, the psychic energy unleashed by our passions may be used for destructive or constructive purposes. Nevertheless, it is a danger zone because of the flood of psychic energy. Flagged energy points in Graph II often reflect a lack of balance in the belief system. There are two possibilities for working with this flow of energy. One is short-term, the other long-term.

Short-term: *Evaluating Intentions*

Plotting points in Graph II are more difficult to alter than plotting points in Graph I. It is easier to change our intentions than what we feel and believe. Thus, for the immediate future, you can exert some control over that energy by reevaluating your intentions. In this approach, there is no alteration of the belief system or reduction of energy. The short-term solution provides you with greater insight into the direction you are heading. This process was discussed in Personal Workshop II, Step Four.

Long-term: *Making the Unconscious Conscious*

This solution is concerned with the character structure and the underlying beliefs. There is a possibility of reducing the flow of energy to a rate that is easier to handle by altering the belief systems. There is also the possibility of redirecting that flow of energy. This is accomplished by making the unconscious conscious.

Some of our ways of interacting with others were developed in the prememory phase—before 4 or 5 years of age. Later experiences and the resulting beliefs that underlie much of our behavior pattern have long since receded into our unconscious. However, these beliefs continue to exert an influence on our behavior.

Reexamining our affective nature—as described in the Graph II interpretation in Personal Workshop I—begins the process of making the unconscious conscious. It helps us to reevaluate our "truth" under current circumstances.

Most important: Beliefs are not cast in stone. We are not predetermined. While we do not have complete freedom of will, we do have a significant area of choice. Making choices makes us fully human; it gives us control over our lives.

Graph II is a dynamic graph; it is all our yesteryears. It reveals what we have learned. When you have a balance in your beliefs (Graph II), you are more likely to engage in constructive behavior when your passions are aroused and you have flagged energy points for a period of time. The process for reexamining your beliefs was discussed in Personal Workshop II, Step Four.

Step Four
Red-Flagged Predicted Behavior: *Graph III*

Examine your third graph. Respond to these questions.

- **Do you have any flagged plotting points in the shaded *A* area at the top of the graph?**

           yes _____   no _____

- **Do you have any flagged plotting points in the shaded *F* area at the bottom of the graph?**

           yes _____   no _____

- **If you have one or more yes responses, you will be directed to the specific analysis of your extended pattern. This is an additional interpretation of your Central Pattern. Prior to the analysis, an overview will increase your understanding of the concept of the extended pattern. (You will find it helpful to study the material even if you do not have flagged plotting points in Graph III.)**

What is Meant by the Extended Patterns

Your third graph, or Entry No. III, was used in Personal Workshop I to direct you to your Central Pattern. You were provided an overview of your work and social behavior. But there is more.

Flagged plotting points in Graph III move the Central Pattern in a different direction. The direction depends on whether the flagged plotting points are in the shaded area *A*, at the top of the graph, or the shaded area *F*, at the bottom of the graph, or both.

In figure 6, the Central Pattern is thirteen—Pacesetter. If the person has a flagged plotting point in area *A*, the extended pattern of Taskmaster emerges. If the flagged plotting point is in area *F*, the extended pattern of Troublemaker comes into being.

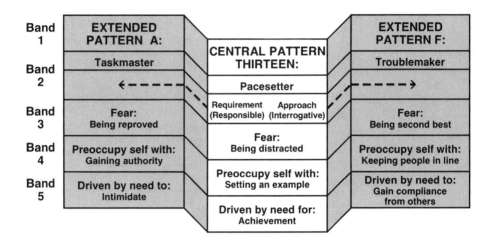

Figure 6.   Central Pattern, Entry Number Thirteen

It is possible, of course, to be identified with all three patterns —the Central Pattern and the two extended patterns— but, in general, the extended patterns will be predominant.

Figure 6 provides an example of how the Central Pattern and the related extended patterns are organized. The analysis compares the behavior of the Central Pattern to the extreme behavior in the extended patterns. The preferred pattern, of course, is the Central Pattern. It represents a more balanced attempt on the part of the individual to handle life's problems.

The major headings of the analysis are presented within bands of information.

Band 1: *Number and Area.* This band is the major reference guide. It alerts you to the Central Pattern number and to the *A* and *F* extended patterns. Even if you do not have a flagged plotting point in Graph III, you will want to locate and study the analysis. It is not unusual to move into an extended pattern during a period of stress. The analysis will help you to better understand and deal with your behavior when that occurs.

Band 2: *Title.* This band identifies the title of each pattern. It also includes the *requirement* and *approach* for the Central Pattern and the extended patterns. This will be discussed after the other three bands.

Band 3: *Fear.* This is the behavior that keeps us running toward or away from people or events. Some individuals run from failure while others run from success. Both may be driven by fear.

Band 4: *Preoccupy Self With.* This band describes the behavior that tends to be on our mind a great deal. It becomes the basis on which we take action.

Band 5: *Driven by Need To.* This band identifies the objective that thrusts us into action.

Requirement and Approach

Band 2 will identify the requirement and approach for the Central Pattern and the extended patterns. Both are based in the person's perception.

Requirement identifies the person's perception of the conditions in the environment. This may or may not be the reality of the situation. But it is the person's perception and the basis for action. In the example of the Pacesetter, band 2 identifies that the individual views the conditions as requiring *responsible* action.

Even when the person has an extended pattern in the flagged area *A* and the Taskmaster emerges, there is a tendency to view "responsible" as the appropriate requirement for the conditions in that environment. The person in the extended pattern, however, experiences anxiety; there is a "tilt" toward distress in meeting the requirement of being responsible.

Approach identifies the person's perception of how to meet that requirement. The Pacesetter takes an interrogative approach. Even when the extended pattern of the Troublemaker emerges, the same approach is used, but intensified. The person uses a suspicious questioning—an indication of increased anxiety.

Strategy and Tactic

The categories of requirement and approach relate to strategy and tactic. As we consider the requirement of the situation, we determine how we will position ourselves in relation to others. That is strategy. It is a process that includes appraisal and planning. On the other hand, the approach we use is related to tactic. It is here that we employ techniques that involve our contact with others.

Requirement of the condition—or strategy—is related to plotting points above the midline. When these plotting points extend into the flagged area *A,* we encounter additional stress in appraising the requirement of the situation and in planning our strategy.

The approach to others—or tactic—is related to the plotting points below the midline. When these plotting points extend into the flagged area *F,* we encounter additional stress in implementing the approach and using tactics.

Procedure for Obtaining Your Extended Pattern Analysis

• Refer to your Entry No. III in table 8 for the page number.

• Study the figure which compares the three patterns.

• Read the interpretation for both extended patterns.

• Concentrate on extended pattern *A* if you have any flagged points in area *A* and on extended pattern *F* if you have any flagged points in area *F.*

Table 8. Analysis for Extended Patterns

Entry No. III	Page
one	414
two	416
three	418
four	420
twelve	422
thirteen	424
fourteen	426
twenty-three	428
twenty-four	430
thirty-four	432
one twenty-three	434
one twenty-four	436
one thirty-four	438
two thirty-four	440

Personal Workshop IV
The Compatibility Factor

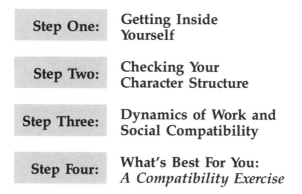

Step One:	Getting Inside Yourself
Step Two:	Checking Your Character Structure
Step Three:	Dynamics of Work and Social Compatibility
Step Four:	What's Best For You: *A Compatibility Exercise*

One of the truths about the human condition is that we cannot live apart from our own kind. And yet, we often find it difficult to live and work with one another.

Work organizations spend millions of dollars in the selection of employees and millions more in helping them to work together productively. In the personal setting, some individuals spend their lives looking for the "right" person. Many more resign themselves to unsatisfying relationships.

All this activity underscores a determination to find some measure of compatibility. In an increasingly interdependent society and world, compatibility—the ability to get along with one another—promises to become a key issue at all levels.

This workshop will introduce dynamic principles of compatibility and new ways of looking at this enduring human problem, which touches every area of our lives. We will focus on the strategy for bringing about compatibility rather than on the specific tactics, or techniques.

While deepening your understanding of the forces that work for or against compatibility, you will have an opportunity to apply this information to a significant person in your work or personal setting. It is an exercise that can be repeated in future situations in which you have need to increase the *climate of compatibility.*

Step One
Getting Inside Yourself

Up to this point, your interpretations have yielded information to help you sort out your overall response to your existing life situation. Additional information has been provided to help you deal with making choices in managing change, conflict, and control. You also learned about the potential danger of extended patterns.

Obviously, this information is important to people compatibility in terms of understanding yourself. But, in this workshop, the interpretation will go one step further. It focuses on your belief system. In other words, you will be identifying those convictions that underlie your character structure.

The appraisal of your belief system will help you to get inside yourself—to discover your basic convictions about the human condition. You'll find answers to such questions as: What belief is reflected when you choose to cooperate? What belief is operating when you express appreciation or disapproval?

Before we turn to the interpretation, a definition of compatibility will provide a common understanding of this important concept.

Compatibility is a harmony that grows from an *appreciation* for what is *similar* and a *respect* for what is *different* in ourselves and in the other person.

Efforts to show appreciation and respect are often impeded by events. Our environment is not always a comfortable one. Stresses and strains—marital discord, concern over children, loss of a work contract, a demanding employer—produce uneven, unpredictable, and sometime difficult behavior.

Faced with personal or work relationships in which incompatibility rears its head, many individuals begin their sentences with "If only he. . . ." or "Why can't she. . . ." There is a strong tendency to think that everything would be all right if only the other person would change his or her behavior. You cannot do a great deal about the other person's behavior by wishful thinking. But you *can* do a great deal about improving the climate of compatibility on your own. By increasing your knowledge about your beliefs—the touchstone of your character—you can appraise your contribution, negative or positive, to the harmony of the relationship.

We turn now to an interpretation of your belief system.

To Receive Your Interpretation

- Turn to *Interpretation Central* on page 443.

- Follow the procedure for obtaining Energetic Flowchart Interpretation, Part II, using Graph II as the reference graph.

- Study Energetic Flowchart Interpretation, Part II.

- Proceed to Step Two of the workshop.

Step Two

Checking Your Character Structure

The second step will assist you in applying the interpretation from Energetics Flowchart, Part II. Table 9 provides a summary of the fourteen Central Patterns and the recommended compatibility patterns for each Central Pattern.

In Personal Workshop I, you completed a compatibility review of your Central Pattern with one social and one work compatibility pattern. In this step, you are asked to study the recommended choice in social compatibility and the second choice in work compatibility. Completing the Compatibility Review will help you to identify the essential differences from and similarities to your own strengths. Then you will be able to evaluate whether your belief system permits or discourages the *appreciation* for the *similarities* and the *respect* for the *differences*.

To Complete Your Compatibility Review

- **Write in your compatibility patterns by referring to table 9.**

  Work: 2nd choice _____ page _____

  Social: recommended _____ page _____

- **Write in the page numbers by referring to table 4 on page 56.**
- **Study the interpretations.**
- **Complete the Compatibility Review.**

Table 9. Identification of Work and Social Compatibility Patterns Assigned to a Central Personality Pattern

CENTRAL PATTERN	WORK COMPATIBILITY		SOCIAL COMPATIBILITY	
	FIRST CHOICE	SECOND CHOICE	NATURAL CHOICE	RECOMMENDED CHOICE
One... Dominator	234 Special Advisor	24 Strategic Planner	3 Stabilizer	34 Standard Bearer
Two... Inducer	134 Designer	13 Harmonizer	4 Conformer	234 Special Advisor
Three... Stabilizer	124 Negotiator	12 Front-runner	1 Dominator	12 Front-runner
Four... Conformer	123 Administrator	23 Harmonizer	2 Inducer	23 Harmonizer
Twelve... Front-runner	34 Standard Bearer	134 Designer	34 Standard Bearer	234 Special Advisor
Thirteen... Pacesetter	24 Strategic Planner	34 Standard Bearer	234 Special Advisor	12 Front-runner
Fourteen... Originator	23 Harmonizer	12 Front-runner	24 Strategic Planner	34 Standard Bearer
Twenty-three... Harmonizer	14 Originator	12 Front-runner	134 Designer	34 Standard Bearer
Twenty-four... Strategic Planner	13 Pacesetter	234 Special Advisor	124 Negotiator	34 Standard Bearer
Thirty-four... Standard Bearer	12 Front-runner	124 Negotiator	23 Harmonizer	123 Administrator
One Twenty-three... Administrator	24 Strategic Planner	234 Special Advisor	14 Originator	234 Special Advisor
One Twenty-four... Negotiator	23 Harmonizer	24 Strategic Planner	34 Standard Bearer	234 Special Advisor
One Thirty-four... Designer	12 Front-runner	123 Administrator	23 Harmonizer	13 Pacesetter
Two Thirty-four... Special Advisor	12 Front-runner	24 Strategic Planner	123 Administrator	23 Harmonizer

Compatibility Review

On the basis of your own behavior interpretations and the interpretations of your work and social compatibility persons, respond to the following items.

List five of your personal strengths. (Ex.: communicate high standards)

1. _____
2. _____
3. _____
4. _____
5. _____

List five of your personal limitations. (Ex: prefer win-lose situations)

1. _____
2. _____
3. _____
4. _____
5. _____

List five personal strengths of your work compatibility person (2nd choice) that *differ* from your strengths.

1. _____
2. _____
3. _____
4. _____
5. _____

List five personal strengths of your social compatibility person (recommended choice) that are *similar* to your strengths.

1. _____
2. _____
3. _____
4. _____
5. _____

In the *social* situation, regarding your compatibility person:

1. What can you do for the person that he/she would find difficult to do for himself or herself?

_____

_____

_____

2. What common limitations do you observe in the other person and yourself?

_____

_____

_____

3. Is there one aspect of the other person's personality that would negate an ongoing linkage?

_____

_____

_____

In the *work* situation, regarding your compatibility person:

1. What can you do for the person that he/she would find difficult to do for himself or herself?

_____

_____

_____

2. What common limitations do you observe in the other person and yourself?

_____

_____

_____

3. Is there one aspect of the other person's personality that would negate an ongoing linkage?

_____

_____

_____

Step Three
Dynamics of Work and Social Compatibility

As an aid in applying principles of compatibility to your personal or work situation, you are asked to respond to the following statements. Rank the statements in order of importance according to how you perceive your behavior. Use a 1 to 4 response with 1 being the highest rank. Place your responses under the "self" column.

	self	other
1. I expend energy to maintain relationships.	____	____
2. I expend energy to restore order.	____	____
3. I expend energy to control events.	____	____
4. I expend energy to build alliances.	____	____

In the column marked "other," rank the statements according to how you think a significant person (spouse, close friend) might rate the items. Or you might ask the person to appraise himself or herself directly.

A comparison of the rankings on the four statements is often revealing. Our experiences with these rankings have been instructive. We have found a significant tendency toward similarity in rankings when the "other" comes from the personal setting. Conversely, there is a tendency toward differences in rankings when the "other" comes from the work setting. What are the explanations?

Work Compatibility

All of us have the opportunity to establish our own identity, to project a uniqueness in the way we approach life's problems. The material on the Energetics Flowchart provides you with descriptive information that further documents your behavior pattern.

But you also learn quickly that your survival and your success depend upon your relationship with other people. And they, in turn, need the qualities that you represent. In fact, your personality characteristics are strongly determined and influenced by your relations with others.

You also learn that, in given situations, according to the purpose of the events or activities, people whose personality patterns are different from yours are a valuable asset to your ambitions. Persons with different patterns help you to meet your objective, enabling you to fulfill the expectations that others have of you.

In the case of work compatibility, you need to clearly identify your purpose. What is it that you want to do? It is this purpose that most often determines the kind of persons who can best work together to achieve optimum results.

During the development of a group that is designed to fulfill a task, three essential questions should be raised.

1) Is the purpose of the group to develop a creative solution?

2) Is the task to develop a structured solution, for example, procedural guidelines?

3) What is the deadline? How long will the group be in existence?

The answers to these questions determine whether the group should be composed of individuals with personality *differences* or personality *similarities.*

Recent research studies support our findings in the area of people compatibility and our recommended assignments to work groups. One such study was conducted at the University of Arkansas by M. Aamodt and W. Kimbrough (1982). They used The Personal Profile System developed by J. Geier (1979) to identify behavioral style patterns.

The conclusions drawn from the results indicate that team heterogeneity or *personal differences* is a superior base for assembling a work team when creative solutions are desired. Conversely, the researchers concluded that homogeneity or *personal similarities* may be better when dealing with structural problems.

Assignment to Work Groups

When two, three, or more persons are assigned to work groups, *Graph III personality patterns are recommended.* The assignments are based upon the purpose of the group. Figure 7 includes teams that have different objectives. The assignments of individuals with similar or different patterns reflect those varying objectives.

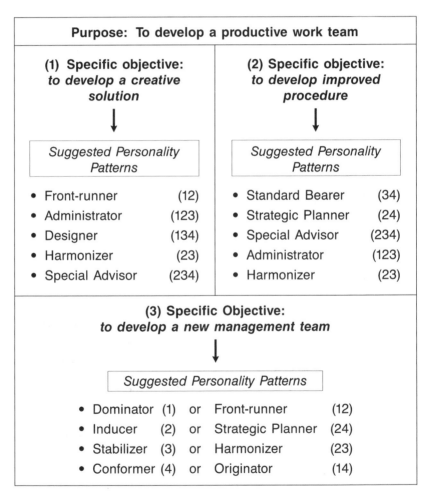

Purpose: To develop a productive work team	
(1) Specific objective: *to develop a creative solution* ↓ *Suggested Personality Patterns*	**(2) Specific objective:** *to develop improved procedure* ↓ *Suggested Personality Patterns*
• Front-runner (12) • Administrator (123) • Designer (134) • Harmonizer (23) • Special Advisor (234)	• Standard Bearer (34) • Strategic Planner (24) • Special Advisor (234) • Administrator (123) • Harmonizer (23)

(3) Specific Objective:
to develop a new management team

↓

Suggested Personality Patterns

- Dominator (1) or Front-runner (12)
- Inducer (2) or Strategic Planner (24)
- Stabilizer (3) or Harmonizer (23)
- Conformer (4) or Originator (14)

Figure 7.　Work Team Alignments

Figure 7 identifies the composition of team members by the personality patterns that are most apt to fulfill the objective of the team. The basic line of reasoning can be demonstrated in the (3) grouping—a new management team. Strong differences should exist in such a team. Thus, the four primary patterns are listed: Dominator (Taking/Dominance), Inducer (Attracting/Inducement), Stabilizer (Responding/Submission), Conformer (Preserving/Compliance).

However, it is even more important to enlist people who combined this primary behavior with another strong attribute. Thus, there is also a listing of the four patterns that possess those personality characteristics (patterns 12, 24, 23, and 14).

We turn now from a discussion of principles of compatibility in the work setting to principles of compatibility in the personal setting. Consideration in this area of our lives entails different goals and objectives.

Social Compatibility

As a result of our research into the area of people compatibility with the Behavior Indicator, we have included both a recommendation for work *and* social compatibility. Your reference to table 9 and your assigned reading has prepared you to better understand the reason for two sets of compatibility persons. But a major question must still be considered: How are we to explain the preference for one person over another?

Three principles grew out of our research into this question with the Behavior Indicator. These are:

• Opposites attract.

• Purpose decides union.

• Character creates people cohesiveness.

A brief analysis of each principle will assist you in understanding the personal preferences you have regarding special people in your life.

Opposites Attract. This first principle is perhaps the most frequent reason given for our affinity to another person. We often discover something in that person that may be lacking in ourselves.

One of the oldest accounts of a "matched pair" is found in the story of Adam and Eve. Their obvious mutual attraction is not difficult to understand. Given the situation, they really didn't have that much choice. When the field is more open, the decisions that people make in selecting companions are intriguing.

Carl Jung (1936) strongly believed that opposites do attract and even fascinate each other. Our research into social compatibility generally supports Jung's belief. The inclusion of the *natural choice* as one of the two compatibility patterns for the social setting attests to our research findings.

However, our research also indicated that additional factors enter into the preferences for one person over another. Focused interviews were employed as the research method to identify the participants' rationale for their preferences in persons.

Differences were cited by people as an initial attention factor. However, it was *similarities* that tended to prolong the interactions and to make them more interesting and vigorous. When this occurs, relationships begin to develop.

It is understandable that individuals would tend to prefer some common ground that would help them to bridge the gap created by their differences. This need is reflected in the second principle of social compatibility: Purpose decides union.

Purpose Decides Union. We have already observed that a sense of purpose is the key ingredient in compatibility when considering work units. Clearly defined goals and stated objectives dictate the kind of personnel who are needed for satisfactory performance or completion of the task.

In the social or personal setting, individuals also have hopes and aspirations that are best satisfied by people who have similar expectations. We may not be "turned on" by an opposite physical appearance or personality trait.

Instead, we seek a *partnership* with someone who is proceeding in the same direction as we ourselves. There is a potential meshing of purpose. In this sense, we are more compatible in both interest and in method.

However, the possibility that our interests may suddenly change or even modify gradually over a period of time may alter the compatibility that is primarily based upon purpose. For example, a marriage that is based solely on the purpose of rearing children may encounter difficulties when the children are reared. The spouses have lost their common purpose.

The first two principles that support the idea of preferences and compatibility recede in importance in light of our most recent findings. We refer to the third principle as: Character creates people cohesiveness.

Character Creates People Cohesiveness. This principle has long been neglected. This is due, in part, because of the lack of an instrument that could identify the elements of character.

In the past, it has been largely assumed that people simply were seeking an external factor in the other person that they could "tune into." There was a search for factors that would permit observable comparisons. These conclusions are true to a certain point. However, our study indicated that people form strong alliances when their personal characters are compatible.

Compatibility that promotes cohesiveness does not purport that *positive* character is the common denominator. In fact, two persons or a group of individuals may form a strong alliance on the basis of *negative* character. An extreme example is the pair of Bonnie and Clyde. This union suggests similar character elements that brought them together until their death at the hand of law officers.

The premise of the character cohesive principle is that individuals are united by their private logic. The principle operates in this manner:

**Cohesive compatibility occurs when
the character structures of the persons
are unfolding in a similar manner.**

Character appears to be a more important determinant of compatibility than either of the other two principles—opposites attract and mutual purpose. The cohesiveness arises in the commonality of evaluation—a similar way of looking at the world. Their personal beliefs—their truths—are validated.

Step Four

What's Best for You: *A Compatibility Exercise*

The fourth step contains a compatibility exercise that will help you to apply the principle that "character creates cohesive compatibility." The exercise enables you to identify and share your beliefs—your "truth" about how you see the world.

We sometimes conceal, even from ourselves, that a "partner" has a totally different perception about life problems than we do. Sharing truths begins the process of meshing them. This is the processs that occupies young married or engaged couples either consciously or unconsciously. The longer it is delayed, the greater the stress and strain in the relationship.

Some people never quite identify their disparity in beliefs. Marriage and business partners often separate on the basis of incompatibility without understanding what the incompatibility is all about. Sometimes there is recognition. When the character of the other person is undergirded with negative character traits, the reason for severing ties is clearer.

You are encouraged to use the following exercise to check out the character compatibility between you and another person in your work or social environment. You will be able to determine how well you understand the private logic of the one with whom you are presently interacting. You will discover the expectations that you have for the person whom you most desire to be close to you. You will be able to communicate the areas of difference between your ideal and the real that exists in the relationship.

Compatibility Exercise

A. Choose a significant person from your social or work environment.

B. Use the Behavior Indicator to develop these patterns:

Step 1 You respond to the indicator based upon your interactions with that person. Develop the graphs and determine your entry numbers.

Step 2 Your compatibility person responds to the indicator based upon his or her interactions with you.

Step 3 You respond to the indicator based upon what you would like that person to be—your ideal.

Step 4 Your compatibility person responds to the indicator based upon what he or she would like you to be—the ideal.

C. Study the resulting interpretations that are available in Personal Workshop I for each of the three graphs. Begin with the interpretations that are based on the real.

D. Give particular attention to the interpretation that is available through the Energetics Flowchart II—The Belief System. *It is generally considered a potentially effective compatibility arrangement when your Graph II configuration is similar to the other person's Graph II.*

E. Consider the total pattern identified in Graph III. Graph III enlarges the view by providing an overall summary; hence the pivotal use of Graph III in suggesting your compatibility person in both work and social situations. The selection of the work or social interpretation will depend on whether your compatibility person is from the social or work setting.

F. Study the interpretations that are based upon the ideal. Compare the ideal and the real for yourself and the other person.

It is recommended that this compatibility exercise be used at least once during a six-month period of time. Obviously, change may occur within one's belief system—albeit slowly. With this change comes a potential difference in our preference for significant work and social persons. While we do not turn off, and on, to other people according to every new whim we develop, it is helpful to exchange new perceptions.

Personal Workshop V
Persuasion as a Quality Action

Step One: Your Persuasion Mode:
How You Take Charge

Step Two: Your Persuasion Mode:
How You Affect Others

Step Three: Quality Persuasion:
The Principles

Step Four: Persuasion Analysis:
An Exercise

Many people associate persuasion primarily with marketing and sales. But, in reality, all of us engage in the persuasion process in every area of our lives. Here is how we view persuasion:

Persuasion is the process whereby we gain attention, express needs, and explore the most satisfying ways to mutually assist one another.

For those in an authority position—executive, manager, supervisor, teacher, parent—persuasion is a tool for involving the other person in the larger purpose.

Persuasion is a complement to providing direction. It diminishes the need to give orders, make demands, and issue ultimatums. The ability to persuade enables you to humanize the coercive potential that is inherent in any position of authority.

For those who are not in a position of authority—employee, student, or minor—persuasion is a direct way to get your message to those in authority. It is a positive alternative to silence, unfair manipulation, clashes, slowdowns, strikes, or physical violence.

For those on an equal basis—friends, spouses, or work associates—persuasion is the way you make the other person aware of your convictions and what you think needs to be done.

Persuasion is truly a significant part of our lives. Unfortunately, the persuasion factor is often overlooked and in some cases minimized. We may even deny being persuasive. Failure to recognize the critical role of persuasion can have negative effects.

First, if we fail to appreciate the power of persuasion, we may rely unduly upon our power or authority or, conversely, on our power to resist authority. Second, we may fail to develop skill in the persuasion process. Third, we may fail to recognize when we use the persuasion process or the responsibility we have toward the person we persuade.

This workshop takes a systems approach. It focuses on you as the persuader, upon the person you hope to persuade, upon the process itself. Finally, you will have an opportunity to apply the principles of quality persuasion and the knowledge of you and the other person in a simulated persuasion exercise. The goal of this workshop can be stated in this way:

The purpose of the workshop is to turn the persuasion process into a *quality action* between you and the other person.

We begin with you as the focus in Step One.

Step One

Your Persuasion Mode: *How You Take Charge*

The persuasion process demands knowledge of self and knowledge of the other person. The urgency of this message is based in part upon two truisms:

Truism I:　If another person knows you better than you know him or her, the other person can control the persuasive process.

Truism II:　If another person knows you better than you know yourself, the other person can control you.

From these two truisms, we can conclude that, while knowledge of the other person is important to the persuasive process, knowledge of self is critical in maintaining control of one's destiny.

Of course, not everyone who has knowledge of you wishes to control you. And you may not wish to control the person or persons of whom you have greater knowledge. Still, the potential for control or *use* of the other person is there. With knowledge of others comes power—and responsibility toward the other person. (This point will be discussed in Step Three of the workshop.) Knowledge of self is an important step to assuming that responsibility.

Certainly, just living in a consumer-oriented society requires knowledge of self. We are all potential persuadees of the larger processes of our society. Millions of dollars are spent in researching target populations and developing products or persuasive messages tailored for major impact. Even though you have the final control over what you choose to accept or buy, it is well to be aware of the continuing effort to persuade you toward certain ends.

Over and above those efforts are the specific attempts by individuals to persuade you. They scrutinize your behavior carefully—seeking an edge, small or large—to persuade you to their point of view.

It is in your interest as a potential "persuadee" that you have as much knowledge about yourself as they have about you. And, if you wish to spend part of your time as a persuader, it is essential to increase your self-insight.

Both Step One and Two of this workshop focus on you. Step One emphasizes your intentions. In the very first personal workshop, you were introduced to your intentions. Now the interpretation will be extended into the persuasion realm. You will be able to view your intentions as they apply to your attempts to influence the motivations of others.

The importance of intentions in the persuasion process can be identified in this key statement:

Intentions precede change in action.

This has a two-fold application. First, if you wish to take charge, altering your actions toward greater effectiveness in the persuasion process, you will need to alter your intentions, if they are inappropriate to that goal. A careful scrutiny of the interpretation will be helpful to you.

Second, if you wish to persuade others, your efforts need to be directed at their intentions, not at their actions. Persuasion which attempts to influence action alone misses the point entirely. Persuasion begins, instead, with the person's intention.

The interpretation will acquaint you with your intentions in regard to influencing the motivations of others. It begins the two-step process of gaining self-insight that will increase your effectiveness as a persuader.

To Obtain Your Interpretation

- Turn to Interpretation Central on page 443.
- Follow the procedure for obtaining Energetic Flowchart, Part I interpretation. Use Graph I as your reference.
- Complete the following exercise. It will be used in Step Three of the Workshop.
- After completing the items, proceed to Step Two.

After Reading Your Interpretation

Take Charge Exercise

1. Record four major ways in which you attempt to influence the motivations of others. Refer to Energetics Flowchart Part I.

    a. _____

    b. _____

    c. _____

    d. _____

2. List four areas from your Energetics Flowchart, Part I interpretation that you consider positive and four that you consider negative. Descriptions that fall in the flagged areas are usually considered negative.

    Positive Areas   Negative Areas

    a. _____   a. _____

    b. _____   b. _____

    c. _____   c. _____

    d. _____   d. _____

Step Two
Your Persuasion Mode: *How You Affect Others*

The second step of the workshop continues the process of providing information about you. Step One focused on your intentions to influence the motivations of others; this step identifies the effect you have on others.

Several key statements will help you to incorporate the interpretation. This statement is pivotal:

All conscious communication is persuasive.

At this point, you may doubt that all your conscious communication is persuasive. An exploration is in order. Let's examine two types of communication as examples.

Structured persuasive messages. These messages are designed to modify others' thoughts and actions. Communication messages in the selling and marketing areas are persuasively structured. That is, there is a deliberate attempt to create an environment in which people will accept the product or message. There is an identifiable strategy and tactics for accomplishing that.

In addition, a structured persuasive message might include carefully preparing for a staff meeting in which you wish to gain acceptance for your ideas. Or a predetermined persuasive message might also include cooking a spouse's favorite dinner as part of a persuasive message.

Structured educational messages. Here the intent is to inform rather than to persuade, and that is where much of the confusion arises both for the listener and for the sender of the message. The failure to recognize the persuasive impact of the educational message has two negative effects:

1) The person fails to anticipate the reaction of the listener.

2) The person neglects to take the responsibility for the persuasive impact.

To fully appreciate the importance of this point, let's explore several examples from different settings. Many teachers view their task as one of instilling knowledge in their students. In their estimation, the intention is to inform. However, ideas can be highly persuasive to students. Teachers who appreciate the persuasive impact of informative ideas are better able to understand the necessity for presenting both sides of a controversial issue. And they are better able to anticipate and deal with the reactions of parents and the community to certain ideas.

Still a different kind of an example can be drawn of a manager in a work setting. This particular manager had the habit of ending each staff meeting by passing on tidbits of information concerning the progress of other departments. Supposedly, his intention was only to inform.

However, the staff interpreted his "tidbits" as persuasion to greater efforts. They judged him as a manager who would never be satisfied with their efforts no matter how hard they worked. He was at a loss to understand their reaction to his unstructured message. He failed to appreciate that all conscious communication is persuasive.

Interestingly enough, the total effect of both structured and unstructured messages may often be the same—that is, they are understood and acted upon.

The *structured* message is received and is acted upon as it was intended. The *unstructured* message is received and is perceived as the *listener* desires it to be and acts accordingly.

Conscious and Unconscious Persuasion

But it can be even more complex. The interpretation that you will receive in this step of the workshop will reflect both the conscious and the unconscious levels of your persuasive efforts. Thus, a portion will not be as familiar to you. You may send different messages on that unconscious level and be totally unaware of it.

For example, you may inform your spouse that there is a documentary on television tonight. At the conscious level, you are simply giving the other person some information. Unconsciously, you have sent a persuasive message that you wish to watch that program.

This can evolve into a no-win situation for one or both of you. The persuasive message is not explicit and is unconscious on your part. It is difficult for either you or your spouse to comment on the persuasive message.

If your spouse reacts to your unconscious persuasion by insisting upon watching another program, you feel perfectly within your rights to ask in wide-eyed astonishment: "What are you getting so upset about? I didn't say you couldn't." Or, if your spouse accepts your unconscious persuasion and goes along with it only to later accuse you of being insensitive, you can come back with: "Why didn't you tell me you wanted to watch something else?"

The messages that we send on the conscious and unconscious levels are often mixed. They distort and impede the message and cause all kinds of problems in relating to others. At times, you may be at a loss to know if you have offended or pleased another person. By probing the way in which your messages are communicated and received, you will gain greater awareness of your behavior.

Keep in mind that many aspects of unconscious communication are also persuasive. Even our most innocuous statements have persuasive impact. Consider the following: "Dinner is ready." "It's hot in here." "I hear a noise downstairs."

It is both beneficial and necessary to increase your understanding of the way you affect others. What kind of message are you sending? What impact do you have on others? How are you being shaped in this persuasive process? These questions lead to a key statement:

We understand ourselves largely from the response we receive from others.

It is difficult, if not impossible, to simply ask countless numbers of persons: "How am I doing?" If you are very fortunate, you may have one or even two confidantes who are willing and competent to give you direct, unbiased feedback. But often these persons do not see you at critical points. And of course, that kind of frankness can strain a relationship.

A more effective way to determine your effect on others is to use such devices as the Behavior Indicator and receive an interpretation from the Energetics Flowchart.

To Obtain Your Interpretation

- Turn to Interpretation Central on page 443.
- Follow the procedure for obtaining Energetics Flowchart, Part III interpretation. Use Graph III as your reference point.
- Complete the following exercise. It will be used in Step Three of the workshop.
- After completing the items, proceed to Step Three.

After Reading Your Interpretation

Persuasion Feedback Exercise

1. Record four major ways in which you affect others. Refer to Energetics Flowchart, Part III.

   a. _____

   b. _____

   c. _____

   d. _____

2. List four areas from your Energetics Flowchart, Part III interpretation with which you strongly *agree* and four areas with which you are less familiar.

Agree

a. _____

b. _____

c. _____

d. _____

Less Familiar

a. _____

b. _____

c. _____

d. _____

Step Three

Quality Persuasion: *The Principles*

In this third step, you may wish to refer to the exercises that you completed at the end of Steps One and Two. You may also refer to the past knowledge you have of yourself. Using these sources of information, respond to the Quality Action Inventory.

Quality Action Inventory

Part A. **Place a check (✓) by the four words that you consider your most important qualities as a person.**

a __ discipline	f __ joy of life	k __ honesty
b __ love	g __ cleanliness	l __ sincerity
c __ patriotism	h __ punctuality	m__ intelligence
d __ obedience	i __ clarity	n __ moderation
e __ defense of honor	j __ consideration of others	o __ respect for rights of others

Part B. **Record your selection of the four qualities in the quality column. Then go to Part C for scoring instructions.**

	Quality	Score
1.	_____	_____
2.	_____	_____
3.	_____	_____
4.	_____	_____
	Total	_____

Part C. • Give each of the four qualities a score in terms of how frequently you incorporate each specific quality as part of your persuasion of others. Use a grade of 1-10 with 10 as the highest frequency.

• Total your points.

• Refer to the Quality Action Scale for a rating of your score.

Quality Action Scale
Score 36 - 40 Very Effective
31 - 35 Effective
26 - 30 Somewhat Effective
21 - 25 Somewhat Ineffective
16 - 20 Ineffective
0 - 15 Poor

The qualities that you selected in Part A of the Quality Action Inventory are representative of your beliefs about yourself. By combining the qualities with the frequency, you arrive at your Quality Action Score in the persuasion process.

The Quality Action Score registers the intensity of your beliefs. The intensity creates the force of convictions that energize your persuasive actions. Effective persuasion is directly related to the use of personal conviction—either good or bad. It is here that the energy necessary to take plans and turn them into action is generated.

These two aspects of Quality Action involve: 1) what you believe, and 2) the intensity with which you develop conviction. Together, they make up your character structure, to which both Freud and Fromm made significant reference.

Erich Fromm (1947) stated: "The forces by which man (sic) is motivated...the way a person acts, feels, and thinks is to a large extent determined by the specificity of his character and is not merely the results of rational responses to realistic situations."

As we have already noted, character structure is deeply rooted in the affective nature—feelings, emotions, and passions. But it is not enough to simply acknowledge that fact. The significance is that we are guided by a private logic that is inherent and unique to our affective nature. This is the first of three principles that are related to persuasion via the character structure:

Principle One:
**To modify or to change the behavior of another,
we must tap the private logic of the other person.
We must touch the character.**

Private logic is our "makes sense" system. It arises out of our feelings, emotions, and passions. It is a filtering system that determines what should be added to or subtracted from our convictions and beliefs.

The character structure, of which our private logic is an extension, was viewed by Freud as the *determinant of motivation.* He developed a theory of character as a system of strivings which underlie our behavior action. These strivings influence the character traits that we develop and, in the final analysis, determine our public logic.*

The way in which you use Graph II of the Behavior Indicator is vital to the *persuasion via character process.* This graph reflects the private logic. It reflects how a person can be motivated and persuaded. In the last step of this workshop, you will have an opportunity to use Graph II with the person you wish to persuade. At that time, you will decide how and if you will use Quality Action in your *persuasion via character.*

---

*Public logic is a mixture of definitions, rules, concepts, and prejudices. It is the accumulated "common sense" of the individuals in that society. Public logic takes on the veneer of "truth and right" because it embodies familiar and accepted practices.

Deciding how you will respond to another's private logic, and in what manner you will develop a studied approach, is the substance of principle two and principle three. The second principle is stated in this manner:

Principle Two:
The persuasion of strategy and tactics is dependent upon our ability to discriminate between character traits and behavior traits.

While it may be difficult for an untrained person to observe the difference in a list of behavior traits as compared to a list of character traits, the Behavior Indicator has been developed with a fine distinction between the two.

Still, you may wish to acquaint yourself with the theory and method behind the instrument. Professional Workshop II is recommended for this purpose. But for now let's consider Graph II.

Graph II reflects your choice of character traits. The configuration determines the psychic energy that can be tapped. It indicates how you seek to gain importance and to discover productive meaning. Graph II represents your belief system.

Principle one and principle two interact when you use your conscious intelligence to analyze how the character traits evaluate the best course of action for yourself. Whatever the pattern in Graph II, it is logical for you and it is the basis on which you act. It may lead you to sainthood or devilhood. But it "makes sense" to you.

The final activity in this workshop will include an opportunity for you to utilize your conscious intelligence to effectively plan a strategy that results in understanding and persuading the other person according to that person's private logic—the character. This type of analysis necessitates the inclusion of the third principle:

Principle Three:
We use our personal reputation as a distinguishing feature to exercise consistent, responsible action.

The responsible person with a reputation to safeguard sees *persuasion via character* as more than a "bag of tricks." There is little question that the persuasive techniques discussed in this workshop can have far-reaching effects. To probe another person's character, the unconscious, and the private logic is to demonstrate a desire to *know.*

And with that knowledge comes a responsibility to that person.

There are any number of reasons to understand another person in the persuasion process. But to *use* or to control the other person for your own ends is unethical. To help the person further his or her self-interest is a legitimate goal of the *persuasion process via character.* To assist in the individual growth of another person is admirable.

Hopefully, the latter two reasons are consistent with your purpose to persuade. But for all of us, perhaps the greatest safeguard we have in avoiding exploitation of the other person is our own reputation.

This is not to say that we have forgotten the skills which a persuadee can develop against unscrupulous persuasion. But a great persuader can be hard to resist.

It is our responsibility as effective persuaders to keep the welfare of the other person before us constantly. It cannot be passed off to the other person by trite explanations such as: "He's an adult." "That's what she wanted."

It is unethical to place the other person in a constant state of defense. It is a misuse of the persuasion process. However, even though misuse of persuasion brings harm to the other person, its greatest harm collectively accrues to ourselves. We minimize what can be our greatest asset—our credibility and our reputation.

Aristotle's term *ethos* means reputation. It is a goal to which we can aspire. Even as we learn that true persuasion is through another person's character, we discover that its roots are also found in our own character. It is character-to-character persuasion.

Step Four

Persuasion Analysis: *An Exercise*

The fourth step provides an opportunity for applying the three principles that can make persuasion a quality action between you and the other person. You are asked to select a significant person—client, spouse, employer, associate, or friend—whom you wish to persuade. To facilitate the experience, we'll review the key statements. They summarize the highlights of this workshop.

Summary: Key Statements on Persuasion

☐ All conscious communication is persuasive.

☐ We understand ourselves largely from the response we receive from others.

☐ Changing the person's intentions precedes influencing action.

☐ People act only on the basis of their private logic.

☐ Strategy and tactics are employed in a consistent and responsible manner.

Persuasion Exercise

Focused Information

1. Select an individual whose behavior you would like to influence.

2. Write in the person's name _____
   (name)

3. Use an 8½ by 11 sheet of paper, referred to as the Strategic Planning Sheet.

   a. Label one side of the sheet "A," and draw a line down the middle, creating two columns. (See example.)

FRONT SIDE   **BACK SIDE**

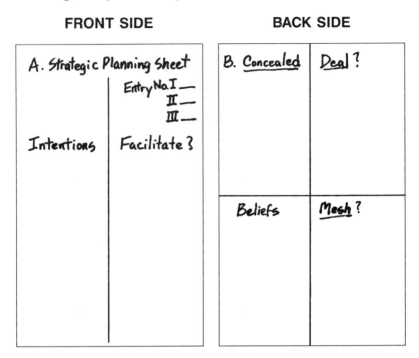

Example

b. Label the opposite side of the sheet "B." Draw a line
    down the middle to create two columns. Draw a line
    across the middle to create four sections. (See example.)

Guided Activity

1. Use the Behavior Indicator.

2. Respond to Part I and Part II, using the following statements as a lead-in to your selection of responses.

   Part I: As I view _____,
            (name)

   I believe that he/she is *most:*

   Part II: As I view _____,
             (name)

   I believe that he/she *feels least:*

3. Develop the configurations for Graph I, II, and III as instructed.

4. Determine the person's three entry numbers.

5. Place the entry numbers on your Strategic Planning Sheet, Side A, upper right-hand corner. (See example, front side.)

Read Interpretation

1. Refer to _____ 's Entry No. I,
   (name)

   and read the person's *intended behavior.*

2. Record the person's *10* intentions in the left column on Side A, Strategic Planning Sheet.

3. Use the right column on Side A to record the ways in which your proposal will *facilitate* the other person's intentions, that is, what your proposal will do to ensure that the intentions will succeed.

Relate to the Other Person's Private Logic

1. Refer to _____ 's Entry No. II,
   (name)

   and read the other person's *concealed behavior.*

2. Summarize and record the feelings of the other person in the upper left column of Side B, Strategic Planning Sheet.

3. Summarize and record how your proposal will *deal* with the other person's feelings in the upper right-hand section of Side B.

4. Refer to page 443 for the Energetic Flowchart in Interpretation Central.

5. Use the other person's Graph II to identify the belief system. Follow procedures to arrive at the correct interpretation in the Flowchart.

6. Summarize and record the other person's beliefs in the lower left column of Side B, Strategic Planning System.

7. Summarize and record in the lower right section how your proposal will *mesh* with the other person's belief system.

Summary Interpretation

1. Refer to the other person's Entry No. III.

2. Read the Central Pattern—both work and social—of the other person.

3. Plan your summary strategy and tactics by completing the following items:

   a. How can I get this person's attention?

   _____

   _____

   b. What are the specific needs of this person?

   _____

   _____

   c. What should be my plan to meet this person's needs?

   _____

   _____

   d. Which of the other person's intentions, if any, do I want to change?

   _____

   _____

   e. How will I request a change of action in this person?

   _____

   _____

Personal Workshop VI
Energetics of Leadership

Step One: Leadership in a
           Different Voice

Step Two: Seeking
           Self-Importance

Step Three: Dealing with
             Right and Wrong

Step Four: Pursuing a
            Course of Action

All of us face challenges in our work and personal lives that demand leadership. If we see ourselves as leaders, we rise to the challenge. If we do not see ourselves as leaders, the challenge makes us uneasy; we look to others for direction.

The myths that surround leadership influence how we see ourselves. Many are elitist conceptions; they are remnants from other eras, other cultures. They include such beliefs as: Only a few have leadership ability; people would rather follow than lead; a leader must be a strong individualist.

These myths fail to recognize the leadership potential in all of us. Exercising our leadership brings this important result:

Leadership enables us to take control of our lives. It gives us a voice in building a shared existence that is constructive for everyone.

Developing and exercising our leadership potential has implications far beyond ourselves. A *nation of followers* produces primarily the negative example—the celebrity—who is committed only to self-interest. A *nation of leaders* produces primarily heroes and heroines who make outstanding contributions. They provide needed examples of how we should relate to one another ideally.

Education for leadership is a necessity in a democratic society. This workshop, *Energetics of Leadership,* will focus on the most vital factor of leadership—character. It is character that evaluates and energizes our actions; character empowers our leadership efforts.

This workshop will replace the old myths with a new model—the Energetics of Leadership. It will provide a way for you to evaluate the leadership of others and to create a positive leadership in your daily life. The interpretation of your behavior will enable you to identify and shape the forces of social change—a critical insight for a leader.

Step One
Leadership in a Different Voice

We are witnessing a profound evolution in the way leadership is viewed. In the past, leadership has been most often associated with such factors as age, authority, influence, personality, or charisma.

We first identified this changing concept of leadership in an early research study (Geier, 1963). Continuing investigation and analysis into leadership provides strong documentation for a major conclusion: The *appointed "leader"* does not necessarily perform in a leadership capacity.

Rather, leadership shifts to that member of the group who has the knowledge and the ability to cope with the task facing the group. This phenomenom has come to be known as *emerging* or *shifting* leadership.

Shifting Leadership

In responding to this conclusion, some corporations have restructured their organizations to facilitate the exercise of leadership at all levels. Workers and managers are being educated to this concept. Relieved of traditional oversight responsibilities, managers are being positioned as facilitators and developers—educating workers for leadership. They are discovering that the person closest to the task often has the best solution.

Shifting leadership can also be observed in the family setting. Responsibility and initiative are taken by the spouse who has the greatest knowledge and skill in specific areas. When encouraged, children practice their fledgling skills in finding solutions to family problems.

In our exploration of leadership, we observed that the lack of knowledge and skill in leadership resulted not only in an evasion of the challenge, but also in a twisted approach to the selection of leaders. We had assumed that people would tend to select and follow the direction of those they perceived to have positive attributes.

This was not necessarily true. In fact, the untrained followers used a process of elimination—identifying those attributes they didn't like about people, and ending up, in most cases, with a leader who had the fewest *negative* characteristics.

The in-depth interviews that probed the reasons for supporting one contender for leadership over another revealed interviewee comments that contained envy, jealousy, and resentment. Those who have not had the opportunity to develop leadership ability are reluctant to give power to another. Hostility creates a negative environment for task completion.

Authority and Leadership

How then can we develop a different voice in our appraisal of leaders? How can we prepare ourselves to lead with a positive voice? Let us begin by making a significant distinction between authority and leadership:

An authority does things right.
A leader does the right thing.

An authority, such as a parent, teacher, or manager, does things in accordance with established policies, traditional expectations, or approved procedures...doing things right.

A leader looks beyond the established, the accepted, the approved way of doing things—to what could be, might be, should be. Knowing that change is the one constant in life, the leader anticipates and responds to challenges—developing the leadership abilities of others and directing efforts for mutual benefits. The leader strives to do the right thing.

Energetics of Leadership is based upon "doing the right thing." The leadership model (figure 8) identifies six tension points of character which are essential to effective leadership.

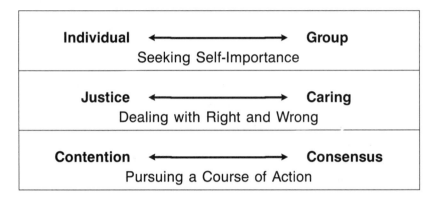

Figure 8. Energetics of Leadership Model

The tension points are at either end of the continuum of behaviors that are implicit in leadership. For example, in pursuing a course of action, we tend to demonstrate a preference for either contention or consensus. Our choices have significant results on others when we exercise leadership.

The arrows indicate that these tension points are most frequently viewed as polarities. Energetics of Leadership proposes that a centering of one's character along that continuum has the most positive impact.

Centering: The Basis of Leadership

The centering of one's character between the six tension points is not viewed as achieving a constant equilibrium. For example, it is quite possible to be a member of the group and not be just a face in the crowd. However, sometimes it is necessary to move outside the group and take a stance that is different.

Centering between the tension points can be defined in this way:

Centering is the ability to choose either tension point for a limited time according to the needs of the situation, while remaining conscious of the overall need to swing back to the other polarity.

The person who chooses the tension point of contention is taking a definite stance. The leader who employs the "centering" concept does not remain in an adversary mode for long. There is an immediate move to educate and to move others toward a new consensus.

The centering leader achieves a dynamic interplay between the tension points. Comfortable in using either, the leader remains flexible and open to change. The remaining steps in this workshop concentrate on the essential movement along the polarity points of three major leadership areas. The first is Seeking a Sense of Self-Importance.

Step Two
Seeking a Sense of Self-Importance

Exercising leadership is one of the most significant ways we have of gaining a sense of self-importance. Concerned about others, we are contributing our time and effort to a purpose beyond ourselves.

Gaining self-importance is a part of the Life Plan and the Self Affirmation System that were discussed in Personal Workshop I. The choices that we make on these tension points have implications that reverberate beyond the immediate leadership challenge.

The tension points of character on this leadership behavior are *individual* and *group*. In preparation for your interpretation, place an X on that point on the continuum that best indicates your preference for either individual or group behaviors. That is, do you tend to seek self-importance as an individual, or do you receive your feeling of importance as a member of the group?

Individual  **Group**

Seeking a Sense of Self-Importance

A leader who shows a preference for individual or group behaviors has different forces with which to contend. They can be stated in this way:

Seeking self-importance as an *individual* provides opportunities for new experiences and personal expression. The leadership potential is an independent, innovative voice.

Seeking self-importance as a *member of a group* provides opportunities for instruction, evaluation, and validation. The leadership potential is an intimate connection with a larger meaning.

A leader who is "stuck" on the polarity of individual may come up with an innovative solution that is neither relevant nor acceptable to the group. A leader who is "stuck" on the polarity of group may have acceptance but lacks an idea for a solution.

There are many reasons why polarities are common on these tension points and why centering is sometimes difficult.

Socializing for Polarities

In the not too distant past, males were socialized for the independence and autonomy that are associated with individuality. There was an expectation of leadership in the larger world. On the other hand, females were socialized for a subordinate role that was supportive to the male. Leadership within that environment was often unrecognized and sometimes not allowed.

This socialization for polarities—the male for individuality, the female for group membership—kept both sexes ignorant. Obviously, some men and women have modified that social stereotype. But to many it remains a powerful force. It influences the leadership voice. Table 10 depicts the negative behaviors associated with marked preferences for individual or group.

Table 10. Negative Behaviors Associated with an Imbalance on Individual or Group

Individual	Group
one-upmanship	blind loyalty
overly competitive	obeys without question
demands privileged position	rejects new experiences
dictates to subordinates	anxious over mistakes
limits commitments	dependent upon approval
seeks control over others	suppresses personal needs

In a very real sense, individuals who place primarily at one tension point or another have developed only one half of their beings. They bring only half a voice to the leadership role.

Centering: Seeking a Sense of Self-Importance

Over the past two decades, individuals are taking steps along that continuum of self-importance toward the other polarity. It has been a difficult period and will continue to be so for some time. Both men and women are beginning to realize the importance of "centering" their character between the poles of individual and group.

Table 11 identifies the positive behavior that occurs when individuals center their character when seeking self-importance.

Table 11. Positive Behaviors Associated with a Balance between Individual and Group

Individual	Group
develop uniqueness	have a common purpose
independent	interdependent
take initiative	cooperate with one another
express creativity	find meaning in togetherness

A leader who is centered has ties to the group. There is intimate knowledge of the needs of others and a willingness to involve others in the process of deliberation. There is active development of the leadership potential of others. There is also the individual ability to mobilize that leadership to meet the challenge.

The interpretation for leadership is contained in three parts that coincide with three steps of the workshop. They are:

Part I: Seeking self-importance

Part II: Dealing with right and wrong

Part III: Pursuing a course of action

To obtain your interpretation for Part I, use the following procedure.

To Obtain Your Interpretation

- **Use your Entry No. III.**
- **Locate the page number in table 12.**
- **Read and study Part I: Seeking a Sense of Self-Importance— Individual and Group.**
- **Complete the Self-Importance Exercise.**

Table 12. Interpretation for Seeking a Sense of Self-Importance—Individual and Group

Entry No. III	Page
one	461
two	466
three	471
four	476
twelve	481
thirteen	486
fourteen	491
twenty-three	496
twenty-four	501
thirty-four	506
one twenty-three	511
one twenty-four	516
one thirty-four	521
two thirty-four	526

After Reading Your Interpretation

• Evaluate your interpretation according to the positive and negative behaviors with individual and group.

• Identify three behaviors under both individual and group that you would like to retain in exercising leadership. List these on the following chart under the headings labeled *retain*.

• Identify three behaviors under both individual and group that you would like to alter in exercising leadership. List these on the following chart under the headings labeled *alter*.

Exercise: Seeking a Sense of Self-Importance

Individual

Group

Retain

1. _____

2. _____

3. _____

Retain

1. _____

2. _____

3. _____

Alter

1. _____

2. _____

3. _____

Alter

1. _____

2. _____

3. _____

Step Three
Dealing with Right and Wrong

Coming to grips with right and wrong is always important. But, when we exercise leadership, the stakes are higher.

All of us have experienced the tension points of justice and caring within the family unit. In the traditional family of a generation or two ago, the two modes were clearly identified in either the mother or the father—at least in our memory of that time.

The father was the disciplinarian. He not only enforced the rules, but he also made them. He represented "justice." In contrast, the mother usually personified the caring mode. She not only cared for our needs, but she interceded for us when punishments were due. Table 13 depicts some of the basic differences between the justice and the caring modes.

Table 13. Distinguishing Features of Justice and Caring Modes

Factors	Justice	Caring
condition	separate from others	interrelated with others
purpose	regulate negative behavior; protect human rights	support and aid; strengthen ties
nature	formal, abstract, and rational	informal, contextual, and emotional
premise	equality	inequality

Based upon the foregoing description of the justice and caring mode, place an X on that point on the continuum that you think best describes your preference for justice or caring when exercising leadership.

Justice  **Caring**

Dealing with Right and Wrong

Justice is based upon the premise of equality. That premise is congruent with a democratic society in which everyone is considered equal and accountable before the law. In our society, as in the family, "justice" is used to protect us from one another. It is based upon "thou shall not."

Without question, the justice mode is the primary framework for dealing with right and wrong in American society; it has been institutionalized. We usually discuss controversial issues that pertain to right and wrong within the justice mode.

In contrast, caring is based upon the premise of inequality. This premise strikes a discordant note in a society that ascribes to a myth of equality. Growing old, becoming ill, being out of luck, having less talent or opportunity threatens that myth. In defense, such occurrences are explained as a lack of effort or planning, or even punishment for previous misdeeds.

American society has a very uneasy relationship with the caring mode. Outside the family, caring efforts are not firmly institutionalized, but often left to voluntary efforts. Those that have a firmer base are often attacked as undermining moral fiber. Most important, controversial issues that touch on right and wrong are not usually discussed in the caring mode.

Justice and caring involve two very different perceptions of right and wrong. Individuals who have a marked preference on justice or caring have difficulty seeing the other point of view. Both sides are afflicted with a strong sense of self-righteousness that impedes discussion.

A Sex-Linked Preference

Research studies have revealed that there is some relationship between the person's sex and preference for justice or caring. Lawrence Kohlberg (1964) formulated and researched a model for stages of moral development. Based on research with boys, the model has some similarity to our conception of justice.

Carol Gilligan (1982) has challenged this attempt to base a moral model solely on male development. Her work indicates that there are different models of moral development and that girls proceed along different lines.

The most striking result of this research is the attention that is being given to the need for socialization of children by both parents. If there is a strong connection between the two modes of justice and caring and sex, the child, socialized by both parents, would have a better chance for a "centered character."

Table 14 identifies the negative behaviors that often occur when individuals are primarily justice or caring oriented.

Table 14. Negative Behavior Associated with an Imbalance on Justice and Caring

Justice	Caring
demonstrates a vengeful "eye for an eye" retaliation	fails to hold others accountable for their actions
views punishment as a deterrent	does for others what they should be doing for themselves
equates what is legal with what is right	has unrealistic expectations and hopes for others
uses law and order as synonymous with law and justice	gains self-affirmation by increasing the dependency of others

Unlike many societies, American society does not have a strong mythology that identifies how we should act toward one another. The accent is on the strong individualist. As a result, we are extremely dependent upon our system of laws. Still, the laws have limits; they cannot legislate what we should do.

A person who is imbalanced on the justice mode will tend toward a setting where there is danger of the person serving the system. A person who is imbalanced on the caring mode will tend toward a setting where there is a danger of undermining individual responsibility. Such persons bring only half a voice to the leadership role.

Centering: Dealing with Right and Wrong

Centering our character on the justice-caring continuum has been difficult. We have not made as much progress along that continuum as we have on the self-importance continuum. Still, there is movement on a personal level.

Table 15 identifies those behaviors that are associated with achieving a balance between the polarities of justice and caring.

Table 15. Positive Behaviors Associated with a Balance between Justice and Caring

Justice	Caring
regulate negative behavior	help others
apply rules evenly	stengthen the human bond
reward and punish	identify the context
protect individual rights	understand, empathize, forgive

The person who centers his or her character between the polarities of justice and caring compensates for the weakness that is inherent in each. The centered leader recognizes the need for standards and the need for compassion.

A personal analysis of your behavior regarding the tension points of justice and caring is contained in Part II of the leadership interpretation. It is obtained by using the following procedure.

To Obtain Your Interpretation

- **Return to your leadership interpretation.**
- **Read and study Part II: Dealing with Right and Wrong—Justice and Caring.**
- **Complete the Exercise.**

After Reading Your Interpretation

• Evaluate your interpretation according to the positive and negative behaviors on justice and caring.

• Identify three behaviors under both justice and caring that you would like to retain in exercising leadership. List these on the following chart under the headings labeled *retain.*

• Identify three behaviors under both justice and caring that you would like to alter in exercising leadership. List these on the following chart under the headings labeled *alter.*

Exercise: Dealing with Right and Wrong

Justice	Caring
Retain	Retain
1. _____	1. _____
2. _____	2. _____
3. _____	3. _____
Alter	Alter
1. _____	1. _____
2. _____	2. _____
3. _____	3. _____

Step Four
Pursuing a Course of Action

The interpretation in this step will identify your preference for contention or consensus behavior when pursuing a course of action.

The Importance of Contention and Consensus

These two tension points are reflections of our democratic heritage—the right to freedom of speech and lawful assembly. One or both are present when we come together for political purposes in an election campaign, when we apply for a position of employment, when we present a marketing proposal to our clients, when we meet with our associates in formal and informal settings.

Contention and consensus are also of critical importance in the personal setting. We use one or both when deciding on a family vacation, allocating scarce resources, settling a marital argument, or disciplining a child.

There is great value in learning the positive language of contention. The individual begins to understand what he or she really thinks; the resulting increase in depth and scope attracts others. And, each time two or more persons come together to achieve a voluntary consensus, they are immeasurably strengthened and enriched.

We can think of contention and consensus as two "languages" whereby we exert character in leadership. Our selection of the language depends upon the "country"—the situation. If we choose the wrong language—contention or consensus—we are speaking in a foreign language that is incomprehensible to others. And, of course, some situations demand an ability to be bilingual, to speak in both the language of contention and that of consensus.

In preparation for your interpretation, place an X on that point on the continuum that best indicates your preference for either contention or consensus behavior. That is, do you tend to pursue a course of action by contending, seeing others as adversaries? Or by consensus, seeking agreements?

Contention |___|___|___|___|___|___|___| **Consensus**

Pursuing a Course of Action

The Language of Contention

While we can expect an expenditure of psychic energy in both contention and consensus, our emotions and passions are more apt to be involved in contention. In the drive to take a position, we usually have a greater degree of psychic energy at our disposal.

Table 16 identifies some of the differences between positive and negative contending. This comparison will help you to evaluate the negative and positive aspects of your interpretation.

Table 16. Ways of Contending

Positive Contention	Negative Contention
informed position	strongly held opinions
considers self and others	considers only self
points or leads the way	claims a corner on the truth
speaks with a strong voice	refuses to compromise

Positive Contention

The basic purpose of positive contention is to problem-solve and to implement solutions. It draws the listener into the process. In using positive contention, you disarm a potential adversary with facts that are useful to the other person. You propose a solution that is of mutual benefit.

Negative Contention

The basic purpose of the person who uses negative contention is to disable the opposition and to achieve unilateral benefits. Some of the behaviors that are associated with negative contention are clouding the issues, distorting information, exaggerating claims, and intimidating rivals. Negative contention has the potential to create lasting enemies.

The Language of Consensus

While there is great value in being willing to take a stance and to use contention, it is equally important to know when to provide leadership in obtaining a consensus.

Consensus usually is propelled by the flow of psychic energy from feeling rather than from the surges of energy from our emotions and passions. Even so, there are positive and negative ways to reach consensus. The differences listed in table 17 will help you to evaluate your consensus behaviors.

Table 17. Ways of Reaching Consensus

Positive	Negative
discussion of possibilities	concealing differences
negotiating a compromise	compromising self
abiding by the agreement	experiencing hostility or reluctance
working toward the common goal	complaining after the fact

Positive Consensus

Discussion is the primary tool of the person who seeks a positive consensus. There is an active sharing of views, opinions, and preferences. Questions and answers clarify important points. Negotiating a compromise in which both sides are satisfied is a time-consuming task that defines what is expected on both sides.

Negative Consensus

An individual uses negative consensus when concealing differences. A predictable response is a compromise of oneself. Eventually, the person becomes hostile and experiences difficulty in living up to an agreement that does not reflect his or her active participation.

Centering: Pursuing a Course of Action

Achieving a balance between the character tension points of contention and consensus is apt to give us the best of both worlds. When there is comfort in selecting either tension point, there is a dynamic movement along the continuum.

Some of the positive behaviors that are associated with a balance between contention and consensus are identified in table 18.

Table 18. Positive Behaviors Associated with a Balance between Contention and Consensus

Contention	Consensus
commit to a position	display openness
hold to the principle	listen and question
speak forcefully	negotiate and reach agreement

A person who centers his or her character between contention and consensus uses the best of both "languages." There is a new language that allows the leader an informed, thoughtful voice.

A personal analysis of your behavior regarding the tension points of contention and consensus is contained in Part III of the leadership interpretation. Use the following procedure.

To Obtain Your Interpretation

- Return to your leadership interpretation.
- Read and study Part III: Pursuing a Course of Action—Contention and Consensus.
- Complete the exercise.

After Reading Your Interpretation

- Evaluate your interpretation according to the positive and negative behaviors on contention and consensus.
- Identify three behaviors under both contention and consensus that you would like to retain in exercising leadership. List these on the following chart under the headings labeled *retain*.
- Identify three behaviors under both contention and consensus that you would like to alter in exercising leadership. List these on the following chart under the headings labeled *alter*.

Exercise: Pursuing a Course of Action

Contention	Consensus
Retain	**Retain**
1. _____	1. _____
2. _____	2. _____
3. _____	3. _____
Alter	**Alter**
1. _____	1. _____
2. _____	2. _____
3. _____	3. _____

Professional Workshop I

Understanding
Your Graphs

Part I:	Contrasting Graphs I and II
Part II:	Single Plotting Point Pattern
Part III:	Unusual Patterns

This workshop provides explanation and clarification of variant graphs. The most obvious ones are on the next page. Check to determine if you have any of the configurations. If so, turn to the page indicated.

Part I: Contrasting Graphs I and II (page 163)

Graph I	Graph II		Graph I	Graph II

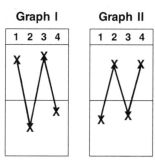

Opposite Graphs

All plotting points are different in Graph I from Graph II

Dissimilar Graphs

Two plotting points are different in Graph I from Graph II

Part II: Single Plotting Point Pattern (page 168)

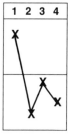

Example

Part III: Unusual Patterns (page 173)

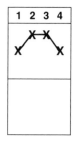 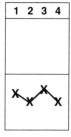 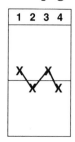

Overdrive	Underdrive	Neutral
All plotting points above the midline	All plotting points below the midline	Plotting points clustered around the midline

Part I

Contrasting Graphs I and II

In figure 9, you will find two examples of contrasting Graphs I and II. They are Comparison A and B. In Comparison A, note that all of the plotting points in Graph I are the opposite of those found in Graph II. For example, the first placement, (1) in Graph I is *above* the midline. The first placement, (1) in Graph II is *below* the midline.

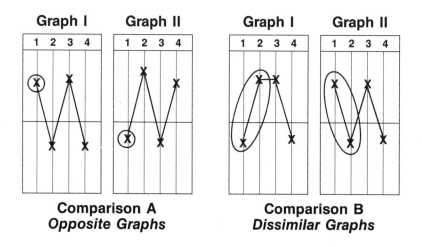

Figure 9. Contrasting Graphs I and II

In contrast, Comparison B is an example of dissimilar graphs in which only two of the plotting points are different in Graph I than they are in Graph II.

When contrasting patterns occur in Graph I and II, we can immediately draw two conclusions:

Change is occurring.
Conflict is present.

It is obvious that in Comparison A (Opposite Patterns) the degree of change and conflict is high. In Comparison B (Dissimilar Patterns) change and conflict are present, but to a lesser degree.

Opposite Patterns: *Comparison A*

In Graph I of Comparison A, the plotting point in column 1 (t – taking) indicates that the person is expected to reach out and forcefully assume a commanding position. Yet, in Graph II, the plotting point in column 1 (D – Dominance) is quite average in terms of energizing this intention.

In effect, the person lacks the feeling and the emotion—psychic energy—needed for taking on the task. In driving toward the powerful individual effort that is expected, he or she will be engaging in different behavior, but will be operating primarily on physical energy—a fraction of the needed requirement.

Note that in Comparison A, there is a similar lack of feelings and emotions—psychic energy—when comparing the plotting points on column 3 (r – responding) in Graph I with column 3 (S – Submission) in Graph II. The individual is balking at the intention to be overly responsive. Indeed, the energy is actually being directed toward separateness rather than togetherness.

Overall, none of the four plotting points on Graph I are in agreement with those in Graph II. They are all on opposite sides of the midline. The person is either being subjected to or is undertaking far-reaching changes. Considerable conflict can be expected. Opposite patterns do not happen that frequently, but they do occur.

Dissimilar Patterns: *Comparison B*

In the example shown in Comparison B, only two of the plotting points on Graph I—column 1 (t – taking) and column 2 (a – attracting) are quite different from the plotting points on Graph II—column 1 (D – Dominance) and column 2 (I – Inducement).

In this case, the person has the energy to reach out and make the powerful individual effort but lacks the intention or the opportunity. While conflict and change are present in dissimilar patterns, they are not as pronounced as in opposite graph patterns. However, they should not be underestimated. In either case, certain results can be anticipated. Here is one real possibility:

**Differences between Graph I and II
can lead to inconsistent behavior and
the Contrasting Graph Syndrome.**

If you have dissimilar or opposite patterns in Graph I and II, you are apt to be experiencing a struggle between what is expected of you and what you expect of yourself. Sometimes it flows from the conflict of trying to adapt to those with whom you work or live and being true to yourself. Sometimes it involves a struggle between what you have been and what you wish to be.

Graph I reflects your intention—the course of action you plan to pursue. Graph II indicates the path you have followed in the past. For a time—a shorter or longer period—you are acting against yourself. You are temporarily a *divided self.*

Under these circumstances, almost every act is the result of conscious deliberation. You are no longer able to fall back on the automatic response of the past. You are trying out new actions and your responses are unfamiliar. Behavior under those conditions tends to be inconsistent.

Within the *Contrasting Graph Syndrome,* you may choose either a positive or negative response to change. Change is a given of life; it is a part of the human condition. And conflict is a close companion; we seldom have one without the other in some form. The importance of opposite or dissimilar patterns in Graphs I and II is the *opportunity* it presents. Our response to change and conflict may be one of growth or regression.

**A negative response to change results
in a divided or diminished self.
A positive response to change
results in character unfoldment.**

Negative Response: *A Divided Self*

When change is thrust upon us from the outside, we are most apt to respond negatively if we feel that we have little choice or control over the change or the outcome.

In the work setting, we may decide to accept the change to "get along," "keep my job," "put food on the table," or because the "boss knows best."

In the personal setting, we may accept the change to "avoid quarreling," "for the children's sake," or to "keep the marriage together."

The danger of a negative response to change is that we retreat from our own self. We make little, if any, effort to share how we feel or think with the other person. Unwilling to risk the rejection or the confrontation, we may decide to endure the continuing conflict. Wearing a mask, we may even congratulate ourselves on keeping the peace. But the self is divided.

Or we may deny our feelings and emotions and run headlong to embrace the change, proclaiming: "I feel just like you do." Then we are in danger of increasing the division of self.

The physiological and psychological effects of negative responses to change are many. These include feelings of being tired, exhausted, and drained of energy. There is difficulty in making a decision or in sustaining action. Mistakes are frequent, and inconsistency may be pronounced. Sometimes there is a marked anxiety about mistakes, with a rigid adherence to requirements. Energy is expended in worrying about the future or in looking back at what used to be.

Positive Response: *Putting It Together*

We are most apt to demonstrate a positive response to change under two conditions—when we initiate the change or when we become actively involved in the change proposed by others. Instead of retreating from ourselves, we are in the forefront. We ask questions about the purpose of the change, the methods, the potential outcome.

If we decide that the change is for the better, we can begin the process of adapting to it. But if we judge that the outcome is negative, we begin the process of trying to modify the negative effects. If it is not possible, our response may even involve leaving the situation.

Positive response to change means affirming ourselves as persons with the ability to think, feel, and act. We become actors instead of being acted upon.

Positive change can also have physical and emotional effects on the individual. We can expect to feel tired and sometimes drained from the exertions. But this is balanced by feelings of satisfaction with exerting some control over our destiny.

Deliberation over actions will be required, and the same inconsistencies and mistakes will occur. But these can be tolerated because of the sense of strength we gain in holding to our convictions—in standing up to be counted.

Gradually, as our psychic energy is redirected, our mistakes decrease and the consistency of our behavior returns. Positive response to change involves the unfolding of our character in a dynamic new alignment—between what we have been and what we are becoming—between ourselves and others.

Part II

Single Plotting Point Patterns

A single plotting point pattern occurs when only one of the factors is above the midline. Figure 10 provides an example of a single plotting point, (1) or t/D in Graph III.

Graph III

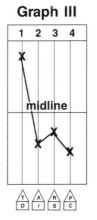

Figure 10. Single Plotting Point Pattern

A single plotting point may occur in any of the three graphs. It may involve an orientation factor, an energy factor, or a combination.

Any one of these orientation factors:	**t, a, r, p**
Any one of these energy factors:	**D, I, S, C**
Any one of these combinations:	**t/D, a/I, r/S, p/C**

Review your graphs to see if you have a single plotting point (SPP) pattern in any one of the three graphs:

Check (✓) the graph where the SPP occurs:	
Graph I	☐ yes ☐ no
Graph II	☐ yes ☐ no
Graph III	☐ yes ☐ no

If your Graph III has a single plotting point above the midline, you have company. Twenty-three percent (23%) of the research population that totaled 1,150 had a single plotting point pattern in Graph III. The single plotting point pattern is explained according to the graph in which it occurs. Let's examine the difference.

Graph I: If you have an SPP in Graph I, you tend to be inordinately influenced by a powerful person or event in your present environment. The high expectations dictate your direction in regard to *taking, attracting, responding,* or *preserving.*

Graph II: If you have an SPP in Graph II, you are experiencing an intense inner struggle to maintain and defend your personal beliefs. You tend to respond with a psychic energy of singular intensity in the form of *Dominance, Inducement, Submission,* or *Compliance.*

Graph III: If you have an SPP in Graph III, you are inclined toward an imbalance in identifying issues. That tilt is also evident in the methods you employ in relating to others.

Since Graph III represents the dynamics occurring in Graphs I and II, any changes in those graphs are reflected in Graph III. For example, the redirection of an overly emphasized energy factor in Graph II has a significant influence in the prediction of behavior in Graph III.

How you direct your psychic energy and how you make possible changes in your intentions will significantly impact your behavior. Often, the result is a single plotting point pattern—SPP.

How does an SPP pattern develop? And what is the effect when a second plotting point appears above the midline and unites to form a combination pattern? Let's follow the process.

Personality Pattern Development

Figure 10 shows the single plotting point on Graph III to be the t/D factor. The t/D is, of course, the result of combining the t factor of Graph I and the D factor of Graph II.

This SPP, represented by t/D, reveals a high degree of taking orientation that is heavily energized by the Dominance factor. The individual with this pattern has chosen to respond to life situations with an excessive amount of Dominance psychic energy.

Consequently, other energy factors, such as I (Inducement), S (Submission), and C (Compliance) are somewhat depleted. There is an imbalance in how this person responds to life situations.

Figure 11 shows how a return to balance is possible. When the I (Inducement) energy factor is aligned with the D (Dominance) energy factor, a combination pattern appears.

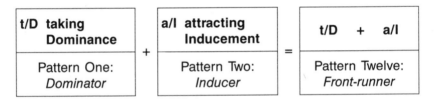

Figure 11. Energizing More than One SPP

In addition to a move toward balance, the t/D + a/I combination also provides an effective back-up system. For example, if the situation requires increased contact with people, the energy is available. This, in effect, is the presence of the a/I factor. Without this back-up, the person with the Dominator pattern must solicit "people-oriented" assistance from others. The combination, however, provides for people-networking in the form of the Front-runner pattern.

In summary, figure 11 displays a combination pattern that facilitates a more balanced approach than is possible with a single plotting point pattern. When we need power, we draw from the energy of the Dominator pattern. When we need the persuasive element, we draw from the energy of the Inducer pattern. Here is the result.

Assertive plus people-conscious = The Front-runner

(Pattern Twelve).

A breakout of all fourteen Central Patterns is contained in figure 12. Only four patterns—one, two, three, and four—are SPP. The percentages relate to the research population (1,150) and apply only to Graph III.

SPP Pattern	Combination		Personality Pattern	No.	Percent of Population
Dominance			Dominator	1	4.0
Inducement			Inducer	2	5.0
Submission			Stabilizer	3	9.0
Compliance			Conformer	4	5.0
Dominance	+ Inducement	=	Front-runner	12	8.0
Dominance	+ Submission	=	Pacesetter	13	2.0
Dominance	+ Compliance	=	Originator	14	1.0
Inducement	+ Submission	=	Harmonizer	23	23.0
Inducement	+ Compliance	=	Strategic Planner	24	3.0
Submission	+ Compliance	=	Standard Bearer	34	17.0
Dominance	+ Inducement	+ Submission =	Administrator	123	2.0
Dominance	+ Inducement	+ Compliance =	Negotiator	124	2.0
Dominance	+ Submission	+ Compliance =	Designer	134	1.0
Inducement	+ Submission	+ Compliance =	Special Advisor	234	18.0
					100.0

Figure 12. Combination of Personality Patterns

Part III

Unusual Patterns

This part of the workshop is designed to help you identify and understand unusual patterns. These are contained in figure 13.

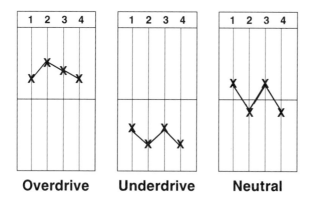

Overdrive   **Underdrive**   **Neutral**

Figure 13. The Unusual Patterns

Earlier, we stated that the *extended* personality patterns (Personal Workshop III) occur frequently. And single plotting point patterns occur in about 25 percent of the population. But the unusual pattern is just that—unusual. These patterns occur infrequently.

Unusual patterns may appear on any one of the three graphs. Sometimes, they occur in all three of the graphs. Although they are relatively rare, they provide important information to the individual. To understand the unusual patterns, it is necessary to examine the point at which they start—the Behavior Indicator.

The instrument to which you have responded, the Behavior Indicator, is designed to elicit responses that result in a multifaceted view of personality. This, of course, is why we use two distinct response forms and three graphs as a basis for the interpretations. Your response to the groups of traits on the indicator is based upon the way you feel, think, and act in life situations. Everyone responds from a unique perspective. Responding to the indicator at intervals reflects the evolving aspect of your personality.

Usually, the response to the Behavior Indicator reveals a preference for one, two, or sometimes three factors or clusters of traits. The result is a clearly identifiable configuration of plotting points that indicates a specific interpretation. Those are the *usual* or the Central Patterns. Occasionally, we encounter a life situation to which we respond in a different manner. The result is an *unusual* pattern.

**An unusual pattern indicates
a preference for all four factors.**

Let's Make Sure

Before beginning with the clarification of the unusual pattern, let's make sure that an unusual pattern *is* present. The check list below will help to ensure your accuracy in developing the tally sheet and the plotting of the graphs.

Place a (✓) in the box after you have completed each check point:
☐ 1) Is the tally correct? Both the first and second row should equal 22.
☐ 2) Are the numbers in the third row the difference between rows 1 and 2? Did you remember the plus and minus?
☐ 3) Is each graph plotted correctly? The third graph with the pluses and minuses?

The Unusual Patterns

The presence of an unusual pattern in any one of the three graphs provides an opportunity for learning about yourself. In Graph I, it may indicate the overpowering effect of individuals or events on your life. In Graph II, an unusual pattern may be related to changes that you are experiencing in deeply held beliefs. In Graph III, an unusual pattern may indicate an intense program of self-discovery.

It is well to remember that these unusual patterns are possible when certain dynamics are present in your life situation. An unusual pattern is temporary because life is always changing. Responding to the Behavior Indicator in several weeks will enable you to determine if the pattern is still present. Chances are good that it will not occur the second time around.

To more specifically comprehend the unusual pattern when it does appear, it is important to distinguish the difference in three sets of traits. The traits and their purposes can be stated in this way:

Behavior traits: *adaptive action*
Character traits: *evaluated response*
Temperament traits: *immediate reaction*

We begin life with an inherited set of traits—our temperament. Temperament traits constitute our *reactive* mode—related to time and intensity. As we proceed through life, we learn what is necessary to survive and to succeed. Along the way we also learn to condition our temperament with some kind of an evaluative process that will allow us to *respond* as well as to react.

However, from time to time, we perceive a life situation from a very basic point of view: We *react* more frequently than we *respond*. During those periods, the temperament traits are more apparent than the behavior or the character traits. This condition is present in both the Overdrive and the Underdrive modes that were depicted in figure 13.

Two questions can be asked. The first is: What does this temperament view imply? This can be answered by considering our search for life's meaning. The first two unusual patterns— Overdrive and Underdrive—appear when there is a desire to "open up"—attempting to get at the very basics of behavior and identifying how you do things. If you have the third unusual graph—Neutral—the desire is just the opposite. You tend to "close up," trying to keep apart from others.

The second question to be asked is: Does the presence of an unusual pattern have a different meaning according to the graph in which it occurs? Yes, it does. With that in mind, review your three graphs. Compare your graph configuration with figure 13.

Check (✓) the type of unusual pattern:			
Graph I	☐ Overdrive	☐ Underdrive	☐ Neutral
Graph II	☐ Overdrive	☐ Neutral	
Graph III	☐ Overdrive	☐ Underdrive	☐ Neutral

The Overdrive Mode:
Clarifications for Graphs I, II, and III

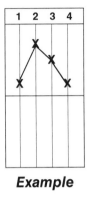

Example

In the overdrive mode, all four factors are above the midline of the graph. You appear to have a need to prove to yourself and others that you have skill in a number of areas. You have had previous opposition that even now is a constant reminder that you must work harder than others to achieve. You tend to overprepare or be oversolicitous in your attempts to receive the "right invitation," appearing with the "in" crowd, and searching for those things that appear to be just out of reach.

The Overdrive Mode: *Graph I Clarification*

You seek attention and desire favors from other people. There is a tendency to go beyond the appropriate or more acceptable methods of securing recognition. Rather ingeniously, you develop unusual ways to act in the hope of discovering immediate solutions to the problems.

You pose questions, often blunt and direct, to arrive at a clear understanding of your position in relation to that of others. Moving from the general to the specific is an approach that you tend to use in clarifying the purpose of activities. You sense a certain ambiguity in the situation and react in order to find meaning.

Others in the environment are viewed as stumbling blocks to your success. You had hoped to identify those who could be helpful. But these very people appear to remain separate and unexpressive. At times, you believe that you expected too much from the situation.

The Overdrive Mode: *Graph II Clarification*

You project a concerted effort to gain a stronger foothold than you usually do. In most situations, you tend to be less outward in your expression. But, at this time, you are taking advantage of new opportunities to add to your beliefs.

You are tending toward a reexamination of your beliefs. But, at the same time, you feel impelled to establish a base of influence that will allow you to project yourself and your ideas.

You experience a surge to enlist others to your purpose. Desiring to share what you have with others, you are willing to exert pressure on them to join you if it is necessary. You show a willingness to oppose the world to protect the principles that you cherish.

The Overdrive Mode: *Graph III Clarification*

You are faced with issues that, at times, appear to be overwhelming. You react to those you perceive as intolerant, even though your own actions may be seen as repressive to them.

Attempting to assume a position, you hope to satisfy a multitude of obligations with one mighty swoop. You try to be all things to all people, making promises that are, at times, difficult to fulfill.

Frustration occurs when others make regulations with little participation on your part. While you appear to move vigorously, you sometimes "spin your wheels." Doors that you thought were open seem to close just as you move to enter. Even though you acknowledge the need for balance, you tend to force issues. You display impatience.

The Underdrive Mode:
Clarifications for Graphs I and III

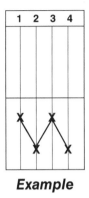

Example

In the Underdrive mode, all four plotting points are below the midline of the graph. There appears to be a marked tendency to "wait and see." While there is a certain tension to create a new experience or a new method, you appear to lack the final drive to complete a project or to gain closure on what you are doing.

The Underdrive Mode: *Graph I Clarification*

You have been slow in reacting to the communicative signs from others. While you tend to desire networking with people, you have difficulty doing it. You become disillusioned by superficial displays of friendship from those who promise to assist you. You may entertain thoughts of going in a different direction.

Others view you as being overly tense. But you deliberately try to play down any overt action that may be misread by them. Waiting for others to make the first move, you become silent and watchful.

When it appears that others will have the first opportunity at things, you become sensitive; you have a tendency to believe that it rightfully belonged to you. The opportunity was one that you coveted. Or you may seriously contemplate taking action, only to be held back by a feeling that you are acting out of step. Not knowing what is wrong, you find it difficult to move forward. You appear to lack energy, or at least sustained energy, to get up and do things.

The Underdrive Mode: *Graph III Clarification*

You believe in respecting authority that appears greater than yourself. Looking to those who have expertise, you seek direction from their specialized skills.

You tend to involve yourself with trivia, losing sight of the bigger picture. Preferring familiar things, you deal with those issues which you have comfortably handled in the past. You are intent on doing things according to an accepted procedure. Desiring to avoid the limelight, you equivocate—failing to take a stance or to be forthright in your opinions.

You sense the need to overcome the anxiety of taking on more than you can do. Accepting responsibility yourself, you hope that others will be equally accountable for their obligations.

The Neutral Mode:
Graphs I, II, and III

Graph I

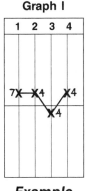

Example

In this mode all of the plotting points cluster around the mid-line of the graph. Figure 14 contains the numbers that make up the Neutral Mode according to the graph in which it appears.

Column	1	2	3	4
Graph I	*7/6	4*	5/4*	*4/3
Graph II	5/6	4	6	6/7
Graph III	+ 1/ − 0	+ 0/ − 1	− 1/ − 2	− 2/ − 3

Figure 14. Numbers that Create the Neutral Mode

The numbers with *s in figure 14 for Graph I are, of course, the numbers that appear in the example in this section.

Check your graphs once more. Do you observe a potential Neutral Mode? A clustering around the midline? If so, check the numbers in the corresponding graph in figure 14. If, for example, your Graph II appears to be in the Neutral Mode, you must have a 5 or 6 plotting point in column 1, a 4 plotting point in column 2, a 6 plotting point in column 3, and a 6 or 7 in column 4. Now let's consider the clarifications for the Neutral Mode.

The Neutral Mode: *Clarification*

Whether the Neutral Mode exists in Graphs I, II, or III, it is obvious that you hesitate to disclose too much information that might reveal your strengths or your limitations. There exists, as well, a possibility that you lack consistency in how you view yourself. Do you really know yourself? More specifically, is it *important* that you know yourself? Let's assume that you have answered in the affirmative. And we will make a few suggestions.

Since the Neutral Mode is infrequently observed, two things can be helpful:

1) Request another person to respond to the Behavior Indicator, using you as the subject; that is, respond as he or she sees you. The results will enable you to see how one other person views you. The two results—your self-perception and the other person's perception—can then be compared. It is a valuable way of gaining self-insight.

2) Respond to the Behavior Indicator a second time—within an interval of 2 to 3 weeks.

The Neutral Mode in any one of the three graphs may be present for one of several reasons. Some of the possibilities include:

1) The meaning of the traits was unclear. The glossary in appendix A should be consulted.

2) An excessive amount of time may have been used in responding to the traits and making a selection. Studying the words puts you in a strategic position of trying to figure out how the instrument works. Don't go over the suggested response time.

3) A bad mood or a bad attitude can have an effect. Be spontaneous. Go with your first inclinations when responding to the words. Learning about yourself can be fun.

4) Perhaps the most frequent reason for the occurrence of the Neutral Mode is an attempt to reveal only what you desire to reveal. This halfway disclosure will result in a limited view of that aspect of your personality.

    If the Neutral Mode is in Graph I, you will not have a clear picture of your adaptive behavior or your intentions.

    If the Neutral Mode is in Graph II, you will have a limited view of how your character structure evaluates and energizes behavior.

    If the Neutral Mode is in Graph III, you will be unable to fully understand your predicted behavior.

Professional Workshop II

Understanding Aristos Personality Theory

Part I:	**How Are Character Traits Different from Behavior Traits?**
Part II:	**How Does the Category of Temperament Differ from Character?**
Part III:	**The Behavior Indicator:** *A Trait Approach to Analyzing Character*

This workshop is designed for the professional or the interested student of personality. It is concerned with the differences and interrelationships among three sets of traits: behavior, character, and temperament.

Part I

How Are Character Traits Different from Behavior Traits?

Do the differences change our understanding of the human personality?

Our behavior traits give rise to action—*what we do.* Our character traits provide the answer—*why we do it.* Character traits underlie behavior traits and subtly alter the action.

In figure 15, the behavior traits are identified with the plain bar, which indicates that actions flowing from our behavior traits are observable to others. This is how we present ourselves.

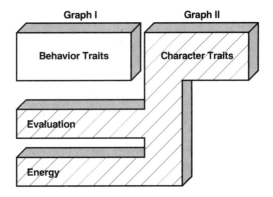

Figure 15.   The Relationship of Character Traits to Behavior Traits

Character traits are identified in figure 15 with the lined area to indicate that they are not as apparent as our behavior traits. The two lined zones beneath the behavior traits represent the two functions of our character traits: evaluating and energizing.

Table 19 provides a further clarification of the differences between behavior traits and character traits.

Table 19. Differences between Behavior and Character Traits

Description of Behavior Traits	Description of Character Traits
• conscious	• unconscious
• observable to others	• underlie our behavior traits, our behavior action
• learned or acquired	• learned or acquired
• changeable	• changeable
• selected by us to meet the objectives of our life plan	• stem from our feelings, emotions, and passions
• correspond to our intentions, which in turn trigger actions	• viewed as desirable, (i.e., polite) or undesirable (i.e., hateful)
• observed in a single factor or a blending of four factors of orientation:	• functioning as evaluative and energy giving
taking	• depicted in a single factor or a blending of four factors of energy:
attracting	Dominance
responding	Inducement
preserving	Submission
	Compliance

Behavior Traits

The selection of behavior traits in Part I of the Behavior Indicator determines the configuration of plotting points in Graph I. The configuration indicates the individual's unique blending of the four orientation factors—taking, attracting, responding, and preserving. It represents the person's intentions in coping with life situations.

The four orientation factors are derived from the work of E. Fromm (1947). The factors are described in table 20 according to their basic premise.

Table 20. Description of the Four Orientation Factors

taking:	The basic premise of the taking orientation is a feeling that the source of all that is desirable lies outside the self. Persons with this orientation, looking outside, expect to take things by force rather than to receive them from others. They tend to judge others by their usefulness, often viewing them as objects of exploitation—the means to an end. Persons with this orientation tend to overrate what others have and underrate what they have.
attracting:	The basic premise of the attracting orientation is a feeling that individuals are commodities with a market value. Persons with this orientation view success as getting their personality across and having the right attributes—joyful or neighborly. They are concerned with how nice a "package" they are. Persons with this orientation tend to feel that who you know is often more important than what you do. Family background, membership in certain clubs, and knowing the right people are regarded as valuable assets.

responding:	The basic premise of the responding orientation is that things of value can only be received from an outside source. This is true whether it is something material or immaterial. Affection, love, pleasure, even knowledge, come from the outside. Exceedingly sensitive to any withdrawal or rebuff on the part of others, persons with this orientation show a particular kind of loyalty. At the bottom of it is a gratitude for the hand that feeds. They have a fear of losing favor with those who give.
preserving:	The basic premise of the preserving orientation is the feeling that not too much good can come from the outside world. Security is based upon saving; spending is viewed as a threat. Persons with this orientation tend to surround themselves with a protective wall. The main aim is to bring as much as possible into this fortified position and to let as little as possible out of it. Persons with this orientation are sentimental; the past appears golden. They hold on to it and indulge in the memories of bygone experiences. A constant "no" is the almost automatic defense against intrusion; sitting tight is the answer to the danger of being pushed.

No one functions in one orientation only. Every human being, in order to survive and to move toward meaningful success, engages in many actions—to take things and to attract and to exchange, to give and to accept, to save and to protect. It is also necessary to follow authority or to guide others, to be alone or to be together. However, individuals do show a preference for certain activities over others. They operate primarily in a unique blending of the orientations.

Character Traits

As important as this understanding of behavior traits is, character traits are the critical key to understanding Aristos Personality Theory. Character traits provide the why—the evaluation and the energy of our intentions. They determine the degree of constructiveness or destructiveness of each orientation. Table 21 lists the four orientation factors and how the resulting action can be energized by either positive or negative character traits.

Table 21. Energizing the Four Orientations

Orientation Factors	Character Traits	
Action	*Negative*	*Positive*
taking	exploitive ———————— ambitious	
attracting	tactless ———————— open-minded	
responding	possessive ———————— loyal	
preserving	anxious ———————— cautious	

Each of the character traits listed in table 21 represent the end points of a continuum that may energize the person's action. If the character trait of *exploitive* underlies the person's action of taking, the result is apt to be destructive. If the character trait of *ambitious* underlies the person's action of taking, the results are apt to be constructive.

The selection of character traits in Part II of the Behavior Indicator is the basis for the configuration of plotting points in Graph II. The choice of character traits is made upon the basis of what we *feel least*.

Feelings are the messengers between our inner and outer worlds. In addition, our *least* choices are less subject to change in response to day-to-day occurrences. These two factors facilitate tapping the unconscious. A composite of our preference regarding character traits can be referred to as the self-ideal.

The self-ideal is an integral part of the character structure. It is a set of beliefs about how we should behave. We state these beliefs in terms of self-expectations or self-demands.

The private logic of our character is instrumental in formulating the self-ideal. Altering or changing our self-ideal occurs only when we begin to reconstruct the private logic of our character.

Private logic has its beginnings in early childhood in the form of demands and expectations that parents and other significant persons have of us. As we grow older, our private logic, with our self-ideal, continues to form. It is always in the process of reformulation. Our self-ideal provides a standard by which we appraise our conduct.

In addition to the evaluative mode of Graph II, we also may observe our energy directed mode. It is through our character traits that we determine the energetics of our personality.

We differ widely in our awareness of the striving that makes up the evaluative and energy directed modes of our character. But these largely unconscious strivings play a significant role in forming our character traits. They channel our psychic energy into a unique blend of the four energy factors—Dominance, Inducement, Submission, and Compliance. These factors are derived from the work of W. Marston (1928). They are described in table 22.

Table 22. Description of the Four Energy Factors

Energy Factor	Affects Action by:
Dominance	• drives for results • seeks power • uses information to control others • accelerates efforts • displays strength
Inducement	• expects rewards • uses outward appearances • shows willingness to share strengths • demonstrates excitability • promotes what is best for self
Submission	• expects security • develops inward satisfaction • builds a reserve of strength • remains calm, composed • develops union with others
Compliance	• stores information • warns of impulsiveness • systematizes efforts • prepares for onslaught of power • protects domain

Each of the four energy factors derives its psychic energy from the affective nature—feelings, emotions, and passions. *The four factors are regulated by the self-ideal contained in the private logic of the character structure.* While energy is expended in all of the factors, most individuals show a unique preference for a blending of the factors. This preference is the result of life experiences that are both conscious and unconscious. With increased awareness, the individual can discover a constructive balance among the energy factors.

Significant differences are apparent between behavior traits and character traits. Those efforts that only employ behavior traits are severely limited in understanding personality, particularly when interpreting individual behavior. Aristos Personality Theory incorporates both character and personality traits.

Without character traits, it would not be possible to accurately analyze the way in which the belief system is activated to energize intentions. Without character traits, it would not be possible to understand the evaluative mode of character that initiates, impedes, or halts individual action.

The third set of traits that is incorporated into Aristos Personality Theory is discussed in Part II of the workshop.

Part II

How Does the Category of Temperament Differ from Character?

This is an intriguing question since there is a resurgence of interest in the old category of temperament in some quarters of our society. In addition, we believe that it is necessary to consider temperament in understanding Aristos Personality Theory.

A portion of the interpretation for each personality pattern focuses, to some degree, on temperament. Understanding temperament and how it fits into our total personality can assist us in orchestrating the full development of the personality.

But how far can we go in terms of the temperament analysis? To what extent can we identify our personal behavior and motivation as it relates to temperament? Let's begin with a brief historical perspective.

The category of temperaments is an old classification of psychic phenomena and traits. Present-day scholars tend to dismiss temperament as an inadequate way to discuss behavior. Social scientists such as A. Adler (1959) concluded that clearly defined temperaments are seldom found. He observed that in dealing with the "four temperaments," one seemed to dissolve into another. In his estimation, this lack of a sharp separation robbed the lore of temperament of all value.

What, then, is temperament? What can we hope to discover? Is temperament the quickness with which we think, speak, or act? Is it the power or the rhythm with which we perform a task? What can be said for the current revival in the use of temperament to describe personality? Is it a justified way to view human behavior?

First, let's clarify the four temperaments. Despite Adler's position regarding the classification of temperaments, he also reminded us that science has been unable to get away from the concept that there are four temperaments—a concept that goes back to antiquity, when scholars first began to study psychic life.

The first identification of temperaments dates from ancient Greece. Hippocrates viewed the temperaments as *modes of reaction* connected with different somatic or bodily sources. It is interesting to note that, in popular usage, only the negative aspects of his descriptions survive. Choleric today is interpreted as easily angered; melancholic means depressed; sanguine is viewed as overly optimistic; phlegmatic is interpreted as slow. The meanings of these four temperaments are obviously too limited. And, in retaining only the negative aspect of the original meaning, they are somewhat unfair. However, it is dangerous to go too far the other way and use temperament to describe the major aspects of personality. Two eminent social scientists— C. Jung and E. Fromm—viewed that prospect as ill-advised.

Carl Jung (1923) expressed his opinion on the four temperaments by moving beyond the four classifications to develop the mechanisms of introvert and extravert. His viewpoint is expressed thus:

"The differentiation of the four temperaments which we took from the ancients, hardly rates as a psychological typology since the temperaments are scarcely more than psychophysical colorings."

Erich Fromm (1947) sounded a warning bell in his criticism of temperaments. While open to a study of temperaments, he was far more intent upon his effort to gain a fresh perspective on character. Fromm felt it was necessary to clearly distinguish between character and temperament. The confusion between the two concepts had impeded progress in characterology as well as in the study of temperament.

Fromm's point is well taken. We view both character and temperament as entities of the personality. Understanding the differences in the more specific areas of temperament traits and character traits is useful at this point in our discussion. In this way, we can identify what can and cannot be changed.

A review of table 23 clarifies the significant differences between character traits and temperament traits. Character is essentially formed by our experiences. In comparison to temperament, character is far more changeable. Character is more encompassing than temperament; it comprises more qualities on which humans differ. Finally, character is primarily a *responsive* mode.

Table 23. Comparing Temperament and Character Traits

Temperament Traits	Quality	Character Traits
yes	conscious?	partially
yes	unconscious?	yes
yes	innate, inherited?	no
partially	fixed, unchangeable?	no
yes	used in a reactive mode?	partially
yes	used as speed, intensity, and perseverance?	no
no	intelligence?	yes
no	power of will?	yes

In contrast, temperament is a *reactive* mode. It is inborn and only partially changeable. However, temperament has a definite effect upon our character and other aspects of our personality. In the reactive mode, temperament is related to time intensity (Ti) and time concentration (Tc).

Our propensity to anger is an example of time intensity and the duration of our anger is an example of time concentration.

Further clarification of *Ti* and *Tc* as part of the reactive mode is possible as you respond to and review the temperament model below.

Respond to the Temperament Model

Step One: **Place *one* (✔) to the left of the model regarding time intensity that is most representative of your propensity to anger.**

Step Two: **Place *one* (✔) at the top of the model regarding time duration that is most representative of your propensity to appeasement.**

The Temperament Model

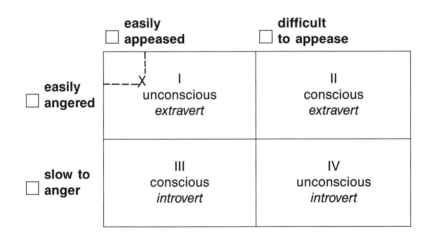

Step Three: **Determine the area for the intersecting point— use an X to mark the spot. (See example in model.)**

The roman numeral in each square of the model is the axis that radiates out to the horizontal and vertical descriptions of the entity contained in the square. See dotted line in Area I for an example.

The italicized word in each of the four areas is *extravert* or *introvert*. These are the two most well-known aspects of temperament. The originator of the terms, C. Jung (1923), succinctly defined the terms:

"The outward reaction characterizes the extravert, just as the inward reaction is the mark of the introvert."

Both terms are fundamentally part of the reactive mode. While none of us are pure introverts or pure extraverts, many people show a tendency toward one or the other.

In addition, as we adapt to our environment, we tend to show a preference for one temperament and push the other into unconsciousness. Let's examine how this may occur.

Conscious and Unconscious Extravert and Introvert

It is important to briefly expand on the explanation of extravert and introvert before examining the conscious and unconscious factors.

The Extravert. The consciousness of the extraverted person looks out into the external world for meaning and value. Generally, the orientations of extraverted persons are compatible with societal values, which makes them rather easy to be around. At their best, extraverted persons are affable, adaptable, and can get projects and tasks accomplished—in some way. At their worst, extraverts do not seem to have a sense of themselves, and thus, they pursue "popularity" and lack self-direction.

The Introvert. In contrast to the extraverted person, the introverted individual focuses on his or her internal thoughts, ideas, and fantasies. These persons appear to be more motivated by their subjective experiences. They are less interested in the practical tasks to be accomplished than in the stimulation they experience from new ideas and theories. The introvert is less outgoing than the extravert—more solitary, more independent of thought, and able to take firm stands on issues regardless of public approbation or disapproval. The introvert is harder to understand and get along with, and requires more time to weigh decisions.

The temperament model includes the aspect of the conscious and unconscious in regard to extravert and introvert. *Keep in mind that the extravert has an introverted side. Conversely, the introvert has an extraverted side.*

The *preferred* attitude or mechanism, whether introvert or extravert, will be expressed in the conscious personality. It will reflect the aim, determination, and achievement of our consciousness.

On the other hand, the suppressed attitude or mechanism is only partly in our consciousness. At times, it reflects behavior that is quite surprising and startlingly to oneself. This less preferred side of a person's temperament is less differentiated and less activated, and, according to Jung, "is apt to be more primitive and undeveloped."

Jung even claimed that if, through concentrated pressure on the part of the mother, the child is coerced into living out his or her less preferred side, this may result in the individual's becoming disturbed in later life. This possibility regarding "others' expectations" of our behavior is a rationale for exploring energetics of personality. Our character—the manner in which we direct our energy to satisfy our survival and success needs—enables us to question and review all aspects of personality—including our temperament.

The response keys of the temperament model provide us with an example of our temperament.

Easily angered: *easily appeased*

Easily angered: *difficult to appease*

Slow to anger: *easily appeased*

Slow to anger: *difficult to appease*

These keys were used over two thousand years ago and are described in the Talmud, in a passage from *Pirke Aboth.* They provide a focus for us regarding our mental disposition, extravert and introvert. Let's examine your results based upon the selection of the response keys.

Results of your Response to
The Temperament Model

Earlier, you determined the intersecting point in one of the four areas of the temperament model. In which area did your intersection occur? Following is an explanation for each of the four areas.

If your X occurred in:

Area I: Unconscious Extravert

While the extravert attitude is considered the less preferred one by the person in comparison to the introvert, there is a note of urgency to meet the expectations of others. Consequently, this person, while projecting a fairly consistent introvert pattern, makes strong attempts to appear extraverted even though it is often difficult.

Area II: Conscious Extravert

This person appears to accommodate to others relatively easily and manages the economic and practical areas of living with some efficiency. On the down side, there is a tendency to be oversuggestible and pushed to the extreme. The individual may be prone to hysterical and physical ailments.

Area III: Conscious Introvert

An attitude reflecting conscious introversion may indicate a person who does not value status or economic achievement as much as the pursuit and understanding of underlying and universal meanings of life not readily apparent or understood in everyday living. On the down side is a possible extreme in which the most frequent neuroses are morbid fantasy, depression, and a tendency to become an isolated recluse.

Area IV: *Unconscious Introvert*

> The individual feels repressed when expressing self-hood, appearing shy and reluctant to project a confident stance. Experiences have reinforced the individual to push the introvert deeper into the unconscious and to instead project the conscious extravert. The person resurrects contacts with others and openly expresses discontent when hostility occurs.

While these general interpretations provide an insight into what Jung referred to as "biological differences," it is important to remember that these mechanisms are, in essence, the "bare bones." True, these appear to be basic characteristics that the person exhibits immediately at birth. There is some wisdom in the urging to avoid forcing people to project what we would like them to be. Children can be forced to act against their temperament mechanism by one or the other parent, just as children can be forced to switch from using their left hand to using their right hand.

Some forms of stuttering have been attributed to this switching of hands since (presumably) it forces the neurological system to act in reverse. In just such a way, people acting contrary to their temperament may be more prone to neurosis, since they are falsifying their own reactive modes.

Still, as we move through life, we consider the necessity to adapt in an appropriate and effective manner. Some of us may exhibit speed or quickness. Others may demonstrate less intensity. Over time, we may find it necessary to alter these reactions—to some degree. And, while temperament is inborn, some change is possible. But it is change that requires significant effort. It must be sustained and constant.

Temperament is more apparent if the other aspects of our personality—character and thinking—are slow in developing. Then our "bare bones" stand out. Temperament is what we start out with in life, but it is only the beginning.

As we grow and develop, other aspects of our personality begin to form and to build a structure around the "bare bones" of our temperament. Some of our experiences occurred because of our temperament. But a great deal of what we learn is spontaneous and results from the people and events in our environment. As our thinking system develops, we begin to recognize our difference in temperament and the influence it has on our behavior.

The unfolding of our character is also affected by our temperament. For example, our mode of reaction—our temperament—may be "quick and strong." But what we are quick and strong about depends upon what kind of character we are developing.

If we are creative, just, and loving, we will act quickly and strongly when we love, or quickly and strongly when we see injustice, or quickly and strongly when we pursue an idea. Conversely, if our character is mean-spirited and hateful, we will be quick and strong to be mean and hateful.

Gaining perspective on temperament and its relationship to character is helpful in knowing what can and cannot be changed. While temperament is largely unchangeable, it contributes to our uniqueness. We can come to know, respect, and appreciate our temperament. In so doing, we make the best use of our reactive modes.

We can conclude, then, that the three sets of traits—behavior, temperament, and character—relate to each other in a unique and fascinating manner. All three must be appropriately considered in viewing our individual behavior.

Describing personality patterns that incorporate the three sets of traits is, indeed, a necessity if the human personality is to be accurately and scientifically appraised. The method of doing so is contained in the third part of this workshop.

Part III

The Behavior Indicator:
A Trait Approach to Analyzing Personality

This book contains over 130 different patterns of interpretation that provide an in-depth analysis of the personality. They are the result of a carefully structured instrument—the Behavior Indicator—that utilizes clusters of traits.

Three sets of traits are used in the Behavior Indicator: behavior, character, and temperament. Temperament traits are employed as a neutral, but meaningful, component in Part I and Part II of the Behavior Indicator.

To provide perspective on our work, it is necessary to take a historical view of the study of personality. In this way, it is possible to trace the accumulation of knowledge in the effort to understand human behavior. For example, in attempting to understand human aggression, early researchers used a single S→R (Stimulus→Response) model in testing a frustration→aggression hypothesis. This approach revealed that individuals reacted in a number of different ways when frustrated. Aggression was not the only response.

Along this same cause and effect line, early researchers in the trait approach attempted to understand character by describing it with a single trait, for example, *ambitious.* Or they attempted to describe behavior with a single trait, for example, *courageous.* The single trait approach was soon discarded because of the incompleteness of the explanation.

Later researchers employed a listing of traits under several major headings. Their method was to use a cluster approach—simply grouping items that appeared to go together. Again, the results were less than satisfying and the conclusions were questionable.

Our research design included work in classifying behavior traits, character traits, and temperament traits through factor analysis. The research procedure was to group the three sets of traits according to the frequency of their selection by research participants. In-depth interviews, utilizing the focus interview technique (Geier 1963) were an integral part of the research design.

This approach enabled us to identify the commonality of traits that have a high correlation with each other. It also permitted us to assign to one factor some traits that did not have as high a correlation with each other. Finally, this research method revealed the extent to which each of the traits reflected the other factors.

These factors around which common traits were discovered are the basis for the Behavior Indicator. Graph I reflects the selection of behavior traits from Part I of the instrument. It is the Orientation System with four factors: taking, attracting, responding, and preserving. Graph II depicts the selection of character traits from Part II of the Behavior Indicator. It is the Energy System with four points: Dominance, Inducement, Submission, and Compliance.

The Orientation System is combined with the Energy System to form the basis of interpretation for Graph III—predicted behavior. It, of course, is not prophetic in foretelling the future. It does, however, permit us to carefully analyze how we affect others and our desired course of action. And in this process we accept the very basis of Energetics of Personality—that is, responsibility for the direction we choose to assume.

The Responsible Direction

We have the potential to shape our character—or Energetics of Personality. If we assume that one's moral qualities are rooted in one's character, then we also acknowledge the responsibility to shape our moral qualities.

Obviously, from the content of this book and the design of the Behavior Indicator, we take the position that the more insight we have into the conditions responsible for the formation of character and its dynamics, the less able we are to escape a sense of responsibility for our actions. In a very real sense, the pursuit of insight becomes a moral act.

Character, the energy we direct toward survival and success, determines our decisions. We are the only creatures endowed with reason, the only beings who are capable of understanding the very forces to which we are subjected. And we are the only creatures who, by our power of understanding, can take an active part in what we will become. We have the power of choice—the free will to decide.

Book II
Interpretation

Intended Behavior

PATTERN ONE
Intended Behavior
Your intentions in the present situation include:

☐ Setting the pace and prodding those who move slowly.
☐ Claiming territory even though it is in dispute or occupied by others.
☐ Winning in competitions that make you feel important.
☐ Developing a single-minded intensity that focuses concentration on an all-consuming project.
☐ Living life intensely; getting what you feel that you deserve.
☐ Directing activity toward a conquest; viewing life as winning and losing.
☐ Stating your ideas exactly as you see them; refraining from holding anything back.
☐ Securing the services of people who will do precisely what you want them to do.
☐ Establishing an authoritative base to show that you mean business.
☐ Instilling fear in others; threatening to remove your support from them if they resist you.

Chart 1 depicts the percentage breakdown and the rank of the amount of time and effort that you devote to the listed intentions. Your top three intentions are: to gain a power base and strongly voice your opinion (25%), to taste success (16%), and to take a risk (15%).

Chart 1

investment of effort:	intentions in this situation	
	intensity of effort	
intentions	% weight	rank
hope to create	10.0	5
desire to please	6.0	7
free to act	11.0	4
take a risk	15.0	3
awake to reality	7.0	6
gain power	25.0	1
develop harmony	2.0	10
have fun	3.0	9
proceed with caution	5.0	8
taste success	16.0	2
total %	100.0	

PATTERN TWO
Intended Behavior

Your intentions in the present situation include:

☐ Discovering aspects of life that are enjoyable; being selective in what you let bother you.

☐ Moving easily between seriousness and lightheartedness.

☐ Displaying "social assertiveness" in circumstances that are favorable or nonthreatening.

☐ Using emotional appeal to change a course of action, playing to the soft spot of others.

☐ Organizing to make yourself look good or, better yet, convincing others to organize for you.

☐ Selecting and associating with others on the basis of their pleasantness and receptiveness to your ideas.

☐ Taking assignments that bring out your uniqueness and talents.

☐ Laughing easily, seeking to avoid events that remind you of past disappointments.

☐ Rolling with the punches, turning the other cheek, if necessary.

☐ Being nonchalant about pressing difficulties.

Chart 2 depicts the percentage breakdown and the rank of the amount of time and effort that you devote to the listed intentions. Your top three intentions are: to act freely (20%), to engage in fun activities (18%), and to develop harmony (15%).

Chart 2

investment of effort:	intentions in this situation	
	intensity of effort	
intentions	% weight	rank
hope to create	3.0	9
desire to please	8.0	6
free to act	20.0	1
take a risk	7.0	7
awake to reality	5.0	8
gain power	10.0	5
develop harmony	15.0	3
have fun	18.0	2
proceed with caution	2.0	10
taste success	12.0	4
total %	100.0	

PATTERN THREE
Intended Behavior
Your intentions in the present situation include:

☐ Finding a way to show your affection and devotion.

☐ Fulfilling the expectations of others, doing what must be done to satisfy them.

☐ Setting limits on those who exploit your generous acts, defending your vulnerability to others.

☐ Protecting yourself by anticipating unforeseen disturbances.

☐ Resisting impulsive moves of others, preferring your own deliberate course of action.

☐ Seeking a way to make things more equitable, viewing yourself as a victim of injustice.

☐ Outwardly showing a patient attitude toward others.

☐ Demonstrating a willingness to give up your high aspirations for the good of others.

☐ Trusting others to support you when you need them.

☐ Joining with others in a spirit of togetherness.

Chart 3 depicts the percentage breakdown and the rank of the amount of time and effort that you devote to the listed intentions. Your top three intentions are: to please others (25%), to face reality by accepting facts (18%), and to develop harmony (15%).

Chart 3

investment of effort:	intentions in this situation	
	intensity of effort	
intentions	% weight	rank
hope to create	6.0	7
desire to please	25.0	1
free to act	4.0	8
take a risk	5.0	6
awake to reality	18.0	2
gain power	2.0	10
develop harmony	15.0	3
have fun	10.0	5
proceed with caution	12.0	4
taste success	3.0	9
total %	100.0	

PATTERN FOUR
Intended Behavior

Your intentions in the present situation include:

☐ Losing yourself in the impulsive activities and presentations of others.
☐ Refraining from active participation in social activity.
☐ Doing things in which you can demonstrate your talent and ability in private surroundings.
☐ Restricting the number of people who hold you accountable, preferring only one.
☐ Giving homage to those who show a greater sense of importance than you feel.
☐ Extolling the successes of others while devaluing your own.
☐ Depending upon others to cheer you up; relying on their good will.
☐ Yielding your position to avoid conflict; insisting, however, that full restitution be made.
☐ Demanding complete surety as a protection against the extremes of aggressiveness from those in authority positions.
☐ Seeking to align yourself with another who is equally sensitive.

Chart 4 depicts the percentage breakdown and the rank of the amount of time and effort that you devote to the listed intentions. Your top three intentions are: to proceed with caution (30%), to please others (20%), and to awake to reality (12%).

Chart 4

investment of effort:	intentions in this situation	
intentions	% weight	rank
hope to create	8.0	5
desire to please	20.0	2
free to act	6.0	6
take a risk	4.0	8
awake to reality	12.0	3
gain power	3.0	9
develop harmony	10.0	4
have fun	2.0	10
proceed with caution	30.0	1
taste success	5.0	7
total %	100.0	

PATTERN TWELVE
Intended Behavior
Your intentions in the present situation include:

☐ Expecting help from those who are obligated for past favors.
☐ Assigning menial tasks to those who have more patience than you.
☐ Promising others a place in your hopes and aspirations.
☐ Selecting opportunities that will potentially add to your possessions.
☐ Accepting any new responsibility that enhances your reputation.
☐ Exerting greater influence on others than they exert on you.
☐ Developing a greater vision that includes a bigger role for you in the future.
☐ Extending yourself in attempts to back up your words with actions.
☐ Establishing a uniqueness that will separate you from the group.
☐ Understanding others better than they understand you.

Chart 5 depicts the percentage breakdown and the rank of the amount of time and effort that you devote to the listed intentions. Your top three intentions are: to gain a power base (20%), to act freely and minimize restraints (16%), and to taste success (15%).

Chart 5

investment of effort:	intentions in this situation	
	intensity of effort	
intentions	% weight	rank
hope to create	8.0	6
desire to please	6.0	7
free to act	16.0	2
take a risk	12.0	4
awake to reality	5.0	8
gain power	20.0	1
develop harmony	4.0	9
have fun	11.0	5
proceed with caution	3.0	10
taste success	15.0	3
total %	100.0	

PATTERN THIRTEEN
Intended Behavior
Your intentions in the present situation include:

☐ Attempting to involve yourself in a satisfying and harmonious relationship.

☐ Weeding out the unpleasant past, when you felt compelled to assume the lion's share of the responsibility.

☐ Seeking reliable persons with whom to share tasks and achieve a high degree of satisfaction.

☐ Interacting with others who appreciate the attention you give to details.

☐ Refusing to say "no," fearing possibilities of missed opportunities.

☐ Treating with contempt those who criticize you; demanding that others show devotion similar to your own.

☐ Using retreat as a viable option to get away from people, permitting you to pull yourself together.

☐ Employing strategies in which you deliberately make others uncomfortable, hoping they view you as unpredictable.

☐ Placing blame on others for not making you happy, chiding them for unfulfilled promises.

☐ Checking on others to ensure that obligations are fulfilled.

Chart 6 depicts the percentage breakdown and the rank of the amount of time and effort that you devote to the listed intentions. **Your top three intentions are: to take a risk (20%), to develop a power base and increase your influence (15%), and to act freely (14%).**

Chart 6

investment of effort:	intentions in this situation	
	intensity of effort	
intentions	% weight	rank
hope to create	12.0	4
desire to please	6.0	8
free to act	14.0	3
take a risk	20.0	1
awake to reality	10.0	5
gain power	15.0	2
develop harmony	8.0	6
have fun	5.0	9
proceed with caution	3.0	10
taste success	7.0	7
total %	100.0	

PATTERN FOURTEEN
Intended Behavior

Your intentions in the present situation include:

☐ Accepting responsibility for being in the corrective role, getting people to strive for excellence.

☐ Remaining immovable until strong opinions and facts warrant a change in your thinking.

☐ Waiting to impose your will on those who didn't take your advice.

☐ Seeking to arrive at the *best* answer rather than just *any* answer.

☐ Forcing people to think through their reasoning and actions.

☐ Striving equally for accomplishments and quality.

☐ Pursuing a plan with intensity that does not allow a deflection from your purpose.

☐ Avoiding dependence on the good will of others.

☐ Calculating the best time to withdraw from the clutches of overly aggressive people.

☐ Displaying logical arguments that weaken the emotional appeal of others.

Chart 7 depicts the percentage breakdown and the rank of the amount of time and effort that you devote to the listed intentions. Your top three intentions are: to awake to reality in light of new information (20%), to fulfill your desire to create (17%), and to take a risk (15%).

Chart 7

investment of effort:	intentions in this situation	
	intensity of effort	
intentions	% weight	rank
hope to create	17.0	2
desire to please	8.0	6
free to act	6.0	7
take a risk	15.0	3
awake to reality	20.0	1
gain power	10.0	5
develop harmony	4.0	9
have fun	3.0	10
proceed with caution	12.0	4
taste success	5.0	8
total %	100.0	

PATTERN TWENTY-THREE
Intended Behavior
Your intentions in the present situation include:

☐ Avoiding intense struggles with others, giving in to those who desire control—at least on the surface.

☐ Developing respectful relationships, building upon those which offer fulfillment and happiness.

☐ Giving warmth and understanding to others in exchange for their approval.

☐ Demonstrating an independent attitude, overshadowed only by your willingness to avoid confrontations.

☐ Accepting blame and responsibility for others, even if, at times, you suffer harmful effects.

☐ Requesting and gaining a portion, spiritual and material, of what others receive.

☐ Using your close involvement with others to gain an appropriate reward.

☐ Committing yourself to the present, but keeping your options open to a change in the future.

☐ Developing thoughts of grandiose schemes, fully realizing that you must depend upon the entrepreneurial skills of others.

☐ Showing a cooperative attitude in the present, but prepared to be confrontive when your rights are denied.

Chart 8 depicts the percentage breakdown and the rank of the amount of time and effort that you devote to the listed intentions. Your top three intentions are: to develop harmony (25%), to please others (18%), and to satisfy the need for fun (15%).

Chart 8

investment of effort:	intentions in this situation	
	intensity of effort	
intentions	% weight	rank
hope to create	7.0	6
desire to please	18.0	2
free to act	12.0	4
take a risk	2.0	10
awake to reality	9.0	5
gain power	3.0	9
develop harmony	25.0	1
have fun	15.0	3
proceed with caution	5.0	7
taste success	4.0	8
total %	100.0	

PATTERN TWENTY-FOUR
Intended Behavior

Your intentions in the present situation include:

☐ Accepting broader responsibility while resisting assignments that require you to perform mundane and trivial activities.

☐ Developing a base from which you can operate; getting settled in a place you can call your own.

☐ Encouraging rivalry as part of motivating yourself to successful efforts.

☐ Closely observing those who are gaining on you, attempting to understand their motivations.

☐ Moving with an air of authority, making people accountable for what they do.

☐ Drawing close to people who possess skills you lack, asking for their assistance and testing their loyalty to you.

☐ Sorting out what is important, carefully picking your battles.

☐ Acknowledging the need to be competitive; increasing your intensity.

☐ Planning a strategy that will place you closer to the center of power.

☐ Being critical when others fail to fulfill their commitments to you, threatening to withdraw your support from them.

Chart 9 depicts the percentage breakdown and the rank of the amount of time and effort that you devote to the listed intentions. Your top three intentions are: to taste success (22%), to develop harmony (18%), and to act freely (15%).

Chart 9

investment of effort:	intentions in this situation	
	intensity of effort	
intentions	% weight	rank
hope to create	5.0	8
desire to please	4.0	9
free to act	15.0	3
take a risk	12.0	4
awake to reality	8.0	5
gain power	7.0	6
develop harmony	18.0	2
have fun	6.0	7
proceed with caution	3.0	10
taste success	22.0	1
total %	100.0	

PATTERN THIRTY-FOUR
Intended Behavior
Your intentions in the present situation include:

☐ Acknowledging the need to be firm when necessary, but assigning tough tasks to those who are more combative.

☐ Showing respect to those in authority, withholding criticism when you disagree.

☐ Waiting for events to develop, hoping to see them go your way.

☐ Getting others to share in your final decisions, believing that blame can be spread evenly.

☐ Showing a sense of pride in handling difficult and complex problems.

☐ Readily accepting details and responsibilities that others view as narrow and cumbersome.

☐ Observing the ways in which others react to your success so that you can repeat it.

☐ Withstanding criticism from those who ridicule the higher moral laws to which you ascribe.

☐ Withholding unpopular suggestions for improvement of systems and methods in the face of strong opposition.

☐ Showing loyalty to those who appear to move with conviction.

Chart 10 depicts the percentage breakdown and the rank of the amount of time and effort that you devote to the listed intentions. Your top three intentions are: to proceed with caution (25%), to please others (23%), and to awake to reality in light of new information (15%).

Chart 10

investment of effort:	intentions in this situation	
	intensity of effort	
intentions	% weight	rank
hope to create	6.0	6
desire to please	23.0	2
free to act	5.0	7
take a risk	3.0	9
awake to reality	15.0	3
gain power	7.0	5
develop harmony	10.0	4
have fun	4.0	8
proceed with caution	25.0	1
taste success	2.0	10
total %	100.0	

PATTERN ONE TWENTY-THREE
Intended Behavior
Your intentions in the present situation include:

☐ Developing a back-up system; finding a way to save face when difficulties arise.

☐ Rejecting people without hurting them, letting them down easily.

☐ Searching for answers that are best for you; protecting your interests as a primary concern.

☐ Admitting weakness so that recognition of limitations becomes one of your key strengths.

☐ Selecting people who have interests similar to your own, checking their sources and credibility.

☐ Comparing your strength with others to note your improvement.

☐ Discovering new ways to bring increased excitement to your life; hoping to overcome sameness.

☐ Showing strength to deal with those who appear envious and who attempt to oppose your ideas.

☐ Developing and even inventing a common enemy to solicit the effort of others.

☐ Keeping in mind that the created foe is one that you and others can defeat.

Chart 11 depicts the percentage breakdown and the rank of the amount of time and effort that you devote to the listed intentions. Your top three intentions are: to act freely (18%), to develop harmony (16%), and to please others (15%).

Chart 11

investment of effort:	intentions in this situation	
	intensity of effort	
intentions	% weight	rank
hope to create	5.0	9
desire to please	15.0	3
free to act	18.0	1
take a risk	6.0	8
awake to reality	7.0	7
gain power	12.0	4
develop harmony	16.0	2
have fun	10.0	5
proceed with caution	3.0	10
taste success	8.0	6
total %	100.0	

PATTERN ONE TWENTY-FOUR
Intended Behavior

Your intentions in the present situation include:

☐ Driving hard for completion of tasks, refusing to relax or give in when you have the advantage.

☐ Developing escape routes from uncomfortable commitments.

☐ Following a routine that is predictable to you.

☐ Deliberately creating pressure so as to increase your production.

☐ Seeking people with like-minded interests, hoping to assign nitty gritty details to them.

☐ Confronting people when they fail to meet the requirements you set for them, withholding favors from those who displease you.

☐ Letting people know that there is more to you than meets the eye; viewing yourself as attractive *and* reflective.

☐ Moving to different and higher levels of interest; showing variety in thought and action.

☐ Displaying respect for risk takers, preferring to let them go out on the limb rather than doing so yourself.

☐ Cultivating your spirit to be more free to explore new opportunties.

Chart 12 depicts the percentage breakdown and the rank of the amount of time and effort that you devote to the listed intentions. Your top three intentions are: to fulfill a desire to create (22%), to gain power (17%), and to face the reality of the situation (15%).

Chart 12

investment of effort:	intentions in this situation	
	intensity of effort	
intentions	% weight	rank
hope to create	22.0	1
desire to please	2.0	10
free to act	12.0	4
take a risk	10.0	5
awake to reality	15.0	3
gain power	17.0	2
develop harmony	3.0	9
have fun	8.0	6
proceed with caution	5.0	8
taste success	6.0	7
total %	100.0	

PATTERN ONE THIRTY-FOUR
Intended Behavior
Your intentions in the present situation include:

☐ Keeping interactions at a minimum and limiting the number of people with whom you deal.

☐ Playing down your sentimental side, permitting that view of you to be seen only by those close to you.

☐ Showing the strength of your determination when others appear to be weakening.

☐ Displaying tenacity in completion of tasks.

☐ Eliminating hidden agendas, asking questions that bring issues into the open, putting your cards on the table.

☐ Using the silent treatment on those who oppose you, withdrawing in order to have more time to consider the response of people toward you.

☐ Protecting yourself against risks and failure by "overpreparing" yourself.

☐ Showing caution regarding promises made to you by others.

☐ Developing a logical procedure to plan both home and work activities.

☐ Including a "personal time" in your schedule to develop individual skills.

Chart 13 depicts the percentage breakdown and the rank of the amount of time and effort that you devote to the listed intentions. Your top three intentions are: to awake to reality as new information becomes available (21%), to proceed with caution (19%), and to please others (15%).

Chart 13

investment of effort:	intentions in this situation	
	intensity of effort	
intentions	% weight	rank
hope to create	10.0	5
desire to please	15.0	3
free to act	4.0	8
take a risk	12.0	4
awake to reality	21.0	1
gain power	8.0	6
develop harmony	6.0	7
have fun	3.0	9
proceed with caution	19.0	2
taste success	2.0	10
total %	100.0	

PATTERN TWO THIRTY-FOUR
Intended Behavior

Your intentions in the present situation include:

☐ Opting for a fixed environment, eliminating, when possible, sudden and abrupt changes.

☐ Revising your goals and expectations to bring them in line with realistic opportunities.

☐ Adjusting your level of activity to correspond with your energy level.

☐ Selecting people who demonstrate loyalty to you.

☐ Avoiding direct confrontations that endanger your security.

☐ Acknowledging your limited resources, indicating that you can do only so much.

☐ Publicly stating that, without contributions from others, you feel depleted of energy, believing that small tasks seem to turn into major chores.

☐ Requesting predictable events that provide a high comfort level.

☐ Attempting to see the situation more objectively, viewing others in terms of their helpfulness to you.

☐ Dealing with your personal frustration, which is a warning of your dissatisfaction.

Chart 14 depicts the percentage breakdown and the rank of the amount of time and effort that you devote to the listed intentions. Your top three intentions are: to please others (22%), to proceed with caution by weighing options (18%), and to develop harmony (15%).

Chart 14

investment of effort:	intentions in this situation	
	intensity of effort	
intentions	% weight	rank
hope to create	4.0	8
desire to please	22.0	1
free to act	10.0	5
take a risk	3.0	9
awake to reality	12.0	4
gain power	6.0	7
develop harmony	15.0	3
have fun	8.0	6
proceed with caution	18.0	2
taste success	2.0	10
total %	100.0	

Concealed Behavior

PATTERN ONE
Concealed Behavior

Your affective nature* in the present situation is reflected as:

Description	*Consequences, Observable Actions*
☐ vengeful	Showing others they were wrong about you; wearing down the opposition; simply refusing to relax or to give in; holding exhaustion at bay by keeping active.
☐ angry	Believing that others have exaggerated their claims; insisting that they have no more right to privileges than you do; consequently, attempting to establish an irrefutable position.
☐ exhausted	Resisting attempts by others to make you look weak; threatening, instead, to expose their shortcomings; refusing to let others see your weariness in overcoming feelings of inferiority.
☐ self-pitying	Exploring all avenues to gain what is deservedly yours; refusing to accept any form of consolation; concluding that you have invested time and effort that have gone unnoticed.

You choose to be

driven

---

*Feelings, emotions, passion

PATTERN TWO
Concealed Behavior

Your affective nature* in the present situation is reflected as:

Description	Consequences, Observable Actions
☐ joyful	Viewing life as having much to offer; anxiously hoping that others enjoy that which is a delight to you.
☐ worrying, concerned	Dreading signals that indicate the end of this pleasurable period of your life; trying to find an effective use of your time and extend the experience.
☐ envying	Favorably comparing yourself to others who seek the same fulfillment as you do; wondering why you've had to expend more effort than others.
☐ freeing	Responding wholeheartedly to the approval and acceptance of others; experiencing relief in this favorable reception, but yearning, at times, for the suspense of the unknown.

You choose to be

unstructured

*Feelings, emotions, passion

PATTERN THREE
Concealed Behavior

Your affective nature* in the present situation is reflected as:

Description	*Consequences, Observable Actions*
☐ rejected	Taking on tasks with fervor in the hope of pleasing others; wishing you would have contributed more at an earlier time.
☐ skeptical, doubtful, questioning	Sulking over snide remarks made by those who contend that you go out of your way to be sacrificial; giving hints that you are annoyed at others who fail to carry their fair share.
☐ steadfast	Projecting an unruffled appearance; approaching circumstances with care and concentration, nervous and anxious on the inside but putting on a good front.
☐ empathetic	Accepting assignments with little outward objection, determined to outdo previous acts of service; giving up your own self-interests to ensure that care is given to those who need you.

You choose to be

sacrificial

*Feelings, emotions, passion

PATTERN FOUR
Concealed Behavior

Your affective nature* in the present situation is reflected as:

Description

Consequences, Observable Actions

☐ withdrawing

Directing attention to the unfair dealings of others, doubting that things will get any better; making exaggerated demands that you believe others cannot meet—testing their concern for you; drawing back from others before they have the opportunity to respond; contending that your active participation may only make things worse.

☐ disbelieving

Fearing that you will miss opportunities available to others, sensing that events are not what you had expected—concluding that they will not improve.

☐ unforgiving

Refusing to accept apologies—they do not appear sincere; seeking to find ways to protect yourself from being hurt again.

☐ resentful

Believing that others gain what they desire by stepping over people and using them; questioning why you must accede to the wishes of others.

You choose to be

irritable

*Feelings, emotions, passion

PATTERN TWELVE
Concealed Behavior

Your affective nature* in the present situation is reflected as:

Description	*Consequences, Observable Actions*
☐ trapped	Becoming impatient and irritable with slow-moving events; planning a move, any kind, just to start momentum—hitting more than retreating; pushing more than pulling, but getting off square one.
☐ overwhelmed	Feeling drained of your resources, but still hopeful of getting, having, and keeping things; making attempts to convince others to assist you in your efforts, sensing that the final burden still rests with you.
☐ arousing	Recognizing that every minute counts; anxiously depending upon excitement, desiring to make your vision a reality.
☐ fragmented	Assuming excessive responsibility; going in many different directions; lacking in continuity; believing that you can do a variety of things, but being forgetful of priorities.

You choose to be

intense

---

*Feelings, emotions, passion

PATTERN THIRTEEN
Concealed Behavior

Your affective nature* in the present situation is reflected as:

Description	*Consequences, Observable Actions*
☐ retreating	Pulling back occasionally for the purpose of contemplation; preferring this aloneness as a means to show independence.
☐ worrying, concerned	Dealing with the pressure from those who insist that you make a choice; considering what others want for you and what you desire for yourself; admitting to yourself that, whatever you decide, others will view you as selfish.
☐ doubting	Avoiding disappointment by doing things for yourself because others may refuse your requests; depending upon your own resources rather than risking rejection.
☐ showing anxiety	Pursuing trivialities to avoid dealing with and confronting real issues and deadlines; keeping yourself busy by assigning work to others.

You choose to be

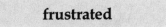

frustrated

---

*Feelings, emotions, passion

PATTERN FOURTEEN
Concealed Behavior

Your affective nature* in the present situation is reflected as:

Description	*Consequences, Observable Actions*
☐ doubting	Keeping a careful and critical watch to determine if motives toward you are sincere; investing in yourself rather than in others who show little inclination to develop standards.
☐ self-protecting	Determining the trustworthiness of those around you; wishing to establish a relationship of mutual respect; seeking to form a bond with anyone who has similar tasks.
☐ anxious	Postponing critical decisions; desiring to make the right move and to avoid the wrath of others.
☐ respectful	Accepting authority, believing that leadership must come from those with unique skills; expecting that others treat you with similar respect for your ability; referring to others by their titles or positions—Mr., Mrs., Ms., Dr.; wishing to avoid intimacy.

You choose to be

severe

*Feelings, emotions, passion

PATTERN TWENTY-THREE
Concealed Behavior

Your affective nature* in the present situation is reflected as:

Description	*Consequences, Observable Actions*
☐ rebellious	Hoping to make things fair between those who have and those who have not; taking sides against those who take advantage of the underdog.
☐ unassertive	Becoming upset when you give in too easily to the excessive demands of others; kicking yourself when you show dependence on those who are more stern and demanding than you.
☐ disappointed	Experiencing helplessness when you cannot convince others that they need your assistance; feeling that you cannot control events; learning that you can, instead, control your reaction to events; desiring to do more for those who need you; consoling yourself when your way is not the best way for others.
☐ joyful	Showing satisfaction with what you have and your need to share with others; making people aware of their potential for personal growth.

You choose to be

helpful

*Feelings, emotions, passion

PATTERN TWENTY-FOUR
Concealed Behavior

Your affective nature* in the present situation is reflected as:

Description	*Consequences, Observable Actions*
☐ accepting	Showing tolerance for others who contribute less than you; hoping to redirect their efforts and overcome their negative and nonchalant attitudes.
☐ self-appraising	Comparing yourself to people who are doing similar tasks; judging both yourself and others; identifying the point of difference; more often giving the advantage to yourself.
☐ disappointed	Analyzing your wins and losses; dwelling on reasons for recent setbacks.
☐ superior	Determining the best methods to increase your chances of receiving approval for your efforts; discovering ways to actively participate in your best events; putting others at a disadvantage by downplaying your preparation time—deliberately minimizing the importance of the event to you.

You choose to be

critical, but proper

---

*Feelings, emotions, passion

PATTERN THIRTY-FOUR
Concealed Behavior

Your affective nature* in the present situation is reflected as:

Description	*Consequences, Observable Actions*
☐ anxious	Deciding to suffer, believing that others will understand the difficulty you experience; showing your dismay at events that cause you to become indecisive.
☐ worrying, concerned	Desiring approval for extra effort; hoping to avoid setbacks by complying with the wishes of others; developing ideas designed to please critics.
☐ nourishing	Doing for others what they find difficult to do for themselves; pleading with others to avoid pitfalls that you have experienced; sacrificing things you desire in order to ensure the pleasure and well-being of others.
☐ agitated	Strongly hinting to others that they could not do better than you under similar circumstances; trying to impress others and comparing with them the time and effort you devote to common projects.

You choose to be

long-suffering

---

*Feelings, emotions, passion

PATTERN ONE TWENTY-THREE
Concealed Behavior

Your affective nature* in the present situation is reflected as:

Description	*Consequences, Observable Actions*
☐ unyielding	Evaluating the possible directions that best suit your purpose; determining to follow through on your commitment and remain steadfast in your position to show the strength of your conviction.
☐ exhausted	Reluctantly admitting that you need creative support; hoping that others will lead in attempts to resolve differences in existing conflicts; preferring a way out; feeling that, while you like to get things started, you have difficulty in final completion.
☐ critical	Becoming disillusioned by the unfulfilled promises of others; giving thoughts to changing a course of action that would affect people who are presently influencing your decisions.
☐ impatient	Deciding to demand more of those who have performed less well than you; preferring to confront those who take advantage of your efforts.

You choose to be

self-sufficient

---

*Feelings, emotions, passion

PATTERN ONE TWENTY-FOUR
Concealed Behavior

Your affective nature* in the present situation is reflected as:

Description	*Consequences, Observable Actions*
☐ obligated	Acknowledging that others have contributed to your well-being; making attempts to accede to their wishes, hoping that they will not take advantage of your situation.
☐ exhausted	Refusing to concede that you have a desire to achieve beyond your skills and capabilities; trying to make a profound impression upon those whom you respect; deliberately withholding from them your need to rest and regroup; desiring instead to be seen as active and alert.
☐ idealizing	Believing that many more options are open to you than actually exist; passing on specific details to others; making plans for merriment and celebration of your achievements.
☐ heartwarming	Sensing that the present situation is desirable, but disguising the feeling to ward off those who would upset a "good thing," refusing to show too much satisfaction for a good situation.

You choose to be

imaginative

*Feelings, emotions, passion

PATTERN ONE THIRTY-FOUR
Concealed Behavior

Your affective nature* in the present situation is reflected as:

Description	Consequences, Observable Actions
☐ excelling	Questioning your ability compared to that of others; seeking a role model that can be validated and respected.
☐ self-protective	Seeking to feel secure; guarding against disappointment in those who have had an influential impact on your life; weighing their promises and offers of commitment; turning down opportunities where success depends on a high-risk factor; running from any prospect of failure.
☐ doubtful	Placing pressure on yourself to ensure a favorable outcome, believing that you can never be overprepared; searching for confirmation that you are an expert in areas in which you have chosen to excel.
☐ disappointed	Making exaggerated demands on those who are expected to fulfill your needs; showing disapproval with even slight shortcomings; deciding that success will largely come from your own efforts.

You choose to be

self-critical

*Feelings, emotions, passion

PATTERN TWO THIRTY-FOUR
Concealed Behavior

Your affective nature* in the present situation is reflected as:

Description	*Consequences, Observable Actions*
☐ resentful	Questioning the reasons for working at a fast pace and receiving so little credit; probing the possibility of spending more time on yourself and less on others.
☐ suspicious	Believing that events may not immediately improve since you have too little control; realizing that things may get worse before they get better; insisting that others are withholding their plans from you.
☐ disillusioned	Giving thought to adjusting the heavy burden you carry, doing what others are satisfied to accomplish; becoming irritated because you had hoped for something better.
☐ protective of others	Taking on concern for others, who you believe have lost their will to protest; showing a willingness to voice complaints on their behalf.

You choose to be

self-regulating

*Feelings, emotions, passion

Central Pattern:
Predicted Behavior

PATTERN ONE — DOMINATOR*
Predicted Social Behavior

Home Management:
Take charge; frequently assign responsibilities to others; desire comfortable surroundings more than pretentious symbols; demand punctual scheduling; watch the growth and development of your children from the sideline.

Mate Relationship:
View ongoing relations with a mate as secondary to a strong career interest; desire, however, to have a sense of quietude, satisfying a need to retreat; place high demands on this person; give direct orders, often abrupt and impatient.

Sociability:
Extraverted more often than introverted—desire contact with a variety of people; initiate controversial topics; find satisfaction in discussing yourself.

Communication:
Tend to be tense, compact, and logical in sharing ideas; avoid stating the obvious; restrict comments to a minimum; desire to be precise in the choice of language—want others to do the same.

Decision Making:
Use *contention* more than *consensus;* inform others once the decision is made; show imagination in developing new proposals.

Response To Opposition:
Act positively and directly in the face of questioning; conceal inner impulses of irritation; wait for an appropriate time to reveal personal points of view; scrutinize the credibility of the critic.

Social Issues:
Thrive on complex social and economic problems that can be solved by creative analysis; encourage your mate to attend public discussion meetings as a personal representative.

Use of Energy:
Pour energy into meeting higher standards of personal performance; tax your personal physical and mental resources in an attempt to show constant improvement.

*4% of Research Population

Social Situation Overview:
Take a forceful stand, willingly fighting for your personal beliefs; tend to use any and all means to reach goals; demonstrate mobility and flexibility in approaching problems.

Preferred Areas of Relaxation:
★ Reading (biographical) ★ competitive sports ★ viewing T.V. documentaries ★ designing new methods.

Social Compatibility Person:
Natural Choice — Pattern Three, *Stabilizer,* page 246.
Recommended — Pattern Thirty-four, *Standard Bearer,* page 267.

Predicted Work Behavior

Ideal Work Situation:
Want authority and important assignments; desire opportunity for advancement and challenge; wish to set priorities, give orders to others, achieve high personal performance.

Task Approach:
Rearrange the environment; make visible the dream of expansion; introduce new systems; initiate and accept changes that make sense.

People Approach:
Tend to be straightforward in dealing with others; state personal opinions; appear to be blunt and critical with people; use emotionally charged words designed to control the actions of others.

Response To Negative People:
Become stimulated rather than weighed down by the prospect of confronting uncooperative people; identify their difficulties as a problem of incompetence and lack of information on what to expect.

Problem Solving:

ANALYTICAL					INTEGRATED				INTUITIVE
5	4	3	2	1	1	2	3	4	5
		Left Brain				Right Brain			

Appear to be more *intuitive* than analytical; think beyond what is; elicit innovative suggestions from others; make final choices based on *thinking* more than on feeling; tend to be insensitive to the complexities of interpersonal relations when implementing decisions.

Time Intensity:
Seek immediate action; complain that there is never enough time to accomplish objectives; cite the slowness of others as a possible problem.

Use of Character Factors:

Chart I

emphasize	*individual*	over	*group*
	88%		12%
emphasize	*contention*	over	*consensus*
	76%		24%
emphasize	*justice*	over	*caring*
	70%		30%

Character Development:

+ Express personal convictions; take firm action even if it is necessary to over-step rulings of others; seldom deviate once committed to a course of action—sometimes going to the extreme.

– Reveal an imbalance when stressing individual behavior (see chart I); demonstrate selfish concerns; tend to be self-centered and lacking in empathy; judge others hastily before considering the total context.

Work Situation Overview:
Organize yourself and others into a smooth-functioning system, planning in advance, keeping short-term and long-term objectives in mind; become a versatile self-starter who responds readily to competition.

Preferred Areas of Responsibility:
★ Design and engineering ★ research and development ★ management technology ★ executive management.

Work Compatibility Person:
First Choice — Pattern Two Thirty-four, *Special Advisor,* page 279.
Second Choice — Pattern Twenty-four, *Strategic Planner,* page 264.

PATTERN TWO — INDUCER*
Predicted Social Behavior

Home Management:
Seek new outlets of expression; search for the "right house" to display; give little attention to routines of daily maintenance or security measures—life insurance, savings accounts; use a democratic approach to run a carefree operation.

Mate Relationship:
Prefer a mate who is stable and firm in making demands; put this individual to a test by living on the edge of adventure; tend to be overly generous; give presents simply out of a desire to please or to evoke surprise.

Sociability:
Extraverted; make mundane events exciting; tend to be impulsive in like and dislike of others; display social aggressiveness in situations not perceived to be threatening; use and respond to various degrees of seduction.

Communication:
Display an impressive flow of expression, verbal and nonverbal; use banter, wit; respond exceptionally well to auditory and visual sexual stimuli that are concrete, real, and graphic.

Decision Making:
Use *consensus* more than *contention;* prefer that others assume the final responsibility for crucial decisions; believe in compromise as a guiding principle.

Response To Opposition:
Rephrase objectives; vow to correct misunderstandings; show reluctance, however, to give up your personal point of view; argue that setbacks—if indeed they do exist—are only temporary.

Social Issues:
Desire that changes in political and social action occur periodically—just to have new blood; tire of sameness; avoid personal involvement unless a leadership role is available.

Use of Energy:
Exert yourself to gain attention from others; use energy for self-gratification; receive new energy by creating excitement, a circular response—the more excitement, the more energy.

*5% of Research Population

Social Situation Overview:
Admit to a good amount of self-indulgence; display self-confidence in most dealings with others; exude charm and establish rapport at first contact with people.

Preferred Areas of Relaxation:
★ Novel adventures ★ sporting events ★ reading ★ theater, partying functions.

Social Compatibility Person:
Natural Choice — Pattern Four, *Conformer*, page 249.
Recommended — Pattern Two Thirty-four, *Special Advisor*, page 279.

Predicted Work Behavior

Ideal Work Situation:
Gravitate toward jobs in which interpersonal skills are needed; desire freedom to respond to the demands of the moment; wish to use your ability to get people together; desire projects that can become a cause.

Task Approach:
Use whatever resources are available; believe that new situations demand new methods; delegate detailed responsibilities to others; challenge procedures and policies by taking the side of employees.

People Approach:
Tend to seek out people with enthusiasm and spark; use personal warmth; desire to uncover hidden talents in others; show fierce loyalty to people you view as disciples.

Response To Negative People:
Try to win uncooperative people through persuasiveness and emotional appeal; display a contagious optimism; share willingly in advice, material possessions, and possible successes.

Problem Solving:

ANALYTICAL					INTEGRATED				INTUITIVE
5	4	3	2	1	1	2	3	4	5
Left Brain						**Right Brain**			

Appear to be more *intuitive* than analytical; rely on an intuitive ability to improvise instead of preparing in advance; make choices based on *feeling* more than on thinking; show readiness to help anyone with a problem; tend to reach conclusions too quickly and ignore some relevant facts.

Time Intensity:
Show awareness of possibilities; tend to be open and willing to converse at any time; accept telephone or personal interruptions; encourage continual contacts.

Use of Character Factors:

Chart II

emphasize	*individual*	more than	*group*
	59%		**41%**
emphasize	*consensus*	more than	*contention*
	73%		**27%**
emphasize	*caring*	more than	*justice*
	69%		**31%**

Character Development:

+ Sincerely desire to consider the needs of people over excessive rules and regulations (see chart II); protect those who are vulnerable to unfair regulations.

− Leap before looking; subject yourself to more temptation than do others; reject the notion that personal actions are governed by established policies, rules, or natural laws.

Work Situation Overview:
Adapt easily to new situations; show impatience with goal statements and theories; tend to find reasons for whatever is desired; turn to one new interest after another.

Preferred Areas of Responsibility:
★ Public relations ★ marketing and sales ★ advertising ★ social service.

Work Compatibility Person:
First Choice — Pattern One Thirty-four, *Designer,* page 276.
Second Choice — Pattern Twenty-three, *Harmonizer,* page 261.

PATTERN THREE — STABILIZER*
Predicted Social Behavior

Home Management:
Develop routines that make the home a safe haven; frequently prefer the friendships of family members over others; strive to stabilize the environment by screening people who become close to the family.

Mate Relationship:
Display loyalty and genuine love for your mate; provide gifts that are symbolic, reminding your mate of cherished events; occasionally may search for new relationships rather than work at deepening those that exist.

Sociability:
Introverted; demonstrate a cool reserve toward others; show a caring and passionate emotion for special persons; project a relatively unruffled, unconcerned appearance.

Communication:
Reflect an extraordinary sensitivity and ability to communicate emotionally; use a sense of touch and eye contact rather than an emphasis on colorful and emotional speech; move with moderation and deliberateness in physical action.

Decision Making:
Use *contention* slightly more than *consensus;* prefer that major decisions be made by those who are more decisive than yourself—except decisions regarding values; refuse to budge on issues related to values.

Response To Opposition:
Conceal the hurt and hostility caused by those who are unfriendly to your personal proposals; defer to experts when encountering difficult problems or conflict with others.

Social Issues:
Pledge to assist groups that support personal convictions; lack sustained, strong leadership to influence opinionated people; advocate conservative positions when intense conflicts arise.

Use of Energy:
Appear to have an unusual store of energy; demonstrate bursts of enthusiasm generated by feelings for nature and surrounding beauty.

---

*9% of Research Population

Social Situation Overview:
Tend to be steady, consistent, preferring to deal with each issue—one at a time; approach most situations with care and concentration; set your own pace and stick to it.

Preferred Areas of Relaxation:
★ Reading ★ travel ★ dance ★ outdoor activities.

Social Compatibility Person:
Natural Choice — Pattern One, *Dominator,* page 240.
Recommended — Pattern Twelve, *Front-runner,* page 252.

Predicted Work Behavior

Ideal Work Situation:
Prefer activities that result in meaningful contributions; desire to be of assistance to people in search of improved health, security, and understanding; direct your skills into areas requiring depth and specialization.

Task Approach:
Tend to be persistent and persevering—not easily swayed once a decision has been made; become rigidly independent when force is applied to change direction.

People Approach:
Develop the potential of each person; place organizational goals in second place—after people; show sympathy and willingness to listen, often taking the side of people against the organization.

Response To Negative People:
Excel in redirecting uncooperative people; create a positive attitude by attending to their needs; develop their sense of importance.

Problem Solving:

ANALYTICAL					INTEGRATED				INTUITIVE
5	4	3	2	1	1	2	3	4	5
	Left Brain					Right Brain			

Appear to be more *analytical* than intuitive; consider it important to use expert testimony and generally good common sense to solve problems; make human choices based on *feeling* more than on thinking or pure logic; work to develop loyalty in people by viewing a decision from their perspective.

Time Intensity:
Keep possibilities open; stress the importance of gathering more data, take time to carefully follow through on potential leads; hope that, given time, something new will occur.

Use of Character Factors:

Chart III

emphasize	*group*	more than	*individual*
	82%		**18%**
emphasize	*contention*	more than	*consensus*
	58%		**42%**
emphasize	*caring*	more than	*justice*
	78%		**22%**

Character Development:

+ Develop consistency in the defense of personal convictions (see chart III); gather strength and renewed energy in support of personal values.

− React unfavorably to those opposing your personal principles; become overly sensitive to criticism; interpret questions as personal attacks; project a self-righteous nature; regard others' investigations as poorly motivated.

Work Situation Overview:
Respect facts and the responsibilities that the facts create; tend to underestimate and understate yourself; continually ward off obligation and confinement; strive to be uncomplicated in motivation.

Preferred Areas of Responsibility:
★ Counseling ★ social work ★ language study ★ teaching.

Work Compatibility Person:
First Choice — Pattern One Twenty-four, *Negotiator,* page 273.
Second Choice — Pattern Twelve, *Front-runner,* page 252.

PATTERN FOUR — CONFORMER*
Predicted Social Behavior

Home Management:
Desire a neat, orderly, and functional home; select practical and durable clothes; develop close bonds with children; tend to hover—may become overprotective.

Mate Relationship:
Show devotion; tend to be private, not always open to physical approaches, preferring to select scheduled times for "close encounters."

Sociability:
Introverted; delight in family gatherings, festive occasions; receive comfort in structured activity; prefer an atmosphere free from antagonism.

Communication:
Appear quiet, detached until conversation centers on personal interests; excel in written language; project greater self-confidence in social conversations with advanced preparation.

Decision Making:
Use *consensus* more than *contention;* project decisiveness in practical matters; discuss major problems with experts; make final choices in cooperation with others.

Response To Opposition:
Respond to queries by asking questions in return; place others on the defensive; feel prepared to defend proposals, ideas.

Social Issues:
Want to make a difference in the world; believe your personal positions are superior to what others believe; closely follow controversial events; participate in the electoral process.

Use of Energy:
Appear to have spurts of intense energy, generated from a need to defend yourself; rise to the occasion when your convictions are tested by others.

*5% of Research Population

Social Situation Overview:
Like to please others; welcome harmony and happy occasions; tend to be crushed by too much criticism; honor contracts of business dealings and friendship agreements.

Preferred Areas of Relaxation:
★ Mechanical hobbies ★ spectator, news events ★ mystery novels ★ community organization involvement.

Social Compatibility Person:
Natural Choice — Pattern Two, *Inducer,* page 243.
Recommended — Pattern Twenty-three, *Harmonizer,* page 261.

Predicted Work Behavior

Ideal Work Situation:
Seek responsibility requiring solitude and concentration; hope to excel in competing with "things" rather than with human beings; want to avoid risk or trouble.

Task Approach:
Determine what might be done and work toward it steadily; develop standards; improve your skills, becoming an expert in at least one area of responsibility.

People Approach:
Tend to win cooperation rather than to demand it; appear willing to modify or compromise with others in order to achieve your personal goals.

Response To Negative People:
Look for "hidden meanings" in the statements of uncooperative people; attempt to separate their actions from their threats; overcome tension through absolute confirmation of the correctness of their actions.

Problem Solving:

ANALYTICAL					INTEGRATED				INTUITIVE
5	4	3	2	1	1	2	3	4	5
	Left Brain					Right Brain			

Appear to be more *analytical* than intuitive; use known facts and proven precedent; make choices based on *thinking* more than on feeling; desire to be cautious and conservative in examining alternative solutions; show capacity for analysis and logic; display patience with detail and routine.

Time Intensity:
Seek immediate action, believe in putting work first; make judgments on the basis of existing data; appear matter-of-fact, realistic in assessing time limits.

Use of Character Factors:

Chart IV

emphasize	**group**	more than	**individual**
	65%		**35%**
emphasize	**consensus**	more than	**contention**
	72%		**28%**
emphasize	**justice**	more than	**caring**
	84%		**16%**

Character Development:

+ Regard the rights and privileges of others as sacred (see chart IV); protect the behavior of others through the support of a strong justice system.

− Lack a deep understanding of yourself and others; set priorities to satisfy immediate physical needs; refuse to let difficult issues penetrate within, i.e., prefer to accept predetermined solutions.

Work Situation Overview:
Gain success by concentration and follow-through; use excellent organizational skills; tend not to take chances with money—your own or someone else's.

Preferred Areas of Responsibility:
★ Corporate unit support ★ financial management ★ planning ★ corrections.

Work Compatibility Person:
First Choice — Pattern One Twenty-three, *Administrator,* page 270.
Second Choice — Pattern Twenty-three, *Harmonizer,* page 261.

PATTERN TWELVE — FRONT-RUNNER*
Predicted Social Behavior

Home Management:
Feel at home with the complexity of changing factors—even some disorganization; expect others to put things in order and do the work; tend to get irritable when others don't respond.

Mate Relationship:
Provide for economic necessities; affect your relationship by engaging in career brinkmanship; appear more business-minded at home than at work; select a mate for both affectionate and practical purposes; expect your partner to assist in business when needed; require freedom to receive attention from more than one person.

Sociability:
Extraverted; show great congeniality when meeting people; often tend to be the center of attraction; show interest in others' ideas; appear easy-going—seldom critical in public.

Communication:
Use well-chosen words; adapt to situations with a comprehensive grasp of well-timed, nonverbal action; tend to be a bit condescending.

Decision Making:
Use *contention* balanced with *consensus;* frequently fail to establish guidelines, consequently, needing to arrive at a decision for each new incident.

Response To Opposition:
Refuse to be pinned down; use a direct method in making responses; consider people; convince others through persuasiveness when necessary; turn objections into opportunities by offering a new twist to an idea.

Social Issues:
Understand the inner workings of the political and social system; aim to determine the motivation of key people; pride yourself in "realism and understanding of people."

Use of Energy:
Focus on what is useful and what can benefit yourself; take risks; use personal reserves of energy to improvise solutions in crises—often very successfully.

*8% of Research Population

Social Situation Overview:
    Reject personal involvement in situations that fail to provide immediate satisfaction; tend to be agitated and unpredictable in the midst of boring events; lack interest in a project once the challenge is gone.

Preferred Areas of Relaxation:
    ★ New adventure, such as sky diving ★ applied psychology ★ sports ★ travel.

Social Compatibility Person:
Natural Choice — Pattern Thirty-four, *Standard Bearer*, page 267.
Recommended — Pattern Two Thirty-four, *Special Advisor*, page 279.

Predicted Work Behavior

Ideal Work Situation:
    Desire to replicate previous successes; want to modify or take a creative idea and make it serve a practical purpose.

Task Approach:
    Plan well ahead; integrate activities to get results; leave details and clarification to others; build in variety and change; want the independence and challenge of a wide scope of operations.

People Approach:
    Seek earned respect from associates; act positively; harness people to assist in personal goal satisfaction; reward others, often beyond the value of the assignment.

Response To Negative People:
    Make a concerted effort to understand those who are uncooperative; identify their roadblocks; run interference—get them to believe in themselves and in others.

Problem Solving:

ANALYTICAL					INTEGRATED				INTUITIVE
5	4	3	2	1	1	2	3	4	5
		Left Brain				Right Brain			

    Appear to be more *intuitive* than analytical; involve others in brainstorming activities; look at the problem as a whole; make choices based on alternating *thinking* with *feeling*; follow the complex verbalizations of others; interpret facts for other key decision makers.

Time Intensity:
Keep possibilities open; develop an information channel to collect data; encourage others to share new insights; downplay hectic, dramatic urgency.

Use of Character Factors:

Chart V

emphasize	*individual*	more than	*group*
	71%		**29%**
use	*contention*	balanced with	*consensus*
	52%		**48%**
use	*justice*	balanced with	*caring*
	54%		**46%**

Character Development:

+ Buy deeply into the win-win concept; combine personal interest with concerns of others; recognize that the human system is severely tested when others are oppressed by injustice or by an overuse of emotional impulses (see chart V).

– Believe that, to avoid chaos and panic, truth may have to be withheld; run the risk of appointing yourself as sole judge to receive personal benefit.

Work Situation Overview:
Demonstrate initiative, with an eye to the future; desire to bring about "what could be"; tend to break promises made to others; make do with what is at hand; count on ingenuity to resolve disappointments.

Preferred Areas of Responsibility:
★ Innovative teaching ★ sales and marketing ★ international diplomacy ★ entrepreneurial activity.

Work Compatibility Person:
First Choice — Pattern Thirty-four, *Standard Bearer,* page 267.
Second Choice — Pattern One Thirty-four, *Designer,* page 276.

PATTERN THIRTEEN — PACESETTER*
Predicted Social Behavior

Home Management:
Tend to be single-minded in designing the home environment; ignore the views and wishes of others; rely on family members for personal "creature" comforts—physical health, emotional well-being.

Mate Relationship:
Desire to confide in someone who can be trusted; look for both a friend and a lover; find it difficult to build intimate trust; develop strong, romantic—and even passionate—feelings for your mate.

Sociability:
Introverted; tend to be quiet, reserved, detachedly curious; withhold emotional reactions; neglect the observation of small rituals designed to put others at ease; become decisive and aggressive when personal ideas are at stake.

Communication:
Tend to be coldly blunt and tactless with many people; apt to be undemonstrative; find it difficult to sell abstract ideas or to generate enthusiasm in others; express yourself through action rather than through people.

Decision Making:
Use *contention* more than *consensus;* employ facts and details to arrive at decisions; share select information with others; encourage more listening than spirited discussion; want to accept the brunt of making the final choice.

Response To Opposition:
Pride yourself on being ready for any eventuality; carefully prepare for objections; answer questions in a firm but restrained manner.

Social Issues:
Influence the course of events; desire to have an impact on political and social thinking—exert a strategic power and pressure behind the scenes.

Use of Energy:
Aggressively seek new ideas, always open to new concepts; become tenacious after starting a project; place your credibility on the line.

*2% of Research Population

Social Situation Overview:
   Appear at times to be complicated, however, revealing great depth of person-ality; possess understanding of others; desire challenges regarding independ-ent and penetrating analysis.

Preferred Areas of Relaxation:
   ★ Mechanical hobbies ★ outdoor sports ★ unusual hobbies ★ disciplined activity; exercise.

Social Compatibility Person:
Natural Choice — Pattern Two Thirty-four, *Special Advisor,* page 279.
Recommended — Pattern Twelve, *Front-runner,* page 252.

Predicted Work Behavior

Ideal Work Situation:
   Want to set an individual pace; desire freedom from close supervision; prefer to develop a systematic approach, ensuring a continuity of effort; accept work of a technical nature more often than involvement with people.

Task Approach:
   Create an environment where things should run smoothly; develop and accept assignments that can be followed through to completion on an independent basis; correct inefficient procedures, i.e., overlapping functions.

People Approach:
   Show an unwillingness to change your personal approach or pace to accom-modate others; respect those who have skills equal to yours; accept those who contribute a quality effort.

Response To Negative People:
   Probe the thinking and the actions of uncooperative people; take a question-ing and sometimes critical approach; convert those who have a logic that is similar to yours.

Problem Solving:

ANALYTICAL					INTEGRATED				INTUITIVE
5	4	3	2	1		1	2	3	4	5
		Left Brain					Right Brain		

   Combine *analytical* thought with an *intuitive* experience; trust insight as to the relationship and meaning of things, regardless of authority or popular beliefs; proceed to document ideas with facts; make choices based on *thinking* more than on feeling; want to work from well-thought-out plans; like to use engineered operations.

Time Intensity:
Seek immediate action; tend to minimize outside evaluation; press to move quickly on ideas—often appearing stubborn and opinionated.

Use of Character Factors:

Chart VI

use	*individual*	balanced with	*group*
	53%		**47%**
emphasize	*contention*	more than	*consensus*
	75%		**25%**
use	*caring*	balanced with	*justice*
	55%		**45%**

Character Development:

+ Value integrity; show courage to follow personal convictions (see chart VI); fight hard and fair for personal objectives.

− Display a heated and sometimes misplaced tendency to hold a grudge; tend to be unforgiving; plan for ways to retaliate.

Work Situation Overview:
Show little interest in pleasing people; appear to be more motivated by logic than by emotion; prove successful at many things—through determination rather than versatility.

Preferred Areas of Responsibility:
★ Systems consulting ★ engineering ★ business ★ administration ★ physical sciences.

Work Compatibility Person:
First Choice — Pattern Twenty-four, *Strategic Planner,* page 264.
Second Choice — Pattern Thirty-four, *Standard Bearer,* page 267.

PATTERN FOURTEEN — ORIGINATOR*
Predicted Social Behavior

Home Management:
Desire harmony, order in the home; insist on having things in place; appear firm and intent on disciplining others; apply ingenuity to planning events, but frequently fail to consider the details of the action.

Mate Relationship:
Seek an intellectually challenging mate; show affection, but may not always be open to physical approaches; tend to be demonstrative at times, but desire to choose the occasion.

Sociability:
Introverted; resemble extraverted individuals in your sympathetic handling of people and in a tendency to ignore unpleasant news; express strong need for privacy; submerge inner impulses by appearing socially spontaneous; use structured spontaneity.

Communication:
Relate with people in a personalized way; express yourself in an elegant and complex manner; occasionally appear withdrawn, giving a physical presence of cold reserve.

Decision Making:
Use *contention* balanced with *consensus;* struggle for the right choice; carefully weigh both sides; share information with others—finally say, "that's it!"

Response To Opposition:
Become silent; seek to redefine terminology; assume responsibility to clarify positions; show hints of being agitated and rude.

Social Issues:
View yourself as above most political and community issues; complain, threatening to change the course of events; use excuses to avoid involvement.

Use of Energy:
Exert strong efforts to please others; tend to contribute your personal best efforts in all situations; exhibit overperfectionism and accentuate tasks that, in themselves, may not justify such efforts.

*1% of Research Population

Social Situation Overview:
Tend to have a vivid imagination reflected in memory and intuition; irritate others by refusing to commit while in a lengthy decision-making process; vacillate in making choices.

Preferred Areas of Relaxation:
★ Stimulating conversation ★ complex games ★ reading (mystery or humorous) ★ assembly of parts.

Social Compatibility Person:
Natural Choice — Pattern Twenty-four, *Strategic Planner,* page 264.
Recommended — Pattern Thirty-four, *Standard Bearer,* page 267.

Predicted Work Behavior

Ideal Work Situation:
Find challenge in working with complex problems; desire to be recognized as a unique person making an unusual contribution; seek to invent "better mousetraps" than others.

Task Approach:
Work ideas out in practice; gain approval from those in authority; subject every idea to the test of usefulness; back up original insight with determination; rise above others as an outstanding innovator of ideas.

People Approach:
Expect a high level of achievement from others; tend to irritate others by playing favorites; appear unemotional and dispassionate with all but a few employees.

Response To Negative People:
Assign challenging and satisfying work to uncooperative people; attempt to get them to "stretch"—reach for the unreachable.

Problem Solving:

ANALYTICAL				INTEGRATED				INTUITIVE
5	4	3	2	1	1	2	3	4	5
		Left Brain				Right Brain		

Combine *analytical* and *intuitive*; use intuition along with reason to come up with a solution that is both visionary and practical; make choices based on *thinking* slightly more than on feeling; select the option that seems most possible and most logical.

Time Intensity:
Seek immediate action; demand quick answers; expect closure when there is a singleness of purpose; become upset when others disrupt your personal timetable.

Use of Character Factors:

Chart VII

emphasize	*individual*	more than	*group*
	58%		42%
use	*contention*	balanced with	*consensus*
	52%		48%
emphasize	*justice*	more than	*caring*
	65%		35%

Character Development:

+ Show good balance between contending for ideas and gathering pertinent data from others (see chart VII); work for consensus agreement when others have equal thinking ability.

− Place excessive emphasis upon rules and regulations—largely to indicate the lack of discipline in others; show less concern for the caring aspect when administering justice.

Work Situation Overview:
Drive others, as well as yourself, to the point of exhaustion; become single-minded in concentrating on projects; tend to reject judgment from outside of yourself.

Preferred Areas of Responsibility:
★ Scientific research ★ human engineering ★ graduate teaching ★ curriculum design.

Work Compatibility Person:
First Choice — Pattern Twenty-three, *Harmonizer,* page 261.
Second Choice — Pattern Twelve, *Front-runner,* page 252.

PATTERN TWENTY-THREE — HARMONIZER*
Predicted Social Behavior

Home Management:
Reflect orderliness without fussiness; adhere to traditional values of the home; enjoy a houseful of friends; involve children in decision making; believe in "share and share alike."

Mate Relationship:
Show respect for marriage vows; express affection in standard ways, verbalizing expressions of love in ritualistic language; bring gifts on appropriate occasions; share new ideas and work problems with your mate.

Sociability:
Extraverted; possess a casual kind of poise; impress most people with a display of warmth, sympathy, and understanding; attend to the needs of others; keep conversations alive; strive for a proper place in the social strata.

Communication:
Display a pleasing manner; speak fluently, but often in generalizations; take an inordinate amount of time to state your personal beliefs; appear to be a good listener.

Decision Making:
Use *consensus* balanced with *contention;* tend to conform to those who are more assertive; discuss routine decisions at length—finally resolve issues through mutual agreement.

Response To Opposition:
Tend to take criticism as a personal affront; pride yourself in responding with the right word in the right place; assure critics that things are proceeding according to plan; remain calm.

Social Issues:
Depend on higher authority as source of personal opinions and formation of attitudes; consider experts, elected officials, and respected friends as authorities to be trusted.

Use of Energy:
Devote considerable effort to self-validation, finding ways to be needed, loved, and appreciated; receive approval from your mate, children, friends, and relatives.

*23% of Research Population

Social Situation Overview:
Occasionally appear to be bound and obligated; display restlessness when isolated from people; seek to give and to care for others; tend to be too indirect in issuing orders or making demands on others.

Preferred Areas of Relaxation:
★ Group involvement ★ reading (novels) ★ sports attractions ★ family vacations.

Social Compatibility Person:
Natural Choice — Pattern One Thirty-four, *Designer,* page 276.
Recommended — Pattern Thirty-four, *Standard Bearer,* page 267.

Predicted Work Behavior

Ideal Work Situation:
Prefer to focus on negotiable problem areas; want freedom to exchange ideas and opinions; respond to duty and service; desire responsibility requiring patience with others in an established framework.

Task Approach:
Determine with others the purpose of an assignment; prefer team effort; set goals consistent with the organization's purpose; lead discussions with originality.

People Approach:
Make great sacrifices for others; inspire deep loyalty; prefer to deal with people on a personal, intimate basis in a low-pressure situation.

Response To Negative People:
Explore the condition in which uncooperative people work, as well as their attitude; determine ways in which to change either the environment or the individual's perception of the situation.

Problem Solving:

ANALYTICAL					INTEGRATED				INTUITIVE
5	4	3	2	1		1	2	3	4	5
		Left Brain					Right Brain		

Combine *analytical* thought with *intuitive* experience; use objective methods—factual data—to build the team types that can best solve problems; make final choices based on *feeling* more than on thinking; emphasize the usefulness of things to people; use personal appeal to gain acceptance of solutions.

Time Intensity:
Keep possibilities open; prolong events in order to gain improved results; believe people suffer when they close their minds; graciously attend to telephone or personal interruptions.

Use of Character Factors:

Chart VIII

emphasize	**group**	more than	**individual**
	63%		**37%**
use	**consensus**	balanced with	**contention**
	51%		**49%**
emphasize	**caring**	more than	**justice**
	81%		**19%**

Character Development:

+ Carefully consider all actions on the basis of means to the end; find a desirable balance in the involvement of people both to contend and to discuss the moral implication of an action (see chart VIII).

– Attribute negative feelings to others; blame them for your unhappiness, thereby removing personal control and responsibility from yourself.

Work Situation Overview:
Sell personality rather than showing the merits of an idea or proposal; tend to be inattentive to the little things; appear to be overly optimistic regarding the possible results of personal projects or the potential of people.

Preferred Areas of Responsibility:
★ Service occupations ★ tangible and intangible sales ★ administration ★ personality development.

Work Compatibility Person:
First Choice — Pattern Fourteen, *Originator,* page 258.
Second Choice — Pattern Twelve, *Front-runner,* page 252.

PATTERN TWENTY-FOUR — STRATEGIC PLANNER*
Predicted Social Behavior

Home Management:
Desire to have family decisions settled efficiently and quickly; want family living routinized, scheduled, and correctly executed; show devotion to the traditional values of home; take charge when others fail.

Mate Relationship:
Show discrimination in selecting a mate; respect the marriage vows; depend upon your mate when mutual respect exists; view partnership as a success when both a proper place in the social strata and an accumulation of material possessions are possible.

Sociability:
Extraverted; enjoy interacting with others; keep a lively circle of contacts through versatility; show an uncanny knowledge in being able to influence others, receiving deep commitments from friends.

Communication:
Laugh easily; become at times overly talkative; use expressions designed to attract attention—tasteful clothing, physical movement; appear attentive when listening to others.

Decision Making:
Use *consensus* more frequently than *contention;* resort to emotional argument when necessary; become most convincing when comparing yourself to others; prepare to compromise and "give in" when financial issues are to be settled.

Response To Opposition:
Display quick but short bursts of temper when your ideas are questioned; become sensitive; respond with conviction by using illustration with factual material.

Social Issues:
Evaluate community and political leaders in terms of their "personal motivation"; seek clear, open discussion; tend to be a moderate.

Use of Energy:
Place emphasis on the acquisition of monetary rewards—channel finances into immediate security measures, personal health, family projects; solicit others to assist in nonfinancial priority areas.

*3% of Research Population

Social Situation Overview:

Tend to be hypersensitive and overly alert to personal and family welfare; express concern for independence; appear to be anticipative—often forecasting impending gloom, but sprinkling it with an optimistic determination to do something about it.

Preferred Areas of Relaxation:

★ Competitive athletic contests ★ entertaining friends ★ community involvement ★ contemplation.

Social Compatibility Person:

Natural Choice — Pattern One Twenty-four, *Negotiator,* page 273.

Recommended — Pattern Thirty-four, *Standard Bearer,* page 267.

Predicted Work Behavior

Ideal Work Situation:

Desire a challenge in an environment of excitement—and even adversity; seek to persuade others, using counseling and persuasive communication; find satisfaction in appraising the efforts of others.

Task Approach:

Design new procedures; evaluate tasks; show agility and ability to move from one project to another with ease and composure; respect and obey the rules and regulations—expect others to do the same.

People Approach:

Show skill in working with talented people; take pride in coaching people to improve their performance; occasionally fail to see the other person's point of view; judge too harshly.

Response To Negative People:

Outline the overall purpose of a project; show how the uncooperative person fits in; become overly optimistic in efforts to make changes in negative individuals—tend to overestimate your personal ability to influence their behavior.

Problem Solving:

ANALYTICAL					INTEGRATED				INTUITIVE
5	4	3	2	1	1	2	3	4	5
			Left Brain			**Right Brain**			

Combine *analytical* thought with *intuitive* experience; explore several actions with limited information at hand; wish to avoid a miscalculation, leaning on others as well as on yourself; make choices based on *feeling* slightly more than on *thinking*; attempt to be critical, but often give way to an emotional consideration.

Time Intensity:
Seek immediate action; show anxiety until a decision has been reached; make an effort to get "something" going just to have it in motion.

Use of Character Factors:

Chart IX

use	*individual*	balanced by	*group*
	51%		49%
emphasize	*consensus*	more than	*contention*
	69%		31%
emphasize	*justice*	more than	*caring*
	57%		43%

Character Development:

+ Openly state your personal beliefs; remind others that it is imperative to stick by convictions; believe that, in the long-run, justice will rule (see chart IX).

− Blame others when your personal goals are thwarted; reject the possibilities that objectives may be unattainable.

Work Situation Overview:
Stretch yourself by setting extremely high goals, hoping for extraordinary recognition; occasionally select "bad" projects and fail to finish them, squandering your inspiration and sapping your energy.

Preferred Areas of Responsibility:
★ Advertising executive ★ service representative ★ social psychology ★ education, training.

Work Compatibility Person:
First Choice — Pattern Thirteen, *Pacesetter,* page 255.
Second Choice — Pattern Two Thirty-four, *Special Advisor,* page 279.

PATTERN THIRTY-FOUR — STANDARD BEARER*
Predicted Social Behavior

Home Management:
Expect your home to be well-kept both inside and outside—meticulously maintained; actively assist in caring for the house and raising children; prefer to handle finances or to be kept well-informed.

Mate Relationship:
Impose standards of right and wrong on your mate and children; view yourself as the one to insist on adherence to standards; require things and people to be consistent and stable, appropriately in harmony with traditional ways.

Sociability:
Introverted; appear to be uncomfortable with new acquaintances; prefer modest, quiet friends; seek to avoid situations that could uncover personal guilt, weaknesses, or failure.

Communication:
Appraise inner thoughts without sharing them with others; swing conversations to early reminiscences of youth or former times; mentally rehearse before verbalizing thoughts.

Decision Making:
Use *consensus* balanced with *contention;* share available information with others; respect differences of opinion; use personal judgment in the final analysis; make independent moves after much deliberation.

Response To Opposition:
Remain silent for a deliberate length of time when others show disagreement; state your personal position only when answers are readily available; use direct and sincere expression.

Social Issues:
Complain about events; yearn for a return to traditional values; become prophetic with the use of historical examples; resist change; plead for time to adjust.

Use of Energy:
Set priorities; limit areas according to available energy; use extensive effort in activities in which previous success has occurred.

*17% of Research Population

Social Situation Overview:
 Show artistic taste and judgment; display irritation with others who put on "airs"—those who act either above or below their social or economic level.

Preferred Areas of Relaxation:
 ★ Refurbishing, renovating ★ hobbies involving collecting ★ family recreation ★ sports attractions in which individuals excel.

Social Compatibility Person:
 Natural Choice — Pattern Twenty-three, *Harmonizer,* page 261.
 Recommended — Pattern One Twenty-three, *Administrator,* page 270.

Predicted Work Behavior

Ideal Work Situation:
 Expect a hostility-free situation; like things to be well-defined, settled, and in order; want firm and timely decisions made by others regarding material, personnel, and procedure.

Task Approach:
 Develop clear lines of communication—who does what and when; make a studied analysis of policies, contracts, and standards or procedures; assure the stability of your effort over a reasonable length of time.

People Approach:
 Align yourself with those who are loyal and have similar work habits; stroke only those who are deserving; insist on penalties for people who perform poorly; tend to identify personally with a boss rather than with the institution.

Response To Negative People:
 Declare an intent to have clear-cut dealings; show the discrepancy between "what is" and "what should be"; examine reasons given for failure to cooperate.

Problem Solving:

ANALYTICAL					INTEGRATED				INTUITIVE
5	4	3	2	1	1	2	3	4	5
Left Brain						Right Brain			

Appear to be more *analytical* than intuitive; dissect tasks into "do-able" parts; simplify the complexity of a problem by examining the details; make choices based on *thinking* slightly more than on feeling; avoid impulses; use firm standards to assess the quality of a final solution.

Time Intensity:
Seek immediate action; show a high level of anxiety when faced with responsibility; become hostile and critical when others fail to respond to personal requests.

Use of Character Factors:

Chart X

emphasize	*group*	more than	*individual*
	76%		**24%**
use	***consensus***	balanced with	***contention***
	54%		**46%**
use	*caring*	balanced with	*justice*
	52%		**48%**

Character Development:

+ Desire that others be treated fairly; make efforts to be available to people; associate with those who demonstrate a similar sense of caring (see chart X).

− Back down to authority figures even when their ultimatums are inappropriate; rely, instead, on your personal reputation and work skills; occasionally permit others to take advantage of your fears and your unassertive stance.

Work Situation Overview:
Preserve the traditions of an organization; create rituals where they are lacking; show sentimentality in relating with friends at work, viewing them as family.

Preferred Areas of Responsibility:
★ Business administration ★ training, skill development ★ health maintenance ★ accounting.

Work Compatibility Person:
First Choice — Pattern Twelve, *Front-runner,* page 252.
Second Choice — Pattern One Twenty-four, *Negotiator,* page 273.

PATTERN ONE TWENTY-THREE —
ADMINISTRATOR*
Predicted Social Behavior

Home Management:
Insist that the home be an extension of your personality—comfortable, with intellectual symbols as part of the surroundings; like to have things settled and organized.

Mate Relationship:
Dream of the perfect relationship; relate with your mate often by taking on his or her personal emotions and beliefs; tend to overidentify; avoid domination of mate and offspring; feel responsible when home life goes awry.

Sociability:
Extraverted; build influence with large or small groups; relate particularly well in face-to-face situations; plan social engagements ahead, fulfilling commitments; handle people with charm and concern.

Communication:
Use tactful language; express just the correct feelings, but can also be assertive with commanding and persuasive communication; respond to others with ease in a leadership role or in a follower role.

Decision Making:
Use *contention* more than *consensus;* verbalize feelings regarding the cause of problems; show reluctance to reach a decision when others appear disagreeable; push ahead, however, to assume a strong position.

Response To Opposition:
Appear thoughtful, serious, and anxious to clarify any misunderstandings; respond with clear and concise statements; carefully avoid the use of misleading statements.

Social Issues:
Willingly take sides on issues that have far-reaching effects; invest time and money to ensure that your personal views are expressed.

Use of Energy:
Place a high value on cooperation from others; invest energy to cooperate in joint ventures; believe that people will eventually do what is right for others.

*2% of Research Population

Social Situation Overview:
Feel security in others' warmth of feeling, consequently, conforming to their views within reasonable limits; tend to be tolerant of others; view yourself as trustworthy.

Preferred Areas of Relaxation:
★ Reading (history and novels) ★ fine arts appreciation ★ travel ★ social organization.

Social Compatibility Person:
Natural Choice — Pattern Fourteen, *Originator,* page 258.
Recommended — Pattern Two Thirty-four, *Special Advisor,* page 279.

Predicted Work Behavior

Ideal Work Situation:
Want to put the gift of expression to work, both in speaking and in writing; seek to develop others; desire to execute useful ideas, i.e., cost-effective proposals and procedures.

Task Approach:
Provide activities and tasks for groups and individuals; find adequate functions for team members—can often organize without planning; promote exceptional team productivity through openness and clarification of goals.

People Approach:
Assist in the growth and development of people; listen to opposing views; learn to be brief and businesslike, being sociable at appropriate times.

Response To Negative People:
Bring uncooperative people in line by extolling the virtues of the institution; maintain a strong belief that employees should respect their place of employment; encourage people to suggest realistic changes that will profit themselves and others.

Problem Solving:

ANALYTICAL					INTEGRATED			INTUITIVE	
5	4	3	2	1	1	2	3	4	5
Left Brain					**Right Brain**				

Appear more *intuitive* than analytical; show irritation with the sameness of methods that often appear boring and stagnant; speculate regarding several solutions; make choices based on *feeling* slightly more than on thinking; place emotional appeal and objective evaluation in proper perspective in developing acceptance of solutions.

Time Intensity:
Keep possibilities open; show a willingness to consider options; develop a "wait and see" attitude regarding the seriousness of a situation; avoid being pushed against a deadline.

Use of Character Factors:

Chart XI

use	*individual*	balanced with	*group*
	53%		**47%**
emphasize	*contention*	more than	*consensus*
	59%		**41%**
use	*caring*	balanced with	*justice*
	54%		**46%**

Character Development:

+ Combine personal high standards—fairness, equality, love, rules—with company growth and profit; seek a good balance (see chart XI); desire to have a positive effect on the world, promoting understanding and happiness; work to change the organization, if necessary.

– Cite the complication of natural and inappropriate behavior as a way to interpret personal shortcomings; believe that humans will be "human"— accepting failure as part of the human condition.

Work Situation Overview:
Act on assumptions; occasionally jump to conclusions; may miss the mark; eventually bring action into a specifically designed routine and schedule.

Preferred Areas of Responsibility:
★ Education ★ executive management ★ business partnership ★ direct supervision.

Work Compatibility Person:
First Choice — Pattern Twenty-four, *Strategic Planner,* page 264.
Second Choice — Pattern Two Thirty-four, *Special Advisor,* page 279.

PATTERN ONE TWENTY-FOUR — NEGOTIATOR*
Predicted Social Behavior

Home Management:
Seek comfort in home surroundings; create a stimulating living environment, a place for exciting communication; dislike mundane chores and routines; encounter difficulty with offspring.

Mate Relationship:
Tend to be possessive without appearing overly demanding; make the other person feel needed; serve as counselor and friend; test mate's patience by unusual humor; may be viewed as threatening to a mate with low self-esteem.

Sociability:
Extraverted; deal imaginatively by using spontaneous action; project yourself as an expert on a variety of subjects.

Communication:
Express opinions easily; respond quickly to others' changing position; show ready and open discussion with new acquaintances; project witticism and cleverness; use specific instances more often than generalities to prove a point.

Decision Making:
Use *consensus* more than *contention;* involve others in discussion, but show a tendency to prearrange plans and thoughts before deliberation; show a masterful technique of "persuasion" in the format of discussion.

Response To Opposition:
Become annoyed—sometimes outwardly; show irritation when others appear doubtful and questioning; hold grudges for a short time—respond with quality information.

Social Issues:
Ignore the conventional and traditional approaches to community and national problems; advocate ideas that would be workable at home and have universal application as well.

Use of Energy:
Apply sustained energy, with a balance between career and personal life; deal imaginatively with social relationships as well as with physical and mechanical properties.

*2% of Research Population

Social Situation Overview:
Demonstrate keen observation, memory of factual information; appear to be several steps ahead of others, anticipating the position they will adopt.

Preferred Areas of Relaxation:
★ Home and equipment renovation ★ unique hobbies ★ artistic development ★ friends and conversation.

Social Compatibility Person:
Natural Choice — Pattern Thirty-four, *Standard Bearer,* page 267.

Recommended — Pattern Two Thirty-four, *Special Advisor,* page 279.

Predicted Work Behavior

Ideal Work Situation:
Desire to turn losing situations into winners; seek to show observable results; want innovative projects; avoid dull routine; insist on working with real things that can be taken apart or put together.

Task Approach:
Recommend fresh starts; discard old methods with proper caution; always look for a better way; seek new projects, new activities, new procedures.

People Approach:
Show discrimination and insight in the selection of people; get high performance by working closely with talented people; delegate broad creative projects to others.

Response To Negative People:
Openly state the harmful effects of uncooperative behavior; show a more effective way to proceed; set time limits on behavior change.

Problem Solving:

ANALYTICAL					INTEGRATED				INTUITIVE
5	4	3	2	1	1	2	3	4	5
		Left Brain					Right Brain		

Appear more *intuitive* than analytical; look beyond yourself and others to receive broader answers; follow inspirations; make final choices based on *thinking* more than on feeling; appear insensitive to others when your personal reputation is on the line; document choices with exact facts.

Time Intensity:
Seek immediate action; make demands on associates, employees, and employers; desire quick satisfaction in knowing how management will solve difficulties.

Use of Character Factors:

Chart XII

emphasize	*individual*	more than	*group*
	68%		**32%**
emphasize	*consensus*	more than	*contention*
	57%		**43%**
use	*justice*	balanced with	*caring*
	53%		**47%**

Character Development:

+ Combine caring for others with the aspects of justice (see chart XII); attempt to view the social context as a way to evaluate and deal with inappropriate behavior.

– Occasionally take credit for others' effort; increase your personal value, sometimes at the expense of others.

Work Situation Overview:
Demonstrate a broad base of unconventional interests; bring people to the negotiating process; sell ideas, but dislike following through on the tedious details.

Preferred Areas of Responsibility:
★ Executive management ★ personnel evaluation ★ corrections— law and order ★ entrepreneurial activity

Work Compatibility Person:
First Choice — Pattern Twenty-three, *Harmonizer,* page 261.
Second Choice — Pattern Twenty-four, *Strategic Planner,* page 264.

PATTERN ONE THIRTY-FOUR — DESIGNER*
Predicted Social Behavior

Home Management:
Desire an organized environment; willingly assist in efforts to make the home functional and attractive; enjoy children and are serious about their upbringing; appear calm, low-key in applying discipline.

Mate Relationship:
Show consideration when your mate can be serious and responsive in working together; desire mutual respect; appear willing and compliant to a loved one— easy to live with.

Sociability:
Introverted; resent the use of valuable time that is needed in social activities; depend upon your mate to manage your social life; tend to be misunderstood by casual listeners; project sharply defined interests.

Communication:
Experience some difficulty in expressing emotions verbally; state technical ideas directly and clearly; appear shy except when discussing personal convictions or when with close friends.

Decision Making:
Use *contention* more than *consensus;* take the lead in advocating major positions; depend upon others to share domestic information and to make social decisions; absent yourself from minor choices.

Response To Opposition:
Encourage a direct exchange on controversial issues; want opponents to talk— in fact, talk themselves out; correct errors in their information; help them to reinterpret data and possibly form new conclusions.

Social Issues:
Identify distinctions and inconsistencies in the conclusions made by political and community leaders; use their shortcomings as a reason to avoid personal involvement with their activities.

Use of Energy:
Use both mind and body to express creativity; gain the best results when your energy is balanced between mental and physical exertion.

*1% of Research Population

Social Situation Overview:
Possess exceptional precision in thought and language; display strong will; show reluctance for spontaneous physical contact; become impatient with those who tend to be emotional.

Preferred Areas of Relaxation:
★ Creative renovation ★ reading (biographies) ★ travel (short visits) ★ designing projects.

Social Compatibility Person:
Natural Choice — Pattern One Twenty-three, *Administrator,* page 270.
Recommended — Pattern Twenty-three, *Harmonizer,* page 261.

Predicted Work Behavior

Ideal Work Situation:
Desire to build data and human systems; translate theory into practical, workable units; want to join diverse elements together.

Task Approach:
Want guarantees of minimal interference, insist on proving hunches with supporting data; invent methods; prefer to leave building and production processes to others.

People Approach:
Minimize personal contacts with others; avoid developing deep ties with people, fearing loss of time; want to work quietly and alone.

Response To Negative People:
Prefer to ignore uncooperative people; prepare reports, excluding them from important considerations—give cursory attention only to the exact role they could assume in the project; expect higher authority to resolve their difficulties.

Problem Solving:

ANALYTICAL					INTEGRATED				INTUITIVE
5	4	3	2	1	1	2	3	4	5
		Left Brain				Right Brain			

Combine *analytical* thought with *intuitive* experience; supply ingenuity to problems; deal with and solve complex issues where data is incomplete; make choices based on *thinking* slightly more than on feeling; implement solutions, seldom counting personal cost in terms of time and energy.

Time Intensity:
Seek immediate action; feel pressure from those who push for results; respond with more intensity.

Use of Character Factors:

Chart XIII

use	*individual*	balanced with	*group*
	54%		**46%**
emphasize	*contention*	more than	*consensus*
	58%		**42%**
use	*justice*	balanced with	*caring*
	53%		**47%**

Character Development:

+ Demonstrate openness in the search for enlightenment; pursue ways to find the centering point in which extremes can be effectively balanced (see chart XIII); probe universal principles for a possible application to current problems.

− Appear smug when involved with your search for truth; show obsession with your analyses; occasionally downgrade the efforts of those who assist in your investigative processes.

Work Situation Overview:
Seek understanding of complex problems; appear impatient with routine details once the project gets underway; become more cooperative when given an efficient support staff; use intuition rather than pure logic to increase your understanding.

Preferred Areas of Responsibility:
★ Engineering ★ systems development ★ medical science ★ conceptual consultation.

Work Compatibility Person:
First Choice — Pattern Twelve, *Front-runner,* page 252.
Second Choice — Pattern Twenty-four, *Strategic Planner,* page 264.

PATTERN TWO THIRTY-FOUR — SPECIAL ADVISOR*
Predicted Social Behavior

Home Management:
Tend to be possessive regarding your family and home—"my spouse, my children"; cherish loved ones instead of claiming ownership; maintain property and equipment; budget carefully; plan for the future.

Mate Relationship:
Desire a predictable, caring mate; occasionally show a lack of understanding of your mate's needs, putting your interests first; confront others with sarcasm, scolding, criticism; use silence as a weapon.

Sociability:
Extraverted; enjoy opportunities to visit with friends; tend to make quick decisions on strangers; start conversations easily; keep an emotional distance; want social events preplanned in an orderly manner; avoid loud parties.

Communication:
Enjoy talk; appear friendly, tactful, and supportive of others; use judgmental language at times—parent style—putting people in their place; fail to listen, at times, to opposing views.

Decision Making:
Use *consensus* more than *contention;* prefer the participation of others in major decisions; become emotional when discussions take an undesirable turn; keep calm, but direct the conversation to improve your personal advantage.

Response To Opposition:
Become "formal," treating objections with some disdain; show disappointment in those who raise negative issues; believe that most opposition occurs as a result of failure to communicate.

Social Issues:
Take a position on crucial issues; appear serious and sensitive to the acknowledged, official decision makers, tending to identify with them; feel drawn to established institutions and their beliefs, accepting their "line" until you can develop a personal approach.

Use of Energy:
Exert an unusual amount of effort to conserve resources—health, security, savings; place the highest priority in the protection of self and family.

*18% of Research Population

Social Situation Overview:
Appear softhearted, sentimental—usually observing special events, birthdays, anniversaries, important occasions; need harmony and advise others on how to create it; appear warm, talkative, and conscientious.

Preferred Areas of Relaxation:
★ Weekend travel ★ house decoration ★ family activities ★ reading (novels).

Social Compatibility Person:
Natural Choice — Pattern Twenty-three, *Harmonizer,* page 261.
Recommended — Pattern Thirteen, *Pacesetter,* page 255.

Predicted Work Behavior

Ideal Work Situation:
Desire to organize and direct the activities of others; want to use effective communication to relate with others—selling, advising, consoling; enjoy being part of a team, discovering roles for yourself and others.

Task Approach:
Organize facts, situations, and operations well in advance; make systematic efforts to reach your objectives on schedule; insist on orderly procedures.

People Approach:
Establish human relations through traditions and rituals; appreciate the value of others' opinions; bring people together despite differences; speak sternly when expressing disapproval.

Response To Negative People:
Concentrate on the reason for their indifference; often take sides with uncooperative people, but oppose their actions if they are unproductive; attempt to show them an alternative to negativism.

Problem Solving:

ANALYTICAL					INTEGRATED				INTUITIVE
5	4	3	2	1	1	2	3	4	5
		Left Brain				Right Brain			

Appear more *analytical* than intuitive; tend to be more curious about new devices and procedures than about new principles and theories; view problems from this practical approach; make choices based on *feeling* slightly more than on thinking; show greater interest in facts about people than facts about things.

Time Intensity:
Seek immediate answers; want things settled and decided; believe in planning ahead; dislike surprises, hoping to prevent an unexpected complication or larger problem.

Use of Character Factors:

Chart XIV

emphasize	**group**	more than	**individual**
	68%		**32%**
emphasize	**consensus**	more than	**contention**
	60%		**40%**
use	**caring**	balanced with	**justice**
	55%		**45%**

Character Development:

+ Become involved in activities that are consistent with your personal value system; challenge unfair regulatory practices; show willingness to consider the behavior of others in light of circumstances (see chart XIV).

− Move slowly to action when your convictions are threatened by others; often wait to discover how others in your group will respond to criticism—then personal actions are evoked.

Work Situation Overview:
Perform best when dealing with people and in any situation where needed cooperation can be won by good will; think best when talking with people.

Preferred Areas of Responsibility:
★ Health related fields ★ teaching ★ production management ★ management, accounting.

Work Compatibility Person:
First Choice — Pattern Twelve, *Front-runner,* page 252.
Second Choice — Pattern One Twenty-three, *Administrator,* page 270.

Behavior Dynamics

— Key No. 1 —

BEHAVIOR DYNAMICS

Part I — Behavior and Change

☐ **Your Behavior Description** — *the real you.* Key word is *practical.* You rely upon self-designed guidelines; weigh actions against stated goals; effectively cope with emergencies that require work against time; assume people think alike when given the same information.

☐ **Your Behavior Objectives** — *what you desire to be.* Key word is *inventive.* You hope to combine logic with emotion to satisfy existing needs; are anxious to show imagination; invent practical methods; use impulsive energy to achieve results.

☐ **Your Behavior Change**

Degree of Change Occurring in Your Behavior		
Little	Some	Much
1.0 2.0	3.0 4.0	5.0

☐ **Your New Behavior** — *where you're going.* Key word is *improvising.* You experience little behavior change; continue to accumulate material goods to enhance your personal growth rather than for their own sake; use persuasiveness from within the system to evoke needed change rather than criticizing from the outside.

Part II — Behavior and Conflict

☐ **Your Behavior Under Pressure** — *how you handle objections.* You remove petty misunderstandings; become clear about what comes next; show readiness to handle a sequence of problem-solving steps; see the big picture and the possibilities in the situation.

☐ **Your Internal Conflict** — *source of personal frustration.* You tend to improvise as events develop; often neglect necessary preparation; open yourself to greater possibilities for failure — this procrastination may lead to *situation avoidance,* implying that, rather than gear yourself up for the preparation of the task, you will turn down the challenge as "just another event which requires additional effort." You may even blame others for placing you on the spot when a decision is needed to accept or refuse requests.

Part III — Behavior and Control

☐ **Your Internal Motivation** — *how others may exert control with you.* Your motivation increases when others provide opportunities for you to: maintain vibrant relationships; explore ways in which people can effectively interact; heighten interest in forming people networks — bring people together.

☐ **Your Motivation of Others** — *how you exert control.* You influence others by the way in which you handle crisis; prove leadership ability in chaotic situations; gain respect and adulation for being cool under stress.

Part IV — Behavior and Predictive Action

☐ **Your Behavior Overview —**
how you adapt to existing circumstances.

Communicating decisiveness	1	2	3	(4	5)	+	1
Ability to stimulate and activate others	1	2	3	(4	5)	+	1
Self-control	1	2	3	(4	5)	+	1
Awareness of others' feelings	1	(2	3)	4	5	+	1
Fairness	1	2	(3	4)	5	+	1
Ability to see the whole, not merely the parts	1	2	(3	4)	5	+	1
Working facts into a logical whole	1	2	3	(4	5)	+	1
Sense of humor	1	2	(3	4)	5	+	1
Handling of complex problems	1	2	3	(4	5)	+	1
Concern for practical details	1	(2	3)	4	5	+	1
Ability to size up another's character	1	2	(3	4)	5	+	1

Calculation Section

	line 1 ____83____ %	
Total of (+1)	line 2 _____ %	
Add lines 1 & 2	line 3 _____ %	
Total of plotting points in shaded graph areas	line 4 _____ %	
Subtract line 4 from line 3	line 5 _____ %	
	(GRAND TOTAL)	

(See page 80 for directions.)

— Key No. 2 —
BEHAVIOR DYNAMICS

Part I — Behavior and Change

☐ **Your Behavior Description** — *the real you.* Key word is *inspiring.* You prefer that others express firmly stated opinions; attempt to win friends on both sides of an issue; expect tacit approval of your plans; take credit for ideas—your own and sometimes the ideas of others; believe your experiences can be transferred to both similar and dissimilar areas of decision-making.

☐ **Your Behavior Objectives** — *what you desire to be.* Key word is *indispensable.* You make attempts to appear formidable; refuse impersonal or minor roles; accept responsibilities which others find difficult to take on; put failure behind you; make known the need for fresh starts; become the difference in situations which need your talent and skill.

☐ **Your Behavior Change**

Degree of Change Occurring in Your Behavior		
Little	Some	Much
1.0 2.0	3.0 4.0	5.0

☐ **Your New Behavior** — *where you're going.* Key word is *unflappable.* You experience little behavior change; continue to project uniqueness of personality; emphasize "self-made person image"; maintain your mystique; show impatience and forcefulness with slow and aimless associates; tend to be more aware of the need to follow through on your verbal commitments.

Part II — Behavior and Conflict

☐ **Your Behavior Under Pressure** — *how you handle objections.* You instantly respond when others disagree with your conclusions; convince yourself that difficulties are less important than they appear to be; tend to use humor to decrease tension; put off distasteful decisions; make promises; assign unpopular actions to others.

☐ **Your Internal Conflict** — *source of personal frustration.* You tend to be easily bored, desire to escape sameness by intense activity— this restlessness may lead to *endless searching,* implying activity directed toward either success or variety of experiences, which may result in exhaustion or fatigue.

Part III — Behavior and Control

☐ **Your Internal Motivation —** *how others may exert control with you.* Your motivation increases when others provide opportunities for you to: develop freely and independently; claim ownership; set a fast-moving pace; prove self-worth; show up critics.

☐ **Your Motivation of Others —** *how you exert control.* You influence others through the use of convincing argument; provide more emotional than rational leadership; make others curious about your new and varied interests; promise them excitement and fulfillment of purpose.

Part IV — Behavior and Predictive Action

☐ **Your Behavior Overview —**
how you adapt to existing circumstances.

Communicating decisiveness	1	2	3	(4	5)	+	1
Ability to stimulate and activate others	1	2	3	(4	5)	+	1
Self-control	1	2	(3	4)	5	+	1
Awareness of others' feelings	1	2	(3	4)	5	+	1
Fairness	1	2	(3	4)	5	+	1
Ability to see the whole, not merely the parts	1	2	(3	4)	5	+	1
Working facts into a logical whole	1	(2	3)	4	5	+	1
Sense of humor	1	2	3	(4	5)	+	1
Handling of complex problems	1	2	(3	4)	5	+	1
Concern for practical details	1	(2	3)	4	5	+	1
Ability to size up another's character	1	2	3	(4	5)	+	1

Calculation Section

	line 1 ____81____ %
Total of (+1)	line 2 _____ %
Add lines 1 & 2	line 3 _____ %
Total of plotting points in shaded graph areas	line 4 _____ %
Subtract line 4 from line 3	line 5 _____ %
	(GRAND TOTAL)

(See page 80 for directions.)

— Key No. 3 —
BEHAVIOR DYNAMICS

Part I — Behavior and Change

☐ **Your Behavior Description** — *the real you.* Key word is *discriminating.* You reject the opinions of those who prejudge before viewing facts; seek answers from higher authority; join with those who have experience in solving complicated problems; rely on others to verbalize your requests.

☐ **Your Behavior Objectives** — *what you desire to be.* Key word is *methodical.* You seek ways to communicate the high standards you set for yourself and others; desire to be the source of authority; directly challenge others with your matter-of-fact statements; put others on the defensive; hope to assume an investigative role; question others' methods in solving problems.

☐ **Your Behavior Change**

Degree of Change Occurring in Your Behavior		
Little	Some	Much
1.0 2.0	3.0 4.0	5.0

☐ **Your New Behavior** — *where you're going.* Key word is *reliability.* You bring increased credibility to the existing environment, which, without your influence, would tend to be unsteady and disorganized; become increasingly more relaxed once friendships are developed; adhere to rules and regulations; continue to reserve the right to judge others by your guidelines.

Part II — Behavior and Conflict

☐ **Your Behavior Under Pressure** — *how you handle objections.* You minimize those who exclusively use emotional responses; develop a carefully designed plan to prove your belief; refer to documentation and expert testimony.

☐ **Your Internal Conflict** — *source of personal frustration.* You tend to be cool and calculating in resolving problems, often overlooking the human element; believe this is a trade-off for a "right" solution—this practice may lead to *conscious distancing,* implying a detachment that is designed to fend off the emotional needs of people. For you, those needs may be difficult to satisfy.

Part III — Behavior and Control

☐ **Your Internal Motivation** — *how others may exert control with you.* Your motivation increases when others provide opportunities for you to: receive recognition and rewards for unusual achievements; gain respect from peers; have sufficient time to make quality the top priority.

☐ **Your Motivation of Others** — *how you exert control.* You influence others by performing activities for them that are difficult or unpleasant; emphasize your contributions as the vital link; project yourself as one who has in-depth understanding.

Part IV — Behavior and Predictive Action

☐ Your Behavior Overview —
how you adapt to existing circumstances.

Communicating decisiveness	① ②	3	4	5	+	1
Ability to stimulate and activate others	1 ② ③	4	5	+	1
Self-control	1 2 3 ④ ⑤	+	1
Awareness of others' feelings	① ②	3	4	5	+	1
Fairness	1 2 ③ ④	5	+	1
Ability to see the whole, not merely the parts	1 2 ③ ④	5	+	1
Working facts into a logical whole	1 2 3 ④ ⑤	+	1
Sense of humor	1 ② ③	4	5	+	1
Handling of complex problems	1 2 3 ④ ⑤	+	1
Concern for practical details	1 2 3 ④ ⑤	+	1
Ability to size up another's character	1 ② ③	4	5	+	1

```
                    Calculation Section

                                    line 1 ____71____ %
                 Total of (+1)      line 2 _____ %
               Add lines 1 & 2      line 3 _____ %
          Total of plotting points in
             shaded graph areas     line 4 _____ %
          Subtract line 4 from line 3   line 5 _____ %
                                          (GRAND TOTAL)

                 (See page 80 for directions.)
```

— *Key No. 4* —
BEHAVIOR DYNAMICS

Part I — Behavior and Change

☐ **Your Behavior Description** — *the real you.* Key word is *inquisitive.* You criticize impulsive people; dislike overly emotional acts you observe in yourself; distance yourself from those who demand quick fixes or fast answers; desire to be reasoned and thoughtful; pride yourself on being blunt and truthful.

☐ **Your Behavior Objectives** — *what you desire to be.* Key word is *helpful.* You welcome opportunities to express yourself on subjects with which you are comfortable; seek familiar people contact to gain confidence in relating; hope to demonstrate an open and cooperative attitude when attempting to position yourself with others; attempt to provide explanations; negotiate; make commitments; build new ideas with increased support.

☐ **Your Behavior Change**

Degree of Change Occurring in Your Behavior		
Little	Some	Much
1.0 2.0	3.0 4.0	5.0

☐ **Your New Behavior** — *where you're going.* Key word is *empathizing.* You show an increased trust in your dealings; become more spontaneous; cope with frustration and disappointment; grasp the value in developing personal interests; avoid being tied down; encourage others to seek equality and independence.

Part II — Behavior and Conflict

☐ **Your Behavior Under Pressure** — *how you handle objections.* You resort to critical analysis under pressure; verbally compare your achievements with those of others; employ slow, measured speech patterns; ponder answers more carefully before responding; request additional time to prepare.

☐ **Your Internal Conflict** — *source of personal frustration.* You tend to avoid confrontation; restrain impulsive acts and withhold opinions that may result in ongoing tension; keep negative evaluations of others to yourself—this practice may lead to *conscious concealment,* implying that you deliberately keep others curious. Evaluations can be helpful only if shared with others; private judgments can feel like secret weapons.

Part III — Behavior and Control

☐ **Your Internal Motivation** — *how others may exert control with you.* Your motivation increases when others provide opportunities for you to: pursue equality for yourself and others; resolve conflict by employing problem-solving skills; create self-developing programs.

☐ **Your Motivation of Others** — *how you exert control.* You influence others through reasoned and critical discourse; emphasize thinking ability; move others through sincerity and a logical course of action.

Part IV — Behavior and Predictive Action

☐ Your Behavior Overview —
how you adapt to existing circumstances.

Communicating decisiveness	1	(2	3)	4	5	+	1
Ability to stimulate and activate others	1	2	(3	4)	5	+	1
Self-control	1	(2	3)	4	5	+	1
Awareness of others' feelings	1	2	(3	4)	5	+	1
Fairness	1	2	3	(4	5)	+	1
Ability to see the whole, not merely the parts	1	2	(3	4)	5	+	1
Working facts into a logical whole	1	2	3	(4	5)	+	1
Sense of humor	1	(2	3)	4	5	+	1
Handling of complex problems	1	(2	3)	4	5	+	1
Concern for practical details	1	(2	3)	4	5	+	1
Ability to size up another's character	1	2	3	(4	5)	+	1

Calculation Section

	line 1 ___73___ %	
Total of (+1)	line 2 _____ %	
Add lines 1 & 2	line 3 _____ %	
Total of plotting points in shaded graph areas	line 4 _____ %	
Subtract line 4 from line 3	line 5 _____ %	
	(GRAND TOTAL)	

(See page 80 for directions.)

— Key No. 5 —
BEHAVIOR DYNAMICS

Part I — Behavior and Change

☐ **Your Behavior Description** — *the real you.* Key word is *stimulating.* You develop a variety of interests; search for new ideas and ways to express hopes and ambitions; readily reinforce those who assist you in your efforts; conclude that the only information and advice that you trust must come from those you respect.

☐ **Your Behavior Objectives** — *what you desire to be.* Key word is *systematic.* You hope to set an example for others; discipline yourself; are anxious for others to complete tasks; seek ways to persuade others to think more rationally; oppose ill-devised ideas; relentlessly seek proof for your beliefs; avoid extensive explanations of your plan; share secrets with a select group of people.

☐ **Your Behavior Change**

Degree of Change Occurring in Your Behavior		
Little	Some	Much
1.0 2.0	3.0 4.0	5.0

☐ **Your New Behavior** — *where you're going.* Key word is *tenacity.* You are becoming more conscious of unfinished projects in the present situation; accept increased responsibility for humdrum, detailed work; check more carefully the accuracy of efforts assigned to others; criticize ineptness of others' methods.

Part II — Behavior and Conflict

☐ **Your Behavior Under Pressure** — *how you handle objections.* You calculate moves of the opposition; use energy to plan ahead of those whom you manipulate; protect your possessions; design back-ups for unexpected failure; develop ongoing communication chains to keep friends informed.

☐ **Your Internal Conflict** — *source of personal frustration.* You tend to withhold expressions of warmth and appreciation; feel that others are demanding more than they deserve; intend to show that your contribution is more essential than that of others—this maneuver may lead to *directed superiority,* implying a need to impress others with your single-handed efforts. You desire to ensure that you receive proper credit.

Part III — Behavior and Control

☐ **Your Internal Motivation —** *how others may exert control with you.* Your motivation increases when others provide opportunities for you to: create something of quality; solve difficult problems; stay with an activity from conception to completion.

☐ **Your Motivation of Others —** *how you exert control.* You influence others by making them feel obligated; emphasize your power to single them out for appreciation and participation; stress importance of their having a friend in the right place.

Part IV — Behavior and Predictive Action

☐ **Your Behavior Overview —**
how you adapt to existing circumstances.

Communicating decisiveness	1	2	③	④	5	+	1
Ability to stimulate and activate others	1	2	③	④	5	+	1
Self-control	1	2	3	④	⑤	+	1
Awareness of others' feelings	1	②	③	4	5	+	1
Fairness	1	2	③	④	5	+	1
Ability to see the whole, not merely the parts	1	2	3	④	⑤	+	1
Working facts into a logical whole	1	2	3	④	⑤	+	1
Sense of humor	1	2	③	④	5	+	1
Handling of complex problems	1	2	③	④	5	+	1
Concern for practical details	1	2	③	④	5	+	1
Ability to size up another's character	1	2	③	④	5	+	1

Calculation Section

line 1 ___81___ %

Total of (+1)   line 2 _____ %

Add lines 1 & 2   line 3 _____ %

Total of plotting points in shaded graph areas   line 4 _____ %

Subtract line 4 from line 3   line 5 _____ %
(GRAND TOTAL)

(See page 80 for directions.)

— Key No. 6 —
BEHAVIOR DYNAMICS

Part I — Behavior and Change

☐ **Your Behavior Description** — *the real you.* Key word is *selective.* You assume a low-risk posture when decisions must be made; use discernment in selecting the most advantageous position; correct systems which have been ineffective; show reluctance to participate in people-problem solving processes; urge others to solve problems related to troublesome individuals; feel that most people around you are overly demanding in their requests, concluding that you will reject their demands.

☐ **Your Behavior Objectives** — *what you desire to be.* Key word is *diplomatic.* You hope to develop greater skills in working with and through people; desire to clearly articulate your purpose; promote better understanding between individuals; consider flattering those who have some control of your activities.

☐ **Your Behavior Change**

Degree of Change Occurring in Your Behavior		
Little	Some	Much
1.0 2.0	3.0 4.0	5.0

☐ **Your New Behavior** — *where you're going.* Key word is *assurance.* You gain increased self-confidence in the worth of your inspiration; demonstrate surprising leadership; provide increased reinforcement for underachievers; effectively deal with varied opinions; respond more vocally and more boldly to your critics.

Part II — Behavior and Conflict

☐ **Your Behavior Under Pressure** — *how you handle objections.* You worry—sometimes needlessly; question the wisdom of responding too quickly when others become demanding; resist moving too fast or too soon.

☐ **Your Internal Conflict** — *source of personal frustration.* You tend to experience difficulty with those who oppose your unusual methods; show irritation for those who promise support but are reluctant to follow through—this hesitancy may lead to *rejection anxiety,* implying slow acceptance and approval from your critics. However, while your "mousetrap" is usually superior, you need to clear things with the establishment.

Part III — Behavior and Control

☐ **Your Internal Motivation** — *how others may exert control with you.* Your motivation increases when others provide opportunities for you to: develop creative systems and ideas; replace existing tools, operations, or enterprises with better ones.

☐ **Your Motivation of Others** — *how you exert control.* You influence others by developing practical systems; emphasize and operate on the principle of utilitarianism; provide what people can see, touch, and use.

Part IV — Behavior and Predictive Action

☐ Your Behavior Overview —
how you adapt to existing circumstances.

Communicating decisiveness	1 2 ③ ④ 5 + 1	
Ability to stimulate and activate others	1 2 3 ④ ⑤ + 1	
Self-control	1 2 3 ④ ⑤ + 1	
Awareness of others' feelings	1 ② ③ 4 5 + 1	
Fairness	1 2 ③ ④ 5 + 1	
Ability to see the whole, not merely the parts	1 2 ③ ④ 5 + 1	
Working facts into a logical whole	1 2 3 ④ ⑤ + 1	
Sense of humor	1 2 ③ ④ 5 + 1	
Handling of complex problems	1 2 3 ④ ⑤ + 1	
Concern for practical details	1 2 3 ④ ⑤ + 1	
Ability to size up another's character	1 2 ③ ④ 5 + 1	

Calculation Section	
	line 1 ___85___ %
Total of ⊕1	line 2 _____ %
Add lines 1 & 2	line 3 _____ %
Total of plotting points in shaded graph areas	line 4 _____ %
Subtract line 4 from line 3	line 5 _____ %
	(GRAND TOTAL)
(See page 80 for directions.)	

— *Key No. 7* —
BEHAVIOR DYNAMICS

Part I — Behavior and Change

☐ **Your Behavior Description** — *the real you*. Key word is *critical*. You demand a great deal of yourself; gain a sense of relief with practical operating procedures; seek to know what others expect of you; become investigative when things don't feel "just right"; show curiosity in the origination of things and events; identify problems; examine options.

☐ **Your Behavior Objectives** — *what you desire to be*. Key word is *persuasive*. You desire the ability to convince others; hope to employ a full range of emotions to become persuasive; show renewed attempts to be accepting of others and less judgmental of their conclusions; demonstrate insight tempered by judgment; hope to emphasize the importance of developing relationships.

☐ **Your Behavior Change**

Degree of Change Occurring in Your Behavior		
Little	Some	Much
1.0 2.0	3.0 4.0	5.0

☐ **Your New Behavior** — *where you're going*. Key word is *fervent*. You appear more futuristic in the presentation of your ideas; combine action with your thinking; show more optimism and understanding; willingly share more responsibility for crucial planning than others do; make dreams a reality; become unpredictable; dislike being pinned down.

Part II — Behavior and Conflict

☐ **Your Behavior Under Pressure** — *how you handle objections*. You respond to difficulty and stress with a stern and determined attitude; demonstrate a reluctance to engage in lengthy discussion; use short, concise retorts; employ logically based replies.

☐ **Your Internal Conflict** — *source of personal frustration*. You tend to move into new areas of authority and prestige, but remain somewhat detached; desire to preserve unique interests and retain a degree of conventionality—this attitude may lead to *separative self-sufficiency*. implying a sense of superiority, but also an unwillingness to test your self-esteem by close contact over a period of time.

Part III — Behavior and Control

☐ **Your Internal Motivation** — *how others may exert control with you.* Your motivation increases when others provide opportunities for you to: innovate procedures; stimulate others through introduction of new ideas; accept assignments at any point of the problem-solving process.

☐ **Your Motivation of Others** — *how you exert control.* You influence others by probing their interests and testing their conclusions; compare your achievements with others'; show strength in your adaptation to both social and technical aspects of a situation.

Part IV — Behavior and Predictive Action

☐ **Your Behavior Overview** —
how you adapt to existing circumstances.

Communicating decisiveness	1	2	③	④	5	+	1
Ability to stimulate and activate others	1	2	③	④	5	+	1
Self-control	1	2	3	④	⑤	+	1
Awareness of others' feelings	1	②	③	4	5	+	1
Fairness	1	2	③	④	5	+	1
Ability to see the whole, not merely the parts	1	2	3	④	⑤	+	1
Working facts into a logical whole	1	2	3	④	⑤	+	1
Sense of humor	1	2	③	④	5	+	1
Handling of complex problems	1	2	3	④	⑤	+	1
Concern for practical details	1	2	3	④	⑤	+	1
Ability to size up another's character	1	②	③	4	5	+	1

```
                    Calculation Section

                                    line 1 ____83____ %
            Total of (+1)           line 2 _____ %
          Add lines 1 & 2           line 3 _____ %
   Total of plotting points in
         shaded graph areas         line 4 _____ %
     Subtract line 4 from line 3    line 5 _____ %
                                    (GRAND TOTAL)

            (See page 80 for directions.)
```

— Key No. 8 —
BEHAVIOR DYNAMICS

Part I — Behavior and Change

☐ **Your Behavior Description** — *the real you.* Key word is *confident.* You prefer fresh, spirited activity; shake off the effects of intense rivalry; make clear statements of purpose; seldom appear winded or tired; develop a calm presence—relaxed and in control.

☐ **Your Behavior Objectives** — *what you desire to be.* Key word is *careful.* You wish to be cautious in making overtures of friendship; desire to position yourself to monitor the activities of others; show a need to be investigative; view yourself, in comparison to others, as superior in thinking; use inner vision for support; gain inner strength; wish to view goals more clearly than in the past; question the impulses of others; show hesitancy with high-risk ideas.

☐ **Your Behavior Change**

Degree of Change Occurring in Your Behavior		
Little	Some	Much
1.0 2.0	3.0 4.0	5.0

☐ **Your New Behavior** — *where you're going.* Key word is *hesitant.* You show greater concern for the safety and security of yourself and close friends and associates; resist impulsive suggestions for change and movement; think twice before expressing unpopular views; appear to miss opportunities for acceptance of your unusual proposals; show increased anxiety.

Part II — Behavior and Conflict

☐ **Your Behavior Under Pressure** — *how you handle objections.* You move in and out of arguments, fearful that others will pin you down; reduce the sharp effects of competitors with wit and humor; use confrontational skills; are unresponsive to requests for additional specific facts and explanations.

☐ **Your Internal Conflict** — *source of personal frustration.* You tend to become overly sensitive; feel uncomfortable in new situations; clash with those who are overly critical and negative; hold more grudges than you have in the past—this attitude may lead to *selective retention,* implying the remembrance of those negative aspects which made you uneasy. This tendency may cause you to isolate yourself and to reject new experiences.

Part III — Behavior and Control

☐ **Your Internal Motivation** — *how others may exert control with you.* Your motivation increases when others provide opportunities for you to: test and review specific results; influence the motivation of others; use intuitive insights concerning the true relationship and meaning of things.

☐ **Your Motivation of Others** — *how you exert control.* You influence others by weighing both sides of an argument before attempting to convince others; show vigor and vitality when committed to an idea; demonstrate an ability to bounce back; appear helpful at any time, providing ongoing assistance.

Part IV — Behavior and Predictive Action

☐ Your Behavior Overview —
how you adapt to existing circumstances.

Communicating decisiveness	1	2	3	(4 5)	+	1
Ability to stimulate and activate others	1	2	3	(4 5)	+	1
Self-control	1	2	(3 4)	5	+	1
Awareness of others' feelings	1	(2 3)	4	5	+	1
Fairness	1	2	(3 4)	5	+	1
Ability to see the whole, not merely the parts	1	2	3	(4 5)	+	1
Working facts into a logical whole	1	2	(3 4)	5	+	1
Sense of humor	1	2	(3 4)	5	+	1
Handling of complex problems	1	2	3	(4 5)	+	1
Concern for practical details	(1 2)	3	4	5	+	1
Ability to size up another's character	1	2	(3 4)	5	+	1

Calculation Section

	line 1 ___79___ %
Total of (+1)	line 2 _____ %
Add lines 1 & 2	line 3 _____ %
Total of plotting points in shaded graph areas	line 4 _____ %
Subtract line 4 from line 3	line 5 _____ %
	(GRAND TOTAL)

(See page 80 for directions.)

— Key No. 9 —
BEHAVIOR DYNAMICS

Part I — Behavior and Change

☐ **Your Behavior Description** — *the real you.* Key word is *arousing.* You evaluate others according to ways in which they settle differences among themselves; urge others to regulate their own conduct; support a competitive system with winners sharing with those who lose; make preparation and develop skills in designing unique systems in which to learn and play—at work or at home.

☐ **Your Behavior Objectives** — *what you desire to be.* Key word is *adventurous.* You desire to be the center of attention; wish to make unusual efforts; make adventure out of mundane events; demand that credit be given for personal achievement.

☐ **Your Behavior Change**

Degree of Change Occurring in Your Behavior		
Little	Some	Much
1.0 2.0 3.0 4.0		5.0

☐ **Your New Behavior** — *where you're going.* Key word is *competing.* You increasingly place your self-interest above the interest of others; seek ways to exert your authority; struggle for things which, up to now, were out of your reach; become more demanding when requests are refused.

Part II — Behavior and Conflict

☐ **Your Behavior Under Pressure** — *how you handle objections.* You react with sensitivity to criticism; separate yourself from those who are overly outspoken; handle controversial issues while letting others attend to specific details; demand mutual accountability.

☐ **Your Internal Conflict** — *source of personal frustration.* You tend to place a premium on competitiveness; use regulation to your advantage, particularly when it is in your interest to create or protect existing rules—this practice may lead to *exaggerated competition,* implying that you may effectively gain through both competition and the way in which rules are made to ensure your success.

Part III — Behavior and Control

☐ **Your Internal Motivation** — *how others may exert control with you.* Your motivation increases when others provide opportunities for you to: develop long-term strategies; evaluate the result of efforts; solicit others who have potential for missionary zeal to assist in your quest for excitement.

☐ **Your Motivation of Others** — *how you exert control.* You influence others by determining the basis for competition; emphasizing the way in which activities are to be governed; setting yourself up as a referee.

Part IV — Behavior and Predictive Action

☐ Your Behavior Overview —
how you adapt to existing circumstances.

Communicating decisiveness	1	2	3	④ ⑤	+	1
Ability to stimulate and activate others	1	2	③ ④	5	+	1
Self-control	1	2	③ ④	5	+	1
Awareness of others' feelings	1	② ③	4	5	+	1
Fairness	1	2	③ ④	5	+	1
Ability to see the whole, not merely the parts	1	2	③ ④	5	+	1
Working facts into a logical whole	1	2	3	④ ⑤	+	1
Sense of humor	1	2	③ ④	5	+	1
Handling of complex problems	1	2	3	④ ⑤	+	1
Concern for practical details	1	2	③ ④	5	+	1
Ability to size up another's character	1	2	③ ④	5	+	1

Calculation Section

	line 1 ____81____ %	
Total of ⊕	line 2 _____ %	
Add lines 1 & 2	line 3 _____ %	
Total of plotting points in shaded graph areas	line 4 _____ %	
Subtract line 4 from line 3	line 5 _____ %	
	(GRAND TOTAL)	

(See page 80 for directions.)

— *Key No. 10* —

BEHAVIOR DYNAMICS

Part I — Behavior and Change

☐ **Your Behavior Description** — *the real you.* Key word is *cooperative.* You effectively work within the structure of a group; show confidence with group decisions; question one-person rule; believe people in relationships should share equally and work for unity; gain strength in numbers; desire to be accepted on the basis of your work and effort.

☐ **Your Behavior Objectives** — *what you desire to be.* Key word is *recognized.* You wish to be accepted and appreciated for your extraordinary efforts to achieve; desire to solve new and challenging problems; display versatility; gain approval for advanced plans of action; seek ways in which to express yourself directly and forthrightly.

☐ **Your Behavior Change**

Degree of Change Occurring in Your Behavior		
Little	Some	Much
1.0 2.0	3.0 4.0	5.0

☐ **Your New Behavior** — *where you're going.* Key word is *teaching.* You show increased resourcefulness; demonstrate greater proficiency in following complex verbalization; provide increased stimulating conversation; argue for fun on either side of a question.

Part II — Behavior and Conflict

☐ **Your Behavior Under Pressure** — *how you handle objections.* You turn to others for support; respect those with previous experience; accept direction when it is in the best interest and security of yourself and others; volunteer to resolve conflict.

☐ **Your Internal Conflict** — *source of personal frustration.* You tend to move from one concern to another; neglect routine assignments; assume many responsibilities—this practice may lead to *trouble-shooting frustration,* implying that a situation gets your attention only when it represents an emergency. Pressure eventually causes you to specialize and solve problems.

Part III — Behavior and Control

☐ **Your Internal Motivation** — *how others may exert control with you.* Your motivation increases when others provide opportunities for you to: win support for your beliefs; fulfill tasks requiring objective analysis; use skills to convince; plan long-range activities.

☐ **Your Motivation of Others** — *how you exert control.* You influence others by establishing purpose and procedure. You emphasize stability; effectively handle technical concerns; provide clarification and full explanations.

Part IV — Behavior and Predictive Action

☐ Your Behavior Overview —
how you adapt to existing circumstances.

Communicating decisiveness	1 ②③ 4 5	+ 1
Ability to stimulate and activate others	1 ②③ 4 5	+ 1
Self-control	1 2 ③④ 5	+ 1
Awareness of others' feelings	1 2 ③④ 5	+ 1
Fairness	1 2 ③④ 5	+ 1
Ability to see the whole, not merely the parts	1 ②③ 4 5	+ 1
Working facts into a logical whole	1 2 ③④ 5	+ 1
Sense of humor	1 2 ③④ 5	+ 1
Handling of complex problems	1 ②③ 4 5	+ 1
Concern for practical details	1 2 3 ④⑤	+ 1
Ability to size up another's character	1 2 ③④ 5	+ 1

Calculation Section

	line 1 ___71___ %	
Total of (+1)	line 2 _____ %	
Add lines 1 & 2	line 3 _____ %	
Total of plotting points in shaded graph areas	line 4 _____ %	
Subtract line 4 from line 3	line 5 _____ % (GRAND TOTAL)	

(See page 80 for directions.)

— Key No. 11 —
BEHAVIOR DYNAMICS

Part I — Behavior and Change

☐ **Your Behavior Description** — *the real you.* Key word is *coaching.* You make things less complicated; emphasize orderliness; show confidence in your skill development; review past achievements, challenging yourself to do as well or better; provide criteria for self-evaluation; compete against yourself.

☐ **Your Behavior Objectives** — *what you desire to be.* Key word is *acclaimed.* You welcome more opportunities to show charm and persuasiveness; desire to demonstrate a commanding presence; use wit and stimulating conversation; stimulate others to action; use convincing arguments; seek support for your ideas; hope to operate well in hostile environments.

☐ **Your Behavior Change**

Degree of Change Occurring in Your Behavior		
Little	Some	Much
1.0 2.0	3.0 4.0	5.0

☐ **Your New Behavior** — *where you're going.* Key word is *assertive.* You become the center of movement; use more tact and expressiveness; increase your energy level; show increased forcefulness in decision making; seem to have much in reserve; appear tireless.

Part II — Behavior and Conflict

☐ **Your Behavior Under Pressure** — *how you handle objections.* You show impatience for rules that box people; skirt around authority; create ways to gain allegiance from others; generally hand off details and minor questions to others; follow routine, but seek short cuts.

☐ **Your Internal Conflict** — *source of personal frustration.* You tend to push beyond your limits; neglect your own personal needs that otherwise would interfere with the larger plan—this practice may lead to *exalted prestige,* implying that you experience anxiety in moving too fast at too great a risk. You fail to consider your own need for personal growth.

Part III — Behavior and Control

☐ **Your Internal Motivation —** *how others may exert control with you.* Your motivation increases when others provide opportunities for you to: persuade and manage others; assist people in their mental growth and development; initiate change; renew spirit and morale in stagnant environments.

☐ **Your Motivation of Others —** *how you exert control.* You influence others by using persuasive communication—clarification of what is said and what will be; helping others to see how they fit in; providing meaningful explanations.

Part IV — Behavior and Predictive Action

☐ **Your Behavior Overview —**
how you adapt to existing circumstances.

Communicating decisiveness	1	2	3	④	⑤	+	1
Ability to stimulate and activate others	1	2	3	④	⑤	+	1
Self-control	1	2	③	④	5	+	1
Awareness of others' feelings	1	2	③	④	5	+	1
Fairness	1	2	③	④	5	+	1
Ability to see the whole, not merely the parts	1	2	③	④	5	+	1
Working facts into a logical whole	1	2	3	④	⑤	+	1
Sense of humor	1	2	3	④	⑤	+	1
Handling of complex problems	1	2	3	④	⑤	+	1
Concern for practical details	1	2	③	④	5	+	1
Ability to size up another's character	1	2	3	④	⑤	+	1

Calculation Section

	line 1 ____89____ %
Total of ⊕	line 2 _____ %
Add lines 1 & 2	line 3 _____ %
Total of plotting points in shaded graph areas	line 4 _____ %
Subtract line 4 from line 3	line 5 _____ %
	(GRAND TOTAL)

(See page 80 for directions.)

— *Key No. 12* —
BEHAVIOR DYNAMICS

Part I — Behavior and Change

☐ **Your Behavior Description** — *the real you.* Key word is *exciting*. You combine firmness with lightheartedness; use terse thinking, sometimes playful and sometimes in quick flashes; prod others to push themselves beyond their normal pace; evaluate the usefulness of others by their desire to make things easier for you.

☐ **Your Behavior Objectives** — *what you desire to be.* Key word is *renewed*. You desire to set yourself apart from group members; wish to be individualistic; express dissatisfaction constructively; use new ideas and short cuts; wish to influence the motivation of others; seek to be truthful.

☐ Your Behavior Change

Degree of Change Occurring in Your Behavior		
Little	Some	Much
1.0 2.0	3.0 4.0	5.0

☐ **Your New Behavior** — *where you're going.* Key word is *self-developing*. You concentrate more on specialized efforts; gain a greater sense of achievement; respond to work and life as a game in which winning is based on new skills; accept rules and regulations.

Part II — Behavior and Conflict

☐ **Your Behavior Under Pressure** — *how you handle objections.* You show irritation with those who are slower and more cautious; criticize yourself for failing to persuade others to your position; assign a variety of tasks to others; accept responsibility to show the benefits of a proposal.

☐ **Your Internal Conflict** — *source of personal frustration.* You tend to be inconsistent in the use of praise; compliment excessively at times, withholding appreciation at other times—this practice may lead to *frustrated support*, implying that others respond according to how they receive your mixed message.

Part III — Behavior and Control

☐ **Your Internal Motivation** — *how others may exert control with you.* Your motivation increases when others provide opportunities for you to: focus on strategy and tactics; rely upon follow-up support from others; streamline efforts.

☐ **Your Motivation of Others** — *how you exert control.* You influence others by using yourself as an example of growth and satisfaction. You emphasize ideas that others can visualize, providing ways for people to see themselves in what you propose.

Part IV — Behavior and Predictive Action

☐ Your Behavior Overview —
how you adapt to existing circumstances.

Communicating decisiveness	1	2	3	(4	5)	+	1
Ability to stimulate and activate others	1	2	3	(4	5)	+	1
Self-control	1	2	(3	4)	5	+	1
Awareness of others' feelings	1	2	(3	4)	5	+	1
Fairness	1	2	(3	4)	5	+	1
Ability to see the whole, not merely the parts	1	2	(3	4)	5	+	1
Working facts into a logical whole	1	2	(3	4)	5	+	1
Sense of humor	1	2	3	(4	5)	+	1
Handling of complex problems	1	2	(3	4)	5	+	1
Concern for practical details	1	2	(3	4)	5	+	1
Ability to size up another's character	1	2	(3	4)	5	+	1

Calculation Section

	line 1 ____83____ %	
Total of (+1)	line 2 _____ %	
Add lines 1 & 2	line 3 _____ %	
Total of plotting points in shaded graph areas	line 4 _____ %	
Subtract line 4 from line 3	line 5 _____ %	
	(GRAND TOTAL)	

(See page 80 for directions.)

— Key No. 13 —
BEHAVIOR DYNAMICS

Part I — Behavior and Change

☐ **Your Behavior Description** — *the real you.* Key word is *spirited.* You display a multi-sided emotional image ranging from joy to anger; use humor and fun-loving tactics to relieve tension; become talkative when things go your way; avoid difficult questions by responding with your own questions.

☐ **Your Behavior Objectives** — *what you desire to be.* Key word is *well-rounded.* You desire to show a serious and sincere side of your personality; search for activities and approaches which bring people and principles together; hope to construct situations to represent quality time between you and others.

☐ **Your Behavior Change**

Degree of Change Occurring in Your Behavior		
Little	Some	Much
1.0 2.0	3.0 4.0	5.0

☐ **Your New Behavior** — *where you're going.* Key word is *appraising.* You show increased empathy for others' shifting positions; adapt to mood changes in others; set in motion ways for people to evaluate their contributions; encourage greater use of updated accountability methods.

Part II — Behavior and Conflict

☐ **Your Behavior Under Pressure** — *how you handle objections.* You provide information designed to elicit a favorable response; attempt to communicate to the feeling level of people; accept responsibility in a grand style for future assignments; agree to more than you can handle.

☐ **Your Internal Conflict** — *source of personal frustration.* You tend to dwell excessively upon the meaning of life; attempt to find your true self; feel that others may have fallen short in their discovery— your apprehension may lead to obsessive *self-exploration,* implying a search for a goal with little or no help from others. You frequently feel confused and irritable with your progress.

Part III — Behavior and Control

☐ **Your Internal Motivation** — *how others may exert control with you.*
Your motivation increases when others provide opportunities for you
to: tackle complex problems and situations; discover new and unusual
procedures; exchange ideas with others.

☐ **Your Motivation of Others** — *how you exert control.* You influence
others by projecting yourself as an expert; making others responsible
for your happiness by demanding that they satisfy your demands for
their active involvement in your activities, emphasizing their need to
improve, often beyond their existing skill level; compare others'
progress to yours.

Part IV — Behavior and Predictive Action

☐ Your Behavior Overview —
how you adapt to existing circumstances.

Communicating decisiveness	(1	2)	3	4	5	+	1
Ability to stimulate and activate others	1	2	3	(4	5)	+	1
Self-control	1	2	(3	4)	5	+	1
Awareness of others' feelings	1	(2	3)	4	5	+	1
Fairness	1	2	(3	4)	5	+	1
Ability to see the whole, not merely the parts	1	(2	3)	4	5	+	1
Working facts into a logical whole	(1	2)	3	4	5	+	1
Sense of humor	1	2	3	(4	5)	+	1
Handling of complex problems	1	2	(3	4)	5	+	1
Concern for practical details	1	2	(3	4)	5	+	1
Ability to size up another's character	1	2	(3	4)	5	+	1

Calculation Section		
	line 1 ___69___ %	
Total of (+1)	line 2 _____ %	
Add lines 1 & 2	line 3 _____ %	
Total of plotting points in shaded graph areas	line 4 _____ %	
Subtract line 4 from line 3	line 5 _____ %	
	(GRAND TOTAL)	

(See page 80 for directions.)

— *Key No. 14* —
BEHAVIOR DYNAMICS

Part I — Behavior and Change

☐ **Your Behavior Description** — *the real you.* Key word is *realistic.* You trust those who show willingness to be tested; select confidants who share a common purpose, objectives, and values; limit expressions of your intentions; compete with proven skills—calculating, discriminating, and selecting worthwhile information.

☐ **Your Behavior Objectives** — *what you desire to be.* Key word is *fun-loving.* You desire to share burdens with others; hope to find release in a more relaxed environment; seek to show joy in living; reveal a happy face; expect others to feel a similar ebullience; hope to manifest new tastes in style and fashion.

☐ **Your Behavior Change**

Degree of Change Occurring in Your Behavior		
Little	Some	Much
1.0　　2.0	3.0　　4.0	5.0

☐ **Your New Behavior** — *where you're going.* Key word is *winsome.* You perform more to meet the expectations of others; use less time to develop your own goals; use wit, charm, and warmth; initiate a chain of optimistic responses; increase your participation in social events.

Part II — Behavior and Conflict

☐ **Your Behavior Under Pressure** — *how you handle objections.* You awake to reality; demand much of yourself; act correctly, according to standards; become critical of yourself when in the wrong; reject shallowness in others.

☐ **Your Internal Conflict** — *source of personal frustration.* You tend to be overly generous when you are in a state of euphoria; respond with a cooperative and willing attitude; trust others indiscriminately; show leniency to those who make excuses—this practice may lead to *indiscriminate excessiveness,* implying an exaggerated emotion in which it is difficult to know when you will come down and on whom.

Part III — Behavior and Control

☐ **Your Internal Motivation** — *how others may exert control with you.* Your motivation increases when others provide opportunities for you to: fulfill public appearance requests; instruct, teach skills to others; be cooperative, yet highly competitive; be enthusiastic, yet complex; be earnest, yet evasive.

☐ **Your Motivation of Others** — *how you exert control.* You influence others by encouraging them to emulate your activities. You emphasize that your actions may be as successful for them as they were for you; reinforce others' actions by rewarding them with matters you do not like to handle.

Part IV — Behavior and Predictive Action

☐ **Your Behavior Overview —**
how you adapt to existing circumstances.

Communicating decisiveness	1	2	③ ④	5	+	1
Ability to stimulate and activate others	1	2	3 ④ ⑤		+	1
Self-control	1	2	③ ④	5	+	1
Awareness of others' feelings	1	2	③ ④	5	+	1
Fairness	1	2	③ ④	5	+	1
Ability to see the whole, not merely the parts	1	2	③ ④	5	+	1
Working facts into a logical whole	1	2	③ ④	5	+	1
Sense of humor	1	2	③ ④	5	+	1
Handling of complex problems	1	2	③ ④	5	+	1
Concern for practical details	① ②		3	4	5	+	1
Ability to size up another's character	1	2	③ ④	5	+	1

Calculation Section

	line 1 _____75_____ %	
Total of (+1)	line 2 _____ %	
Add lines 1 & 2	line 3 _____ %	
Total of plotting points in shaded graph areas	line 4 _____ %	
Subtract line 4 from line 3	line 5 _____ %	
	(GRAND TOTAL)	

(See page 80 for directions.)

— *Key No. 15* —
BEHAVIOR DYNAMICS

Part I — Behavior and Change

☐ **Your Behavior Description** — *the real you.* Key word is *mediating.* You establish effective relationships; assume a conciliatory role when necessary; work for compromise; insist that others be fair; ensure that people keep their promises.

☐ **Your Behavior Objectives** — *what you desire to be.* Key word is *contesting.* You wish to become more confrontational when necessary; make a concerted effort to gain an edge over others; desire to enhance your image as a forceful presence; hope to assume an assertive leadership role; bring hope and opportuntities for changes; make others believe in themselves.

☐ **Your Behavior Change**

Degree of Change Occurring in Your Behavior		
Little	Some	Much
1.0　　　2.0	3.0　　4.0	5.0

☐ **Your New Behavior** — *where you're going.* Key word is *upward.* You start new ventures; seek greater rewards for your success; place increased value on material goods; believe in taking your share first; decide how benefits should be allotted; increase vitality.

Part II — Behavior and Conflict

☐ **Your Behavior Under Pressure** — *how you handle objections.* You attempt to explain reasons for unfulfilled promises; tend to neglect specific details; find it difficult to be firm and aggressive; become lenient with impulsive people.

☐ **Your Internal Conflict** — *source of personal frustration.* You tend to solicit support from others; surround yourself with generous people; reciprocate by volunteering your personal services—this practice may lead to *over-committed anxiety,* implying great pressure on your resources. You run the risk of developing an ambivalent attitude in which you waver between the desire to interact and the need to be left in peace.

Part III — Behavior and Control

☐ **Your Internal Motivation** — *how others may exert control with you.* Your motivation increases when others provide opportunities for you to: accept challenges which others find difficult to accept; turn events around when the turning point involves people; receive appropriate credit.

☐ **Your Motivation of Others** — *how you exert control.* You influence others through a willingness to share. You emphasize sincerity in meeting personal needs; demonstrate an equality between yourself and others.

Part IV — Behavior and Predictive Action

☐ Your Behavior Overview —
how you adapt to existing circumstances.

Communicating decisiveness	1	②③	4	5	+	1
Ability to stimulate and activate others	1	2 ③④	5		+	1
Self-control	1	②③	4	5	+	1
Awareness of others' feelings	1	2 3	④⑤		+	1
Fairness	1	2 3	④⑤		+	1
Ability to see the whole, not merely the parts	1	2 ③④	5		+	1
Working facts into a logical whole	①②	3	4	5	+	1
Sense of humor	1	2 ③④	5		+	1
Handling of complex problems	1	②③	4	5	+	1
Concern for practical details	1	②③	4	5	+	1
Ability to size up another's character	1	2 ③④	5		+	1

Calculation Section		
	line 1 ____69____ %	
Total of ⊕	line 2 _____ %	
Add lines 1 & 2	line 3 _____ %	
Total of plotting points in shaded graph areas	line 4 _____ %	
Subtract line 4 from line 3	line 5 _____ %	
	(GRAND TOTAL)	
(See page 80 for directions.)		

— *Key No. 16* —
BEHAVIOR DYNAMICS

Part I — Behavior and Change

☐ **Your Behavior Description** — *the real you.* Key word is *open-minded.* You use friendly overtures to convince and persuade; seek out those who can be helpful to your purpose; visualize successful patterns and creative possibilities; reject routine; seek stimulating activity.

☐ **Your Behavior Objectives** — *what you desire to be.* Key word is *conservative.* You sense the need to be calculating and cautious in your risk taking; desire to follow routine procedure; wish to follow exacting plans and details; avoid impulsive and rash moves.

☐ **Your Behavior Change**

Degree of Change Occurring in Your Behavior		
Little	Some	Much
1.0 2.0	3.0 4.0	5.0

☐ **Your New Behavior** — *where you're going.* Key word is *reserved.* You painstakingly follow orders from authority; become more systematic; appear reserved and patient; feel a greater need to be superdependable; make moves to stabilize the environment with corrective measures.

Part II — Behavior and Conflict

☐ **Your Behavior Under Pressure** — *how you handle objections.* You win support for minimizing divisive elements; focus on solidarity rather than diversity; clarify complex issues; disarm others through thoughtful, yet convincing, arguments.

☐ **Your Internal Conflict** — *source of personal frustration.* You tend to take pleasure in pursuing goals by convincing and controlling others; take credit for ideas that have been dormant—this practice may lead to *unresolved envy,* implying that others identify with what you do, but at times feel their contributions are merged too closely with your achievements.

Part III — Behavior and Control

☐ **Your Internal Motivation** — *how others may exert control with you.*
Your motivation increases when others provide opportunities for you
to: sharply define your interests; enjoy what you do best; focus on
your powers of concentration; be accountable for a task.

☐ **Your Motivation of Others** — *how you exert control.* You influence
others by making them feel a part of your cause. You emphasize the
role each person has in what you do; make their effort as important
to them as it is to you.

Part IV — Behavior and Predictive Action

☐ **Your Behavior Overview** —
how you adapt to existing circumstances.

Communicating decisiveness	1	2	3	④	⑤	+	1
Ability to stimulate and activate others	1	2	3	④	⑤	+	1
Self-control	1	2	③	④	5	+	1
Awareness of others' feelings	1	②	③	4	5	+	1
Fairness	1	2	③	④	5	+	1
Ability to see the whole, not merely the parts	1	②	③	4	5	+	1
Working facts into a logical whole	1	2	③	④	5	+	1
Sense of humor	1	2	③	④	5	+	1
Handling of complex problems	1	2	③	④	5	+	1
Concern for practical details	1	②	③	4	5	+	1
Ability to size up another's character	1	2	③	④	5	+	1

Calculation Section

	line 1 ____75____ %	
Total of (+1)	line 2 _____ %	
Add lines 1 & 2	line 3 _____ %	
Total of plotting points in shaded graph areas	line 4 _____ %	
Subtract line 4 from line 3	line 5 _____ %	
	(GRAND TOTAL)	

(See page 80 for directions.)

— Key No. 17 —
BEHAVIOR DYNAMICS

Part I — Behavior and Change

☐ **Your Behavior Description** — *the real you.* Key word is *exacting.* You sense a need to bring new order and improved systems to faltering situations; attempt to correct by intense and concentrated activity; display exacting standards; seek the source of others' dissatisfaction; soothe hurt feelings.

☐ **Your Behavior Objectives** — *what you desire to be.* Key word is *dependable.* You desire to fulfill promises; hope to set a consistent pace; make a diligent effort to resolve differences of opinion among close friends; adapt to routine; wish to prove your sincerity, providing assistance and support when people are in need.

☐ **Your Behavior Change**

Degree of Change Occurring in Your Behavior		
Little	Some	Much
1.0 2.0	3.0 4.0	5.0

☐ **Your New Behavior** — *where you're going.* Key word is *togetherness.* You make greater attempts to build solidarity with a closely knit group of people; clearly state your opinions of others; show increased willingness to assume unpleasant responsibilities; outwardly show a forgiving attitude, but remember wrongs done to you.

Part II — Behavior and Conflict

☐ **Your Behavior Under Pressure** — *how you handle objections.* You brood; keep negative feelings within; fear reprisals; become suspicious; expect the worst; seek to escape into a more peaceful and problem-free situation.

☐ **Your Internal Conflict** — *source of personal frustration.* You tend to assume fault when others fail; prefer to be accountable only for your own faults—this attitude may lead to *defensive superiority,* implying that you doubt the performance of others and feel that they cannot measure up to your level.

Part III — Behavior and Control

☐ **Your Internal Motivation** — *how others may exert control with you.* Your motivation increases when others provide opportunities for you to: view your efforts in comparison to others; receive assurances that your effort is rewarded; avoid surprises.

☐ **Your Motivation of Others** — *how you exert control.* You influence others with your attentiveness to organizing. You emphasize systematic procedure; promise a better way of doing things; assume responsibility to prove your point.

Part IV — Behavior and Predictive Action

☐ Your Behavior Overview —
how you adapt to existing circumstances.

Communicating decisiveness	(1	2)	3	4	5	+	1
Ability to stimulate and activate others	(1	2)	3	4	5	+	1
Self-control	1	2	3	(4	5)	+	1
Awareness of others' feelings	1	2	(3	4)	5	+	1
Fairness	1	2	3	(4	5)	+	1
Ability to see the whole, not merely the parts	1	2	(3	4)	5	+	1
Working facts into a logical whole	1	2	3	(4	5)	+	1
Sense of humor	1	(2	3)	4	5	+	1
Handling of complex problems	1	2	3	(4	5)	+	1
Concern for practical details	1	2	(3	4)	5	+	1
Ability to size up another's character	1	(2	3)	4	5	+	1

Calculation Section

	line 1 ____73____ %
Total of (+1)	line 2 _____ %
Add lines 1 & 2	line 3 _____ %
Total of plotting points in shaded graph areas	line 4 _____ %
Subtract line 4 from line 3	line 5 _____ %
	(GRAND TOTAL)

(See page 80 for directions.)

— Key No. 18 —
BEHAVIOR DYNAMICS

Part I — Behavior and Change

☐ **Your Behavior Description —** *the real you.* Key word is *impatient.* You accept responsibility for tasks; compare yourself favorably with others; express confidence in your ability to outthink and outpace others; question the worth of tedious work needed to nurture team play.

☐ **Your Behavior Objectives —** *what you desire to be.* Key word is *problem-solver.* You desire to project optimism and hope; talk easily and confidently about the future; wish to feel no more anxiety than the situation requires; want sincere and reliable friendships; provide steady and firm guidance in new relationships.

☐ **Your Behavior Change**

Degree of Change Occurring in Your Behavior		
Little	Some	Much
1.0　　　2.0	3.0　　　4.0	5.0

☐ **Your New Behavior —** *where you're going.* Key word is *interactive.* You become more tactful and patient with others; tolerate diversity of opinion; trust your feelings; seek advice from others; show more responsiveness to advice from others; listen and develop a keen interest in others' activities.

Part II — Behavior and Conflict

☐ **Your Behavior Under Pressure —** *how you handle objections.* You speak with authority in refuting objections; find fault with timid and shy individuals who refuse your request for support; doubt the promises of others; rely on the personal strength of your own convictions.

☐ **Your Internal Conflict —** *source of personal frustration.* You tend to orchestrate the feelings of people, using a warmhearted approach when convenient and a hard-driving method when necessary—this approach may lead to *manipulation of emotions,* implying a heightened desire to take what you want and place your needs above those of others.

Part III — Behavior and Control

☐ **Your Internal Motivation** — *how others may exert control with you.* Your motivation increases when others provide opportunities for you to: move freely from one interest to another; generate support from dedicated people; make a lasting impression.

☐ **Your Motivation of Others** — *how you exert control.* You influence others by placing strong demands on their time. You emphasize the need to become a more "complete" person; convince others that time spent in thinking and action will enable them to fulfill themselves.

Part IV — Behavior and Predictive Action

☐ Your Behavior Overview —
how you adapt to existing circumstances.

Communicating decisiveness	1	2	3	④ ⑤	+	1
Ability to stimulate and activate others	1	2	③ ④	5	+	1
Self-control	1	2	3	④ ⑤	+	1
Awareness of others' feelings	1	② ③	4	5	+	1
Fairness	1	② ③	4	5	+	1
Ability to see the whole, not merely the parts	1	2	③ ④	5	+	1
Working facts into a logical whole	1	2	③ ④	5	+	1
Sense of humor	1	2	③ ④	5	+	1
Handling of complex problems	1	2	③ ④	5	+	1
Concern for practical details	1	② ③	4	5	+	1
Ability to size up another's character	1	2	③ ④	5	+	1

Calculation Section

	line 1 ____69____ %
Total of ⊕	line 2 _____ %
Add lines 1 & 2	line 3 _____ %
Total of plotting points in shaded graph areas	line 4 _____ %
Subtract line 4 from line 3	line 5 _____ %
	(GRAND TOTAL)

(See page 80 for directions.)

— Key No. 19 —
BEHAVIOR DYNAMICS

Part I — Behavior and Change

☐ **Your Behavior Description —** *the real you.* Key word is *deliberate.* You make attempts to disguise occasional self-doubt; underestimate yourself in comparison with other achievers; believe your skill is more difficult to develop; stress work ethic; appear to be reflective; work hard; work long; look for recognition.

☐ **Your Behavior Objectives —** *what you desire to be.* Key word is *driving force.* You desire private and public attention for your achievements; hope to be viewed as one with strong leadership potential; encourage people to believe in themselves; wish to keep ahead of others, while insisting they keep pace with you.

☐ **Your Behavior Change**

Degree of Change Occurring in Your Behavior		
Little	Some	Much
1.0 2.0	3.0 4.0	5.0

☐ **Your New Behavior —** *where you're going.* Key word is *expansive.* You make new social contacts; demonstrate more bursts of constructive energy interspersed with periods of fun and relaxation; reveal efforts to work smarter and do things your way.

Part II — Behavior and Conflict

☐ **Your Behavior Under Pressure —** *how you handle objections.* You seek information to justify your position; hope to satisfy queries with evidence of a good memory for facts; listen attentively to others.

☐ **Your Internal Conflict —** *source of personal frustration.* You tend to make a lasting impression on those around you; are anxious to inform others of how far you have come; are eager to encourage others—this desire may lead to *lure of adventure,* implying that you push forward while others attempt to pull you back to them. You may both fail to acknowledge the desirable features on either side.

Part III — Behavior and Control

☐ **Your Internal Motivation** — *how others may exert control with you.* Your motivation increases when others provide opportunities for you to: gain new and different experiences; satisfy a craving for adventure; prove your spirit for experimentation.

☐ **Your Motivation of Others** — *how you exert control.* You influence others by your command of situations. You emphasize the need to understand variety and differences in people; deliberately exert effort to *work* at knowing how to satisfy others.

Part IV — Behavior and Predictive Action

☐ **Your Behavior Overview** —
how you adapt to existing circumstances.

Communicating decisiveness	1	2	③	④	5	+ 1
Ability to stimulate and activate others	1	2	③	④	5	+ 1
Self-control	1	②	③	4	5	+ 1
Awareness of others' feelings	1	2	③	④	5	+ 1
Fairness	1	2	3	④	⑤	+ 1
Ability to see the whole, not merely the parts	1	②	③	4	5	+ 1
Working facts into a logical whole	1	2	③	④	5	+ 1
Sense of humor	1	2	③	④	5	+ 1
Handling of complex problems	①	②	3	4	5	+ 1
Concern for practical details	1	2	3	④	⑤	+ 1
Ability to size up another's character	1	2	③	④	5	+ 1

Calculation Section

	line 1 ____73____ %	
Total of (+1)	line 2 _____ %	
Add lines 1 & 2	line 3 _____ %	
Total of plotting points in shaded graph areas	line 4 _____ %	
Subtract line 4 from line 3	line 5 _____ %	
	(GRAND TOTAL)	

(See page 80 for directions.)

— Key No. 20 —
BEHAVIOR DYNAMICS

Part I — Behavior and Change

☐ **Your Behavior Description** — *the real you.* Key word is *ambitious.* You refuse to acknowledge limitations; orchestrate events to gain advantage; develop competitive angles to motivate yourself; make activity difficult for others, placing them, as well as yourself, at risk; ready yourself for personal challenges; make correct decisions at the appropriate time.

☐ **Your Behavior Objectives** — *what you desire to be.* Key word is *challenged.* You take pleasure in the quickness of your physical movement and mental alertness; use a direct approach; criticize compromising behavior; wish to be forceful in leadership; show little empathy for those who falter while competing with you, referring to them as losers.

☐ **Your Behavior Change**

Degree of Change Occurring in Your Behavior		
Little	Some	Much
1.0 2.0	3.0 4.0	5.0

☐ **Your New Behavior** — *where you're going.* Key word is *driven.* You project a more serious mood; become more detached and withdrawn; reflect a cool demeanor; dare others to match your determination; make fun and games competitive—often an irritant to others.

Part II — Behavior and Conflict

☐ **Your Behavior Under Pressure** — *how you handle objections.* You show ease of movement; calm others; question and draw out a variety of opinions; communicate inspirationally; sprinkle comments with hints of sensitivity and caring.

☐ **Your Internal Conflict** — *source of personal frustration.* You tend to concentrate on a single issue at the expense of other areas in your life; show obsession to succeed where others have failed—this determination may lead to *ultimate frustration,* implying that you separate yourself from friends who often cannot comprehend your endless ambition.

Part III — Behavior and Control

☐ **Your Internal Motivation** — *how others may exert control with you.* Your motivation increases when others provide opportunities for you to: complete a task without a time limit; turn failure into success— almost overnight; struggle against the odds; gain power.

☐ **Your Motivation of Others** — *how you exert control.* You influence others by making yourself "bigger" than life. You express a strong and unwavering belief in yourself; indicate a willingness to totally invest in yourself.

Part IV — Behavior and Predictive Action

☐ **Your Behavior Overview —**
how you adapt to existing circumstances.

Communicating decisiveness	1	2	3	(4	5)	+	1
Ability to stimulate and activate others	1	2	3	(4	5)	+	1
Self-control	1	2	(3	4)	5	+	1
Awareness of others' feelings	1	(2	3)	4	5	+	1
Fairness	1	2	(3	4)	5	+	1
Ability to see the whole, not merely the parts	1	2	(3	4)	5	+	1
Working facts into a logical whole	1	2	(3	4)	5	+	1
Sense of humor	1	2	3	(4	5)	+	1
Handling of complex problems	1	2	(3	4)	5	+	1
Concern for practical details	(1	2)	3	4	5	+	1
Ability to size up another's character	1	2	3	(4	5)	+	1

Calculation Section

	line 1 ___79___ %	
Total of (+1)	line 2 _____ %	
Add lines 1 & 2	line 3 _____ %	
Total of plotting points in shaded graph areas	line 4 _____ %	
Subtract line 4 from line 3	line 5 _____ %	
	(GRAND TOTAL)	

(See page 80 for directions.)

— *Key No. 21* —
BEHAVIOR DYNAMICS

Part I — Behavior and Change

☐ **Your Behavior Description** — *the real you.* Key word is *watchful.* You proceed cautiously with your plan of action; appear more rational than emotional; withhold negative feelings; desire in-depth understanding from close friends and associates; need approval for things you do.

☐ **Your Behavior Objectives** — *what you desire to be.* Key word is *rewarded.* You desire to be free from worry; throw off the shackles of doubt; fear sameness; search for new people contacts, believing that they can be helpful to you; hope to depend upon others' good will.

☐ **Your Behavior Change**

Degree of Change Occurring in Your Behavior				
Little		Some		Much
1.0	2.0	3.0	4.0	5.0

☐ **Your New Behavior** — *where you're going.* Key word is *hopeful.* You search for new ways to channel your increased personal energy; desire to break loose from rigid feeling and thinking; become discontent with the slowness of others; broaden your set of objectives; open yourself to new ideas.

Part II — Behavior and Conflict

☐ **Your Behavior Under Pressure** — *how you handle objections.* You prepare for possible negative consequences; become defensive; display occasional pessimism; show the effects of worrying; contend that others use unfair criticism.

☐ **Your Internal Conflict** — *source of personal frustration.* You tend to seek a balance between deliberate action and spontaneity of movement; experiment with both sides of the spectrum; keep others in doubt—this action may lead to *aggression for self-assurance,* implying that your impulsive need to gain approval is, at times, misdirected and confusing to others.

Part III — Behavior and Control

☐ **Your Internal Motivation** — *how others may exert control with you.* Your motivation increases when others provide opportunities for you to: tap the emotions of others; use convincing arguments; experiment with new ventures; receive respected and credible support.

☐ **Your Motivation of Others** — *how you exert control.* You influence others by cautious determination. You emphasize planning and directing in a controlled setting; impress others by knowing your way through the maze of policy, procedure, and obstacles.

Part IV — Behavior and Predictive Action

☐ **Your Behavior Overview** —
how you adapt to existing circumstances.

Communicating decisiveness	①②③ 3	4	5	+	1
Ability to stimulate and activate others	1 ②③	4	5	+	1
Self-control	1 2 ③④	5	+	1
Awareness of others' feelings	1 2 ③④	5	+	1
Fairness	1 2 3 ④⑤	+	1
Ability to see the whole, not merely the parts	1 ②③	4	5	+	1
Working facts into a logical whole	1 2 ③④	5	+	1
Sense of humor	1 ②③	4	5	+	1
Handling of complex problems	1 2 ③④	5	+	1
Concern for practical details	1 2 3 ④⑤	+	1
Ability to size up another's character	1 ②③	4	5	+	1

Calculation Section

	line 1 ___69___ %
Total of (+1)	line 2 _____ %
Add lines 1 & 2	line 3 _____ %
Total of plotting points in shaded graph areas	line 4 _____ %
Subtract line 4 from line 3	line 5 _____ %
	(GRAND TOTAL)

(See page 80 for directions.)

326 Energetics of Personality

— Key No. 22 —
BEHAVIOR DYNAMICS

Part I — Behavior and Change

☐ **Your Behavior Description** — *the real you.* Key word is *optimistic.* You think positively; rid yourself of doubt; show why things are not as they appear; emphasize favorable aspects; disassociate yourself from the negative; discover ways to add to your self-importance.

☐ **Your Behavior Objectives** — *what you desire to be.* Key word is *warmhearted.* You desire to organize for future activity; use options and participative planning to direct activities; wish to show the desirable effects of relying upon specialized skills of people; identify meaningful ways in which to work with differences in people.

☐ **Your Behavior Change**

Degree of Change Occurring in Your Behavior		
Little	Some	Much
1.0 　　　 2.0	3.0 　　　 4.0	5.0

☐ **Your New Behavior** — *where you're going.* Key word is *understanding.* You increasingly develop close ties of affection with others; satisfy a need to be part of an inner circle of friends and associates; develop more secure relationships with others.

Part II — Behavior and Conflict

☐ **Your Behavior Under Pressure** — *how you handle objections.* You use sentiment more than logic; display anger when pushed to the limit; quickly shift to a more conciliatory mood; move with ease from one emotion to the next.

☐ **Your Internal Conflict** — *source of personal frustration.* You tend to make excessive commitments to others; find it necessary to win support by promising to help; distribute favors with little or no discrimination—this practice may lead to *anxious approval,* implying an overly generous spirit. In the process, however, you may lose recognition; friends may show less faith and trust.

Part III — Behavior and Control

☐ **Your Internal Motivation** — *how others may exert control with you.* Your motivation increases when others provide opportunities for you to: care for others; respect authority which is pro-people; use therapeutic communication—offering a listening ear, giving suggestions.

☐ **Your Motivation of Others** — *how you exert control.* You influence others by being optimistic. You emphasize the good news; associate yourself with favorable forecasts with which others want to identify.

Part IV — Behavior and Predictive Action

☐ Your Behavior Overview—
how you adapt to existing circumstances.

Communicating decisiveness	1	② ③	4	5	+	1
Ability to stimulate and activate others	1	2 3	④ ⑤		+	1
Self-control	① ②	3	4	5	+	1
Awareness of others' feelings	1	2	③ ④	5	+	1
Fairness	1	2	③ ④	5	+	1
Ability to see the whole, not merely the parts	① ②	3	4	5	+	1
Working facts into a logical whole	① ②	3	4	5	+	1
Sense of humor	1	2	3	④ ⑤	+	1
Handling of complex problems	① ②	3	4	5	+	1
Concern for practical details	1	2	③ ④	5	+	1
Ability to size up another's character	1	2	3	④ ⑤	+	1

Calculation Section		
	line 1 ____65____ %	
Total of ⊕	line 2 _____ %	
Add lines 1 & 2	line 3 _____ %	
Total of plotting points in shaded graph areas	line 4 _____ %	
Subtract line 4 from line 3	line 5 _____ %	
	(GRAND TOTAL)	
(See page 80 for directions.)		

— Key No. 23 —
BEHAVIOR DYNAMICS

Part I — Behavior and Change

☐ **Your Behavior Description** — *the real you.* Key word is *growth.* You show firmness when your reputation is at stake; reprimand others for inattentiveness to detail; reflect an independent spirit; refuse to be identified with a cause without appropriate credit; keep your options open.

☐ **Your Behavior Objectives** — *what you desire to be.* Key word is *considerate.* You desire to be more patient with people in complicated situations; show respect for the opinions of close friends and associates; wish to utilize human systems that bring people together; adjust to facts as they are.

☐ **Your Behavior Change**

Degree of Change Occurring in Your Behavior		
Little	Some	Much
1.0 2.0	3.0 4.0	5.0

☐ **Your New Behavior** — *where you're going.* Key word is *reinforcing.* You increase your reliance on compromise and consensus; share the decision-making role; encourage others to explain and clarify reasons for their beliefs; provide greater encouragement for open participation.

Part II — Behavior and Conflict

☐ **Your Behavior Under Pressure** — *how you handle objections.* You welcome the opportunity to defend your position; effectively use counterattack and rebuttal; believe that you, more than your ideas, are on trial; let your feelings enter into the situation.

☐ **Your Internal Conflict** — *source of personal frustration.* You tend to believe that tension is disruptive; view disturbances as blockages to free expression; make efforts to avoid stressful points—this belief may lead to *false peace and tranquility,* implying that others will be fearful of expressing negative feelings. In addition, the elimination of tension may result in the absence of creativity.

Part III — Behavior and Control

☐ **Your Internal Motivation** — *how others may exert control with you.* Your motivation increases when others provide opportunities for you to: facilitate participation of people with differing backgrounds; create situations in which ideas are shared; experiment with communication channels.

☐ **Your Motivation of Others** — *how you exert control.* You influence others by bringing a variety of people together. You emphasize the rainbow effect of people and their skills; sacrifice speed of effort for full participation of others.

Part IV — Behavior and Predictive Action

☐ Your Behavior Overview —
how you adapt to existing circumstances.

Communicating decisiveness	1	2	3	④ ⑤	+	1
Ability to stimulate and activate others	1	2	3	④ 5	+	1
Self-control	1	2	③ 4	5	+	1
Awareness of others' feelings	1	2	③ 4	5	+	1
Fairness	1	2	③ 4	5	+	1
Ability to see the whole, not merely the parts	1	2	③ 4	5	+	1
Working facts into a logical whole	1	2	③ 4	5	+	1
Sense of humor	1	2	3	④ ⑤	+	1
Handling of complex problems	1	2	③ 4	5	+	1
Concern for practical details	1	② ③	4	5	+	1
Ability to size up another's character	1	2	3	④ ⑤	+	1

Calculation Section		
	line 1 ____83____ %	
Total of (+1)	line 2 _____ %	
Add lines 1 & 2	line 3 _____ %	
Total of plotting points in shaded graph areas	line 4 _____ %	
Subtract line 4 from line 3	line 5 _____ %	
	(GRAND TOTAL)	
(See page 80 for directions.)		

— Key No. 24 —
BEHAVIOR DYNAMICS

Part I — Behavior and Change

☐ **Your Behavior Description** — *the real you.* Key word is *constant.* You identify with those who have high standards; rely on getting approval for specialized efforts rather than depending upon your physical presence or public performance; accept realistic limitations on your capabilities.

☐ **Your Behavior Objectives** — *what you desire to be.* Key word is *enlightened.* You desire facts, receiving them in an agreeable fashion; attempt to show an understanding of the value of information; wish to show friendliness and appropriateness; hope to demonstrate liveliness and persistence.

☐ **Your Behavior Change**

Degree of Change Occurring in Your Behavior				
Little		Some		Much
1.0	2.0	3.0	4.0	5.0

☐ **Your New Behavior** — *where you're going.* Key word is *directive.* You increasingly take charge of events in your life; remove obstacles that impede progress; make bold new attempts to gain power in relationships; directly confront opposition.

Part II — Behavior and Conflict

☐ **Your Behavior Under Pressure** — *how you handle objections.* You appear cooperative; become task oriented; comply with requests from those you respect; make demands when necessary; show nervous anxiety; secretly admit personal inadequacies.

☐ **Your Internal Conflict** — *source of personal frustration.* You tend to do more than your share; feel that, at times, it is difficult to control events—this admission may lead to *rebellion and resentment,* implying that unreasonable demands are made on you. Your reluctance to express displeasure with others permits them to assume less than their share.

Part III — Behavior and Control

☐ **Your Internal Motivation** — *how others may exert control with you.* Your motivation increases when others provide opportunities for you to: be true to your beliefs; gain support in your need to act independently and yet be loyal to your benefactors.

☐ **Your Motivation of Others** — *how you exert control.* You influence others by showing dedication to a cause. You emphasize commitment to the task; remind others of your diligent efforts.

Part IV — Behavior and Predictive Action

☐ **Your Behavior Overview** —
how you adapt to existing circumstances.

Communicating decisiveness	1	②③	4	5	+	1
Ability to stimulate and activate others	①②	3	4	5	+	1
Self-control	1	2	③④	5	+	1
Awareness of others' feelings	1	2	③④	5	+	1
Fairness	1	2	③④	5	+	1
Ability to see the whole, not merely the parts	1	2	③④	5	+	1
Working facts into a logical whole	1	2	③④	5	+	1
Sense of humor	1	②③	4	5	+	1
Handling of complex problems	1	2	3	④⑤	+	1
Concern for practical details	1	2	3	④⑤	+	1
Ability to size up another's character	1	2	③④	5	+	1

Calculation Section

	line 1 ____73____ %
Total of ⊕	line 2 _____ %
Add lines 1 & 2	line 3 _____ %
Total of plotting points in shaded graph areas	line 4 _____ %
Subtract line 4 from line 3	line 5 _____ %
	(GRAND TOTAL)

(See page 80 for directions.)

— Key No. 25 —
BEHAVIOR DYNAMICS

Part I — Behavior and Change

☐ **Your Behavior Description** — *the real you.* Key word is *fair-minded.* You wait for events to unfold; permit others to provide active leadership; test the suggestions of others; view yourself as one to say no rather than yes; appear discriminating in decision making.

☐ **Your Behavior Objectives** — *what you desire to be.* Key word is *availability.* You opt for more excitement; desire to take on responsibility for new ventures; assume obligations for expansion and development; lead by offering suggestions; wish to show alertness; observe others' reactions to events; improve the morale of friends and associates.

☐ **Your Behavior Change**

Degree of Change Occurring in Your Behavior		
Little	Some	Much
1.0 2.0	3.0 4.0	5.0

☐ **Your New Behavior** — *where you're going.* Key word is *receptive.* You become more open to things that are new, modern, or intriguing; increase contact with people; verbalize more clearly; show optimism regarding the future; demand more of yourself; emphasize your competence.

Part II — Behavior and Conflict

☐ **Your Behavior Under Pressure** — *how you handle objections.* You view alternatives to gain approval for your actions; show signs of insecurity when lacking specific or technical information; search for additional data to support your claims; show firmness when your preparation is thorough.

☐ **Your Internal Conflict** — *source of personal frustration.* You tend to feel overtaxed when others expect a continuous show of enthusiasm; feel pressure to respond with optimistic support—this concern may lead to *exhausted anticipation,* implying a reluctance to reveal your true feelings. You need time to sort through requests and demands.

Part III — Behavior and Control

☐ **Your Internal Motivation** — *how others may exert control with you.* Your motivation increases when others provide opportunities for you to: develop freely; shake off lingering self-doubts which have plagued you in the past; assume the role of stimulator to others.

☐ **Your Motivation of Others** — *how you exert control.* You influence others by providing insight into existing operations. You emphasize your investigative nature; believe others will save time and effort by relying upon your studied judgment.

Part IV — Behavior and Predictive Action

☐ Your Behavior Overview —
how you adapt to existing circumstances.

Communicating decisiveness	1	2 ③	④ 5	+	1
Ability to stimulate and activate others	1	② 3	4 5	+	1
Self-control	1	② 3	4 5	+	1
Awareness of others' feelings	1	2 ③	④ 5	+	1
Fairness	1	2 3	④ ⑤	+	1
Ability to see the whole, not merely the parts	1	② 3	4 5	+	1
Working facts into a logical whole	1	2 ③	④ 5	+	1
Sense of humor	1	② 3	4 5	+	1
Handling of complex problems	1	② 3	4 5	+	1
Concern for practical details	1	2 3	④ ⑤	+	1
Ability to size up another's character	1	② 3	4 5	+	1

Calculation Section

	line 1 ___69___ %
Total of ⊕1	line 2 _____ %
Add lines 1 & 2	line 3 _____ %
Total of plotting points in shaded graph areas	line 4 _____ %
Subtract line 4 from line 3	line 5 _____ %
	(GRAND TOTAL)

(See page 80 for directions.)

— Key No. 26 —

BEHAVIOR DYNAMICS

Part I — Behavior and Change

☐ **Your Behavior Description** — *the real you.* Key word is *astute.* You project a superiority; regard yourself as having the moral authority to correct others; show firmness of mind and conviction to your ideas; challenge others to review methods of operations.

☐ **Your Behavior Objectives** — *what you desire to be.* Key word is *advocate.* You desire to emphasize equality and protection of rights of others as well as your own; consider the needs of others to be as important as your own; wish to express dissatisfaction constructively; cope with unpleasantness; hope to avoid intense confrontation; project genuineness in your behavior.

☐ **Your Behavior Change**

Degree of Change Occurring in Your Behavior		
Little	Some	Much
1.0 2.0	3.0 4.0	5.0

☐ **Your New Behavior** — *where you're going.* Key word is *accepting.* You show an increased ability to discuss personal feelings; trust others; feel there is some good in everyone; earn rather than expect approval from others; increase your willingness to share in work.

Part II — Behavior and Conflict

☐ **Your Behavior Under Pressure** — *how you handle objections.* You use dramatization to make a salient point; introduce humor or another type of relief in a tense situation; cope with mixed feelings toward people by discovering what is best in each person; critically examine yourself and others.

☐ **Your Internal Conflict** — *source of personal frustration.* You tend to direct attention toward yourself; wish to pursue discussions of personal issues; feel that your concern for individual development should be meticulously explored—this belief may lead to *self-centeredness,* implying that your behavior should be exemplary to others. You aim at handling your own dissatisfaction before giving thought to how others may feel.

Part III — Behavior and Control

☐ **Your Internal Motivation** — *how others may exert control with you.* Your motivation increases when others provide opportunities for you to: prove your trust in others; shape group opinion; nurture growth of individuals; develop activities that serve as models for others.

☐ **Your Motivation of Others** — *how you exert control.* You influence others by making them aware of their responsibilities to each other. You emphasize the need to reexamine reasons why people do things; move others to self-affirmation—belief in who they are.

Part IV — Behavior and Predictive Action

☐ **Your Behavior Overview —**
how you adapt to existing circumstances.

Communicating decisiveness	1	2	3	(4 5)	+	1
Ability to stimulate and activate others	1	2	3	(4 5)	+	1
Self-control	1	2	(3 4)	5	+	1
Awareness of others' feelings	1	2	(3 4)	5	+	1
Fairness	1	(2 3)	4	5	+	1
Ability to see the whole, not merely the parts	1	2	(3 4)	5	+	1
Working facts into a logical whole	1	2	(3 4)	5	+	1
Sense of humor	1	2	(3 4)	5	+	1
Handling of complex problems	1	2	3	(4 5)	+	1
Concern for practical details	1	2	3	(4 5)	+	1
Ability to size up another's character	1	2	(3 4)	5	+	1

Calculation Section

	line 1 ____83____ %	
Total of (+1)	line 2 _____ %	
Add lines 1 & 2	line 3 _____ %	
Total of plotting points in shaded graph areas	line 4 _____ %	
Subtract line 4 from line 3	line 5 _____ %	
	(GRAND TOTAL)	

(See page 80 for directions.)

— Key No. 27 —

BEHAVIOR DYNAMICS

Part I — Behavior and Change

☐ **Your Behavior Description** — *the real you.* Key word is *restrained.* You depend upon expert advice; appear reserved and cautious; plan your responses in advance; make a serious issue all-consuming until a comfort level is reached; question the trust placed in emotional and impulsive people.

☐ **Your Behavior Objectives** — *what you desire to be.* Key word is *trustworthy.* You desire closeness in relationships; expect loyalty from friends and associates; harbor negative feelings for those who betray your trust; expect that affection be returned; show admiration for skilled associates—often tending to idealize them.

☐ **Your Behavior Change**

Degree of Change Occurring in Your Behavior		
Little	Some	Much
1.0 2.0	3.0 4.0	5.0

☐ **Your New Behavior** — *where you're going.* Key word is *sharing.* You show an increasingly more pleasant disposition; radiate warmth; display an ability to understand people; develop harmonious relationships; express a greater desire for sincerity and demonstrations of affection.

Part II — Behavior and Conflict

☐ **Your Behavior Under Pressure** — *how you handle objections.* You weigh options; follow a logical sequence of steps to select alternative solutions; refuse final pronouncements until complete analysis is made; urge others to seek second and even third opinions; refuse to operate with generalizations.

☐ **Your Internal Conflict** — *source of personal frustration.* You tend to have difficulty making crucial decisions; become hesitant and uncertain—this circumstance may lead to *vacillation,* implying an excessive reliance upon the strength and wisdom of others, which may cause them to doubt your ability to move quickly.

Part III — Behavior and Control

☐ **Your Internal Motivation** — *how others may exert control with you.* Your motivation increases when others provide opportunities for you to: demonstrate sympathy for the inadequate efforts of others; think and act independently; give direct supervision.

☐ **Your Motivation of Others** — *how you exert control.* You influence others by identifying with their weak areas. You emphasize the empathy you feel; use your expertise to guide others to a resolution.

Part IV — Behavior and Predictive Action

☐ Your Behavior Overview —
how you adapt to existing circumstances.

Communicating decisiveness	1	② ③	4	5	+	1
Ability to stimulate and activate others	1	② ③	4	5	+	1
Self-control	1	2	③ ④	5	+	1
Awareness of others' feelings	1	2	③ ④	5	+	1
Fairness	1	2	3	④ ⑤	+	1
Ability to see the whole, not merely the parts	1	2	③ ④	5	+	1
Working facts into a logical whole	1	2	3	④ ⑤	+	1
Sense of humor	1	2	③ ④	5	+	1
Handling of complex problems	1	2	3	④ ⑤	+	1
Concern for practical details	1	2	3	④ ⑤	+	1
Ability to size up another's character	1	2	③ ④	5	+	1

Calculation Section

	line 1 ___81___ %	
Total of ⊕	line 2 _____ %	
Add lines 1 & 2	line 3 _____ %	
Total of plotting points in shaded graph areas	line 4 _____ %	
Subtract line 4 from line 3	line 5 _____ %	
	(GRAND TOTAL)	

(See page 80 for directions.)

— Key No. 28 —
BEHAVIOR DYNAMICS

Part I — Behavior and Change

☐ **Your Behavior Description** — *the real you.* Key word is *forceful.* You look beyond existing circumstances and anticipate conflict; develop a predetermined game plan; demonstrate an offensive rather than a defensive stance; prefer win-lose actions; delegate details to others.

☐ **Your Behavior Objectives** — *what you desire to be.* Key word is *serious.* You desire a better way to handle conflict; seek clarification of issues; ask questions instead of forcing answers; wish to follow logical sequences to conclusions; desire to test the water before leaping.

☐ **Your Behavior Change**

Degree of Change Occurring in Your Behavior				
Little		Some		Much
1.0	2.0	3.0	4.0	5.0

☐ **Your New Behavior** — *where you're going.* Key word is *supportive.* You listen more carefully; become increasingly more patient; examine your intentions; deliberately take less from people; give more of yourself; show increased flexibility and accommodation to overcome difficulties.

Part II — Behavior and Conflict

☐ **Your Behavior Under Pressure** — *how you handle objections.* You view others' objections as opportunities to reaffirm yourself; authoritatively state your position; prepare thoroughly; provide more information than is necessary; use physical stamina that outlasts that of others.

☐ **Your Internal Conflict** — *source of personal frustration.* You tend to evoke curiosity with the projection of a two-sided image; show concern for people on one hand, exaggerated self-concern on the other— this attitude may lead to *ambiguous motivation,* implying that you are often misunderstood. Your desires are met with ambivalence; others view you as lacking depth of feeling.

Part III — Behavior and Control

☐ **Your Internal Motivation** — *how others may exert control with you.* Your motivation increases when others provide opportunities for you to: develop carefully designed plans; stick to goals; prove the wisdom of your procedure; gain substantial control of your activities.

☐ **Your Motivation of Others** — *how you exert control.* You influence others by determination. You push or pull to get what you desire; emphasize tenacity; show the fruit of hard labor and negotiation.

Part IV — Behavior and Predictive Action

☐ Your Behavior Overview —
how you adapt to existing circumstances.

Communicating decisiveness	1	2	3	④ ⑤	+	1
Ability to stimulate and activate others	1	2	③ ④	5	+	1
Self-control	1	2	3	④ ⑤	+	1
Awareness of others' feelings	1	② ③	4	5	+	1
Fairness	1	② ③	4	5	+	1
Ability to see the whole, not merely the parts	1	2	③ ④	5	+	1
Working facts into a logical whole	1	2	3	④ ⑤	+	1
Sense of humor	1	② ③	4	5	+	1
Handling of complex problems	1	2	③ ④	5	+	1
Concern for practical details	1	2	3	④ ⑤	+	1
Ability to size up another's character	1	2	③ ④	5	+	1

Calculation Section		
	line 1 ___79___ %	
Total of ⊕	line 2 _____ %	
Add lines 1 & 2	line 3 _____ %	
Total of plotting points in shaded graph areas	line 4 _____ %	
Subtract line 4 from line 3	line 5 _____ %	
	(GRAND TOTAL)	
(See page 80 for directions.)		

BEHAVIOR DYNAMICS

Part I — Behavior and Change

☐ **Your Behavior Description** — *the real you.* Key word is *resourceful.* You identify the exact basis for disagreement; resist emotional outbursts; place high priority on being unruffled; refuse to fully express your intentions or to tax your personal resources; look for better ways to solve complex problems.

☐ **Your Behavior Objectives** — *what you desire to be.* Key word is *original.* You seek reinforcement in your desire to bolster your self-esteem; use self-critical appraisal; wish to develop discrimination in your choice of people and events; complete tasks; urge others to adhere to the same strict schedule as you do.

☐ **Your Behavior Change**

Degree of Change Occurring in Your Behavior				
Little		Some		Much
1.0	2.0	3.0	4.0	5.0

☐ **Your New Behavior** — *where you're going.* Key word is *imaginative.* Little change is occurring in your behavior. You continue to make attempts to simplify complicated activities; stick to your beliefs; reveal a passionate conviction to set facts straight; remain firm in handling problems; tend to assume increased responsibility for specific details.

Part II — Behavior and Conflict

☐ **Your Behavior Under Pressure** — *how you handle objections.* You fight to stay in control; are wary of those who use emotional cliches; refuse to give in when the facts are on your side; use a form of silence; wear down the opposition.

☐ **Your Internal Conflict** — *source of personal frustration.* You tend to have overly high expectations of yourself and others; fail to satisfy personal hopes—this consequence may lead to *unexpressed pessimism,* implying fear of formulating fresh goals. You may fail to satisfy your need for achievement, experiencing stress and anxiety.

Part III — Behavior and Control

☐ **Your Internal Motivation** — *how others may exert control with you.* Your motivation increases when others provide opportunities for you to: solve problems that baffle others; demonstrate faithfulness to obligations; outperform others in design and application.

☐ **Your Motivation of Others** — *how you exert control.* You influence others by your realism. You emphasize the way it is; avoid sugarcoating; stress that an objective is attainable only when it is clearly defined.

Part IV — Behavior and Predictive Action

☐ **Your Behavior Overview** —
how you adapt to existing circumstances.

Communicating decisiveness	1	2	③	④	5	+	1
Ability to stimulate and activate others	1	②	③	4	5	+	1
Self-control	1	2	3	④	⑤	+	1
Awareness of others' feelings	1	2	③	④	5	+	1
Fairness	1	2	③	④	5	+	1
Ability to see the whole, not merely the parts	1	2	3	④	⑤	+	1
Working facts into a logical whole	1	2	3	④	⑤	+	1
Sense of humor	1	2	③	④	5	+	1
Handling of complex problems	1	2	3	④	⑤	+	1
Concern for practical details	1	2	③	④	5	+	1
Ability to size up another's character	1	2	③	④	5	+	1

Calculation Section

	line 1 ____83____ %
Total of (+1)	line 2 _____ %
Add lines 1 & 2	line 3 _____ %
Total of plotting points in shaded graph areas	line 4 _____ %
Subtract line 4 from line 3	line 5 _____ %
	(GRAND TOTAL)

(See page 80 for directions.)

— Key No. 30 —
BEHAVIOR DYNAMICS

Part I — Behavior and Change

☐ **Your Behavior Description** — *the real you.* Key word is *zestful.* You discover joy in living; replace worry with optimism and hope; show flexibility when dealing with solutions to problems; react spontaneously in structured environments; believe time restraints are for others.

☐ **Your Behavior Objectives** — *what you desire to be.* Key word is *approved.* You claim a wide sphere of personal influence; desire to form personal friendships with authority figures; seek new contacts; hope to discover ways to fulfill hopes.

☐ **Your Behavior Change**

Degree of Change Occurring in Your Behavior		
Little	Some	Much
1.0 2.0	3.0 4.0	5.0

☐ **Your New Behavior** — *where you're going.* Key word is *enchanting.* Little change is occurring in your behavior. You continue to select appropriate moods to fit each situation—active, talkative, friendly, or agreeable; develop routine graciousness and courtesy; feel relaxed, needed, and appreciated.

Part II — Behavior and Conflict

☐ **Your Behavior Under Pressure** — *how you handle objections.* You minimize personal attacks; separate yourself from conflict issues; take things in stride; agree that things can always be better; simplify answers; spread blame evenly; promise to get necessary data.

☐ **Your Internal Conflict** — *source of personal frustration.* You tend to spread your efforts over too wide an area; overextend your activities and commitment; make promises easily and often—this practice may lead to *broken hopes,* implying that others become disillusioned. Friends and associates grow wary and refuse to believe in you.

Part III — Behavior and Control

☐ **Your Internal Motivation** — *how others may exert control with you.* Your motivation increases when others provide opportunities for you to: open up new and better possibilities; encourage others to commit themselves to new experiences; stimulate people in proving their worth to themselves.

☐ **Your Motivation of Others** — *how you exert control.* You influence others by giving them a reason to believe, emphasizing the potential of a bright future; visualizing yourself and others as ascending stars; showing willingness to share your dream.

Part IV — Behavior and Predictive Action

☐ **Your Behavior Overview** —
how you adapt to existing circumstances.

Communicating decisiveness	(1 2)	3	4	5	+	1
Ability to stimulate and activate others	1 2 3	(4 5)	+	1
Self-control	(1 2)	3	4	5	+	1
Awareness of others' feelings	1 2	(3 4)	5	+	1
Fairness	1 2	(3 4)	5	+	1
Ability to see the whole, not merely the parts	1 (2 3)	4	5	+	1
Working facts into a logical whole	(1 2)	3	4	5	+	1
Sense of humor	1 2 3	(4 5)	+	1
Handling of complex problems	(1 2)	3	4	5	+	1
Concern for practical details	(1 2)	3	4	5	+	1
Ability to size up another's character	1 2	(3 4)	5	+	1

Calculation Section

	line 1 _____59_____ %
Total of (+1)	line 2 _____ %
Add lines 1 & 2	line 3 _____ %
Total of plotting points in shaded graph areas	line 4 _____ %
Subtract line 4 from line 3	line 5 _____ %
	(GRAND TOTAL)

(See page 80 for directions.)

— Key No. 31 —

BEHAVIOR DYNAMICS

Part I — Behavior and Change

☐ **Your Behavior Description** — *the real you.* Key word is *harmonious.* You place importance upon dates and events; recall memorable and meaningful experiences; reduce tensions between people; encourage cooperation in solving problems; demonstrate patience; meld individualistic ideas into group efforts.

☐ **Your Behavior Objectives** — *what you desire to be.* Key word is *peaceful.* You take delight in satisfying the needs of others; desire to live by the rules of the majority; counsel rather than cajole others to live by the rules and standards that are acceptable to you and your peers.

☐ **Your Behavior Change**

Degree of Change Occurring in Your Behavior		
Little	Some	Much
1.0 2.0	3.0 4.0	5.0

☐ **Your New Behavior** — *where you're going.* Key word is *adapting.* You show deliberateness in your effort; know what it is that you want; appear to be more serious-minded and thoughtful than in previous situations; find greater security through concentration and thoroughness; willingly change plans to fit the situation.

Part II — Behavior and Conflict

☐ **Your Behavior Under Pressure** — *how you handle objections.* You avoid outward signs of stress; respond to questions with full explanations; gather pertinent information; offer to revise or improve operating procedures.

☐ **Your Internal Conflict** — *source of personal frustration.* You tend to lose confidence when others become hostile and unfriendly; avoid challenges that may fall short of others' expectations—this attitude may lead to *anticipated rejection,* implying that excessive criticism hampers your involvement. You may tend to become immobilized in undesirable situations.

Part III — Behavior and Control

☐ **Your Internal Motivation** — *how others may exert control with you.* Your motivation increases when others provide opportunities for you to: prove loyalty to a respected person or cause; receive material compensation for work efforts, believing that words don't always adequately express appreciation.

☐ **Your Motivation of Others** — *how you exert control.* You influence others through your loyalty. You emphasize your acceptance of them, regardless of their behavior; provide support systems on which they can depend.

Part IV — Behavior and Predictive Action

☐ Your Behavior Overview —
how you adapt to existing circumstances.

Communicating decisiveness	① ②	3	4	5	+	1
Ability to stimulate and activate others	1 ② ③	4	5	+	1
Self-control	1 ② ③	4	5	+	1
Awareness of others' feelings	1 2 3 ④ ⑤	+	1
Fairness	1 2 ③ ④ 5	+	1
Ability to see the whole, not merely the parts	1 ② ③	4	5	+	1
Working facts into a logical whole	1 2 ③ ④ 5	+	1
Sense of humor	1 2 ③ ④ 5	+	1
Handling of complex problems	① ②	3	4	5	+	1
Concern for practical details	1 2 ③ ④ 5	+	1
Ability to size up another's character	1 2 ③ ④ 5	+	1

Calculation Section		
	line 1 ____65____ %	
Total of ⊕	line 2 _____ %	
Add lines 1 & 2	line 3 _____ %	
Total of plotting points in shaded graph areas	line 4 _____ %	
Subtract line 4 from line 3	line 5 _____ %	
	(GRAND TOTAL)	
(See page 80 for directions.)		

— *Key No. 32* —
BEHAVIOR DYNAMICS

Part I — Behavior and Change

☐ **Your Behavior Description** — *the real you.* Key word is *strong-willed.* You believe that what is good for you is good for others; arrive at methods that test the loyalty of others—challenge them to show the strength of their convictions; show self-control in your handling of time and effort; take the initiative.

☐ **Your Behavior Objectives** — *what you desire to be.* Key word is *diligent.* You desire to set the record straight; interpret issues; clear up ambiguous ideas and suggestions; desire to keep yourself and others on a direct course; attend to practical concerns such as cost, operations, and implementation of ideas.

☐ **Your Behavior Change**

Degree of Change Occurring in Your Behavior		
Little	Some	Much
1.0 2.0	3.0 4.0	5.0

☐ **Your New Behavior** — *where you're going.* Key word is *consistent.* You become increasingly more patient in dealing with agitation and irritation caused by critical people; begin to build and improve relationships; show restraint; offer meaningful facts and information.

Part II — Behavior and Conflict

☐ **Your Behavior Under Pressure** — *how you handle objections.* You dismiss the importance of the opposition's contention; view difficult questions as a challenge to demonstrate your wisdom; keep others on edge; prepare to spring unexpected responses.

☐ **Your Internal Conflict** — *source of personal frustration.* You tend to gain a position of strength through force; beat down the opposition; use reasoning only after impulsive action has begun—this practice may lead to *misdirected energy,* implying that your clear, concise reasoning is often too late, establishing you as one who thinks after the act.

Part III — Behavior and Control

☐ **Your Internal Motivation** — *how others may exert control with you.* Your motivation increases when others provide opportunities for you to: constructively resurrect floundering situations; assume an expert role in formulating a task or goal; demonstrate an ability to plan.

☐ **Your Motivation of Others** — *how you exert control.* You influence others with your strength to relentlessly pursue the cause of problems. You emphasize your tough-mindedness by testing others before they test you.

Part IV — Behavior and Predictive Action

☐ Your Behavior Overview —
how you adapt to existing circumstances.

Communicating decisiveness	1 2 3 (4 5)	+ 1
Ability to stimulate and activate others	1 2 (3 4) 5	+ 1
Self-control	1 2 3 (4 5)	+ 1
Awareness of others' feelings	(1 2) 3 4 5	+ 1
Fairness	1 (2 3) 4 5	+ 1
Ability to see the whole, not merely the parts	1 2 (3 4) 5	+ 1
Working facts into a logical whole	1 2 (3 4) 5	+ 1
Sense of humor	1 (2 3) 4 5	+ 1
Handling of complex problems	1 2 3 (4 5)	+ 1
Concern for practical details	1 2 (3 4) 5	+ 1
Ability to size up another's character	1 (2 3) 4 5	+ 1

Calculation Section

	line 1 ___73___ %
Total of (+1)	line 2 _____ %
Add lines 1 & 2	line 3 _____ %
Total of plotting points in shaded graph areas	line 4 _____ %
Subtract line 4 from line 3	line 5 _____ %
	(GRAND TOTAL)

(See page 80 for directions.)

— Key No. 33 —

BEHAVIOR DYNAMICS

Part I — Behavior and Change

☐ **Your Behavior Description** — *the real you.* Key word is *merging.* You relate well with people; participate in solving problems; rely upon others to furnish technical and specific detail; appear overly burdened, assuming responsibility for others; desire to be free of excessive tasks.

☐ **Your Behavior Objectives** — *what you desire to be.* Key word is *foresight.* You desire to create new opportunities on your own; hope to obtain an improved position; increase prestige; show unusual skill in communicating with others; plan to impose restrictions on those who neglect responsibility.

☐ **Your Behavior Change**

Degree of Change Occurring in Your Behavior		
Little	Some	Much
1.0 2.0	3.0 4.0	5.0

☐ **Your New Behavior** — *where you're going.* Key word is *liberating.* You show increased determination; make fewer concessions; refuse to compromise when it is not to your advantage; gain new respect and recognition of your achievements.

Part II — Behavior and Conflict

☐ **Your Behavior Under Pressure** — *how you handle objections.* You retreat when hostility is present; avoid confrontation by regrouping; join forces with respected allies; decide on a new course of action.

☐ **Your Internal Conflict** — *source of personal frustration.* You tend to involve yourself in situations beyond your capabilities or reserves of strength; look for outside confirmation of your ability; seek release by assigning high-failure risks to others—this practice may lead to *calculated maneuvering,* implying that you shift responsibility and potential blame from yourself.

Part III — Behavior and Control

☐ **Your Internal Motivation** — *how others may exert control with you.* Your motivation increases when others provide opportunities for you to: increase esteem both in your eyes and in the eyes of others; develop a structure in which individuals plan together and carry out tasks to benefit a common purpose.

☐ **Your Motivation of Others** — *how you exert control.* You influence others by showing proficiency in total operating procedures. You emphasize issues others have overlooked; gain respect for discovering weak links in an otherwise strong chain of activity.

Part IV — Behavior and Predictive Action

☐ Your Behavior Overview —
how you adapt to existing circumstances.

Communicating decisiveness	1	②③	4	5	+	1
Ability to stimulate and activate others	1	2	③④	5	+	1
Self-control	1	②③	4	5	+	1
Awareness of others' feelings	1	2	3	④⑤	+	1
Fairness	1	2	③④	5	+	1
Ability to see the whole, not merely the parts	1	②③	4	5	+	1
Working facts into a logical whole	1	②③	4	5	+	1
Sense of humor	1	2	③④	5	+	1
Handling of complex problems	1	2	3	④⑤	+	1
Concern for practical details	1	2	③④	5	+	1
Ability to size up another's character	1	2	③④	5	+	1

```
                    Calculation Section

                                    line 1 ____73____ %
            Total of (+1)           line 2 _____ %
            Add lines 1 & 2         line 3 _____ %
        Total of plotting points in
            shaded graph areas      line 4 _____ %
        Subtract line 4 from line 3 line 5 _____ %
                                       (GRAND TOTAL)

               (See page 80 for directions.)
```

BEHAVIOR DYNAMICS

Part I — Behavior and Change

☐ **Your Behavior Description** — *the real you*. Key word is *invigorating*. You project a steady and winsome personality; discover ways to please others; request a full explanation for even a hint of rejection of your ideas; show confidence in your specialized abilities; resent those who question your motivation.

☐ **Your Behavior Objectives** — *what you desire to be*. Key word is *credible*. You desire to be knowledgeable about subjects that will increase your influence with others; apply exacting standards to your behavior; wish to show caution in dealing with others; fear being taken advantage of in specialized areas; prepare for loss or disappointment in relationships; use critical appraisal of yourself and others.

☐ **Your Behavior Change**

Degree of Change Occurring in Your Behavior				
Little		Some		Much
1.0	2.0	3.0	4.0	5.0

☐ **Your New Behavior** — *where you're going*. Key word is *skeptical*. You demonstrate increased sensitivity; worry about possible injury to yourself and others; experience a sense of loneliness; discover events and settings where you exchange warmth and understanding with others; seek to prove yourself capable.

Part II — Behavior and Conflict

☐ **Your Behavior Under Pressure** — *how you handle objections*. You assist in solving problems; provide direction to others' thinking; willingly discuss feelings and ideas with accuracy; anticipate the positive and negative feelings of others; avoid overstating your position.

☐ **Your Internal Conflict** — *source of personal frustration*. You tend to feel temporarily cut off from a close friend or family; feel unhappy because of difficulty in achieving the degree of cooperation you desire—this perception may lead to *need for identification*, implying that you must form part of something or feel aligned and secure with someone.

Part III — Behavior and Control

☐ **Your Internal Motivation —** *how others may exert control with you.* Your motivation increases when others provide opportunities for you to: develop a comfortable and safe situation in which to feel secure; discover a peaceful state of harmony; form partnerships with those having a common goal.

☐ **Your Motivation of Others —** *how you exert control.* You influence others by securing a place for them—physically and psychologically. You emphasize the mutual need to satisfy desires of home, work, and social situations; attempt to fulfill your needs as well as those of others.

Part IV — Behavior and Predictive Action

☐ Your Behavior Overview —
how you adapt to existing circumstances.

Communicating decisiveness	1 2 ③ ④ 5 + 1	
Ability to stimulate and activate others	1 2 3 ④ ⑤ + 1	
Self-control	1 2 ③ ④ 5 + 1	
Awareness of others' feelings	1 2 ③ ④ 5 + 1	
Fairness	1 2 ③ ④ 5 + 1	
Ability to see the whole, not merely the parts	1 ② ③ 4 5 + 1	
Working facts into a logical whole	1 ② ③ 4 5 + 1	
Sense of humor	1 2 ③ ④ 5 + 1	
Handling of complex problems	1 ② ③ 4 5 + 1	
Concern for practical details	1 ② ③ 4 5 + 1	
Ability to size up another's character	1 2 ③ ④ 5 + 1	

Calculation Section

	line 1 _____71_____ %	
Total of ⊕	line 2 _____ %	
Add lines 1 & 2	line 3 _____ %	
Total of plotting points in shaded graph areas	line 4 _____ %	
Subtract line 4 from line 3	line 5 _____ %	
	(GRAND TOTAL)	

(See page 80 for directions.)

— *Key No. 35* —

BEHAVIOR DYNAMICS

Part I — Behavior and Change

☐ **Your Behavior Description** — *the real you.* Key word is *self-assured.* You willingly take on challenges; appear direct and bold; resolve conflicts constructively; use knowledge and skills; show self-reliance; plan events to ensure the desired outcome.

☐ **Your Behavior Objectives** — *what you desire to be.* Key word is *popular.* You desire to gain acceptance and immediate approval from others; seek escape from problems, difficulties, and tensions by exploring new experiences; broaden your field of activity; insist that hopes and ideas are realistic.

☐ **Your Behavior Change**

Degree of Change Occurring in Your Behavior		
Little	Some	Much
1.0 2.0	3.0 4.0	5.0

☐ **Your New Behavior** — *where you're going.* Key word is *appealing.* You use a full range of emotions; renew belief in yourself; seek energetic outlets; move willingly to show proof of successful patterns in relating with others—via letters, testimonials; sense a great destiny to influence events.

Part II — Behavior and Conflict

☐ **Your Behavior Under Pressure** — *how you handle objections.* You expect assistance from others; solicit those who are obligated to you for past favors; show self-control; ask others to handle minute details; apply energy and extraordinary effort.

☐ **Your Internal Conflict** — *source of personal frustration.* You tend to use overly optimistic statements; cover up for your frustrations; show impatience with slow development of events—this feeling may lead to *severe distress,* implying that others are to blame for your inability to fulfill promises and meet your personal objectives.

Part III — Behavior and Control

☐ **Your Internal Motivation** — *how others may exert control with you.* Your motivation increases when others provide opportunities for you to: uncover others' hidden potential as well as your own; have a wide sphere of influence; be imaginative; show optimism amidst adversity.

☐ **Your Motivation of Others** — *how you exert control.* You influence others through inspirational verbalization—all can be part of the dream. You emphasize that the success of the past influences the present and future as well; build upon the unique skills of others.

Part IV — Behavior and Predictive Action

☐ **Your Behavior Overview** —
how you adapt to existing circumstances.

Communicating decisiveness	1	2	3	(4	5)	+	1
Ability to stimulate and activate others	1	2	3	(4	5)	+	1
Self-control	1	2	3	(4	5)	+	1
Awareness of others' feelings	1	(2	3)	4	5	+	1
Fairness	1	(2	3)	4	5	+	1
Ability to see the whole, not merely the parts	1	2	(3	4)	5	+	1
Working facts into a logical whole	1	2	(3	4)	5	+	1
Sense of humor	1	2	3	(4	5)	+	1
Handling of complex problems	1	2	(3	4)	5	+	1
Concern for practical details	1	(2	3)	4	5	+	1
Ability to size up another's character	1	2	3	(4	5)	+	1

Calculation Section

	line 1 ____81____ %
Total of (+1)	line 2 _____ %
Add lines 1 & 2	line 3 _____ %
Total of plotting points in shaded graph areas	line 4 _____ %
Subtract line 4 from line 3	line 5 _____ %
	(GRAND TOTAL)

(See page 80 for directions.)

— Key No. 36 —
BEHAVIOR DYNAMICS

Part I — Behavior and Change

☐ **Your Behavior Description** — *the real you.* Key word is *forward-looking.* You show a good-natured, optimistic side; project personal warmth; easily grant and request favors; use connections that are unavailable to others; organize to make yourself look good.

☐ **Your Behavior Objectives** — *what you desire to be.* Key word is *self-reliant.* You desire to showcase your talent and skills; seek to appear self-confident, at times, self-controlling and rebellious toward authority; wish to cast off restrictions that impose on your freedom.

☐ **Your Behavior Change**

Degree of Change Occurring in Your Behavior		
Little	Some	Much
1.0 2.0	3.0 4.0	5.0

☐ **Your New Behavior** — *where you're going.* Key word is *flourishing.* You are increasingly anxious to assume leadership; willingly promote cooperation among friends and associates; withhold specific judgment of others, showing less willingness to share gossip items and more interest in sharing generalized accounts of your achievements.

Part II — Behavior and Conflict

☐ **Your Behavior Under Pressure** — *how you handle objections.* You give and take criticism; insist that negative appraisals are not threatening to your image, viewing them as learning experiences; make a concerted effort to be adaptable.

☐ **Your Internal Conflict** — *source of personal frustration.* You tend to outstrip the efforts of others; criticize the slow, sometimes hesitant movement of friends and associates; refuse to listen to excuses—this action may lead to *self-imposed superiority,* implying that others are not considered in the same league. You use caustic humor to prod them, often without success.

Part III — Behavior and Control

☐ **Your Internal Motivation** — *how others may exert control with you.* Your motivation increases when others provide opportunities for you to: experience upward mobility within a hierarchical system; move toward social activity and work progress at the same time.

☐ **Your Motivation of Others** — *how you exert control.* You influence others by being excited by your activities, attempting to show them how they can be involved as well. You emphasize the need to shed worry and pessimistic thinking; dwell on existing success, showing ways in which it can be extended.

Part IV — Behavior and Predictive Action

☐ Your Behavior Overview —
how you adapt to existing circumstances.

Communicating decisiveness	1	② ③	4	5	+	1
Ability to stimulate and activate others	1	2 3	④ ⑤		+	1
Self-control	1	② ③	4	5	+	1
Awareness of others' feelings	1	2 ③	④	5	+	1
Fairness	1	2 ③	④	5	+	1
Ability to see the whole, not merely the parts	1	② ③	4	5	+	1
Working facts into a logical whole	① ②	3	4	5	+	1
Sense of humor	1	2 3	④ ⑤		+	1
Handling of complex problems	① ②	3	4	5	+	1
Concern for practical details	① ②	3	4	5	+	1
Ability to size up another's character	1	2 ③	④	5	+	1

Calculation Section

	line 1 ____63____ %
Total of (+1)	line 2 _____ %
Add lines 1 & 2	line 3 _____ %
Total of plotting points in shaded graph areas	line 4 _____ %
Subtract line 4 from line 3	line 5 _____ %
	(GRAND TOTAL)

(See page 80 for directions.)

— *Key No. 37* —
BEHAVIOR DYNAMICS

Part I — Behavior and Change

☐ **Your Behavior Description** — *the real you.* Key word is *speculative.* You project yourself as cooperative in decision making but competitive in effort, attached and playful but compulsively driven to succeed; feel superior to those who question your authenticity; participate as a team player but often as a would-be superstar.

☐ **Your Behavior Objectives** — *what you desire to be.* Key word is *risk-taking.* You desire to take risks in the use of innovative methods to organize the efforts of people; demonstrate strength and resilience in chaotic situations; use determination to stabilize and bring order to failing situations; receive credit for results; provide guidance to others; influence consensus of opinion.

☐ **Your Behavior Change**

Degree of Change Occurring in Your Behavior		
Little	Some	Much
1.0 2.0	3.0 4.0	5.0

☐ **Your New Behavior** — *where you're going.* Key word is *vigorous.* You engage more often in competitive contests; find ways to develop skills; initiate a program to self-compare, self-monitor, and self-criticize; avoid deep encounters with yourself and others.

Part II — Behavior and Conflict

☐ **Your Behavior Under Pressure** — *how you handle objections.* You become talkative; downplay the meaningfulness of the event in which others confront you; handle difficult issues by switching the conversation to less tense issues; show willingness to document your position.

☐ **Your Internal Conflict** — *source of personal frustration.* You tend to delegate inventive tasks to others when your creative flair is temporarily restricted; hope others can fill the void even though they are untested—this practice may lead to *energized incompetence,* implying that others may be willing but not capable. This situation may set the stage for disillusionment.

Part III — Behavior and Control

☐ **Your Internal Motivation** — *how others may exert control with you.* Your motivation increases when others provide opportunities for you to: experiment with new projects; demonstrate an ability to initiate change; achieve status and gain monetary reward.

☐ **Your Motivation of Others** — *how you exert control.* You influence others through intense activity. You emphasize that things revolve around you; place others near you at the center of action, making them feel important.

Part IV — Behavior and Predictive Action

☐ Your Behavior Overview —
how you adapt to existing circumstances.

Communicating decisiveness	1	2	3	(4	5)	+	1
Ability to stimulate and activate others	1	2	3	(4	5)	+	1
Self-control	1	2	(3	4)	5	+	1
Awareness of others' feelings	1	(2	3)	4	5	+	1
Fairness	1	(2	3)	4	5	+	1
Ability to see the whole, not merely the parts	1	2	(3	4)	5	+	1
Working facts into a logical whole	1	(2	3)	4	5	+	1
Sense of humor	1	2	(3	4)	5	+	1
Handling of complex problems	1	2	(3	4)	5	+	1
Concern for practical details	(1	2)	3	4	5	+	1
Ability to size up another's character	1	2	(3	4)	5	+	1

Calculation Section

	line 1 ____71____ %
Total of (+1)	line 2 _____ %
Add lines 1 & 2	line 3 _____ %
Total of plotting points in shaded graph areas	line 4 _____ %
Subtract line 4 from line 3	line 5 _____ %
	(GRAND TOTAL)

(See page 80 for directions.)

BEHAVIOR DYNAMICS

Part I — Behavior and Change

☐ **Your Behavior Description** — *the real you.* Key word is *devoted.* You make attempts to fulfill promises; worry about details; show loyalty to close friends; find sympathy, caring, and responsiveness from people with close ties.

☐ **Your Behavior Objectives** — *what you desire to be.* Key word is *influential.* You desire to receive a favorable response from those outside your circle of close associates; respond to differences in people; hope to broaden your interests and become more accepting of people; state your intent to treat people alike.

☐ **Your Behavior Change**

Degree of Change Occurring in Your Behavior		
Little	Some	Much
1.0　　　2.0	3.0　　　4.0	5.0

☐ **Your New Behavior** — *where you're going.* Key word is *compelling.* You increasingly provide visible leadership; openly question others; improvise when necessary; become more talkative; refuse to take "no" for an answer; take greater pride in your personal achievements.

Part II — Behavior and Conflict

☐ **Your Behavior Under Pressure** — *how you handle objections.* You become conventional; confide in close friends; engage in secretive conversations; seek support from those with similar histories and experience; provide a full explanation of events; assume personal responsibility.

☐ **Your Internal Conflict** — *source of personal frustration.* You tend to devote time to developing numerous in-depth contacts with people; put off serious tasks which have high priority; disappoint those to whom you have given a commitment—this attitude may lead to *procrastination,* implying that you find it difficult to deal with your restless dissatisfaction and emotional disappointment.

Part III — Behavior and Control

☐ **Your Internal Motivation** — *how others may exert control with you.* Your motivation increases when others provide opportunities for you to: move a group toward satisfaction with interpersonal relations and goal attainment; use gentle persuasion in offering substantial ideas to others.

☐ **Your Motivation of Others** — *how you exert control.* You influence others through understanding of feelings. You identify the comfort level of people; pride yourself on knowing where people are psychologically and being able to meet them halfway.

Part IV — Behavior and Predictive Action

☐ Your Behavior Overview —
how you adapt to existing circumstances.

Communicating decisiveness	①②3 4 5 + 1
Ability to stimulate and activate others	①②3 4 5 + 1
Self-control	1 2 3④⑤ + 1
Awareness of others' feelings	1 2 3④⑤ + 1
Fairness	1 2 3④⑤ + 1
Ability to see the whole, not merely the parts	1②③4 5 + 1
Working facts into a logical whole	1②③4 5 + 1
Sense of humor	1②③4 5 + 1
Handling of complex problems	①②3 4 5 + 1
Concern for practical details	1 2③④5 + 1
Ability to size up another's character	1 2③④5 + 1

```
               Calculation Section

                              line 1 ___65___ %
        Total of (+1)         line 2 _____ %
      Add lines 1 & 2         line 3 _____ %
  Total of plotting points in
       shaded graph areas     line 4 _____ %
  Subtract line 4 from line 3 line 5 _____ %
                                  (GRAND TOTAL)

             (See page 80 for directions.)
```

— *Key No. 39* —

BEHAVIOR DYNAMICS

Part I — Behavior and Change

☐ **Your Behavior Description** — *the real you.* Key word is *relating.* You know your own feelings; accept and approve of yourself; seek to understand others; use terminology to encourage people—team play, togetherness; resolve conflicts through negotiation.

☐ **Your Behavior Objectives** — *what you desire to be.* Key word is *analytical.* You wish to focus intensely on one or two objectives in work and social activity; refuse to be deflected from personal goals; seek to concentrate on doing a few things well; show appropriate caution.

☐ **Your Behavior Change**

Degree of Change Occurring in Your Behavior		
Little	Some	Much
1.0 2.0	3.0 4.0	5.0

☐ **Your New Behavior** — *where you're going.* Key word is *comprehending.* You show greater discernment in selecting people with whom to share your interests and special projects; begin to socialize with those whose views are similar to your own; refuse to pry into the affairs of others.

Part II — Behavior and Conflict

☐ **Your Behavior Under Pressure** — *how you handle objections.* You surprise the opposition by being pleasant and receptive; search for commonality with those who appear sincere; encourage open expressions of positive and negative feelings.

☐ **Your Internal Conflict** — *source of personal frustration.* You tend to place the burden on others to initiate actions; prefer to wait and see how others react to new proposals; blame others when events move slowly—this attitude may lead to *unsettling indecisiveness,* implying that both you and others become irritable when there is delay in deciding a course of action.

Part III — Behavior and Control

☐ **Your Internal Motivation** — *how others may exert control with you.* Your motivation increases when others provide opportunities for you to: achieve special recognition and standing from people who are knowledgeable; interpret laws, rules, and regulations.

☐ **Your Motivation of Others** — *how you exert control.* You influence others by assuming the role of expert within the group. You emphasize the value of viewing both technical and behavioral components; project yourself as one to consult when either component is needed.

Part IV — Behavior and Predictive Action

☐ Your Behavior Overview —
how you adapt to existing circumstances.

Communicating decisiveness	(1 2) 3 4 5	+ 1
Ability to stimulate and activate others	1 2 (3 4) 5	+ 1
Self-control	1 (2 3) 4 5	+ 1
Awareness of others' feelings	1 2 3 (4 5)	+ 1
Fairness	1 2 3 (4 5)	+ 1
Ability to see the whole, not merely the parts	1 2 (3 4) 5	+ 1
Working facts into a logical whole	1 2 (3 4) 5	+ 1
Sense of humor	1 2 (3 4) 5	+ 1
Handling of complex problems	1 (2 3) 4 5	+ 1
Concern for practical details	1 (2 3) 4 5	+ 1
Ability to size up another's character	1 2 (3 4) 5	+ 1

Calculation Section

	line 1 ___71___ %
Total of (+1)	line 2 _____ %
Add lines 1 & 2	line 3 _____ %
Total of plotting points in shaded graph areas	line 4 _____ %
Subtract line 4 from line 3	line 5 _____ %
	(GRAND TOTAL)

(See page 80 for directions.)

— Key No. 40 —
BEHAVIOR DYNAMICS

Part I — Behavior and Change

☐ **Your Behavior Description** — *the real you.* Key word is *straightforward.* You persuade others to your point of view through factual information; take calculated risks; project strength of conviction in the rightness of your positon; withhold emotional arguments.

☐ **Your Behavior Objectives** — *what you desire to be.* Key word is *objective.* You wish to develop a fine eye for detail; respond when called upon to resolve complicated, detailed issues; avoid impulsiveness; respect those for whom you work; wait for appropriate cues from authority before proceeding; involve yourself as a trouble-shooter, questioning others' ability and effort to handle unexpected events.

☐ **Your Behavior Change**

Degree of Change Occurring in Your Behavior		
Little	Some	Much
1.0 2.0	3.0 4.0	5.0

☐ **Your New Behavior** — *where you're going.* Key word is *discriminating.* You make greater attempts to avoid conflict or disagreement; experience doubt in your ability to convince others in the present situation; seek release from the stress of difficult decision making; become more critical of brash people in your environment.

Part II — Behavior and Conflict

☐ **Your Behavior Under Pressure** — *how you handle objections.* You prepare a stubborn defense; emphasize discipline and control to handle unsolved problems; appeal to logic and reasoning; vigorously contend for your ideas.

☐ **Your Internal Conflict** — *source of personal frustration.* You tend to handle personal matters with meticulous care; maintain strong internal control; become disillusioned with your lack of influence outside your jurisdiction—this inability may lead to *exaggerated mistrust,* implying that you need to openly express your feelings and avoid secretly complaining.

Part III — Behavior and Control

☐ **Your Internal Motivation** — *how others may exert control with you.* Your motivation increases when others provide opportunities for you to: keep longstanding sacred beliefs healthy, steady, balanced, and well-insured; plan before promising; rely upon your own resources for direction.

☐ **Your Motivation of Others** — *how you exert control.* You influence others by promising stability. You remain steadfast and reliable in diversity; set the example for how to proceed; calm those who are impatient in their demands.

Part IV — Behavior and Predictive Action

☐ **Your Behavior Overview** —
how you adapt to existing circumstances.

Communicating decisiveness	(1	2)	3	4	5	+	1
Ability to stimulate and activate others	1	2	(3	4)	5	+	1
Self-control	1	2	3	(4	5)	+	1
Awareness of others' feelings	1	(2	3)	4	5	+	1
Fairness	1	2	(3	4)	5	+	1
Ability to see the whole, not merely the parts	1	2	(3	4)	5	+	1
Working facts into a logical whole	1	2	3	(4	5)	+	1
Sense of humor	1	(2	3)	4	5	+	1
Handling of complex problems	1	2	(3	4)	5	+	1
Concern for practical details	1	2	(3	4)	5	+	1
Ability to size up another's character	1	(2	3)	4	5	+	1

Calculation Section

	line 1 ____71____ %	
Total of (+1)	line 2 _____ %	
Add lines 1 & 2	line 3 _____ %	
Total of plotting points in shaded graph areas	line 4 _____ %	
Subtract line 4 from line 3	line 5 _____ %	
	(GRAND TOTAL)	

(See page 80 for directions.)

— *Key No. 41* —

BEHAVIOR DYNAMICS

Part I — Behavior and Change

☐ **Your Behavior Description** — *the real you.* Key word is *closeness.* You rely upon the strength of "protective" friends; expect others to offer assistance; merge your personal interests with institutions of home, work, and spiritual emphasis.

☐ **Your Behavior Objectives** — *what you desire to be.* Key word is *counselor.* You seek to use diplomatic skills; desire to be articulate in expressing needs and ways to satisfy those conditions; hope to manage life at a steady and purposeful pace; cultivate long-term friendships; nurture deeper relationships with special friends.

☐ **Your Behavior Change**

Degree of Change Occurring in Your Behavior		
Little	Some	Much
1.0 2.0	3.0 4.0	5.0

☐ **Your New Behavior** — *where you're going.* Key word is *unifying.* You increasingly reflect a calm, thoughtful manner in selecting areas of interest; respond more readily to tasteful and aesthetic expression; appear more relaxed, waiting for inspiration; allow events to happen.

Part II — Behavior and Conflict

☐ **Your Behavior Under Pressure** — *how you handle objections.* You make amends; tend to place blame on yourself for shortcomings; seek corrective measures that lie outside yourself; request specialized help; often take the gratitude of others for granted; pay attention to specific details.

☐ **Your Internal Conflict** — *source of personal frustration.* You tend to make others dependent upon your advice and good will; willingly take time to console people, taking the opportunity to discuss your personal problems as well—this practice may lead to *dependency denial,* implying that you rely on others as much as they do on you. You refuse to acknowledge your need, irritating others by your denial.

Part III — Behavior and Control

☐ **Your Internal Motivation** — *how others may exert control with you.* Your motivation increases when others provide opportunities for you to: work for recognition; gain status; help others receive equal opportunity; make sacrifices for close friends.

☐ **Your Motivation of Others** — *how you exert control.* You influence others by being present when they are in need, providing ongoing support. You let others know your availability to listen, to be near.

Part IV — Behavior and Predictive Action

☐ **Your Behavior Overview** —
how you adapt to existing circumstances.

Communicating decisiveness	1	(2 3)	4	5	+	1
Ability to stimulate and activate others	1	2 (3 4)	5		+	1
Self-control	(1 2)	3	4	5	+	1
Awareness of others' feelings	1	2 3 (4 5)			+	1
Fairness	1	2 (3 4)	5		+	1
Ability to see the whole, not merely the parts	1	(2 3)	4	5	+	1
Working facts into a logical whole	1	(2 3)	4	5	+	1
Sense of humor	1	2 (3 4)	5		+	1
Handling of complex problems	(1 2)	3	4	5	+	1
Concern for practical details	1	2 3 (4 5)			+	1
Ability to size up another's character	1	2 (3 4)	5		+	1

Calculation Section

	line 1 ____67____ %	
Total of (+1)	line 2 _____ %	
Add lines 1 & 2	line 3 _____ %	
Total of plotting points in shaded graph areas	line 4 _____ %	
Subtract line 4 from line 3	line 5 _____ %	
	(GRAND TOTAL)	

(See page 80 for directions.)

— Key No. 42 —

BEHAVIOR DYNAMICS

Part I — Behavior and Change

☐ **Your Behavior Description** — *the real you.* Key word is *defensive.* You rely upon keen observation—read, experience, and collect information; provide interpretations of events when it is to your benefit; keep your intentions closely guarded; protect your real feelings.

☐ **Your Behavior Objectives** — *what you desire to be.* Key word is *independent.* You desire to develop original ideas; do things on your own; combine logic and analysis with decisiveness; reject offers from those desiring to be your spokesperson; rely on the ingenuity of your suggestions to guarantee their acceptance.

☐ **Your Behavior Change**

Degree of Change Occurring in Your Behavior				
Little		Some		Much
1.0	2.0	3.0	4.0	5.0

☐ **Your New Behavior** — *where you're going.* Key word is *confronting.* You show increased forcefulness; confront those who desire to look good at your expense; protect the integrity of your ideas, taking appropriate credit.

Part II — Behavior and Conflict

☐ **Your Behavior Under Pressure** — *how you handle objections.* You encourage others to make a final ruling on comparison of facts; hope difficulty will dissipate; avoid emotional confrontation; expect the worst; show a sense of preparation.

☐ **Your Internal Conflict** — *source of personal frustration.* You tend to yield what was gained by struggle for newly acquired freedom and independence; desire to maintain what is rightfully yours—this action may lead to *anxious compliance,* implying that you tend to experience self-effacement and unfair treatment by yielding on certain points.

Part III — Behavior and Control

☐ **Your Internal Motivation** — *how others may exert control with you.* Your motivation increases when others provide opportunities for you to: remodel circumstances; locate the cause of problems; experience different sensations; gain emotional independence and self-reliance.

☐ **Your Motivation of Others** — *how you exert control.* You influence others through the use of essential information. You emphasize your ability to interpret and use data that will open blocked communication.

Part IV — Behavior and Predictive Action

☐ **Your Behavior Overview** — *how you adapt to existing circumstances.*

Communicating decisiveness	1	②③	4	5	+	1
Ability to stimulate and activate others	①②	3	4	5	+	1
Self-control	1	2	③④	5	+	1
Awareness of others' feelings	1	②③	4	5	+	1
Fairness	1	2	3	④⑤	+	1
Ability to see the whole, not merely the parts	1	2	③④	5	+	1
Working facts into a logical whole	1	2	3	④⑤	+	1
Sense of humor	1	②③	4	5	+	1
Handling of complex problems	1	2	③④	5	+	1
Concern for practical details	1	2	③④	5	+	1
Ability to size up another's character	1	②③	4	5	+	1

Calculation Section

	line 1 _____69_____ %
Total of ⊕1	line 2 _____ %
Add lines 1 & 2	line 3 _____ %
Total of plotting points in shaded graph areas	line 4 _____ %
Subtract line 4 from line 3	line 5 _____ %
	(GRAND TOTAL)

(See page 80 for directions.)

— Key No. 43 —
BEHAVIOR DYNAMICS

Part I — Behavior and Change

☐ **Your Behavior Description** — *the real you.* Key word is *alert.* You keep watch of how others react to your activities; maintain a behavior code within general guidelines; desire strict control of your emotions; avoid exaggerated behavior; observe the change in your present work and social environment; weigh options to decide on the best direction.

☐ **Your Behavior Objectives** — *what you desire to be.* Key word is *steadfast.* You desire to set a clear example for others; show a consistency of effort; do for people what they find difficult to do for themselves; check details; organize; establish good will.

☐ **Your Behavior Change**

Degree of Change Occurring in Your Behavior		
Little	Some	Much
1.0 2.0	3.0 4.0	5.0

☐ **Your New Behavior** — *where you're going.* Key word is *committing.* You look to others for stimulation of your activities, acknowledging their uniqueness and originality; improve your self-image by emulating successful associates; attempt to discover personal strength—your uniqueness.

Part II — Behavior and Conflict

☐ **Your Behavior Under Pressure** — *how you handle objections.* You express willingness to negotiate; want to make a favorable impression; desire to be regarded as a special personality; display preventive measures, rules, regulations; commit extra effort to satisfy the demands of others.

☐ **Your Internal Conflict** — *source of personal frustration.* You tend to be ambivalent in selecting your goals and the rewards you desire for your efforts; want to provide human service, yet are anxious for materialistic gain—this quandary may lead to *anxiety and dissatisfaction,* implying uncertainty about the way in which you will become involved with people and how you communicate your dependence upon their assistance in your efforts.

Part III — Behavior and Control

☐ **Your Internal Motivation** — *how others may exert control with you.* Your motivation increases when others provide opportunities for you to: become involved in efforts in which individuals have mutual respect; be free from discord and disunity; support fundamental issues which utilize your uniqueness.

☐ **Your Motivation of Others** — *how you exert control.* You influence others by setting an example of behavior control. You emphasize the importance of balance in life; instill the belief that risks can be taken without a structured environment.

Part IV — Behavior and Predictive Action

☐ **Your Behavior Overview —**
how you adapt to existing circumstances.

Communicating decisiveness	1 2 ③ ④ 5	+ 1
Ability to stimulate and activate others	1 2 ③ ④ 5	+ 1
Self-control	1 ② ③ 4 5	+ 1
Awareness of others' feelings	1 2 ③ ④ 5	+ 1
Fairness	1 2 3 ④ ⑤	+ 1
Ability to see the whole, not merely the parts	1 2 ③ ④ 5	+ 1
Working facts into a logical whole	1 2 ③ ④ 5	+ 1
Sense of humor	1 2 ③ ④ 5	+ 1
Handling of complex problems	1 2 ③ ④ 5	+ 1
Concern for practical details	1 2 ③ ④ 5	+ 1
Ability to size up another's character	1 2 3 ④ ⑤	+ 1

Calculation Section

	line 1 ___79___ %
Total of (+1)	line 2 _____ %
Add lines 1 & 2	line 3 _____ %
Total of plotting points in shaded graph areas	line 4 _____ %
Subtract line 4 from line 3	line 5 _____ %
	(GRAND TOTAL)

(See page 80 for directions.)

— *Key No. 44* —
BEHAVIOR DYNAMICS

Part I — Behavior and Change

☐ **Your Behavior Description** — *the real you.* Key word is *controlling.* You cause uneasiness in others; set yourself up as a source of knowledge; cause others to doubt their ability; downgrade the skill of those who vie with you for control; minimize competitive events in which you do not excel.

☐ **Your Behavior Objectives** — *what you desire to be.* Key word is *admired.* You desire to be selective in your choice of close friends; identify those whom you can trust; improve in your communication with others; become a fascinating conversationalist; use substance of thought; show conscientiousness; adhere to principles that respected friends share.

☐ **Your Behavior Change**

Degree of Change Occurring in Your Behavior		
Little	Some	Much
1.0 2.0	3.0 4.0	5.0

☐ **Your New Behavior** — *where you're going.* Key word is *believable.* You increase your belief in people; look for good in others which can be useful to yourself as well; show increased sensitivity; relate activities to your stated purpose in life.

Part II — Behavior and Conflict

☐ **Your Behavior Under Pressure** — *how you handle objections.* You display anger, hoping that others will retreat; use delaying tactics; slow down the process and progress of activities you dislike; appear to be unsettled by others' impulsive actions.

☐ **Your Internal Conflict** — *source of personal frustration.* You tend to set high standards for people who potentially threaten your position; critically judge others' expectations and inspirations—this tendency may lead to a *defensive posture,* implying that you will separate yourself from the very people who can be most helpful to you.

Part III — Behavior and Control

☐ **Your Internal Motivation** — *how others may exert control with you.*
Your motivation increases when others provide opportunities for you
to: prove emotional stability; order your priorities—self-development
first, followed by financial and material gains.

☐ **Your Motivation of Others** — *how you exert control.* You influence
others by guiding them through difficult times. You emphasize your
ability to be assertive as well as knowledgeable in perceiving danger;
minimize others who make pledges that are similar to yours.

Part IV — Behavior and Predictive Action

☐ Your Behavior Overview —
how you adapt to existing circumstances.

Communicating decisiveness	1	2	3	④ ⑤	+	1
Ability to stimulate and activate others	1	2	③ ④	5	+	1
Self-control	1	2	3	④ ⑤	+	1
Awareness of others' feelings	① ②	3	4	5	+	1
Fairness	1	2	3	④ ⑤	+	1
Ability to see the whole, not merely the parts	1	2	③ ④	5	+	1
Working facts into a logical whole	1	2	③ ④	5	+	1
Sense of humor	1	2	③ ④	5	+	1
Handling of complex problems	1	2	3	④ ⑤	+	1
Concern for practical details	1	② ③	4	5	+	1
Ability to size up another's character	1	2	③ ④	5	+	1

Calculation Section

	line 1 ___79___ %
Total of ⊕1	line 2 _____ %
Add lines 1 & 2	line 3 _____ %
Total of plotting points in shaded graph areas	line 4 _____ %
Subtract line 4 from line 3	line 5 _____ %
	(GRAND TOTAL)

(See page 80 for directions.)

— Key No. 45 —
BEHAVIOR DYNAMICS

Part I — Behavior and Change

☐ **Your Behavior Description** — *the real you.* Key word is *purposeful.* You persuade others to accept your beliefs; gain your objectives by developing a stern, firm position; remove doubts or vulnerable areas; use convincing emotions and facts; show insight into the character of others.

☐ **Your Behavior Objectives** — *what you desire to be.* Key word is *persistent.* You desire to follow through on your commitments; attempt to use common-sense judgment; utilize facts and reasoning to draw conclusions; make inferences; develop feelings in common with friends and associates.

☐ **Your Behavior Change**

Degree of Change Occurring in Your Behavior		
Little	Some	Much
1.0 2.0	3.0 4.0	5.0

☐ **Your New Behavior** — *where you're going.* Key word is *persevering.* You show increased sincerity in relationships; avoid prejudging others; need consideration and understanding from others; become more conventional and private in thinking and acting; protect yourself from arguments and conflict more than before.

Part II — Behavior and Conflict

☐ **Your Behavior Under Pressure** — *how you handle objections.* You give effective rebuttal; appear in a better light than those who provide opposition; take advantage of objections raised; use others' questioning format to raise new issues; launch fresh ideas.

☐ **Your Internal Conflict** — *source of personal frustration.* You tend to insist that people live by your expectations; frown on lifestyles and work methods that differ from the traditional; persuade others to your point of view—tendency may lead to *sameness;* implying that you tend to reject those who march to a different drummer. You fail to stretch your thinking and hamper the originality of those around you.

Part III — Behavior and Control

☐ **Your Internal Motivation** — *how others may exert control with you.* Your motivation increases when others provide opportunities for you to: share ideas, plans, and hopes with those who are trustworthy and loyal; structure a situation by first selecting key people.

☐ **Your Motivation of Others** — *how you exert control.* You influence others through your insight into the motivation of people. You emphasize understanding gained from experiences rather than from theory; startle others with your ability to know people quickly and deeply.

Part IV — Behavior and Predictive Action

☐ Your Behavior Overview —
how you adapt to existing circumstances.

Communicating decisiveness	1	2	3	④ ⑤	+	1
Ability to stimulate and activate others	1	2	3	④ ⑤	+	1
Self-control	1	② ③	4	5	+	1
Awareness of others' feelings	1	2	③ ④	5	+	1
Fairness	1	2	3	④ ⑤	+	1
Ability to see the whole, not merely the parts	1	2	③ ④	5	+	1
Working facts into a logical whole	1	2	③ ④	5	+	1
Sense of humor	1	2	3	④ ⑤	+	1
Handling of complex problems	1	2	③ ④	5	+	1
Concern for practical details	1	2	③ ④	5	+	1
Ability to size up another's character	1	2	3	④ ⑤	+	1

Calculation Section

	line 1 ___85___ %
Total of ⊕	line 2 _____ %
Add lines 1 & 2	line 3 _____ %
Total of plotting points in shaded graph areas	line 4 _____ %
Subtract line 4 from line 3	line 5 _____ %
	(GRAND TOTAL)

(See page 80 for directions.)

— Key No. 46 —
BEHAVIOR DYNAMICS

Part I — Behavior and Change

☐ **Your Behavior Description —** *the real you.* Key word is *street-smart.* You display little, if any, sympathy for those who lose to you in competition; reject claims of innocent mistakes; urge others to take full responsibility for their actions; demand reason above emotion; insist on apology from those who fall short.

☐ **Your Behavior Objectives —** *what you desire to be.* Key word is *opportunistic.* You desire to be accepted for your unusual talents; develop ideas that will fulfill your hopes and ambitions; share ways in which others can effectively develop their potential; excite and move others to action.

☐ **Your Behavior Change**

Degree of Change Occurring in Your Behavior		
Little	Some	Much
1.0 2.0	3.0 4.0	5.0

☐ **Your New Behavior —** *where you're going.* Key word is *industrious.* You show increased talent in handling difficult problems; gain recognition through improved verbal skills; encourage rather than alienate those who are reluctant to accept your ideas.

Part II — Behavior and Conflict

☐ **Your Behavior Under Pressure —** *how you handle objections.* You take criticism personally; vow to get revenge when others are overly combative; firmly state your position, based upon facts; refuse to back down unless forced.

☐ **Your Internal Conflict —** *source of personal frustration.* You tend to encourage others to compete with you for similar goals; believe all can gain by being driven toward success—belief may lead to *ill-considered actions,* implying that allowance is not made for those who perform better in a noncompetitive situation. For some, stress is greatly increased when you make competitive those things which are best set in a cooperative mode.

Part III — Behavior and Control

☐ **Your Internal Motivation** — *how others may exert control with you.* Your motivation increases when others provide opportunities for you to: develop strong leadership ability in people; change motivations of others; occupy yourself with ideas and events of an intensely exciting nature.

☐ **Your Motivation of Others** — *how you exert control.* You influence others by demanding respect for what you have done for them. You emphasize their need to repay obligations. In turn, they learn to relate to others with a similar type of firmness.

Part IV — Behavior and Predictive Action

☐ Your Behavior Overview —
how you adapt to existing circumstances.

Communicating decisiveness	1	2	3	④	⑤	+	1
Ability to stimulate and activate others	1	2	3	④	⑤	+	1
Self-control	1	2	③	④	5	+	1
Awareness of others' feelings	1	②	③	4	5	+	1
Fairness	①	②	3	4	5	+	1
Ability to see the whole, not merely the parts	1	2	③	④	5	+	1
Working facts into a logical whole	1	②	③	4	5	+	1
Sense of humor	1	2	③	④	5	+	1
Handling of complex problems	1	2	③	④	5	+	1
Concern for practical details	①	②	3	4	5	+	1
Ability to size up another's character	1	2	③	④	5	+	1

Calculation Section

	line 1 ____69____ %
Total of (+1)	line 2 _____ %
Add lines 1 & 2	line 3 _____ %
Total of plotting points in shaded graph areas	line 4 _____ %
Subtract line 4 from line 3	line 5 _____ %
	(GRAND TOTAL)

(See page 80 for directions.)

— *Key No. 47* —

BEHAVIOR DYNAMICS

Part I — Behavior and Change

☐ **Your Behavior Description** — *the real you.* Key word is *particular.* You exert relentless pressure on those who cause you discomfort; need to be independent and investigative; determine to be correct; demand an apology when others make mistakes; do not easily forget or forgive those who lead you astray.

☐ **Your Behavior Objectives** — *what you desire to be.* Key word is *personable.* You desire to appear calm in the midst of crisis; develop skills that others lack; appear equally comfortable conversing with groups of people and doing things requiring solitude and concentration; find ways to cope with unpleasantness; excel in keeping promises.

☐ **Your Behavior Change**

Degree of Change Occurring in Your Behavior		
Little	Some	Much
1.0 2.0	3.0 4.0	5.0

☐ **Your New Behavior** — *where you're going.* Key word is *accommodating.* You increasingly combine people problem-solving methods with technical systems; show sensitivity in handling others, reinforcing them through approval and acceptance; develop more satisfying interaction with close friends.

Part II — Behavior and Conflict

☐ **Your Behavior Under Pressure** — *how you handle objections.* You make extensive preparation; anxiously confront the opposition; use counter-arguments; avoid the role of scapegoat; willingly point an accusing finger at disruptive sources.

☐ **Your Internal Conflict** — *source of personal frustration.* You tend to encourage order and acceptance of responsibility; put things in their proper place; penalize those who foul up the system—this action may lead to *discriminating control*, implying that your attempts at precision and exactitude border on the fussy and oversolicitous, making others feel threatened.

Part III — Behavior and Control

☐ **Your Internal Motivation** — *how others may exert control with you.* Your motivation increases when others provide opportunities for you to: develop creativeness in a structured rather than an unstructured environment; assist in personal growth of people with both social and science backgrounds.

☐ **Your Motivation of Others** — *how you exert control.* You influence others through your determination. You emphasize completeness; gain support from those who desire closure in their lives; reduce uncertainty and disorganization.

Part IV — Behavior and Predictive Action

☐ Your Behavior Overview —
how you adapt to existing circumstances.

Communicating decisiveness	1 ②③ 4 5	+ 1
Ability to stimulate and activate others	1 2 ③④ 5	+ 1
Self-control	1 2 3 ④⑤	+ 1
Awareness of others' feelings	1 ②③ 4 5	+ 1
Fairness	1 2 ③④ 5	+ 1
Ability to see the whole, not merely the parts	1 2 3 ④⑤	+ 1
Working facts into a logical whole	1 2 3 ④⑤	+ 1
Sense of humor	1 ②③ 4 5	+ 1
Handling of complex problems	1 2 3 ④⑤	+ 1
Concern for practical details	1 2 ③④ 5	+ 1
Ability to size up another's character	1 ②③ 4 5	+ 1

```
Calculation Section

                                  line 1 ____77____ %
              Total of (+1)       line 2 _____ %
           Add lines 1 & 2        line 3 _____ %
    Total of plotting points in
          shaded graph areas      line 4 _____ %
    Subtract line 4 from line 3   line 5 _____ %
                                      (GRAND TOTAL)

          (See page 80 for directions.)
```

— Key No. 48 —
BEHAVIOR DYNAMICS

Part I — Behavior and Change

☐ **Your Behavior Description** — *the real you*. Key word is *demanding*. You insist on demonstrating superiority in personal thinking and acting; set unrealistic time limits for yourself and others; show impatience with hesitancy and slowness in others; rely on your own strength rather than accepting assistance from others.

☐ **Your Behavior Objectives** — *what you desire to be*. Key word is *precise*. You desire to follow a clear, concise philosophy of work life and social activity; guard against attempts by others to change your personal beliefs and procedures; seek to justify your style of life; insist on clear-cut, unequivocal dealings.

☐ **Your Behavior Change**

Degree of Change Occurring in Your Behavior		
Little	Some	Much
1.0 2.0	3.0 4.0	5.0

☐ **Your New Behavior** — *where you're going*. Key word is *conscientious*. You reason from logical conclusions; increase your ability to understand and evaluate your reality and that of others; place greater attention on your personal achievements; observe the distance between where you are and where you should be; show ingenuity and quick understanding of issues.

Part II — Behavior and Conflict

☐ **Your Behavior Under Pressure** — *how you handle objections*. You challenge accusations; judge the motivations of others; receive criticism for being insensitive; exploit the weakness of others, placing them on the defensive; secretly deny your inner feelings of inferiority in the face of strong opposition.

☐ **Your Internal Conflict** — *source of personal frustration*. You tend to provide a full accounting of any situation; insist on stating the exact truth, as you view it; become overly complicated—this tendency may lead to *obstinate exclusion,* implying defiant obstinacy and rigid adherence to your own point of view.

Part III — Behavior and Control

☐ **Your Internal Motivation** — *how others may exert control with you.* Your motivation increases when others provide opportunities for you to: be valued and respected as an exceptional individual; develop systems with underlying philosophy; communicate deep-seated beliefs and ideas.

☐ **Your Motivation of Others** — *how you exert control.* You influence others with your insistence on being right. You emphasize that an attack on you will be the demise of all that others have worked hard to accomplish.

Part IV — Behavior and Predictive Action

☐ **Your Behavior Overview —**
how you adapt to existing circumstances.

Communicating decisiveness	1	2	3	④	⑤	+	1
Ability to stimulate and activate others	1	2	③	④	5	+	1
Self-control	1	2	3	④	⑤	+	1
Awareness of others' feelings	①	②	3	4	5	+	1
Fairness	1	②	③	4	5	+	1
Ability to see the whole, not merely the parts	1	2	3	④	⑤	+	1
Working facts into a logical whole	1	2	3	④	⑤	+	1
Sense of humor	1	②	③	4	5	+	1
Handling of complex problems	1	2	3	④	⑤	+	1
Concern for practical details	1	2	③	④	5	+	1
Ability to size up another's character	1	②	③	4	5	+	1

Calculation Section		
	line 1 ____77____ %	
Total of ⊕1	line 2 _____ %	
Add lines 1 & 2	line 3 _____ %	
Total of plotting points in shaded graph areas	line 4 _____ %	
Subtract line 4 from line 3	line 5 _____ %	
	(GRAND TOTAL)	

(See page 80 for directions.)

— Key No. 49 —
BEHAVIOR DYNAMICS

Part I — Behavior and Change

☐ **Your Behavior Description** — *the real you.* Key word is *expressive.* You are open to new ideas and possibilities; seek approval from others; extend overly generous offers to contribute time and effort; often refuse to admit your mistakes, dismissing them as minor and unimportant.

☐ **Your Behavior Objectives** — *what you desire to be.* Key word is *amiable.* You desire to make a favorable impression and be recognized for stabilizing situations—home and work; respond to the unique needs of people; unite people into productive units; develop peaceful relationships.

☐ **Your Behavior Change**

Degree of Change Occurring in Your Behavior		
Little	Some	Much
1.0 2.0	3.0 4.0	5.0

☐ **Your New Behavior** — *where you're going.* Key word is *moderate.* You increasingly attend to specific details; remind people of their obligations; encourage others to complete tasks; show willingness to set an example of dedication to work and effort; urge conscientiousness and loyalty to agreements.

Part II — Behavior and Conflict

☐ **Your Behavior Under Pressure** — *how you handle objections.* You win support by charm and amiability; use appropriate timing to coincide with others' mood and disposition; pass over your own shortcomings; insist on moving to the "big picture."

☐ **Your Internal Conflict** — *source of personal frustration.* You tend to be very particular in your choice of partner and associate; believe that you have a wide selection from which to choose; use excessive time in screening candidates—this tendency may lead to *exaggerated importance,* implying that nothing is too good for you. Often it is a one-way street—your way.

Part III — Behavior and Control

☐ **Your Internal Motivation** — *how others may exert control with you.* Your motivation increases when others provide opportunities for you to: use emotional enthusiasm; be helpful in creating a situation in which lasting bonds can be developed; encourage others to peacefully coexist.

☐ **Your Motivation of Others** — *how you exert control.* You influence others by making them see reality. You emphasize your newly gained insight; bring others to an appreciation of each other.

Part IV — Behavior and Predictive Action

☐ Your Behavior Overview —
how you adapt to existing circumstances.

Communicating decisiveness	① ② 3 4 5	+	1
Ability to stimulate and activate others	1 2 3 ④ ⑤	+	1
Self-control	① ② 3 4 5	+	1
Awareness of others' feelings	1 2 3 ④ ⑤	+	1
Fairness	1 2 ③ ④ 5	+	1
Ability to see the whole, not merely the parts	① ② 3 4 5	+	1
Working facts into a logical whole	① ② 3 4 5	+	1
Sense of humor	1 2 3 ④ ⑤	+	1
Handling of complex problems	① ② 3 4 5	+	1
Concern for practical details	1 2 ③ ④ 5	+	1
Ability to size up another's character	1 2 ③ ④ 5	+	1

Calculation Section

	line 1 ___63___ %
Total of (+1)	line 2 _____ %
Add lines 1 & 2	line 3 _____ %
Total of plotting points in shaded graph areas	line 4 _____ %
Subtract line 4 from line 3	line 5 _____ %
	(GRAND TOTAL)

(See page 80 for directions.)

— *Key No. 50* —
BEHAVIOR DYNAMICS

Part I — Behavior and Change

☐ **Your Behavior Description** — *the real you.* Key word is *no-nonsense.* You move decisively; believe in claiming what can be yours; attack rather than defend; accuse others rather than excuse your actions; excite the restless with your ideas and methods.

☐ **Your Behavior Objectives** — *what you desire to be.* Key word is *enthusiastic.* You desire to move close to the limelight; provide inspirational leadership; get others committed to a cause; cross social barriers and social roles with ease.

☐ **Your Behavior Change**

Degree of Change Occurring in Your Behavior		
Little	Some	Much
1.0 2.0	3.0 4.0	5.0

☐ **Your New Behavior** — *where you're going.* Key word is *demonstrative.* You show responsiveness to people with requests; gain favors in return for your assistance; sense increased popularity with supportive people; probe ways to read others' pulse; spend more time on others' problems; learn ways to compromise.

Part II — Behavior and Conflict

☐ **Your Behavior Under Pressure** — *how you handle objections.* You bypass the pleasantries in favor of hard-hitting reality; display a short temper; state what will be done; show reluctance to listen to opposition; aim to prove your versatility.

☐ **Your Internal Conflict** — *source of personal frustration.* You tend to gravitate to those who are quick to praise your effort; seek approval from those who want exciting leadership—this action may lead to *secret self-doubts,* implying a search to identify those who prefer using complimentary reinforcement rather than appropriate constructive criticism. Their misdirected influence may result in your misguided leadership.

Part III — Behavior and Control

☐ **Your Internal Motivation —** *how others may exert control with you.* Your motivation increases when others provide opportunities for you to: reach your true potential; become what you are capable of becoming; extend your self-picture.

☐ **Your Motivation of Others —** *how you exert control.* You influence others by including them in a cause. You emphasize a reason for them to believe; bring thinking and feeling into action; locate yourself at the center of activity.

Part IV — Behavior and Predictive Action

☐ Your Behavior Overview —
how you adapt to existing circumstances.

Communicating decisiveness	1 2 3 ④ ⑤	+ 1
Ability to stimulate and activate others	1 2 3 ④ ⑤	+ 1
Self-control	1 2 ③ 4 5	+ 1
Awareness of others' feelings	1 ② ③ 4 5	+ 1
Fairness	① ② 3 4 5	+ 1
Ability to see the whole, not merely the parts	1 2 ③ ④ 5	+ 1
Working facts into a logical whole	1 2 ③ ④ 5	+ 1
Sense of humor	1 ② ③ 4 5	+ 1
Handling of complex problems	1 2 ③ ④ 5	+ 1
Concern for practical details	① ② 3 4 5	+ 1
Ability to size up another's character	1 2 ③ ④ 5	+ 1

Calculation Section

	line 1 _____69_____ %
Total of ⊕	line 2 _____ %
Add lines 1 & 2	line 3 _____ %
Total of plotting points in shaded graph areas	line 4 _____ %
Subtract line 4 from line 3	line 5 _____ %
	(GRAND TOTAL)

(See page 80 for directions.)

— *Key No. 51* —
BEHAVIOR DYNAMICS

Part I — Behavior and Change

☐ **Your Behavior Description** — *the real you.* Key word is *humility.* You state truth as you see it; seek cooperation and emotional fulfillment through the help of others; admit dependence upon people you respect; acknowledge anxious feelings, running the risk of a weakened position.

☐ **Your Behavior Objectives** — *what you desire to be.* Key word is *disciplined.* You desire to find an environment in which it is possible for single-minded concentration; express yourself with a minimum amount of expression; go directly to the point of an issue; demonstrate analytical and critical examination in problem solving; remain unwavering in actions.

☐ **Your Behavior Change**

Degree of Change Occurring in Your Behavior		
Little	Some	Much
1.0 2.0	3.0 4.0	5.0

☐ **Your New Behavior** — *where you're going.* Key word is *respectful.* There is little change occurring in your behavior. You continue to show commitment to your beliefs by criticizing the actions of those who take what is rightfully yours; make the best of things as they are; use available systems; present yourself as orderly, methodical, and self-contained.

Part II — Behavior and Conflict

☐ **Your Behavior Under Pressure** — *how you handle objections.* You use hard facts; avoid communicating between the lines; meet forceful demands with clear, concise answers; attack ideas rather than people who express them; withhold hostility; minimize open conflict.

☐ **Your Internal Conflict** — *source of personal frustration.* You tend to feel mistreated and left out; question your compensation; doubt that you receive your fair share of attention or reward—this suspicion may lead to *shattered relations,* implying that your silent treatment of those you consider responsible for your plight is ineffective; they do not understand your message.

Part III — Behavior and Control

☐ **Your Internal Motivation** — *how others may exert control with you.* Your motivation increases when others provide opportunities for you to: restore order; develop plans along structured lines; become conscientious, principled, and persistent.

☐ **Your Motivation of Others** — *how you exert control.* You influence others through honesty. You emphasize truthfulness as a means to positively affect the motivation of others—tell it like it is; use peaceful methods based upon shared information.

Part IV — Behavior and Predictive Action

☐ Your Behavior Overview —
how you adapt to existing circumstances.

Communicating decisiveness	1	②③ 4 5	+	1
Ability to stimulate and activate others	①② 3 4 5	+	1
Self-control	1 2 3 ④⑤	+	1
Awareness of others' feelings	1 ②③ 4 5	+	1
Fairness	1 2 3 ④⑤	+	1
Ability to see the whole, not merely the parts	1 2 ③④ 5	+	1
Working facts into a logical whole	1 2 3 ④⑤	+	1
Sense of humor	1 ②③ 4 5	+	1
Handling of complex problems	1 2 3 ④⑤	+	1
Concern for practical details	1 2 ③④ 5	+	1
Ability to size up another's character	1 ②③ 4 5	+	1

Calculation Section		
	line 1 ___73___ %
Total of (+1)	line 2 _____ %
Add lines 1 & 2	line 3 _____ %
Total of plotting points in shaded graph areas	line 4 _____ %
Subtract line 4 from line 3	line 5 _____ %
	(GRAND TOTAL)
(See page 80 for directions.)	

— *Key No. 52* —
BEHAVIOR DYNAMICS

Part I — Behavior and Change

☐ **Your Behavior Description** — *the real you.* Key word is *sympathetic.* You cling to the belief that people basically treat others fairly; tend to give up too much of what is rightfully yours; refuse to deal with personal animosity, envy, or jealousy—discuss noncontroversial issues, when possible.

☐ **Your Behavior Objectives** — *what you desire to be.* Key word is *sincere.* You desire to inspire loyalty; freely exchange ideas and opinions; comfortably handle life problems; take pride in being open-minded as well as fair-minded; establish equality when favors are granted.

☐ **Your Behavior Change**

Degree of Change Occurring in Your Behavior		
Little	Some	Much
1.0 2.0	3.0 4.0	5.0

☐ **Your New Behavior** — *where you're going.* Key word is *agreement.* There is little change occurring in your behavior. You continue to struggle with whether to use competitive or cooperative methods in dealing with people; often follow the path of least resistance; compete when challenged to a fair contest; tend to display sensitivity when others criticize your efforts.

Part II — Behavior and Conflict

☐ **Your Behavior Under Pressure** — *how you handle objections.* You dodge troublesome issues; avoid direct and frontal attack; warn others that their impulsive behavior will have negative consequences; show sensitivity to criticism, fend off your irritable feelings.

☐ **Your Internal Conflict** — *source of personal frustration.* You tend to give positive appraisals; fear offending others—this concern may lead to *artificial feedback,* implying that verbal and nonverbal messages are often confused and misunderstood. Negative feelings are communicated between the lines and seldom reach their destination.

Part III — Behavior and Control

☐ **Your Internal Motivation** — *how others may exert control with you.* Your motivation increases when others provide opportunities for you to: include friendships as part of a working bargain; interact in a cooperative and friendly atmosphere; establish personal interest with hopes for potential long-term relationships.

☐ **Your Motivation of Others** — *how you exert control.* You influence others through genuine friendship. You emphasize commonality and the humanity of people; urge others to reach out to one another.

Part IV — Behavior and Predictive Action

☐ **Your Behavior Overview —**
how you adapt to existing circumstances.

Communicating decisiveness	1	②　③	4	5	+	1
Ability to stimulate and activate others	1	2	③　④	5	+	1
Self-control	1	2	③　④	5	+	1
Awareness of others' feelings	1	2	3	④　⑤	+	1
Fairness	1	2	③　④	5	+	1
Ability to see the whole, not merely the parts	1	2	③　④	5	+	1
Working facts into a logical whole	1	②　③	4	5	+	1
Sense of humor	1	2	③　④	5	+	1
Handling of complex problems	1	②　③	4	5	+	1
Concern for practical details	1	②　③	4	5	+	1
Ability to size up another's character	1	2	③　④	5	+	1

Calculation Section

	line 1 ___71___ %	
Total of ⊕1	line 2 _____ %	
Add lines 1 & 2	line 3 _____ %	
Total of plotting points in shaded graph areas	line 4 _____ %	
Subtract line 4 from line 3	line 5 _____ %	
	(GRAND TOTAL)	

(See page 80 for directions.)

— Key No. 53 —
BEHAVIOR DYNAMICS

Part I — Behavior and Change

☐ **Your Behavior Description** — *the real you.* Key word is *aware.* You refuse to take advantage of those whose skills are inferior to your own, showing sympathy and mindfulness of their anxiety and fear; fight off occasional feelings of helplessness; feel weighed down with the problems of others, finding it difficult to escape from their requests.

☐ **Your Behavior Objectives** — *what you desire to be.* Key word is *businesslike.* You desire to live intensely; shed worry and concern; delegate unpleasant tasks to others; develop spontaneity, viewing quick routes as expedient and necessary when competing for advantage.

☐ **Your Behavior Change**

Degree of Change Occurring in Your Behavior		
Little	Some	Much
1.0 2.0	3.0 4.0	5.0

☐ **Your New Behavior** — *where you're going.* Key word is *to-the-point.* You increase assertiveness; use a tough-minded approach to justify your behavior; find greater excitement in creating; insist on taking new territory—claim ownership.

Part II — Behavior and Conflict

☐ **Your Behavior Under Pressure** — *how you handle objections.* You fend off conflict and disturbance; search for different viewpoints; seek to broaden the reality of others; disguise personal anxiety by suggesting wider issues for discussion.

☐ **Your Internal Conflict** — *source of personal frustration.* You tend to drive yourself beyond the capacity of your resources; become impatient, hectic, and irritable; feel that others fail to do their fair share—this concern may lead to *secret self-doubts,* implying that you are a victim, doing work that others refuse to do. Others tend to resent your attitude, taking offense and leaving you with the task of restoring affinity and natural trust.

Part III — Behavior and Control

☐ **Your Internal Motivation** — *how others may exert control with you.* Your motivation increases when others provide opportunities for you to: be regarded as an exciting and interesting personality; use tactics skillfully; have others place their confidence in your abilities.

☐ **Your Motivation of Others** — *how you exert control.* You influence others through hidden persuasion. You emphasize that the struggle of others is your struggle as well; urge those with a concern for equality and self-respect to place their faith in you.

Part IV — Behavior and Predictive Action

☐ Your Behavior Overview —
how you adapt to existing circumstances.

Communicating decisiveness	1	② ③	4	5	+	1
Ability to stimulate and activate others	1	2	③ ④	5	+	1
Self-control	1	2	③ ④	5	+	1
Awareness of others' feelings	1	2	3	④ ⑤	+	1
Fairness	1	2	3	④ ⑤	+	1
Ability to see the whole, not merely the parts	1	② ③	4	5	+	1
Working facts into a logical whole	① ②	3	4	5	+	1
Sense of humor	1	2	③ ④	5	+	1
Handling of complex problems	1	② ③	4	5	+	1
Concern for practical details	1	② ③	4	5	+	1
Ability to size up another's character	1	2	③ ④	5	+	1

Calculation Section

	line 1 ____69____ %
Total of ⊕1	line 2 _____ %
Add lines 1 & 2	line 3 _____ %
Total of plotting points in shaded graph areas	line 4 _____ %
Subtract line 4 from line 3	line 5 _____ %
	(GRAND TOTAL)

(See page 80 for directions.)

— Key No. 54 —

BEHAVIOR DYNAMICS

Part I — Behavior and Change

☐ **Your Behavior Description —** *the real you.* Key word is *gentle emotion.* You show willingness to discuss differences of opinion; resolve conflict by supporting strong leadership; rely upon strength of those who favorably respond to your contributions; encourage others to express true and sincere feeling—yet you withhold anger.

☐ **Your Behavior Objectives —** *what you desire to be.* Key word is *judgmental.* You desire to develop increased self-confidence; seek to develop self-discipline with hopes of overcoming difficulties; attempt to become more alert and investigative; evaluate activities of others; minimize emotional explanations; desire to appear more critical and discerning.

☐ **Your Behavior Change**

Degree of Change Occurring in Your Behavior		
Little	Some	Much
1.0 2.0	3.0 4.0	5.0

☐ **Your New Behavior —** *where you're going.* Key word is *anxious.* You increasingly become more particular in your choice of friends and associates; become less trusting; avoid open conflict; fear that the prospects of realizing your hopes and ideals are dependent upon the good will of others.

Part II — Behavior and Conflict

☐ **Your Behavior Under Pressure —** *how you handle objections.* You are anxious; take complaints and suggestions seriously—sometimes to the extreme; request time to evaluate your effort; offer to adjust conditions; avoid the struggle for power in relationships—assume an agreeable, participative role.

☐ **Your Internal Conflict —** *source of personal frustration.* You tend to have mental reservations regarding those close to you; desire protection which will ensure a conflict-free environment—this concern may lead to *self-contained orderliness,* implying that relationships do not always measure up to your high emotional expectations. Others view your critical observations as "bossiness." They show disappointment and become suspicious at the start of new relationships.

Part III — Behavior and Control

☐ **Your Internal Motivation** — *how others may exert control with you.* Your motivation increases when others provide opportunities for you to: be faithful; fulfill commitments; work closely with trusted people; receive consideration and unquestioning affection; be understood.

☐ **Your Motivation of Others** — *how you exert control.* You influence others by dealing with overly aggressive people, using personal grievances and unpleasant experiences to rally support from victims like yourself. You tend to be successful in control of others and events when you attack what is, rather than support what will be.

Part IV — Behavior and Predictive Action

☐ Your Behavior Overview —
how you adapt to existing circumstances.

Communicating decisiveness	①② 3 4 5	+	1
Ability to stimulate and activate others	1 ②③ 4 5	+	1
Self-control	1 ②③ 4 5	+	1
Awareness of others' feelings	1 2 ③④ 5	+	1
Fairness	1 2 3 ④⑤	+	1
Ability to see the whole, not merely the parts	1 2 ③④ 5	+	1
Working facts into a logical whole	1 2 ③④ 5	+	1
Sense of humor	1 ②③ 4 5	+	1
Handling of complex problems	1 ②③ 4 5	+	1
Concern for practical details	1 2 3 ④⑤	+	1
Ability to size up another's character	1 ②③ 4 5	+	1

Calculation Section	
	line 1 ___67___ %
Total of ⊕	line 2 _____ %
Add lines 1 & 2	line 3 _____ %
Total of plotting points in shaded graph areas	line 4 _____ %
Subtract line 4 from line 3	line 5 _____ %
	(GRAND TOTAL)
(See page 80 for directions.)	

BEHAVIOR DYNAMICS

Part I — Behavior and Change

☐ **Your Behavior Description** — *the real you.* Key word is *likable.* You communicate openly and persuasively; use appropriate timing with those who are hesitant to act; show sensitivity in knowing when to agree or disagree; avoid interruption; use affirmative responses—nod of head, smile, approving gestures.

☐ **Your Behavior Objectives** — *what you desire to be.* Key word is *logical.* You seek reason over emotion; reject the opinions of those who lead by inspiration only; rely upon step-by-step analysis to determine your direction; desire private time in which to pull yourself together.

☐ **Your Behavior Change**

Degree of Change Occurring in Your Behavior		
Little	Some	Much
1.0 2.0	3.0 4.0	5.0

☐ **Your New Behavior** — *where you're going.* Key word is *yielding.* You identify policy and rules; emphasize the need for clearer operating guidelines; defer more to authority when crucial decisions must be made; become increasingly more reserved; participate upon request.

Part II — Behavior and Conflict

☐ **Your Behavior Under Pressure** — *how you handle objections.* You pace yourself; allow others full opportunity to express themselves; change disposition when others become overly critical—avoid being "overly nice"; speak strongly against those who take unfair advantage.

☐ **Your Internal Conflict** — *source of personal frustration.* You tend to permit others to receive credit for your efforts, believing that eventually you will gain favor with them; feel hurt when requests are later denied—this practice may lead to *offended pride*, implying that hopes are not always fulfilled. You feel pain when new, fresh ideas are incomplete as others fail to cooperate.

Part III — Behavior and Control

☐ **Your Internal Motivation** — *how others may exert control with you.* Your motivation increases when others provide opportunities for you to: solve problems; develop a system that minimizes and reduces errors; create person-to-person evaluation procedures.

☐ **Your Motivation of Others** — *how you exert control.* You influence others by strong support. You emphasize that you will do many of the unpleasant tasks; call the bluff of those who are waiting in the wings but do not perform when needed.

Part IV — Behavior and Predictive Action

☐ Your Behavior Overview —
how you adapt to existing circumstances.

Communicating decisiveness	①②③ 3	4	5	+	1
Ability to stimulate and activate others	1 2 ③④	5	+	1
Self-control	1 2 ③④ 5	+	1
Awareness of others' feelings	1 ②③ 4 5	+	1
Fairness	1 2 ③④ 5	+	1
Ability to see the whole, not merely the parts	1 ②③ 4 5	+	1
Working facts into a logical whole	1 ②③ 4 5	+	1
Sense of humor	1 2 ③④ 5	+	1
Handling of complex problems	①②③ 4 5	+	1
Concern for practical details	1 2 ③④ 5	+	1
Ability to size up another's character	1 2 ③④ 5	+	1

Calculation Section

	line 1 ___63___ %
Total of (+1)	line 2 _____ %
Add lines 1 & 2	line 3 _____ %
Total of plotting points in shaded graph areas	line 4 _____ %
Subtract line 4 from line 3	line 5 _____ % (GRAND TOTAL)

(See page 80 for directions.)

— *Key No. 56* —
BEHAVIOR DYNAMICS

Part I — Behavior and Change

☐ **Your Behavior Description** — *the real you.* Key word is *friendly.* You yearn for a happy, stable environment—consistent over time; insist on fairness in any arrangement; represent the interests of those who lack skills to demand equality; minimize easy formulas or instant gratification; prefer lasting results; show sincerity.

☐ **Your Behavior Objectives** — *what you desire to be.* Key word is *sociable.* You attempt to broaden your base of support; desire to direct communication to a larger audience; wish to let others know your availability; compare yourself favorably with others; solicit compliments to justify your belief in the need to cross social and cultural lines.

☐ **Your Behavior Change**

Degree of Change Occurring in Your Behavior		
Little	Some	Much
1.0 2.0	3.0 4.0	5.0

☐ **Your New Behavior** — *where you're going.* Key word is *emotional.* You begin to live for the excitement of the moment; act spontaneously; do the unpredictable; establish unique behavior patterns that cause you to examine fresh approaches to personal problem-solving; bridge the gap between you and older people, which had set you apart.

Part II — Behavior and Conflict

☐ **Your Behavior Under Pressure** — *how you handle objections.* You listen; take criticism personally; remove anxiety by sharing personal feelings; relate reasons for your apprehension; openly express opinions.

☐ **Your Internal Conflict** — *source of personal frustration.* You tend to be overly generous with others, often at the expense of your personal needs; put others ahead of family at times—this practice may lead to *messianic image,* implying an unrealistic view of self. You expect too much of yourself, displaying frustration, as well, with the ingratitude of those you help.

Part III — Behavior and Control

☐ **Your Internal Motivation** — *how others may exert control with you.* Your motivation increases when others provide opportunities for you to: be treated as the accepted leader of a dedicated, discriminating group of people; receive material recognition in proportion to your contributions.

☐ **Your Motivation of Others** — *how you exert control.* You influence others through the use of enthusiasm. You bring people hope; emphasize partnerships; promote unique activities in which all gain vigor and satisfaction.

Part IV — Behavior and Predictive Action

☐ Your Behavior Overview —
how you adapt to existing circumstances.

Communicating decisiveness	1	(2	3)	4	5	+	1
Ability to stimulate and activate others	1	2	3	(4	5)	+	1
Self-control	(1	2)	3	4	5	+	1
Awareness of others' feelings	1	2	3	(4	5)	+	1
Fairness	1	2	(3	4)	5	+	1
Ability to see the whole, not merely the parts	1	2	(3	4)	5	+	1
Working facts into a logical whole	1	2	(3	4)	5	+	1
Sense of humor	1	2	(3	4)	5	+	1
Handling of complex problems	1	(2	3)	4	5	+	1
Concern for practical details	1	2	(3	4)	5	+	1
Ability to size up another's character	1	2	(3	4)	5	+	1

Calculation Section

	line 1 ___73___ %
Total of (+1)	line 2 _____ %
Add lines 1 & 2	line 3 _____ %
Total of plotting points in shaded graph areas	line 4 _____ %
Subtract line 4 from line 3	line 5 _____ %
	(GRAND TOTAL)

(See page 80 for directions.)

— *Key No. 57* —
BEHAVIOR DYNAMICS

Part I — Behavior and Change

☐ **Your Behavior Description** — *the real you.* Key word is *aggression.* You act with harshness and occasional severity; take commanding leadership; pit yourself against disbelievers; minimize personal weakness; refuse to acknowledge limitations.

☐ **Your Behavior Objectives** — *what you desire to be.* Key word is *self-willed.* You desire to use confrontation as a welcome diversion from boredom or monotony; respond easily to anything which provides stimulation; hope to attract attention by doing the unusual or unexpected.

☐ **Your Behavior Change**

Degree of Change Occurring in Your Behavior		
Little	Some	Much
1.0 2.0	3.0 4.0	5.0

☐ **Your New Behavior** — *where you're going.* Key word is *stubborn.* There is little change occurring in your behavior. You continue to assume an autocratic and determined attitude; use others more than they use you; react rather than act when upsetting events occur.

Part II — Behavior and Conflict

☐ **Your Behavior Under Pressure** — *how you handle objections.* You react with an urgent, hectic intensity; challenge the comments of others; falter, then recover by responding with sharp-witted retorts; escalate skirmishes to full-fledged battles if opponents are combative.

☐ **Your Internal Conflict** — *source of personal frustration.* You tend to ignore pessimistic information; select data that enhances your personal belief—this practice may lead to *selective attention,* implying the possibility that you can become misinformed. Consequently, your leadership suffers and your efforts go unrewarded.

Part III — Behavior and Control

☐ **Your Internal Motivation** — *how others may exert control with you.* Your motivation increases when others provide opportunities for you to: excel at what you do; create new activities that provide for things missed earlier in life; break free from oppressive burdens.

☐ **Your Motivation of Others** — *how you exert control.* You influence others through intimidation, making others fearful that your favor will be withdrawn. You create uncertainty with a promise that your way is best.

Part IV — Behavior and Predictive Action

☐ Your Behavior Overview —
how you adapt to existing circumstances.

Communicating decisiveness	1	2	3	④ ⑤	+	1
Ability to stimulate and activate others	1	2	③ ④	5	+	1
Self-control	1	2	3	④ ⑤	+	1
Awareness of others' feelings	① ②	3	4	5	+	1
Fairness	① ②	3	4	5	+	1
Ability to see the whole, not merely the parts	1	② ③	4	5	+	1
Working facts into a logical whole	1	2	③ ④	5	+	1
Sense of humor	1	② ③	4	5	+	1
Handling of complex problems	1	2	③ ④	5	+	1
Concern for practical details	1	② ③	4	5	+	1
Ability to size up another's character	1	2	③ ④	5	+	1

Calculation Section

	line 1 ____67____ %
Total of ⊕1	line 2 _____ %
Add lines 1 & 2	line 3 _____ %
Total of plotting points in shaded graph areas	line 4 _____ %
Subtract line 4 from line 3	line 5 _____ %
	(GRAND TOTAL)

(See page 80 for directions.)

— *Key No. 58* —
BEHAVIOR DYNAMICS

Part I — Behavior and Change

☐ **Your Behavior Description** — *the real you.* Key word is *softhearted*. You need close friends; require time to identify with differences in people; develop friendships over a period of time; use tension-releasing techniques that are uniquely yours; show unexpected flashes of original humor; use a low-key approach to disarm more aggressive people.

☐ **Your Behavior Objectives** — *what you desire to be.* Key word is *good-natured*. You desire to remain in control of structured situations; attempt to organize by listing separate items to be done; respond to authority in fulfilling tasks; become intent on using objective measures to evaluate your achievements.

☐ **Your Behavior Change**

Degree of Change Occurring in Your Behavior				
Little		Some		Much
1.0	2.0	3.0	4.0	5.0

☐ **Your New Behavior** — *where you're going.* Key word is *unselfish*. There is little change occurring in your behavior. You continue to take your fair share of praise and blame; wisely select activities that are designed to bring you fulfillment; show determination in satisfying your obligations; pay little attention to distractions.

Part II — Behavior and Conflict

☐ **Your Behavior Under Pressure** — *how you handle objections.* You demonstrate resilience; turn deficiencies into strengths the second time around; count on friends' dependability; reproach those who are irresponsible.

☐ **Your Internal Conflict** — *source of personal frustration.* You tend to follow organizational structure; believe that uncertainty is unsettling to people—this belief may lead to *excessive operational control*, implying that behind your outer calm you look at facts from an intensely individual angle. There is concern that the unexpected will disrupt carefully laid plans.

Part III — Behavior and Control

☐ **Your Internal Motivation** — *how others may exert control with you.* Your motivation increases when others provide opportunities for you to: use common sense; apply practical ability; get ahead steadily; receive just compensation.

☐ **Your Motivation of Others** — *how you exert control.* You influence others by using a low-key approach. You emphasize a subtle, push-pull method; nudge people gently, but firmly, toward a new goal—let them set a realistic goal for themselves.

Part IV — Behavior and Predictive Action

☐ **Your Behavior Overview —**
how you adapt to existing circumstances.

Communicating decisiveness	①② 3 4 5	+	1
Ability to stimulate and activate others	1 ②③ 4 5	+	1
Self-control	1 2 ③④ 5	+	1
Awareness of others' feelings	1 2 3 ④⑤	+	1
Fairness	1 2 3 ④⑤	+	1
Ability to see the whole, not merely the parts	1 ②③ 4 5	+	1
Working facts into a logical whole	1 2 ③④ 5	+	1
Sense of humor	1 2 ③④ 5	+	1
Handling of complex problems	①② 3 4 5	+	1
Concern for practical details	1 2 3 ④⑤	+	1
Ability to size up another's character	1 ②③ 4 5	+	1

Calculation Section		
	line 1 _____69_____ %	
Total of ⊕1	line 2 _____ %	
Add lines 1 & 2	line 3 _____ %	
Total of plotting points in shaded graph areas	line 4 _____ %	
Subtract line 4 from line 3	line 5 _____ %	
	(GRAND TOTAL)	
(See page 80 for directions.)		

— Key No. 59 —

BEHAVIOR DYNAMICS

Part I — Behavior and Change

☐ **Your Behavior Description** — *the real you.* Key word is *prepared.* You yield when others firmly state their demands; reappraise criteria for testing others; rethink conclusions; show surface reluctance to accept authority, eventually submitting to bold and respected leadership.

☐ **Your Behavior Objectives** — *what you desire to be.* Key word is *authoritative.* You desire to be in control; attempt to win others to your persuasion and beliefs; bluntly criticize and occasionally prod others to comply with your demands; seek to keep others off balance; vary your demands from low-key to direct and bold.

☐ **Your Behavior Change**

Degree of Change Occurring in Your Behavior		
Little	Some	Much
1.0 2.0	3.0 4.0	5.0

☐ **Your New Behavior** — *where you're going.* Key word is *unhesitating.* You show increased fascination with power; grasp for more opportunities to understand, control, predict, and set the realities for people; use rules and procedures to gain greater advantages.

Part II — Behavior and Conflict

☐ **Your Behavior Under Pressure** — *how you handle objections.* You provide accounting for specific facts; show a sense of preparedness; vacillate in crucial decision making; worry about missing major opportunities; insist that events unfold too slowly.

☐ **Your Internal Conflict** — *source of personal frustration.* You tend to judge hastily, often without sufficient facts and without regard for what friends and associates think and feel—this tendency may lead to *obstinate self-righteousness,* implying that you run the risk of experiencing stress when misjudging and antagonizing others.

Part III — Behavior and Control

☐ **Your Internal Motivation —** *how others may exert control with you.* Your motivation increases when others provide opportunities for you to: minimize confusion and inefficiency; solve complex problems; gain insight, exercise vision in long-range possibilities.

☐ **Your Motivation of Others —** *how you exert control.* You influence others through forceful discipline. You set a pace that is challenging to those selected for relationships; keep people in line by comparing their achievements to those of others.

Part IV — Behavior and Predictive Action

☐ Your Behavior Overview —
how you adapt to existing circumstances.

Communicating decisiveness	1	② ③	4	5	+	1
Ability to stimulate and activate others	1	2	③ ④	5	+	1
Self-control	1	2	3	④ ⑤	+	1
Awareness of others' feelings	1	② ③	4	5	+	1
Fairness	1	2	③ ④	5	+	1
Ability to see the whole, not merely the parts	1	2	3	④ ⑤	+	1
Working facts into a logical whole	1	2	3	④ ⑤	+	1
Sense of humor	1	2	③ ④	5	+	1
Handling of complex problems	1	2	3	④ ⑤	+	1
Concern for practical details	1	2	③ ④	5	+	1
Ability to size up another's character	1	2	③ ④	5	+	1

Calculation Section

	line 1 ____81____ %	
Total of (+1)	line 2 _____ %	
Add lines 1 & 2	line 3 _____ %	
Total of plotting points in shaded graph areas	line 4 _____ %	
Subtract line 4 from line 3	line 5 _____ %	
	(GRAND TOTAL)	

(See page 80 for directions.)

BEHAVIOR DYNAMICS

Part I — Behavior and Change

☐ **Your Behavior Description** — *the real you.* Key word is *willingness.* You share problems with others; gain strength in numbers; provide a way for people to solidify beliefs; help others deal with problems in relationships; avoid lasting scars; seek ways for yourself and others to "fit" into situations.

☐ **Your Behavior Objectives** — *what you desire to be.* Key word is *appropriate.* You search for options; seek new and varied outlets of expression; desire to be practical and gain a realistic view; wish to have a direct impact on others.

☐ **Your Behavior Change**

Degree of Change Occurring in Your Behavior		
Little	Some	Much
1.0 2.0 3.0 4.0		5.0

☐ **Your New Behavior** — *where you're going.* Key word is *accountable.* You appear methodical and matter-of-fact when making an appraisal; become more blunt when others disagree with your intentions, show greater insensitivity to those who offer contrary advice.

Part II — Behavior and Conflict

☐ **Your Behavior Under Pressure** — *how you handle objections.* You appear agreeable and friendly; tend to follow strongly opinionated people—but avoid being a "yes" person; favor early agreement when people are willing to discuss.

☐ **Your Internal Conflict** — *source of personal frustration.* You tend to avoid excitable people; turn off high-energy individuals, believing their comments are hurtful—this concern may lead to *cautious sensitivity,* implying that you protect the investment of your time and prejudge others in light of what you expect them to be.

Part III — Behavior and Control

☐ **Your Internal Motivation** — *how others may exert control with you.* Your motivation increases when others provide opportunities for you to: develop varied interests; remove obstacles affecting clear thinking; systematize exact methods; create new ways of viewing possibilities.

☐ **Your Motivation of Others** — *how you exert control.* You influence others by demonstrating reliability. You emphasize what can be expected from you; stress that what you say is what you do.

Part IV — Behavior and Predictive Action

☐ **Your Behavior Overview** —
how you adapt to existing circumstances.

Communicating decisiveness	(1 2) 3	4	5	+	1
Ability to stimulate and activate others	1 (2 3)	4	5	+	1
Self-control	1 (2 3)	4	5	+	1
Awareness of others' feelings	1 2 (3 4)	5	+	1
Fairness	1 2 3 (4 5)	+	1
Ability to see the whole, not merely the parts	1 (2 3)	4	5	+	1
Working facts into a logical whole	1 2 (3 4)	5	+	1
Sense of humor	1 (2 3)	4	5	+	1
Handling of complex problems	1 2 (3 4)	5	+	1
Concern for practical details	1 2 3 (4 5)	+	1
Ability to size up another's character	1 (2 3)	4	5	+	1

Calculation Section

	line 1 ___67___ %
Total of (+1)	line 2 _____ %
Add lines 1 & 2	line 3 _____ %
Total of plotting points in shaded graph areas	line 4 _____ %
Subtract line 4 from line 3	line 5 _____ %
	(GRAND TOTAL)

(See page 80 for directions.)

— Key No. 61 —
BEHAVIOR DYNAMICS

Part I — Behavior and Change

☐ **Your Behavior Description** — *the real you.* Key word is *vulnerable.* You move to the center; steer away from rugged individualism; seek consensus of thought and action; find solace in others; utilize support systems to gain a sense of security.

☐ **Your Behavior Objectives** — *what you desire to be.* Key word is *formidable.* You attempt to protect your beliefs; participate in competitive activities; desire to gain instant satisfaction; show increased determination to succeed; seek more authority.

☐ Your Behavior Change

Degree of Change Occurring in Your Behavior		
Little	Some	Much
1.0 2.0	3.0 4.0	5.0

☐ **Your New Behavior** — *where you're going.* Key word is *spontaneous.* You show an increased preference for unstructured situations; do things on the spur of the moment; assert your individuality; bring more luster to routine and predictable events; invent new ways of doing things.

Part II — Behavior and Conflict

☐ **Your Behavior Under Pressure** — *how you handle objections.* You identify with those who are sympathetic to you; avoid offending others; inwardly become irritated when you easily give in to adversity; maintaining, however, that hope lies in agreement and understanding rather than in the spoils of manipulation.

☐ **Your Internal Conflict** — *source of personal frustration.* You tend to visualize results before building; think ahead; avoid surprises; occasionally irritate others with your realistic, down-to-earth approach— this attitude may lead to *arrogant attention-getting,* implying that your risk-taking is calculated and you need to inform others how they will be involved. They need to know the amount of credit they will receive for their efforts.

Part III — Behavior and Control

☐ **Your Internal Motivation** — *how others may exert control with you.* Your motivation increases when others provide opportunities for you to: make openings rather than wait for calls; develop and creatively sell ideas; move with unusual and high-achieving people.

☐ **Your Motivation of Others** — *how you exert control.* You influence others through the use of unity. You believe that people should have common purpose; bring individuals into line by demonstrating the potential strength of many.

Part IV — Behavior and Predictive Action

☐ Your Behavior Overview —
how you adapt to existing circumstances.

Communicating decisiveness	1	2	③ ④	5	+	1
Ability to stimulate and activate others	1	2	③ ④	5	+	1
Self-control	1	2	③ ④	5	+	1
Awareness of others' feelings	1	2	③ ④	5	+	1
Fairness	1	2	③ ④	5	+	1
Ability to see the whole, not merely the parts	1	2	③ ④	5	+	1
Working facts into a logical whole	1	2	3	④ ⑤	+	1
Sense of humor	① ②	3	4	5	+	1
Handling of complex problems	1	2	3	④ ⑤	+	1
Concern for practical details	1	2	3	④ ⑤	+	1
Ability to size up another's character	1	2	③ ④	5	+	1

Calculation Section

	line 1 ____79____ %
Total of ⊕	line 2 _____ %
Add lines 1 & 2	line 3 _____ %
Total of plotting points in shaded graph areas	line 4 _____ %
Subtract line 4 from line 3	line 5 _____ %
	(GRAND TOTAL)

(See page 80 for directions.)

— Key No. 62 —
BEHAVIOR DYNAMICS

Part I — Behavior and Change

☐ **Your Behavior Description** — *the real you.* Key word is *collaborating.* You attempt to reconcile disagreements; reduce tension by examining several solutions; indicate by verbal or nonverbal communication your acceptance of others' contributions; show flexibility; sort out real from make-believe.

☐ **Your Behavior Objectives** — *what you desire to be.* Key word is *sensible.* You desire to use logical reasoning to assist in the motivation of people; believe actions should be synonymous with common sense; seek to find ways to avoid costly errors; commit to high standards of performance.

☐ **Your Behavior Change**

Degree of Change Occurring in Your Behavior				
Little		Some		Much
1.0	2.0	3.0	4.0	5.0

☐ **Your New Behavior** — *where you're going.* Key word is *sensitive.* You show increased patience with complicated details; absorb complex information; become more conscientious, precise, and demanding; accept blame when at fault; modify procedures when necessary.

Part II — Behavior and Conflict

☐ **Your Behavior Under Pressure** — *how you handle objections.* You yield when your position conflicts with those held by respected friends and associates; hope to win support by making concessions to those with reasonable requests; appear warm, friendly, and responsive to others.

☐ **Your Internal Conflict** — *source of personal frustration.* You tend to be overly sensitive to invasions of your physical and psychological territory; feel that others take advantage of your good-natured disposition—this concern may lead to *conscious protectiveness,* implying a desire to protect yourself from any disturbing influence. The absence of tension may reduce the essential tension necessary for creativeness.

Part III — Behavior and Control

☐ **Your Internal Motivation —** *how others may exert control with you.* Your motivation increases when others provide opportunities for you to: analyze problems and inconsistencies; assist people in planning and organizing; reflect a high regard for protocol—proper and formal.

☐ **Your Motivation of Others —** *how you exert control.* You influence others through your use of nonverbal communication. You employ meaningful movements, critical looks, or approving gestures to command attention from others; emphasize your willingness to work on others' problems.

Part IV — Behavior and Predictive Action

☐ Your Behavior Overview —
how you adapt to existing circumstances.

Communicating decisiveness	1	②　③	4	5	+	1
Ability to stimulate and activate others	1	2	③　④	5	+	1
Self-control	1	2	③　④	5	+	1
Awareness of others' feelings	1	2	3	④　⑤	+	1
Fairness	1	2	3	④　⑤	+	1
Ability to see the whole, not merely the parts	1	2	③　④	5	+	1
Working facts into a logical whole	1	②　③	4	5	+	1
Sense of humor	1	2	③　④	5	+	1
Handling of complex problems	1	②　③	4	5	+	1
Concern for practical details	1	②　③	4	5	+	1
Ability to size up another's character	1	2	③　④	5	+	1

Calculation Section

	line 1 ___73___ %
Total of (+1)	line 2 _____ %
Add lines 1 & 2	line 3 _____ %
Total of plotting points in shaded graph areas	line 4 _____ %
Subtract line 4 from line 3	line 5 _____ %
	(GRAND TOTAL)

(See page 80 for directions.)

— *Key No. 63* —
BEHAVIOR DYNAMICS

Part I — Behavior and Change

☐ **Your Behavior Description** — *the real you.* Key word is *comfortable.* You put people at ease; use laughter, humor, and good will; entertain and enliven social conversation; believe that personal acceptance is equivalent to acceptance of your ideas.

☐ **Your Behavior Objectives** — *what you desire to be.* Key word is *cautious.* You attempt to be serious in physical mannerisms, using calculated movement; seek strong, meaningful relationships; depend on facts as a basis for arguments; attend to specific rather than general projects.

☐ **Your Behavior Change**

Degree of Change Occurring in Your Behavior		
Little	Some	Much
1.0 2.0	3.0 4.0	5.0

☐ **Your New Behavior** — *where you're going.* Key word is *correct.* You become more cynical and self-sufficient; question the reasons for failure rather than providing excuses for shortcomings; become guarded in expression; fear being overly emotional.

Part II — Behavior and Conflict

☐ **Your Behavior Under Pressure** — *how you handle objections.* You use generalities; avoid specific attacks on those who appear hostile; doubt the seriousness of questions; appear more confident than you are; use language that contains an optimistic flavor—better than ever, unbelievable, super.

☐ **Your Internal Conflict** — *source of personal frustration.* You tend to become suspicious of those close to you; find it increasingly difficult to express loyalties and ideals—the action may lead to *misplaced trust,* implying that you search for those who are dependable, bemoaning the fact that past relationships proved empty and meaningless.

Part III — Behavior and Control

☐ **Your Internal Motivation** — *how others may exert control with you.* Your motivation increases when others provide opportunities for you to: face obstacles with a set of facts combined with inspiration; achieve aims by developing a unique system; use intellectual curiosity.

☐ **Your Motivation of Others** — *how you exert control.* You influence others through your search for meaning. You emphasize that others' needs can be met through the search process with you; generate interest and curiosity.

Part IV — Behavior and Predictive Action

☐ **Your Behavior Overview** —
how you adapt to existing circumstances.

Communicating decisiveness	1	②③	4	5	+	1
Ability to stimulate and activate others	1	2 3	④⑤		+	1
Self-control	①②	3	4	5	+	1
Awareness of others' feelings	1 2	③④	5		+	1
Fairness	1	②③	4	5	+	1
Ability to see the whole, not merely the parts	1 2	③④	5		+	1
Working facts into a logical whole	①②	3	4	5	+	1
Sense of humor	1 2	③④	5		+	1
Handling of complex problems	1	②③	4	5	+	1
Concern for practical details	1	②③	4	5	+	1
Ability to size up another's character	1 2	③④	5		+	1

Calculation Section

	line 1 ___63___ %
Total of (+1)	line 2 _____ %
Add lines 1 & 2	line 3 _____ %
Total of plotting points in shaded graph areas	line 4 _____ %
Subtract line 4 from line 3	line 5 _____ %
	(GRAND TOTAL)

(See page 80 for directions.)

— Key No. 64 —
BEHAVIOR DYNAMICS

Part I — Behavior and Change

☐ **Your Behavior Description** — *the real you.* Key word is *relevant.* You display a serious, restrained composure; demand factual data as a way to predict future events; pour energy into thought; look for alternative solutions; desire to be right.

☐ **Your Behavior Objectives** — *what you desire to be.* Key word is *expectant.* You pursue new opportunities for advancement; become more hopeful; believe you can refute those who are cynical; desire greater recognition for extraordinary achievement; hope to operate with increased energy.

☐ **Your Behavior Change**

Degree of Change Occurring in Your Behavior		
Little	Some	Much
1.0 2.0	3.0 4.0	5.0

☐ **Your New Behavior** — *where you're going.* Key word is *soaring.* You show increased enthusiasm; dismiss negative signals; refer more often to future potential rather than to past reservations; move from the ordinary to the unusual.

Part II — Behavior and Conflict

☐ **Your Behavior Under Pressure** — *how you handle objections.* You appear startled by those who scrutinize your ideas; reverse your opinions in light of new information; tend to immerse yourself in trivialities as an escape route; seek time to consider options.

☐ **Your Internal Conflict** — *source of personal frustration.* You tend to feel burdened with more than your share of problems; accept responsibility for correcting the mistakes of others; attempt to get people involved through occasional charm and frequent wit, taking their refusal as a personal affront—this attitude may lead to *fear of rejection,* implying that you feel others do not always take you seriously. You may prepare to take a hard line with them.

Part III — Behavior and Control

☐ **Your Internal Motivation —** *how others may exert control with you.* Your motivation increases when others provide opportunities for you to: gain prestige; follow your impulses; become involved in exciting events; work people into organizational patterns in which each assumes a role.

☐ **Your Motivation of Others —** *how you exert control.* You influence others with your silent and deliberate manner when pressed to achieve. You emphasize seriousness of purpose; force others to adopt a somber attitude.

Part IV — Behavior and Predictive Action

☐ **Your Behavior Overview —**
how you adapt to existing circumstances.

Communicating decisiveness	1	②③	4	5	+	1
Ability to stimulate and activate others	1	②③	4	5	+	1
Self-control	1	2	③④	5	+	1
Awareness of others' feelings	1	②③	4	5	+	1
Fairness	1	2	③④	5	+	1
Ability to see the whole, not merely the parts	1	2	③④	5	+	1
Working facts into a logical whole	1	2	3	④⑤	+	1
Sense of humor	1	2	③④	5	+	1
Handling of complex problems	1	2	③④	5	+	1
Concern for practical details	1	2	③④	5	+	1
Ability to size up another's character	1	②③	4	5	+	1

Calculation Section

	line 1 ___71___ %	
Total of ⊕	line 2 _____ %	
Add lines 1 & 2	line 3 _____ %	
Total of plotting points in shaded graph areas	line 4 _____ %	
Subtract line 4 from line 3	line 5 _____ %	
	(GRAND TOTAL)	

(See page 80 for directions.)

Extended Pattern
Interpretation

PATTERN ONE
Extended Interpretation

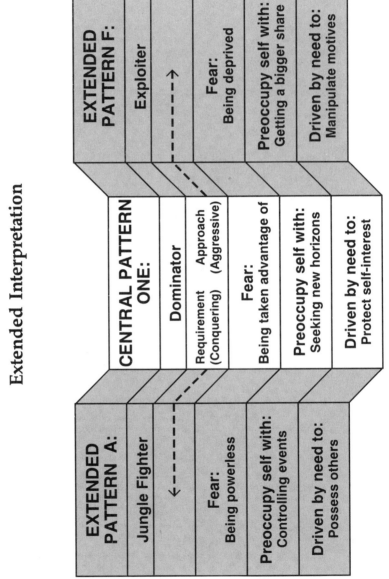

EXTENDED PATTERN F:

Exploiter

- - - - →

Fear: Being deprived

Preoccupy self with: Getting a bigger share

Driven by need to: Manipulate motives

CENTRAL PATTERN ONE:

Dominator

Requirement (Conquering)   Approach (Aggressive)

Fear: Being taken advantage of

Preoccupy self with: Seeking new horizons

Driven by need to: Protect self-interest

EXTENDED PATTERN A:

Jungle Fighter

← - - - -

Fear: Being powerless

Preoccupy self with: Controlling events

Driven by need to: Possess others

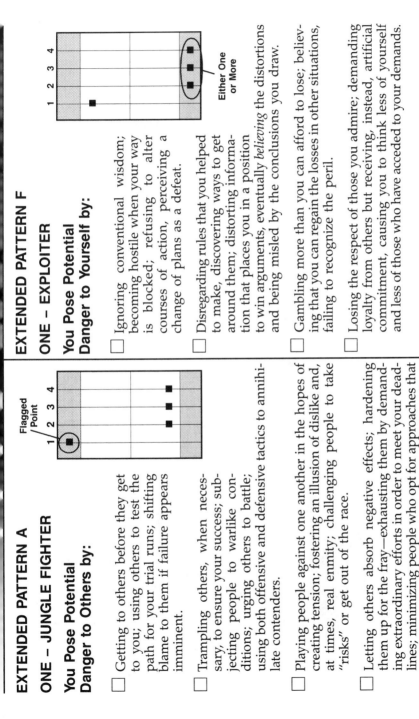

EXTENDED PATTERN A

ONE – JUNGLE FIGHTER

**You Pose Potential
Danger to Others by:**

☐ Getting to others before they get to you; using others to test the path for your trial runs; shifting blame to them if failure appears imminent.

☐ Trampling others, when necessary, to ensure your success; subjecting people to warlike conditions; urging others to battle; using both offensive and defensive tactics to annihilate contenders.

☐ Playing people against one another in the hopes of creating tension; fostering an illusion of dislike and, at times, real enmity; challenging people to take "risks" or get out of the race.

☐ Letting others absorb negative effects; hardening them up for the fray—exhausting them by demanding extraordinary efforts in order to meet your deadlines; minimizing people who opt for approaches that are even-handed or understanding; labeling them weak and naive.

EXTENDED PATTERN F

ONE – EXPLOITER

**You Pose Potential
Danger to Yourself by:**

☐ Ignoring conventional wisdom; becoming hostile when your way is blocked; refusing to alter courses of action, perceiving a change of plans as a defeat.

☐ Disregarding rules that you helped to make, discovering ways to get around them; distorting information that places you in a position to win arguments, eventually *believing* the distortions and being misled by the conclusions you draw.

☐ Gambling more than you can afford to lose; believing that you can regain the losses in other situations, failing to recognize the peril.

☐ Losing the respect of those you admire; demanding loyalty from others but receiving, instead, artificial commitment, causing you to think less of yourself and less of those who have acceded to your demands.

PATTERN TWO
Extended Interpretation

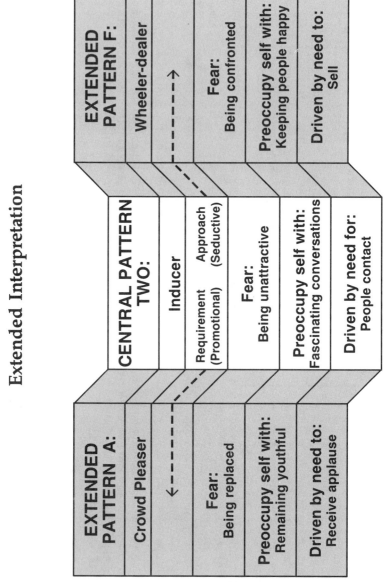

EXTENDED
PATTERN F:

Wheeler-dealer

Fear:
Being confronted

Preoccupy self with:
Keeping people happy

Driven by need to:
Sell

CENTRAL PATTERN
TWO:

Inducer

Requirement   Approach
(Promotional)   (Seductive)

Fear:
Being unattractive

Preoccupy self with:
Fascinating conversations

Driven by need for:
People contact

EXTENDED
PATTERN A:

Crowd Pleaser

Fear:
Being replaced

Preoccupy self with:
Remaining youthful

Driven by need to:
Receive applause

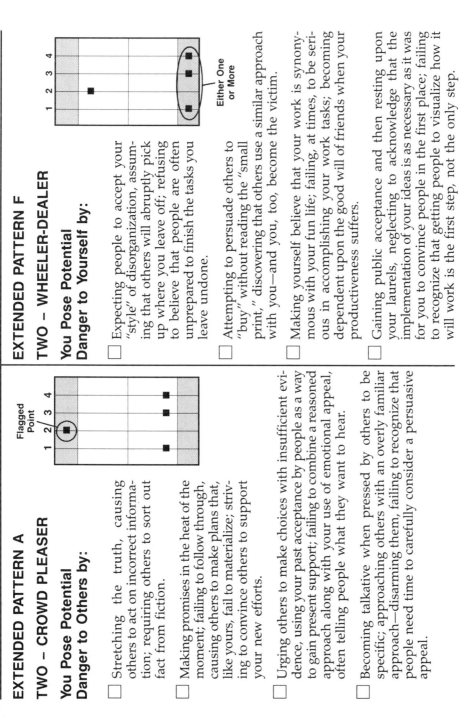

EXTENDED PATTERN A

TWO – CROWD PLEASER

**You Pose Potential
Danger to Others by:**

☐ Stretching the truth, causing others to act on incorrect information; requiring others to sort out fact from fiction.

☐ Making promises in the heat of the moment; failing to follow through, causing others to make plans that, like yours, fail to materialize; striving to convince others to support your new efforts.

☐ Urging others to make choices with insufficient evidence, using your past acceptance by people as a way to gain present support; failing to combine a reasoned approach along with your use of emotional appeal, often telling people what they want to hear.

☐ Becoming talkative when pressed by others to be specific; approaching others with an overly familiar approach—disarming them, failing to recognize that people need time to carefully consider a persuasive appeal.

EXTENDED PATTERN F

TWO – WHEELER-DEALER

**You Pose Potential
Danger to Yourself by:**

☐ Expecting people to accept your "style" of disorganization, assuming that others will abruptly pick up where you leave off; refusing to believe that people are often unprepared to finish the tasks you leave undone.

☐ Attempting to persuade others to "buy" without reading the "small print," discovering that others use a similar approach with you—and you, too, become the victim.

☐ Making yourself believe that your work is synonymous with your fun life; failing, at times, to be serious in accomplishing your work tasks; becoming dependent upon the good will of friends when your productiveness suffers.

☐ Gaining public acceptance and then resting upon your laurels, neglecting to acknowledge that the implementation of your ideas is as necessary as it was for you to convince people in the first place; failing to recognize that getting people to visualize how it will work is the first step, not the only step.

PATTERN THREE
Extended Interpretation

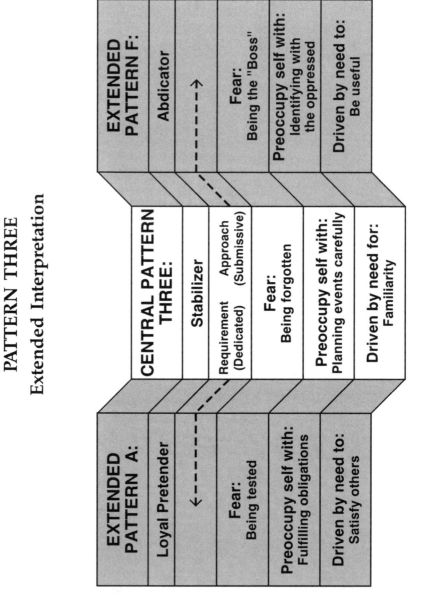

EXTENDED PATTERN F:

Abdicator

Fear:
Being the "Boss"

Preoccupy self with:
Identifying with the oppressed

Driven by need to:
Be useful

CENTRAL PATTERN THREE:

Stabilizer

Requirement   Approach
(Dedicated)   (Submissive)

Fear:
Being forgotten

Preoccupy self with:
Planning events carefully

Driven by need for:
Familiarity

EXTENDED PATTERN A:

Loyal Pretender

Fear:
Being tested

Preoccupy self with:
Fulfilling obligations

Driven by need to:
Satisfy others

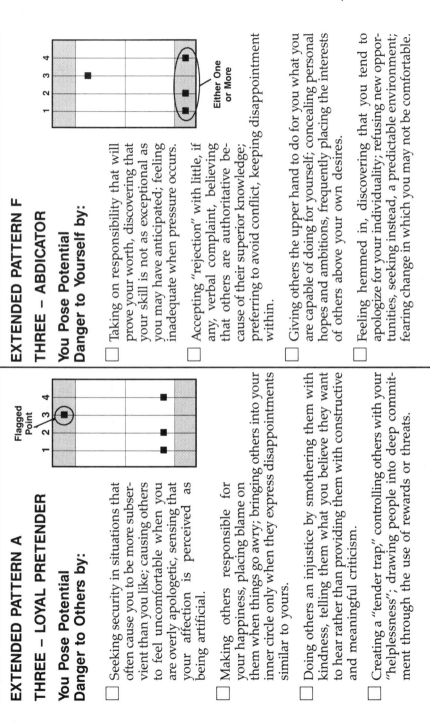

EXTENDED PATTERN A

THREE – LOYAL PRETENDER

You Pose Potential Danger to Others by:

☐ Seeking security in situations that often cause you to be more subservient than you like; causing others to feel uncomfortable when you are overly apologetic, sensing that your affection is perceived as being artificial.

☐ Making others responsible for your happiness, placing blame on them when things go awry; bringing others into your inner circle only when they express disappointments similar to yours.

☐ Doing others an injustice by smothering them with kindness, telling them what you believe they want to hear rather than providing them with constructive and meaningful criticism.

☐ Creating a "tender trap," controlling others with your "helplessness"; drawing people into deep commitment through the use of rewards or threats.

EXTENDED PATTERN F

THREE – ABDICATOR

You Pose Potential Danger to Yourself by:

☐ Taking on responsibility that will prove your worth, discovering that your skill is not as exceptional as you may have anticipated; feeling inadequate when pressure occurs.

☐ Accepting "rejection" with little, if any, verbal complaint, believing that others are authoritative because of their superior knowledge; preferring to avoid conflict, keeping disappointment within.

☐ Giving others the upper hand to do for you what you are capable of doing for yourself; concealing personal hopes and ambitions, frequently placing the interests of others above your own desires.

☐ Feeling hemmed in, discovering that you tend to apologize for your individuality; refusing new opportunities, seeking instead, a predictable environment; fearing change in which you may not be comfortable.

PATTERN FOUR
Extended Interpretation

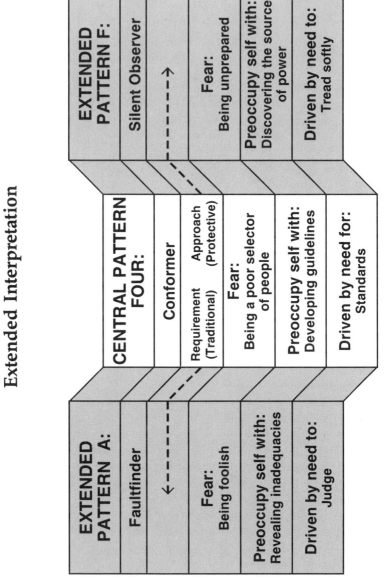

EXTENDED PATTERN F:

Silent Observer

Fear:
Being unprepared

Preoccupy self with:
Discovering the source of power

Driven by need to:
Tread softly

CENTRAL PATTERN FOUR:

Conformer

Requirement (Traditional)   Approach (Protective)

Fear:
Being a poor selector of people

Preoccupy self with:
Developing guidelines

Driven by need for:
Standards

EXTENDED PATTERN A:

Faultfinder

Fear:
Being foolish

Preoccupy self with:
Revealing inadequacies

Driven by need to:
Judge

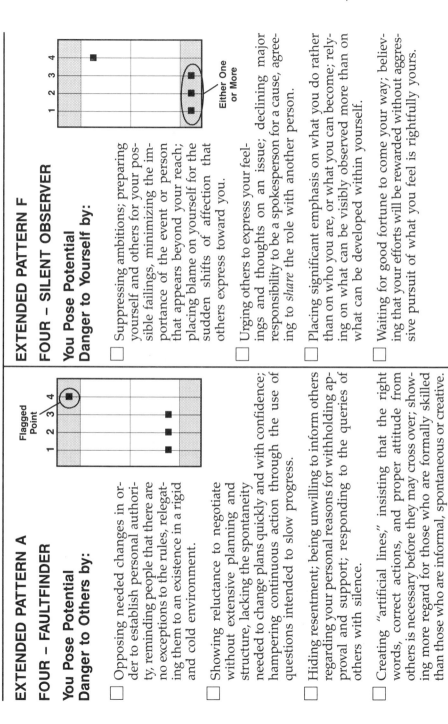

EXTENDED PATTERN A

FOUR – FAULTFINDER

**You Pose Potential
Danger to Others by:**

☐ Opposing needed changes in order to establish personal authority, reminding people that there are no exceptions to the rules, relegating them to an existence in a rigid and cold environment.

☐ Showing reluctance to negotiate without extensive planning and structure, lacking the spontaneity needed to change plans quickly and with confidence; hampering continuous action through the use of questions intended to slow progress.

☐ Hiding resentment; being unwilling to inform others regarding your personal reasons for withholding approval and support; responding to the queries of others with silence.

☐ Creating "artificial lines," insisting that the right words, correct actions, and proper attitude from others is necessary before they may cross over; showing more regard for those who are formally skilled than those who are informal, spontaneous or creative.

EXTENDED PATTERN F

FOUR – SILENT OBSERVER

**You Pose Potential
Danger to Yourself by:**

☐ Suppressing ambitions; preparing yourself and others for your possible failings, minimizing the importance of the event or person that appears beyond your reach; placing blame on yourself for the sudden shifts of affection that others express toward you.

☐ Urging others to express your feelings and thoughts on an issue; declining major responsibility to be a spokesperson for a cause, agreeing to *share* the role with another person.

☐ Placing significant emphasis on what you do rather than on who you are, or what you can become; relying on what can be visibly observed more than on what can be developed within yourself.

☐ Waiting for good fortune to come your way; believing that your efforts will be rewarded without aggressive pursuit of what you feel is rightfully yours.

PATTERN TWELVE
Extended Interpretation

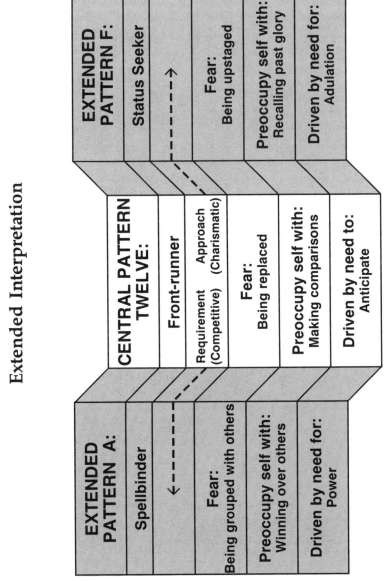

EXTENDED
PATTERN F:

Status Seeker

Fear:
Being upstaged

Preoccupy self with:
Recalling past glory

Driven by need for:
Adulation

CENTRAL PATTERN
TWELVE:

Front-runner

Requirement   Approach
(Competitive)   (Charismatic)

Fear:
Being replaced

Preoccupy self with:
Making comparisons

Driven by need to:
Anticipate

EXTENDED
PATTERN A:

Spellbinder

Fear:
Being grouped with others

Preoccupy self with:
Winning over others

Driven by need for:
Power

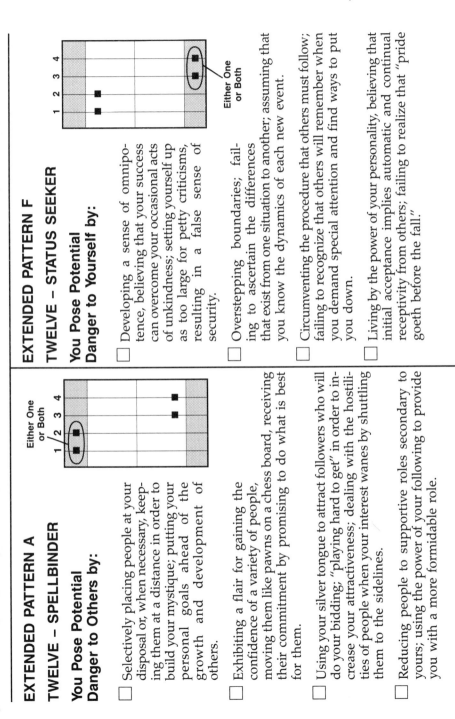

EXTENDED PATTERN A

TWELVE – SPELLBINDER

**You Pose Potential
Danger to Others by:**

Either One
or Both

☐ Selectively placing people at your disposal or, when necessary, keeping them at a distance in order to build your mystique; putting your personal goals ahead of the growth and development of others.

☐ Exhibiting a flair for gaining the confidence of a variety of people, moving them like pawns on a chess board, receiving their commitment by promising to do what is best for them.

☐ Using your silver tongue to attract followers who will do your bidding; "playing hard to get" in order to increase your attractiveness; dealing with the hostilities of people when your interest wanes by shuttling them to the sidelines.

☐ Reducing people to supportive roles secondary to yours; using the power of your following to provide you with a more formidable role.

EXTENDED PATTERN F

TWELVE – STATUS SEEKER

**You Pose Potential
Danger to Yourself by:**

Either One
or Both

☐ Developing a sense of omnipotence, believing that your success can overcome your occasional acts of unkindness; setting yourself up as too large for petty criticisms, resulting in a false sense of security.

☐ Overstepping boundaries; failing to ascertain the differences that exist from one situation to another; assuming that you know the dynamics of each new event.

☐ Circumventing the procedure that others must follow; failing to recognize that others will remember when you demand special attention and find ways to put you down.

☐ Living by the power of your personality, believing that initial acceptance implies automatic and continual receptivity from others; failing to realize that "pride goeth before the fall."

PATTERN THIRTEEN
Extended Interpretation

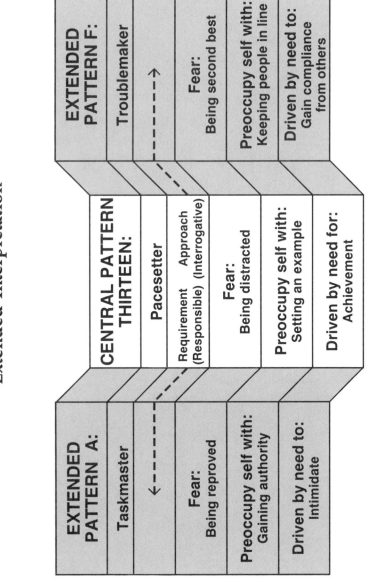

CENTRAL PATTERN THIRTEEN:

Pacesetter

Requirement   Approach
(Responsible)   (Interrogative)

Fear:
Being distracted

Preoccupy self with:
Setting an example

Driven by need for:
Achievement

EXTENDED PATTERN F:

Troublemaker

Fear:
Being second best

Preoccupy self with:
Keeping people in line

Driven by need to:
Gain compliance
from others

EXTENDED PATTERN A:

Taskmaster

Fear:
Being reproved

Preoccupy self with:
Gaining authority

Driven by need to:
Intimidate

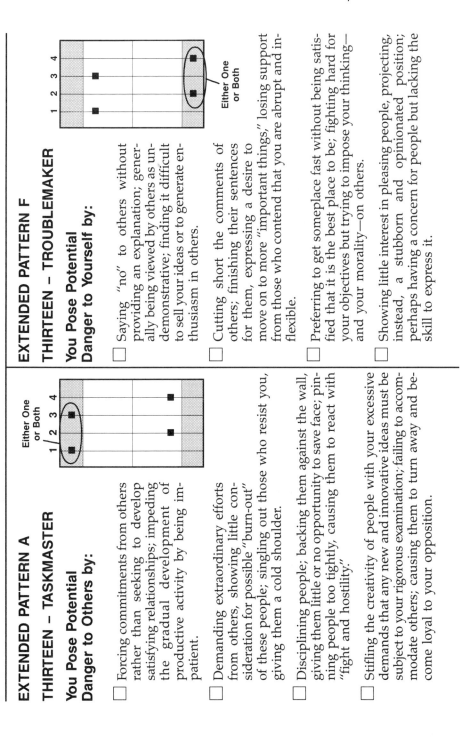

EXTENDED PATTERN A

THIRTEEN – TASKMASTER

Either One or Both

You Pose Potential Danger to Others by:

☐ Forcing commitments from others rather than seeking to develop satisfying relationships; impeding the gradual development of productive activity by being impatient.

☐ Demanding extraordinary efforts from others, showing little consideration for possible "burn-out" of these people; singling out those who resist you, giving them a cold shoulder.

☐ Disciplining people; backing them against the wall, giving them little or no opportunity to save face; pinning people too tightly, causing them to react with "fight and hostility."

☐ Stifling the creativity of people with your excessive demands that any new and innovative ideas must be subject to your rigorous examination; failing to accommodate others; causing them to turn away and become loyal to your opposition.

EXTENDED PATTERN F

THIRTEEN – TROUBLEMAKER

You Pose Potential Danger to Yourself by:

Either One or Both

☐ Saying "no" to others without providing an explanation; generally being viewed by others as undemonstrative; finding it difficult to sell your ideas or to generate enthusiasm in others.

☐ Cutting short the comments of others; finishing their sentences for them, expressing a desire to move on to more "important things," losing support from those who contend that you are abrupt and inflexible.

☐ Preferring to get someplace fast without being satisfied that it is the best place to be; fighting hard for your objectives but trying to impose your thinking—and your morality—on others.

☐ Showing little interest in pleasing people, projecting, instead, a stubborn and opinionated position; perhaps having a concern for people but lacking the skill to express it.

PATTERN FOURTEEN
Extended Interpretation

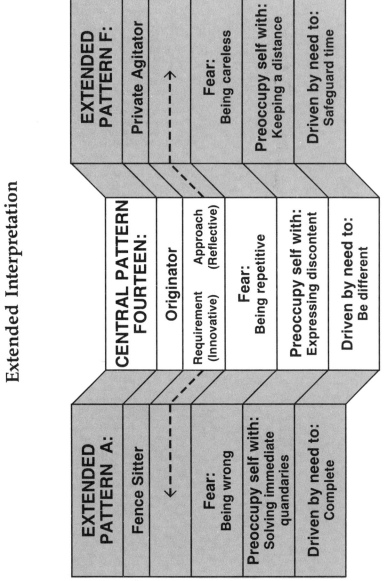

CENTRAL PATTERN FOURTEEN:

Originator

Requirement (Innovative)   Approach (Reflective)

Fear:
Being repetitive

Preoccupy self with:
Expressing discontent

Driven by need to:
Be different

EXTENDED PATTERN F:

Private Agitator

Fear:
Being careless

Preoccupy self with:
Keeping a distance

Driven by need to:
Safeguard time

EXTENDED PATTERN A:

Fence Sitter

Fear:
Being wrong

Preoccupy self with:
Solving immediate quandaries

Driven by need to:
Complete

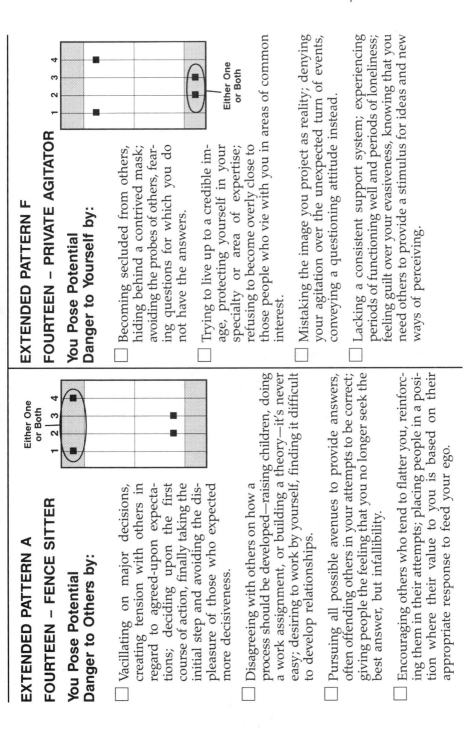

EXTENDED PATTERN A

FOURTEEN – FENCE SITTER

**You Pose Potential
Danger to Others by:**

☐ Vacillating on major decisions, creating tension with others in regard to agreed-upon expectations; deciding upon the first course of action, finally taking the initial step and avoiding the displeasure of those who expected more decisiveness.

☐ Disagreeing with others on how a process should be developed—raising children, doing a work assignment, or building a theory—it's never easy; desiring to work by yourself, finding it difficult to develop relationships.

☐ Pursuing all possible avenues to provide answers, often offending others in your attempts to be correct; giving people the feeling that you no longer seek the best answer, but infallibility.

☐ Encouraging others who tend to flatter you, reinforcing them in their attempts; placing people in a position where their value to you is based on their appropriate response to feed your ego.

EXTENDED PATTERN F

FOURTEEN – PRIVATE AGITATOR

**You Pose Potential
Danger to Yourself by:**

☐ Becoming secluded from others, hiding behind a contrived mask; avoiding the probes of others, fearing questions for which you do not have the answers.

☐ Trying to live up to a credible image, protecting yourself in your specialty or area of expertise; refusing to become overly close to those people who vie with you in areas of common interest.

☐ Mistaking the image you project as reality; denying your agitation over the unexpected turn of events, conveying a questioning attitude instead.

☐ Lacking a consistent support system; experiencing periods of functioning well and periods of loneliness; feeling guilt over your evasiveness, knowing that you need others to provide a stimulus for ideas and new ways of perceiving.

PATTERN TWENTY-THREE
Extended Interpretation

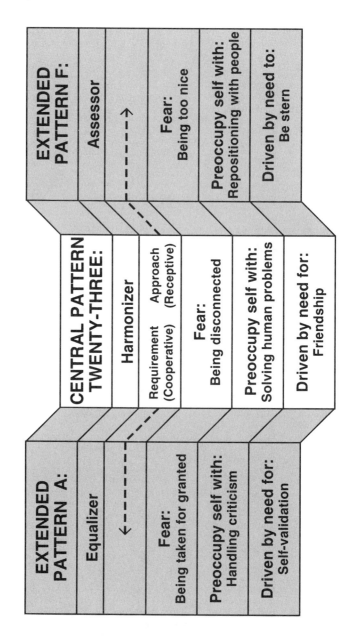

EXTENDED PATTERN A:	CENTRAL PATTERN TWENTY-THREE:		EXTENDED PATTERN F:
Equalizer	Harmonizer		Assessor
	Requirement (Cooperative)	Approach (Receptive)	
Fear: Being taken for granted	Fear: Being disconnected		Fear: Being too nice
Preoccupy self with: Handling criticism	Preoccupy self with: Solving human problems		Preoccupy self with: Repositioning with people
Driven by need for: Self-validation	Driven by need for: Friendship		Driven by need to: Be stern

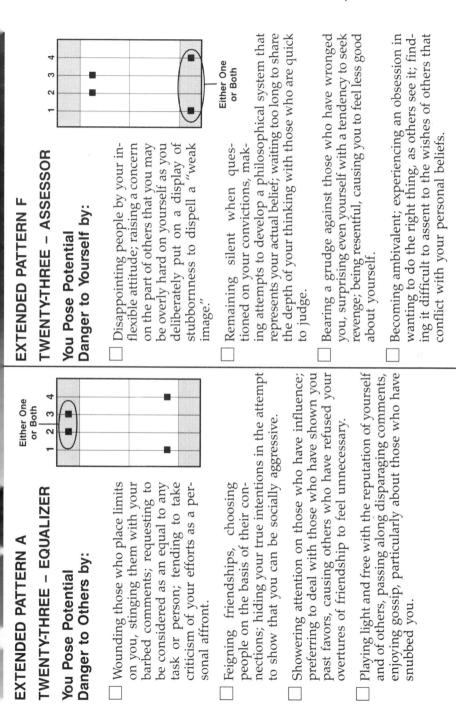

EXTENDED PATTERN A

TWENTY-THREE – EQUALIZER

**You Pose Potential
Danger to Others by:**

☐ Wounding those who place limits on you, stinging them with your barbed comments; requesting to be considered as an equal to any task or person; tending to take criticism of your efforts as a personal affront.

☐ Feigning friendships, choosing people on the basis of their connections; hiding your true intentions in the attempt to show that you can be socially aggressive.

☐ Showering attention on those who have influence; preferring to deal with those who have shown you past favors, causing others who have refused your overtures of friendship to feel unnecessary.

☐ Playing light and free with the reputation of yourself and of others, passing along disparaging comments, enjoying gossip, particularly about those who have snubbed you.

EXTENDED PATTERN F

TWENTY-THREE – ASSESSOR

**You Pose Potential
Danger to Yourself by:**

☐ Disappointing people by your inflexible attitude; raising a concern on the part of others that you may be overly hard on yourself as you deliberately put on a display of stubbornness to dispel a "weak image."

☐ Remaining silent when questioned on your convictions, making attempts to develop a philosophical system that represents your actual belief; waiting too long to share the depth of your thinking with those who are quick to judge.

☐ Bearing a grudge against those who have wronged you, surprising even yourself with a tendency to seek revenge; being resentful, causing you to feel less good about yourself.

☐ Becoming ambivalent; experiencing an obsession in wanting to do the right thing, as others see it; finding it difficult to assent to the wishes of others that conflict with your personal beliefs.

PATTERN TWENTY-FOUR
Extended Interpretation

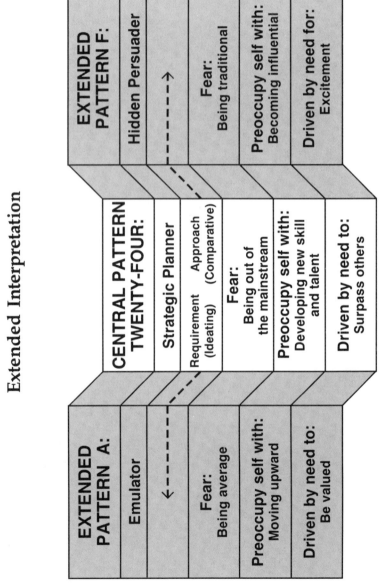

EXTENDED PATTERN F:

Hidden Persuader

Fear:
Being traditional

Preoccupy self with:
Becoming influential

Driven by need for:
Excitement

CENTRAL PATTERN TWENTY-FOUR:

Strategic Planner

Requirement   Approach
(Ideating)   (Comparative)

Fear:
Being out of
the mainstream

Preoccupy self with:
Developing new skill
and talent

Driven by need to:
Surpass others

EXTENDED PATTERN A:

Emulator

Fear:
Being average

Preoccupy self with:
Moving upward

Driven by need to:
Be valued

EXTENDED PATTERN A

TWENTY-FOUR – EMULATOR

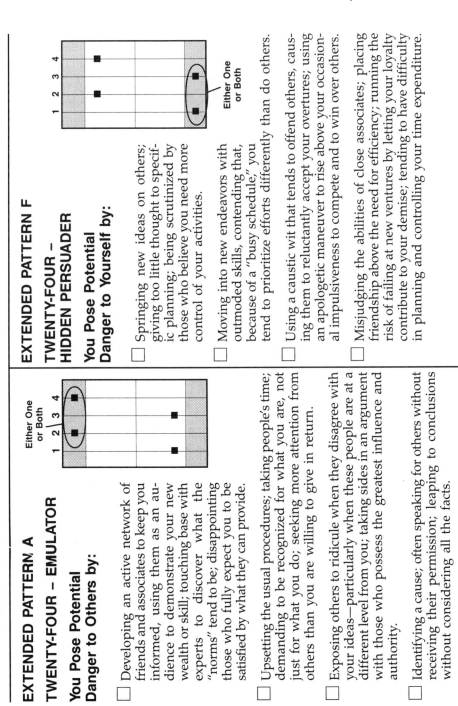

Either One
or Both

**You Pose Potential
Danger to Others by:**

☐ Developing an active network of friends and associates to keep you informed, using them as an audience to demonstrate your new wealth or skill; touching base with experts to discover what the "norms" tend to be; disappointing those who fully expect you to be satisfied by what they can provide.

☐ Upsetting the usual procedures; taking people's time; demanding to be recognized for what you are, not just for what you do; seeking more attention from others than you are willing to give in return.

☐ Exposing others to ridicule when they disagree with your ideas—particularly when these people are at a different level from you; taking sides in an argument with those who possess the greatest influence and authority.

☐ Identifying a cause; often speaking for others without receiving their permission; leaping to conclusions without considering all the facts.

EXTENDED PATTERN F

TWENTY-FOUR – HIDDEN PERSUADER

**You Pose Potential
Danger to Yourself by:**

☐ Springing new ideas on others; giving too little thought to specific planning; being scrutinized by those who believe you need more control of your activities.

☐ Moving into new endeavors with outmoded skills, contending that, because of a "busy schedule," you tend to prioritize efforts differently than do others.

☐ Using a caustic wit that tends to offend others, causing them to reluctantly accept your overtures; using an apologetic maneuver to rise above your occasional impulsiveness to compete and to win over others.

☐ Misjudging the abilities of close associates; placing friendship above the need for efficiency; running the risk of failing at new ventures by letting your loyalty contribute to your demise; tending to have difficulty in planning and controlling your time expenditure.

PATTERN THIRTY-FOUR
Extended Interpretation

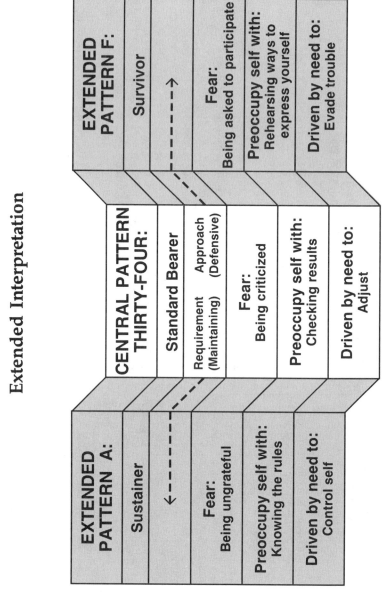

EXTENDED PATTERN A:

Sustainer

←

Fear:
Being ungrateful

Preoccupy self with:
Knowing the rules

Driven by need to:
Control self

CENTRAL PATTERN THIRTY-FOUR:

Standard Bearer

Requirement (Maintaining)   Approach (Defensive)

Fear:
Being criticized

Preoccupy self with:
Checking results

Driven by need to:
Adjust

EXTENDED PATTERN F:

Survivor

→

Fear:
Being asked to participate

Preoccupy self with:
Rehearsing ways to express yourself

Driven by need to:
Evade trouble

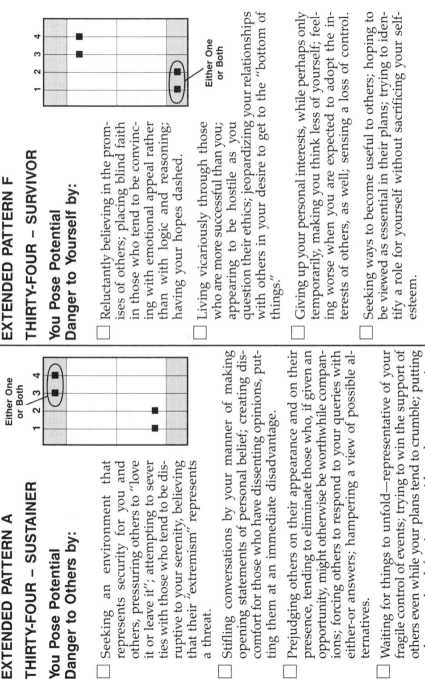

EXTENDED PATTERN A

THIRTY-FOUR – SUSTAINER

You Pose Potential Danger to Others by:

☐ Seeking an environment that represents security for you and others, pressuring others to "love it or leave it"; attempting to sever ties with those who tend to be disruptive to your serenity, believing that their "extremism" represents a threat.

☐ Stifling conversations by your manner of making opening statements of personal belief; creating discomfort for those who have dissenting opinions, putting them at an immediate disadvantage.

☐ Prejudging others on their appearance and on their presence, tending to eliminate those who, if given an opportunity, might otherwise be worthwhile companions; forcing others to respond to your queries with either-or answers; hampering a view of possible alternatives.

☐ Waiting for things to unfold—representative of your fragile control of events; trying to win the support of others even while your plans tend to crumble; putting others on the defensive to avoid unpleasant questions regarding the high standards you've set for yourself.

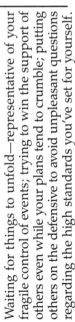

EXTENDED PATTERN F

THIRTY-FOUR – SURVIVOR

You Pose Potential Danger to Yourself by:

☐ Reluctantly believing in the promises of others; placing blind faith in those who tend to be convincing with emotional appeal rather than with logic and reasoning; having your hopes dashed.

☐ Living vicariously through those who are more successful than you; appearing to be hostile as you question their ethics; jeopardizing your relationships with others in your desire to get to the "bottom of things."

☐ Giving up your personal interests, while perhaps only temporarily, making you think less of yourself; feeling worse when you are expected to adopt the interests of others, as well; sensing a loss of control.

☐ Seeking ways to become useful to others; hoping to be viewed as essential in their plans; trying to identify a role for yourself without sacrificing your self-esteem.

PATTERN ONE TWENTY-THREE
Extended Interpretation

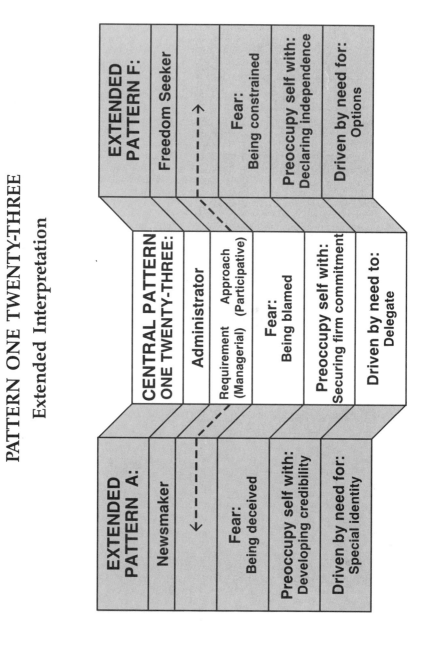

EXTENDED PATTERN A:	CENTRAL PATTERN ONE TWENTY-THREE:	EXTENDED PATTERN F:
Newsmaker	Administrator	Freedom Seeker
	Requirement (Managerial) Approach (Participative)	
Fear: Being deceived	Fear: Being blamed	Fear: Being constrained
Preoccupy self with: Developing credibility	Preoccupy self with: Securing firm commitment	Preoccupy self with: Declaring independence
Driven by need for: Special identity	Driven by need to: Delegate	Driven by need for: Options

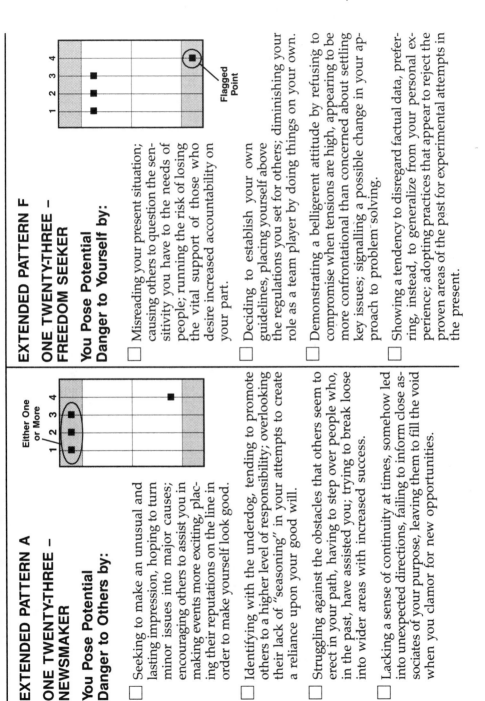

EXTENDED PATTERN A

ONE TWENTY-THREE – NEWSMAKER

Either One or More

You Pose Potential Danger to Others by:

☐ Seeking to make an unusual and lasting impression, hoping to turn minor issues into major causes; encouraging others to assist you in making events more exciting, placing their reputations on the line in order to make yourself look good.

☐ Identifying with the underdog, tending to promote others to a higher level of responsibility; overlooking their lack of "seasoning" in your attempts to create a reliance upon your good will.

☐ Struggling against the obstacles that others seem to erect in your path, having to step over people who, in the past, have assisted you; trying to break loose into wider areas with increased success.

☐ Lacking a sense of continuity at times, somehow led into unexpected directions, failing to inform close associates of your purpose, leaving them to fill the void when you clamor for new opportunities.

EXTENDED PATTERN F

ONE TWENTY-THREE – FREEDOM SEEKER

Flagged Point

You Pose Potential Danger to Yourself by:

☐ Misreading your present situation; causing others to question the sensitivity you have to the needs of people; running the risk of losing the vital support of those who desire increased accountability on your part.

☐ Deciding to establish your own guidelines, placing yourself above the regulations you set for others; diminishing your role as a team player by doing things on your own.

☐ Demonstrating a belligerent attitude by refusing to compromise when tensions are high, appearing to be more confrontational than concerned about settling key issues; signalling a possible change in your approach to problem solving.

☐ Showing a tendency to disregard factual data, preferring, instead, to generalize from your personal experience; adopting practices that appear to reject the proven areas of the past for experimental attempts in the present.

PATTERN ONE TWENTY-FOUR
Extended Interpretation

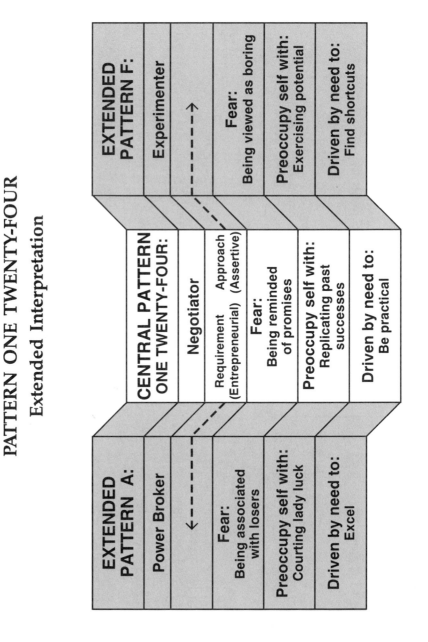

EXTENDED PATTERN A:	CENTRAL PATTERN ONE TWENTY-FOUR:	EXTENDED PATTERN F:
Power Broker	Negotiator	Experimenter
	Requirement (Entrepreneurial) Approach (Assertive)	
Fear: Being associated with losers	Fear: Being reminded of promises	Fear: Being viewed as boring
Preoccupy self with: Courting lady luck	Preoccupy self with: Replicating past successes	Preoccupy self with: Exercising potential
Driven by need to: Excel	Driven by need to: Be practical	Driven by need to: Find shortcuts

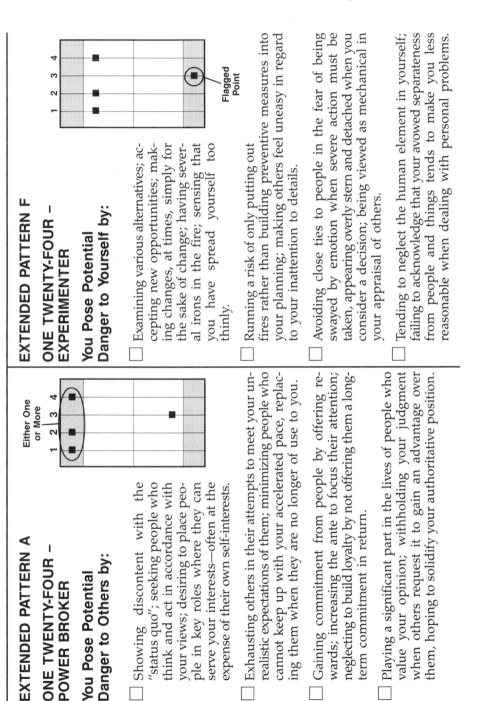

EXTENDED PATTERN A

ONE TWENTY-FOUR – POWER BROKER

You Pose Potential Danger to Others by:

☐ Showing discontent with the "status quo"; seeking people who think and act in accordance with your views; desiring to place people in key roles where they can serve your interests—often at the expense of their own self-interests.

☐ Exhausting others in their attempts to meet your unrealistic expectations of them; minimizing people who cannot keep up with your accelerated pace, replacing them when they are no longer of use to you.

☐ Gaining commitment from people by offering rewards; increasing the ante to focus their attention; neglecting to build loyalty by not offering them a long-term commitment in return.

☐ Playing a significant part in the lives of people who value your opinion; withholding your judgment when others request it to gain an advantage over them, hoping to solidify your authoritative position.

EXTENDED PATTERN F

ONE TWENTY-FOUR – EXPERIMENTER

You Pose Potential Danger to Yourself by:

☐ Examining various alternatives; accepting new opportunities; making changes, at times, simply for the sake of change; having several irons in the fire; sensing that you have spread yourself too thinly.

☐ Running a risk of only putting out fires rather than building preventive measures into your planning; making others feel uneasy in regard to your inattention to details.

☐ Avoiding close ties to people in the fear of being swayed by emotion when severe action must be taken, appearing overly stern and detached when you consider a decision; being viewed as mechanical in your appraisal of others.

☐ Tending to neglect the human element in yourself; failing to acknowledge that your avowed separateness from people and things tends to make you less reasonable when dealing with personal problems.

PATTERN ONE THIRTY-FOUR
Extended Interpretation

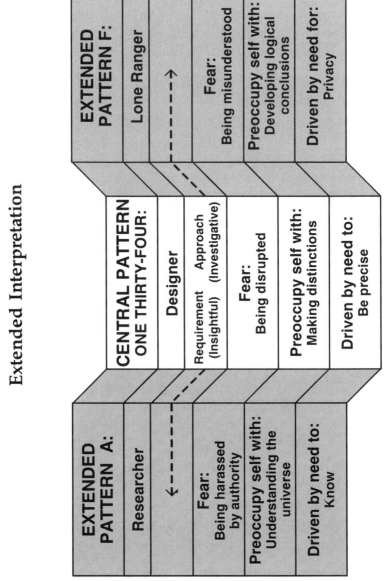

EXTENDED PATTERN A:

Researcher

Fear:
Being harassed by authority

Preoccupy self with:
Understanding the universe

Driven by need to:
Know

CENTRAL PATTERN ONE THIRTY-FOUR:

Designer

Requirement (Insightful)   Approach (Investigative)

Fear:
Being disrupted

Preoccupy self with:
Making distinctions

Driven by need to:
Be precise

EXTENDED PATTERN F:

Lone Ranger

Fear:
Being misunderstood

Preoccupy self with:
Developing logical conclusions

Driven by need for:
Privacy

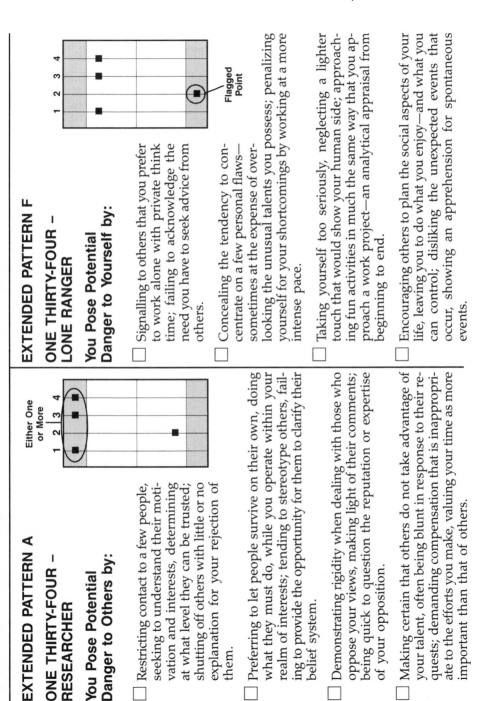

EXTENDED PATTERN A

ONE THIRTY-FOUR – RESEARCHER

Either One or More

You Pose Potential Danger to Others by:

☐ Restricting contact to a few people, seeking to understand their motivation and interests, determining at what level they can be trusted; shutting off others with little or no explanation for your rejection of them.

☐ Preferring to let people survive on their own, doing what they must do, while you operate within your realm of interests; tending to stereotype others, failing to provide the opportunity for them to clarify their belief system.

☐ Demonstrating rigidity when dealing with those who oppose your views, making light of their comments; being quick to question the reputation or expertise of your opposition.

☐ Making certain that others do not take advantage of your talent, often being blunt in response to their requests; demanding compensation that is inappropriate to the efforts you make, valuing your time as more important than that of others.

EXTENDED PATTERN F

ONE THIRTY-FOUR – LONE RANGER

Flagged Point

You Pose Potential Danger to Yourself by:

☐ Signalling to others that you prefer to work alone with private think time; failing to acknowledge the need you have to seek advice from others.

☐ Concealing the tendency to concentrate on a few personal flaws—sometimes at the expense of overlooking the unusual talents you possess; penalizing yourself for your shortcomings by working at a more intense pace.

☐ Taking yourself too seriously, neglecting a lighter touch that would show your human side; approaching fun activities in much the same way that you approach a work project—an analytical appraisal from beginning to end.

☐ Encouraging others to plan the social aspects of your life, leaving you to do what you enjoy—and what you can control; disliking the unexpected events that occur, showing an apprehension for spontaneous events.

PATTERN TWO THIRTY-FOUR
Extended Interpretation

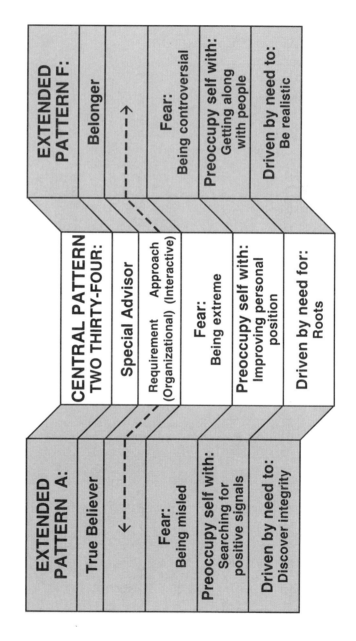

EXTENDED PATTERN A:	CENTRAL PATTERN TWO THIRTY-FOUR:	EXTENDED PATTERN F:
True Believer	Special Advisor	Belonger
	Requirement (Organizational) Approach (Interactive)	
Fear: Being misled	Fear: Being extreme	Fear: Being controversial
Preoccupy self with: Searching for positive signals	Preoccupy self with: Improving personal position	Preoccupy self with: Getting along with people
Driven by need to: Discover integrity	Driven by need for: Roots	Driven by need to: Be realistic

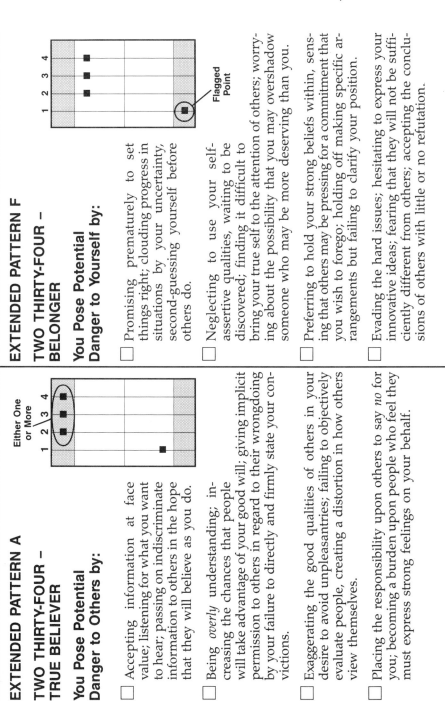

EXTENDED PATTERN A

TWO THIRTY-FOUR – TRUE BELIEVER

You Pose Potential Danger to Others by:

☐ Accepting information at face value; listening for what you want to hear; passing on indiscriminate information to others in the hope that they will believe as you do.

☐ Being *overly* understanding; increasing the chances that people will take advantage of your good will; giving implicit permission to others in regard to their wrongdoing by your failure to directly and firmly state your convictions.

☐ Exaggerating the good qualities of others in your desire to avoid unpleasantries; failing to objectively evaluate people, creating a distortion in how others view themselves.

☐ Placing the responsibility upon others to say *no* for you; becoming a burden upon people who feel they must express strong feelings on your behalf.

EXTENDED PATTERN F

TWO THIRTY-FOUR – BELONGER

You Pose Potential Danger to Yourself by:

☐ Promising prematurely to set things right; clouding progress in situations by your uncertainty, second-guessing yourself before others do.

☐ Neglecting to use your self-assertive qualities, waiting to be discovered; finding it difficult to bring your true self to the attention of others; worrying about the possibility that you may overshadow someone who may be more deserving than you.

☐ Preferring to hold your strong beliefs within, sensing that others may be pressing for a commitment that you wish to forego; holding off making specific arrangements but failing to clarify your position.

☐ Evading the hard issues; hesitating to express your innovative ideas; fearing that they will not be sufficiently different from others; accepting the conclusions of others with little or no refutation.

Interpretation Central

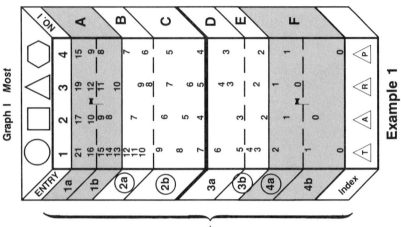

Example 1

Procedure for Developing Your Energetics Flowchart

1. Refer to Graph I, II, or III as directed.

- Note the index to the left of the graph (Example 1).

- Circle the index numbers which are across from the X's in the columns. You may have to circle a number more than once.

Example 1: Note that index numbers 2a, 2b, 3b, and 4a have been circled.

2. Refer to Energetics Flowchart, Part I, II, or III that corresponds to your Graph No.

- Circle the same index numbers on the flowchart that you have circled on the graph.

- Look at the flowchart in terms of columns 1, 2, 3, 4, which match the four columns of the graph.

- Circle that portion of the column on the flowchart that corresponds to the X on the graph.

- Read and study the four areas of the flowchart that you have circled.

- Read the companion area that is in the same block on the flowchart (indicated by the arrow in Example 2).

Example 2: In column 1, the person would read 3a as well as 3b.

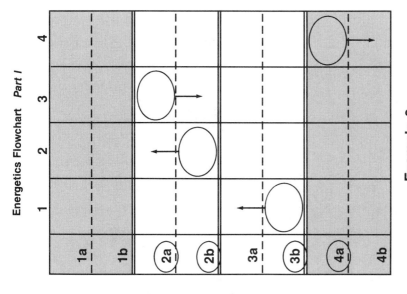

Energetics Flowchart *Part I*

Example 2

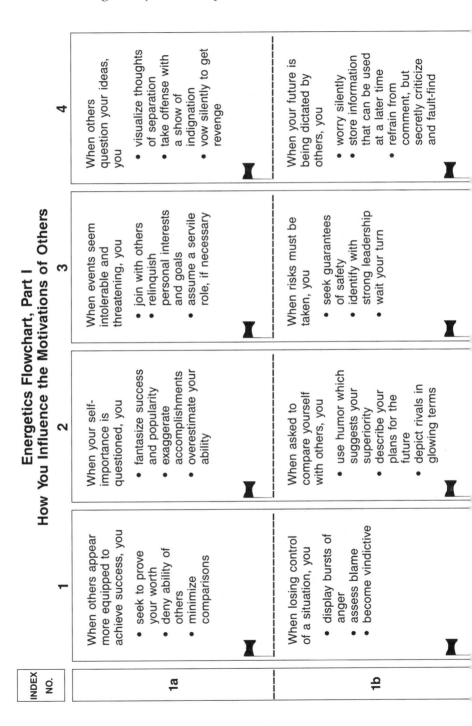

Energetics Flowchart, Part I
How You Influence the Motivations of Others

INDEX NO.	1	2	3	4
1a	When others appear more equipped to achieve success, you • seek to prove your worth • deny ability of others • minimize comparisons	When your self-importance is questioned, you • fantasize success and popularity • exaggerate accomplishments • overestimate your ability	When events seem intolerable and threatening, you • join with others • relinquish personal interests and goals • assume a servile role, if necessary	When others question your ideas, you • visualize thoughts of separation • take offense with a show of indignation • vow silently to get revenge
1b	When losing control of a situation, you • display bursts of anger • assess blame • become vindictive	When asked to compare yourself with others, you • use humor which suggests your superiority • describe your plans for the future • depict rivals in glowing terms	When risks must be taken, you • seek guarantees of safety • identify with strong leadership • wait your turn	When your future is being dictated by others, you • worry silently • store information that can be used at a later time • refrain from comment, but secretly criticize and fault-find

Energetics Flowchart, Part I
How You Influence the Motivations of Others (Continued)

INDEX NO.	1	2	3	4
2a	When your position is challenged, you • use forceful methods • project confidence • employ strategy and competitive skills	When you identify with a cause, you • employ persuasive techniques • project a winsome personality • generate enthusiasm	When cooperation is requested, you • listen attentively • show allegiance to respected associates • use specialized skills	When corrective measures are needed, you • uphold standards • support your new position with facts • adhere closely to rules
2b	When problems demand new solutions, you • develop creative uniqueness • show single-minded intensity • discard old methods	When people need support, you • evoke responsive chords in others • use appropriate timing • give generously of yourself	When others are being disruptive, you • exhibit patience • soothe ruffled feelings • compliment the efforts of others	When emotional appeals sway others, you • dismiss ideas of being shallow and irrational • check and recheck assumptions • express preference for conventional methods

Energetics Flowchart, Part I
How You Influence the Motivations of Others (Continued)

INDEX NO.	1	2	3	4
3a	When unforeseen events occur, you • identify successful methods of the past • create options • employ planned risk taking	When your ideas are opposed, you • meet privately with your critics • request time to explain • take a direct approach	When change occurs, you • Search for personal advantages • press to see how you fit into plans • project firmness and cooperation	When others attempt to treat all people alike, you • point out the different abilities of others • demand that the minority opinion be heard • express yourself forcefully
3b	When personal goals are jeopardized, you • seek encouragement and hopeful signs from others • adjust goals downward • rely on expert opinion	When encountering assertive people, you • take an uncompromising stance • retreat when others are uncooperative • withhold information	When others insist on traditional methods, you • show discontent • move toward independence • use unorthodox ideas	When others lead with a directive approach, you • contest authoritarian attempts • elicit support in criticizing the process • project self-reliance

Energetics Flowchart, Part I
How You Influence the Motivations of Others (Concluded)

INDEX NO.	1	2	3	4
4a	When accepting responsibility, you • demonstrate anxiety • search for acceptance of your contributions • brace yourself for critical appraisal	When pressed to communicate, you • withdraw without explanation • use blunt expressions • rely on others to communicate	When seeking individuality, you • criticize stereotypes • use sarcasm • delegate unpleasant tasks to others	When regulations are imposed, you • question their necessity • assume they are for others • use them to your advantage
4b	When major decisions are made by others, you • depend upon their good will • experience powerlessness • question your ability to lead	When misunderstandings prevail, you • use silence as a strategy • convey disappointment • expect an apology from others	When ties to the group become strained, you • display boredom • search for new acquaintances • seek a new life-style	When conformity is required, you • resist expected behavior • demonstrate belligerence if the request is contrary to your beliefs • become hostile when reminded of your duty

Energetics Flowchart, Part II
Your Belief System

INDEX NO.	1	2	3	4
1a	YOUR BELIEF Only a select few should have power. Motivated to have power over others	YOUR BELIEF Binding people to you ensures approval for who you are and what you do. Motivated to captivate others	YOUR BELIEF Your needs are satisfied through the strengths of others. Motivated to become attached to others	YOUR BELIEF All thinking people should come to the same conclusion. Motivated to judge the actions of others
1b	YOUR BELIEF Claim ownership of whatever you want. Motivated to understand human behavior to gain superiority	YOUR BELIEF You have a high and majestic calling. Motivated to orchestrate feelings of pain and joy to elicit support from others	YOUR BELIEF Help others so that you can feel good about yourself. Motivated to place the interests of others over the interests of yourself	YOUR BELIEF Answers to great problems come from logic, analysis, and systematized experiences. Motivated to value reason over emotion

Energetics Flowchart, Part II
Your Belief System (Continued)

INDEX NO.	1	2	3	4
2a	YOUR BELIEF The highest value is influencing the lives of others. Motivated to effect change and control	YOUR BELIEF The highest value is expressing self and developing individuality. Motivated to assist others in extending themselves beyond their self-imposed limits	YOUR BELIEF The highest value is helping others in meaningful ways. Motivated to hold people together by performing tasks that please even the most critical	YOUR BELIEF The highest value is breaking through ignorance. Motivated to search for knowledge; to withhold support for ill-advised popular ideas
2b	YOUR BELIEF Sustained effort flows from internal forces rather than from outer coercion. Motivated to question direct orders, exceed designated boundaries	YOUR BELIEF Each individual should be part of the decision-making process. Motivated to challenge limitations placed on freedom of expression	YOUR BELIEF Conflict is minimized by showing appreciation to others. Motivated to praise the contributions of loyal and agreeable people	YOUR BELIEF Work to improve the system from within rather than from the outside. Motivated to criticize and perfect according to personal standards

Energetics Flowchart, Part II
Your Belief System (Continued)

INDEX NO.	1	2	3	4
3a	YOUR BELIEF Those with more experience and knowledge should guide the masses. Motivated to question your own judgments	YOUR BELIEF Extreme positions should be avoided. Motivated to curb impulsive desires and strive for stability	YOUR BELIEF If we don't stick together, we will hang separately. Motivated to remain with those who have similar work values	YOUR BELIEF Avoid impatience even when unresolved problems remain. Motivated to operate from a balance of feelings and logic
3b	YOUR BELIEF The unknown is reason for fear and unrest. Motivated to proceed slowly when pushed toward new events	YOUR BELIEF Change is acceptable only when personal benefits are obvious. Motivated to adapt to change in private	YOUR BELIEF Each person is responsible for finding and expressing freedom. Motivated to free yourself from commitment to those who make you feel obligated	YOUR BELIEF New solutions require trial and error. Motivated to develop flexible and proven success methods

Energetics Flowchart, Part II
Your Belief System (Concluded)

INDEX NO.	1	2	3	4
4a	YOUR BELIEF Life, at best, is hopeful, not optimistic. Motivated to depend on present circumstances rather than stretch for new experiences	YOUR BELIEF Feelings play a small part in selecting a correct course of action. Motivated to search for truth apart from the emotional urges of others	YOUR BELIEF Flexible and creative people should be freed from boring activities. Motivated to use responsible people to fulfill mundane tasks	YOUR BELIEF Independence is found by operating from one's own private center. Motivated to ignore rules that regulate human relations
4b	YOUR BELIEF Others attempt to use people for their own ends. Motivated to feel sorry for yourself	YOUR BELIEF Associate only with those of like values. Motivated to be skeptical of those who appear to know more than you do	YOUR BELIEF Escape from boredom justifies extreme action. Motivated to refuse comments or to give reasons for actions	YOUR BELIEF Safe relationships are secondary to the freedom of selecting whomever you choose. Motivated to select controversial associates and use unorthodox methods

Energetics Flowchart, Part III
How You Affect Others

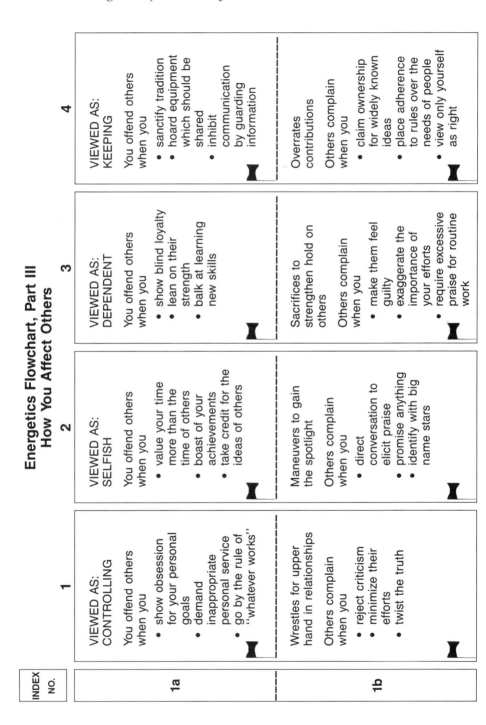

INDEX NO.	1	2	3	4
	VIEWED AS: CONTROLLING	VIEWED AS: SELFISH	VIEWED AS: DEPENDENT	VIEWED AS: KEEPING
1a	You offend others when you • show obsession for your personal goals • demand inappropriate personal service • go by the rule of "whatever works"	You offend others when you • value your time more than the time of others • boast of your achievements • take credit for the ideas of others	You offend others when you • show blind loyalty • lean on their strength • balk at learning new skills	You offend others when you • sanctify tradition • hoard equipment which should be shared • inhibit communication by guarding information
1b	Wrestles for upper hand in relationships Others complain when you • reject criticism • minimize their efforts • twist the truth	Maneuvers to gain the spotlight Others complain when you • direct conversation to elicit praise • promise anything • identify with big name stars	Sacrifices to strengthen hold on others Others complain when you • make them feel guilty • exaggerate the importance of your efforts • require excessive praise for routine work	Overrates contributions Others complain when you • claim ownership for widely known ideas • place adherence to rules over the needs of people • view only yourself as right

Energetics Flowchart, Part III
How You Affect Others (Continued)

INDEX NO.	1	2	3	4
2a	VIEWED AS: DIRECTIVE Others respond because you • treat others as you treat yourself • demonstrate fast reaction time • take the lead	VIEWED AS: PERSUASIVE Others respond because you • generate enthusiasm • demonstrate belief in what you do • verbalize convincingly	VIEWED AS: TRUSTWORTHY Others respond because you • demonstrate follow-through • value truthfulness • show sincerity	VIEWED AS: PROTECTIVE Others respond because you • remember linkages between past and present • demonstrate conscientiousness • represent continuity in values—doing things right
2b	Eager and willing to help others advance You gain support because you • use innovative planning • project vitality • overcome objections	Spontaneous and quick to reduce tension You gain support because you • express with words how others are feeling • create a positive climate • solicit ideas from others	Friendly and cooperative in solving problems You gain support because you • commit self • assume responsibility for specific detail • lead by example	Displays a calming effect on others You gain support because you • reason from evidence • show tactfulness • develop a climate of respect

Energetics Flowchart, Part III
How You Affect Others (Continued)

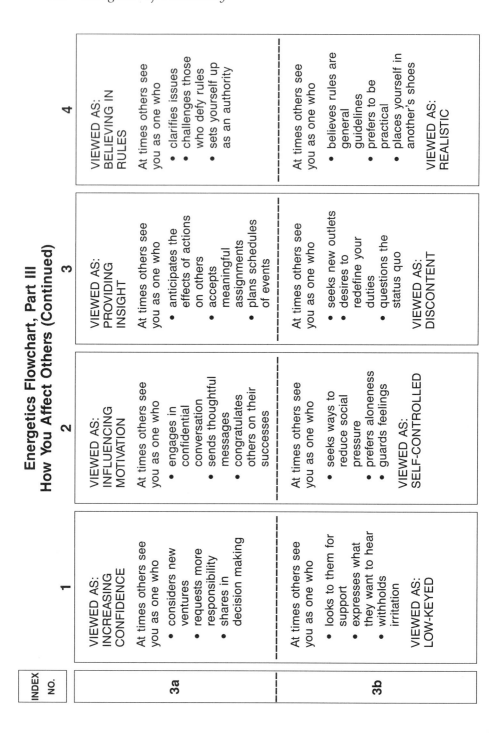

INDEX NO.	1	2	3	4
3a	VIEWED AS: INCREASING CONFIDENCE At times others see you as one who • considers new ventures • requests more responsibility • shares in decision making	VIEWED AS: INFLUENCING MOTIVATION At times others see you as one who • engages in confidential conversation • sends thoughtful messages • congratulates others on their successes	VIEWED AS: PROVIDING INSIGHT At times others see you as one who • anticipates the effects of actions on others • accepts meaningful assignments • plans schedules of events	VIEWED AS: BELIEVING IN RULES At times others see you as one who • clarifies issues • challenges those who defy rules • sets yourself up as an authority
3b	At times others see you as one who • looks to them for support • expresses what they want to hear • withholds irritation VIEWED AS: LOW-KEYED	At times others see you as one who • seeks ways to reduce social pressure • prefers aloneness • guards feelings VIEWED AS: SELF-CONTROLLED	At times others see you as one who • seeks new outlets • desires to redefine your duties • questions the status quo VIEWED AS: DISCONTENT	At times others see you as one who • believes rules are general guidelines • prefers to be practical • places yourself in another's shoes VIEWED AS: REALISTIC

Energetics Flowchart, Part III
How You Affect Others (Concluded)

INDEX NO.	1	2	3	4
4a	VIEWED AS: RESIGNED You are unsettling to others when you • reject challenging assignments • wait for others to make the first move • believe that fate has the best hand	VIEWED AS: SECLUDED You are unsettling to others when you • remain aloof • appear self-conscious • use sarcastic wit and humor	VIEWED AS: UNCOMMITTED You are unsettling to others when you • flaunt your independence • resist overtures for close friendship • find fault with others	VIEWED AS: DEFIANT You are unsettling to others when you • appear obstinate • question the establishment • interpret new meanings of law and order
4b	Withdraws from conflict You are unsettling to others when you • increase tension by avoiding issues • vacillate in your thinking • minimize yourself	Resigns self to absence of joy You are unsettling to others when you • show mistrust and suspicion of others • expect the worst • communicate bluntly	Expects group benefits without assuming obligations You are unsettling to others when you • appear elusive • do only the things you enjoy • miss appointments	Takes advantage to further own needs You are unsettling to others when you • rely exclusively on personal judgment • cite rules that benefit you • chide those who need wisdom outside of self

Leadership Interpretation

PATTERN ONE
Leadership Interpretation

PART I   You Seek A Sense Of Self-Importance by:

☐ Placing a greater emphasis on *individual* behavior than on *group* behavior. See chart 1A.

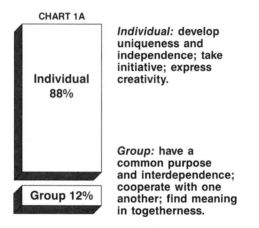

CHART 1A

Individual 88%

Group 12%

Individual: **develop uniqueness and independence; take initiative; express creativity.**

Group: **have a common purpose and interdependence; cooperate with one another; find meaning in togetherness.**

☐ Preferring *individual* behavior (88% of the time) over *group* behavior (12% of the time).

☐ Exercising your personal power; resisting any interference; viewing a democratic process as too slow and constraining.

☐ Taking risks; overcoming obstacles —and, if necessary, dictating to others.

☐ Comparing your assertiveness to others'; evaluating yourself favorably; justifying your overt actions on the basis that others abdicate or refuse to take a position.

☐ Insisting on running the show; being opportunistic in your dealings— arrogant, ostentatious, and showing off potential victories.

☐ Causing others to reconsider the way in which they think and act; forcing them to seek additional time to consider your demands.

☐ Achieving your position through introspective viewing of others; understanding them better than they understand you.

☐ Employing strategy; often withholding thoughts and intentions—causing others to react in a similar manner.

☐ Rewarding those who provide you with structure in which to operate; offering them power positions; placing those positions above the purpose of the structure or the organization.

☐ Showing an *imbalance* when using the character **tension points** of *individual* and *group*.

You Intensify Your Individual-Group Imbalance by:

☐ Believing in your superiority; feeling that you have a right to take control; pointing to your achievements; succeeding where others have failed.

☐ Justifying your effort to gain the upper hand in relationships on the basis of your independent thinking; asserting that eventually *one* person will have the reins of leadership and it might as well be you.

☐ Using the group or a relationship to entice individuals to be responsive to your needs; attempting to accomplish this through the control and distribution of rewards to each person.

☐ Reminding yourself **too infrequently** that you can learn from others who do things differently—working with and through people to reduce the anxiety level. Because you desire to avoid emotional highs and lows, you occasionally consider the methods that involve closer contact with helpful associates who can direct your activities toward a purposeful goal.

PART II   You Deal With Right and Wrong by:

☐ Placing a greater emphasis on *justice* behavior than *caring* behavior. See chart 1B.

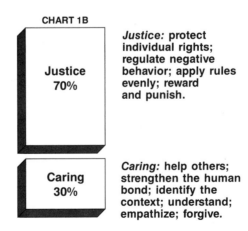

CHART 1B

Justice 70%

Justice: protect individual rights; regulate negative behavior; apply rules evenly; reward and punish.

Caring 30%

Caring: help others; strengthen the human bond; identify the context; understand; empathize; forgive.

☐ Preferring *justice* behavior (70% of the time) over *caring* behavior (30% of the time).

☐ Becoming a law unto yourself; trying to legitimize your actions by drawing up rules "after the fact."

☐ Favoring practices that use law enforcement because they speed your progress; applying them quickly to avoid the questioning and delay that usually accompany the lengthy probes into a person's motivation.

☐ Perceiving wrongdoing as habit-forming; necessitating a penalty; giving little hope to those who need rehabilitation.

☐ Believing that people are unequal in their ability to make decisions; viewing law and legislation as a way to ensure that others' decisions will not be harmful to you.

☐ Moving to lay claim to that which can belong to the strong; believing that the weak lack decisiveness.

☐ Making attempts to enshrine your "zeal" as a virtue in some settings; camouflaging the trampling of others as industriousness.

☐ Viewing others as replicas of yourself; believing that you know what is best for them; deciding how they should gain from others.

☐ Employing the *caring* factor primarily for those who are personally close to you; modifying your stern use of *justice* to maintain their support.

☐ Showing an imbalance when using the character **tension points** of *justice* and *caring*.

You Intensify Your Justice-Caring Imbalance by:

☐ Failing to correctly interpret the deep concerns of others; displaying little sensitivity to their needs.

☐ Viewing others as means to an end rather than people in their own right with feelings and thinking different from your own.

☐ Considering individuals as obstacles in the way, or as things—resources— to be used and discarded.

☐ Using a heavy hand to instill fear in the minds of those who demonstrate opposition; urging them on to at least a show of force against you; knowing that you have an efficient system of rules and retaliation.

☐ Reminding yourself **too infrequently** that your decisions related to right and wrong are only as good as the information on which they are based. There is a need to update your data and even to share your information with others. You entertain the idea of scheduling times to listen to others, hoping to increase understanding of how people with differing personalities respond to rules and regulations.

PART III   You Pursue A Course Of Action by:

☐ Placing a greater emphasis on *contention* behavior than on *consensus* behavior. See chart 1C.

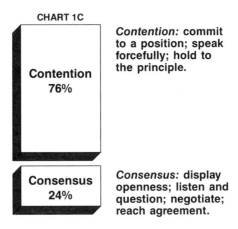

CHART 1C

Contention 76%

Contention: commit to a position; speak forcefully; hold to the principle.

Consensus 24%

Consensus: display openness; listen and question; negotiate; reach agreement.

☐ Preferring *contention* behavior (76% of the time) over *consensus* behavior (24% of the time).

☐ Contending forcefully with a briskness of movement, an economy of verbalization, and a readiness to do battle, if necessary.

☐ Expressing your ideas as decisions that are already made.

☐ Focusing your attempts on possessing and "having"; expressing yourself through money, power, and knowledge.

☐ Putting together your need for "having" with the benefits of ownership; preoccupying yourself with ideas of claiming ownership; posing a threat to those who stand in your way.

☐ Gathering support from those who become excited over the strength of your convictions and the possibilities of sharing in the rewards.

☐ Dismissing those who become uneasy and uncomfortable before the intensity of your argument to *take* rather than to *negotiate.*

☐ Commanding attention and respect from those who have similar convictions and confrontational methods as yourself; giving in to their strength only if it is greater than yours.

☐ Viewing negotiating and compromise only as a last resort; using this avenue only when few individuals support your ideas.

☐ Showing an *imbalance* when using the character **tension points** of *contention* and *consensus.*

You Intensify Your Contention-Consensus Imbalance by:

☐ Being stubborn; employing hard-headed resistance; impeding possible compromise.

☐ Finding it difficult to trust others; viewing their motivations with suspicion; preferring to advise yourself.

☐ Placing a psychological distance between yourself and others; withholding your thoughts and feelings; refusing to carefully study positions that differ from your own.

☐ Causing others to delay or withhold their support from you; refusing their requests to be more flexible in your position.

☐ Reminding yourself **too infrequently** that you appear to show your worst side when people seek clarification or seem to doubt you. People tend to resist you because of your mannerisms rather than because of your ideas. They are apt to make harsh judgments that may or may not be indicated—evaluating your intensity as excitability, your intuitiveness as impulsivity, your self-confidence as self-centeredness.

PATTERN TWO

Leadership Interpretation

PART I   You Seek A Sense Of Self-Importance by:

☐ Placing a greater emphasis on *individual* behavior than on *group* behavior. See chart 2A.

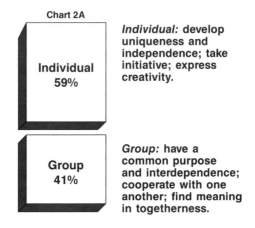

Chart 2A

Individual 59% — *Individual:* develop uniqueness and independence; take initiative; express creativity.

Group 41% — *Group:* have a common purpose and interdependence; cooperate with one another; find meaning in togetherness.

☐ Preferring *individual* behavior (59% of the time) over *group* behavior (41% of the time).

☐ Creating an environment which highlights your best attributes—willing to forgive and understand others; encouraging them to express their feelings and their displeasure with you.

☐ Putting your best foot forward; listing ways to evaluate your magnetism—winning over rivals in attracting the opposite sex, gaining approval from an authority figure, or receiving the recognition of your peers.

☐ Urging others to trust you; giving examples of how you helped others to move ahead quickly; allowing them to use your contacts.

☐ Verbalizing what others are feeling but are afraid to say; making others feel that you are on their side.

☐ Acting as a cheerleader for individuals and groups; guarding, however, your autonomy from the norms and constrictions of the group.

☐ Living in the present; putting unpleasant events in the past; overcoming criticism from those who complain of your broken promises; convincing them of your forgetfulness and dislike of tedious tasks.

☐ Being one step ahead of others; using the opportune time to be viewed as having the winning edge; employing charm and seductiveness to change the course of events, when necessary.

☐ Showing an *imbalance* when using the character **tension points** of *individual* and *group*.

You Intensify Your Individual-Group Imbalance by:

☐ Making yourself look good by giving equal weight to all sides of a conflict; seeking common ground.

☐ Seeking validation as an outstanding person; visualizing yourself in close association with the inner group; refusing the more realistic assessment that you tend to accent your individualism verbally but retain only fleeting commitments to relationships and to groups.

☐ Desiring to win the approval of others; changing your position to mesh with the position of someone you respect; placing your personal convictions second to receiving approval.

☐ Socializing with people at every opportunity; hoping to gain their affection; failing to realize that you need time for inner contemplation.

☐ Reminding yourself **too infrequently** that support and reinforcement from a *few* loyal persons may be more meaningful for you than from *many* persons who only casually give you a nod of approval. It is easy to forget that the "roar of the crowd" is quite temporary and often misleading.

PART II   You Deal With Right and Wrong by:

☐ Placing a greater emphasis on *caring* behavior than on *justice* behavior. See chart 2B.

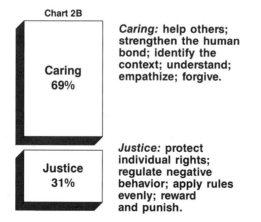

Chart 2B

Caring 69%

Caring: help others; strengthen the human bond; identify the context; understand; empathize; forgive.

Justice 31%

Justice: protect individual rights; regulate negative behavior; apply rules evenly; reward and punish.

☐ Preferring *caring* behavior (69% of the time) to *justice* behavior (31% of the time).

☐ Identifying with the large number of people who, like yourself, fail to observe *all* the details and "small print"; believing that it is impossible to prosecute such large numbers.

☐ Interpreting rules and regulations in a casual way; seeking possible loopholes that place human beings above the law.

☐ Relaxing the rigid application of hard and fast rules; being good-natured with those who appear overly fearful of making mistakes when complying with regulations.

☐ Requesting help from experts to advise you on the intricacies of rules; pleading innocent to misunderstanding because of the complexities of the written documents.

☐ Finding it difficult to administer an "eye for an eye" justice; arguing for the passionate and forgivable incident.

☐ Providing encouragement to people in following the "higher law"; recalling breakthroughs that stress a "law of love."

☐ Placing yourself at the mercy of the "court"; using emotional arguments when you fall short of the mark.

☐ Urging others to believe that you have learned your lesson; willingly "repenting" when sweet talk, charm, and persuasive arguments fail to win your day in court.

☐ Showing an *imbalance* when using the character **tension points** of *justice* and *caring*.

You Intensify Your Justice-Caring Imbalance by:

☐ Believing that laws, in many ways, are only general guidelines; minimizing the importance of holding to the letter of the law.

☐ Using human frailties as an excuse for slighting rules, restrictions, and constraints; finding it difficult to discipline yourself.

☐ Failing to recognize that small infractions of rules and regulations show a disregard for the rights and interests of others; causing others to become irritated over your nonchalant manner.

☐ Leading the way to increased litigation as you discover ways to use the justice system to gain monetary compensation; openly admitting your intentions to "get what you can."

☐ Concealing your fear of the extremity of justice; sensing that other human beings may allow their emotions to push them toward punitive judgments, just as you allow your emotions to propel you to deny your concern about being penalized.

☐ Reminding yourself **too infrequently** that establishments operate more efficiently when people adhere to prescribed limits. When and if your "conversion" occurs, you may become a dedicated zealot to regulatory causes. At that point, others will be able to pass you on the highway because you are obeying the speed limit.

PART III   You Pursue A Course Of Action by:

☐ Placing a greater emphasis on *consensus* behavior than on *contention* behavior. See chart 2C.

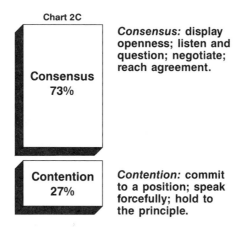

Chart 2C

**Consensus
73%**

Consensus: display openness; listen and question; negotiate; reach agreement.

**Contention
27%**

Contention: commit to a position; speak forcefully; hold to the principle.

☐ Preferring *consensus* behavior (73% of the time) over *contention* behavior (27% of the time).

☐ Responding to others with concern and warmth; urging people to be as open about their opinions as you are.

☐ Selecting emotionally charged words to accompany the enthusiasm in your voice and manner; using the testimony of nationally known people who share your ideas.

☐ Encouraging others to express themselves ahead of you; observing which ideas are well-received; aligning your ideas and showing the similarity to popularly held opinions.

☐ Summarizing the best of ideas; hitchhiking on statements of belief to enhance your potential role as leader or lieutenant to the decision maker.

☐ Using humor to coax people away from a contentious mode—teasing, joking, using lightheartedness to get others to recognize and possibly accept a different point of view.

☐ Using people to support a cause that represents a majority opinion—one that will serve the best interests of many; inspiring others to view themselves as a rallying point.

☐ Showing willingness to give up your opinion in order to create unity; reminding others of your flexibility in dealing with critical issues.

☐ Showing an *imbalance* when using the character **tension points** of *contention* and *consensus*.

You Intensify Your Contention-Consensus Imbalance by:

☐ Projecting yourself as one who accepts a variety of opinions; convincing yourself that you are hardly likely to attract others if your actions are viewed as aggressive, contentious, or judgmental.

☐ Recognizing that quarreling people are not to your advantage; discovering that your desire to look good and bring people together makes you a catalyst in the interchange of ideas.

☐ Giving greater attention to the style of your delivery, which will bring attention and approval, rather than to the soundness of your position or the logic of your opinion.

☐ Accenting the points of agreement rather than dwelling upon the difference of opinion; displaying an optimism that often places you in the role of leadership.

☐ Reminding yourself **too infrequently** that there is a need to secure approval for unpopular ideas as well as those that are easily accepted; forgetting that good problem solving requires a critical approach.

PATTERN THREE
Leadership Interpretation

PART I   You Seek A Sense Of Self-Importance by:

☐ Placing a greater emphasis on *group* behavior than on *individual* behavior. See chart 3A.

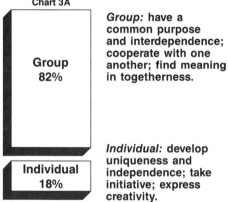

Chart 3A

Group: have a common purpose and interdependence; cooperate with one another; find meaning in togetherness.

Group 82%

Individual 18%

Individual: develop uniqueness and independence; take initiative; express creativity.

☐ Preferring *group* behavior (82% of the time) over *individual* behavior (18% of the time).

☐ Directing your actions toward the welfare of others; following a pattern of steadiness and resourcefulness.

☐ Accepting a sense of responsibility for those tasks or people important to you, regardless of criticism.

☐ Frequently denying yourself the things you want; conforming to the high expectations of others; hoping to avoid hostility.

☐ Forming a coalition with others to ward off people who tend to be aggressive and threatening; developing an obstacle that can be opposed and disliked—ensuring unity against a common enemy.

☐ Verbalizing with the companionable "we" rather than the solitary "I."

☐ Putting down roots with those who have interests and desires similar to your own; even in times of separation, staying in contact with one another and planning for celebrating your reunion.

☐ Remembering special events; keeping track of important dates, places, and times; following the activities of those who are close to you.

☐ Doing for others what they find difficult to do for themselves; accepting kindness from others without feeling obligated.

☐ Showing an imbalance when using the character **tension points** of *individual* and *group*.

You Intensify Your Individual-Group Imbalance by:

☐ Making it difficult for others to associate with you as an individual; tending to come encased in a group—a family, a work group, a profession, a social club.

☐ Insisting that those who deal with you must also relate with those close to you. They must be able to fit into your family or group, tradition, and experience.

☐ Being dependent upon others who give or withhold approval for what you do; drawing them into your problem solving, thus, making you feel inadequate.

☐ Moving against the tide in a competitive economic system; discovering that your trustworthiness, steadfastness, and industriousness can be valued and yet exploited.

☐ Recognizing that, even in the home environment, your consideration, thoughtfulness, and support can be taken for granted.

☐ Reminding yourself **too infrequently** that you tend to turn down opportunities for advancement (particularly in the work setting) for fear of being ostracized by the group if you are successful and because you dislike the thought of separation from those with whom you are familiar.

PART II　You Deal With Right and Wrong by:

☐ Placing a greater emphasis on *caring* behavior than on *justice* behavior. See chart 3B.

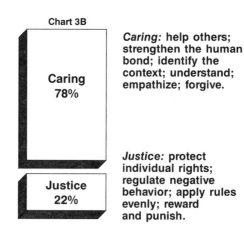

Chart 3B

Caring
78%

Caring: help others; strengthen the human bond; identify the context; understand; empathize; forgive.

Justice
22%

Justice: protect individual rights; regulate negative behavior; apply rules evenly; reward and punish.

☐ Preferring *caring* behavior (78% of the time) over *justice* behavior (22% of the time).

☐ Placing high value upon the worth of the individual; believing that rules, regulations, and laws are made for the benefit of people—to protect rather than to infringe on their power.

☐ Being attentive to the right and wrong of each human action; believing that people are responsible for the choices they make.

☐ Using your sense of kindness and fairness to be available when others experience rejection for failing to live up to standards; providing a source of understanding to those who feel weakness and temptation.

☐ Listening to those who would contemplate wrong actions; hoping to prevent unacceptable behavior; trying to help them avoid the potential penalties administered through a regulating system.

☐ Doing more than just talking about the need to care for people; becoming involved in causes that represent your feelings.

☐ Taking on the responsibility for others when dealing with the basics of physical comfort—food to eat, a place to sleep, and adequate clothing.

☐ Making an attempt to be responsible for your own behavior; setting your own code of conduct which is consistent with the larger cultural, universal laws of living.

☐ Showing an *imbalance* when using the character **tension points** of *justice* and *caring*.

You Intensify Your Justice-Caring Imbalance by:

☐ Becoming, at times, overly involved with law and regulation violators; feeling drained both physically and psychologically.

☐ Fearing that your tendency toward protecting the interests of others may overstep the line on occasion, diminishing your respect for the rightness of the law and for regulations.

☐ Worrying that those whom you have assisted will fall back into their non-conformist behavior, making them vulnerable to increased temptation.

☐ Sensing that your caring attitude has created a no-win situation for you at times. Those you help become irritable when you set limits on them, making you the "bad guy" when they fail to live up to mutually accepted standards.

☐ Feeling repercussions when others free themselves from dependency on you. You become remorseful and resentful that their separation removes events, persons, and activities to which you have become attached.

☐ Reminding yourself **too infrequently** that, in your good intentions to resolve the conflicts of others, you may stunt your own growth. Involved in the lives of others, you may find it too easy to live your life through them. Giving attention to your own development is vital.

PART III   You Pursue A Course Of Action by:

☐ Placing a greater emphasis on *contention* behavior than on *consensus* behavior. See chart 3C.

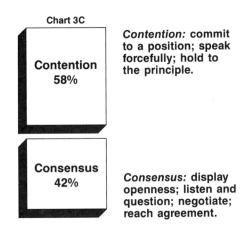

Chart 3C

Contention 58%

Contention: commit to a position; speak forcefully; hold to the principle.

Consensus 42%

Consensus: display openness; listen and question; negotiate; reach agreement.

☐ Preferring *contention* behavior (58% of the time) over *consensus* behavior (42% of the time).

☐ Being deliberate and intent on a course that brings you peace of mind.

☐ Stating your conviction with sincerity; vowing to remain true to your commitment; believing that it is right for you.

☐ Staying in control even though others pressure you to check with them on your course of action; showing resistance and stubbornness when your mind is made up; discouraging others from contesting your will.

☐ Displaying loyalty to people who have kept faith with you.

☐ Directing your major efforts to the development and maintenance of deep and lasting friendships; showing determination in keeping your word.

☐ Following through on specific details in the hope of setting an example of discipline and thoroughness.

☐ Associating with others who have attitudes and values similar to yours; gaining confidence and strength by an increase in numbers.

☐ Desiring to protect your own interests; considering others' welfare as important, but concluding that survival is possible only if self-interest is also a priority.

☐ Showing an *imbalance* when using the character **tension points** of *contention* and *consensus*.

You Intensify Your Contention-Consensus Imbalance by:

☐ Being defensive when asked to provide examples of how your way is more effective than other possibilities; causing you to disassociate yourself from critical or "liberal oriented" elements.

☐ Placing loyalty and commitment before the essence of your belief on some occasions; causing some people to question whether you support the stated opinion or whether you protect your friendships.

☐ Insisting that outsiders conform to the procedures and purposes of your private organizations or groups; questioning them on their beliefs even though they desire a casual or one-time contact with you.

☐ Dismissing criticisms of your beliefs as being too general or appearing to be derogatory; showing an unwillingness to regard investigation as a realistic probing of ideas.

☐ Reminding yourself **too infrequently** that you are overly critical of those who draw different conclusions from the same set of facts. When people draw different interpretations, it is an indication that more open communication is needed.

PATTERN FOUR

Leadership Interpretation

PART I   You Seek A Sense Of Self-Importance by:

☐ Placing a greater emphasis on *group* behavior than on *individual* behavior. See chart 4A.

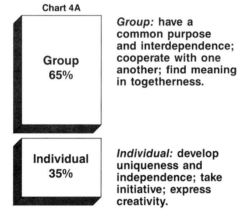

Chart 4A

Group 65%

Group: have a common purpose and interdependence; cooperate with one another; find meaning in togetherness.

Individual 35%

Individual: develop uniqueness and independence; take initiative; express creativity.

☐ Preferring *group* behavior (65% of the time) over *individual* behavior (35% of the time).

☐ Projecting orderliness and predictability in the development of products and relationships; believing that structured roles and a division of responsibility minimize confusion.

☐ Cooperating with set plans and expectations; preferring to attract the attention of people who respect your self-discipline; casting yourself in the role of expert.

☐ Helping people to know their place and what is expected of them; controlling the behavior of others through silence; effectively utilizing the nonverbal: a reproving glance, a frown, or a nod of the head.

☐ Striving for correctness; reflecting your skill in the comprehensiveness of your information, the accuracy of your facts—the thoroughness of your preparation. You do not like mistakes. Striving for a fail-safe environment, you leave no stone unturned.

☐ Adapting a conciliatory, diplomatic attitude; changing to a combative attitude in critical areas where mistakes could be devastating.

☐ Probing how others feel about you; attempting to discover your value; projecting the accuracy and scope of your contribution in terms of appropriate compensation and rewards.

☐ Placing trust in a few, selected friends and associates after a lengthy period of association; exposing only what will match their estimation of your personality; making a few exceptions to that general rule.

☐ Showing an imbalance when using the character **tension points** of *individual* and *group.*

You Intensify Your Individual-Group Imbalance by:

☐ Communicating through your critical thinking pattern; ascertaining how the world should be ordered and where people, including you, fit into the scheme of things.

☐ Adapting to a hierarchical arrangement with persons classified according to rank; believing that equality is reserved for the group environment.

☐ Conveying an outward appearance of exchanging pleasantries with familiar and comfortable associates; yearning inwardly to openly compete with wit and wisdom; desiring to be viewed as a winner; choosing instead to be cooperative.

☐ Refraining from expressing your emotions; fearing that you may project an impulsive side; desiring to be in control at all times.

☐ Reminding yourself **too infrequently** that it is enticing to remain within the group or within relationships that safeguard you in your corner of the world and allow you to do what you see fit. You sense that it is imperative to assume a more assertive role. You recognize the need to move from your customary critical thinking role or expert role into a setting where you move in and out of leadership functions and increased social participation.

PART II   You Deal With Right and Wrong by:

☐ Placing a greater emphasis on *justice* behavior than on *caring* behavior. See chart 4B.

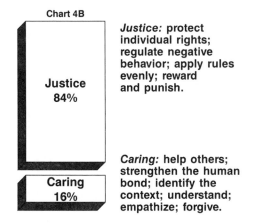

Chart 4B

Justice
84%

Justice: protect individual rights; regulate negative behavior; apply rules evenly; reward and punish.

Caring
16%

Caring: help others; strengthen the human bond; identify the context; understand; empathize; forgive.

☐ Preferring *justice* behavior (84% of the time) over *caring* behavior (16% of the time).

☐ Being hard-nosed in your judgment and criticism; expecting others to comply, without exception, to rules and regulations.

☐ Demanding attention and respect for your own authority; deferring to experts when difficulties arise.

☐ Showing a passion for exactness; absorbing complex statements regarding rules; demonstrating tenacity in observing details related to procedure.

☐ Observing rules of conduct when officiating at meetings; being careful to use titles; showing civility when interacting with others.

☐ Demonstrating courtesy and diplomacy in regard to law officers and other respected officials in authority.

☐ Searching for qualified elected or appointed officials who represent order and predictability; refusing opportunities, however, to assume these significant roles for yourself.

☐ Putting aside, in quick fashion, those thoughts which tempt you to gain advantage by discarding your personal law or a formal law; believing that the more you talk and stand on the "right side," the greater your chances of overcoming temptation.

☐ Upholding the purpose of institutions that serve as regulators of conduct—government, church, school, work organization; recognizing differences in the teaching of each; reconciling the variance as due to different objectives and environments.

☐ Showing an imbalance when using the character **tension points** of *justice* and *caring*.

You Intensify Your Justice-Caring Imbalance by:

☐ Antagonizing others by setting yourself in judgment—often without mercy, compassion, or rebuttal.

☐ Tending to reject new information that may cause you to waver in your judgment; believing that additional information, particularly if you are dealing with a highly emotional issue, may cause confusion.

☐ Placing excessive pressure on yourself when temptation occurs; making it necessary to recall your strong and exacting views on what constitutes correct and incorrect behavior; being vulnerable in your dislike of yourself for being tempted.

☐ Admitting that your desire for perfection is unrealistic; coming to grips with human experience—we are born; we live; we die; coming to recognize that human stories come in endless variation with difficult beginnings, uneven middles, and untidy endings.

☐ Reminding yourself **too infrequently** that people do make mistakes—and you occasionally fall short of the mark. You may question, at times, why you are drawn more to stories of justice and penalty than to stories of forgiveness and absolution.

PART III   You Pursue A Course Of Action by:

☐ Placing a greater emphasis on *consensus* behavior than on *contention behavior.* See chart 4C.

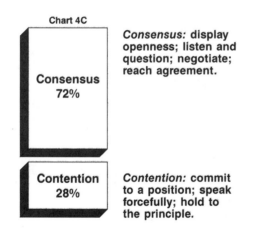

Chart 4C

Consensus 72%

Consensus: display openness; listen and question; negotiate; reach agreement.

Contention 28%

Contention: commit to a position; speak forcefully; hold to the principle.

☐ Preferring *consensus* behavior (72% of the time) over *contention* behavior (28% of the time).

☐ Using specialized competencies and skills; developing systematic methods; employing a question-answer format.

☐ Directing the attention of others to the quality of your contributions; focusing on the content rather than on how it is delivered; highlighting the central issue; downplaying the importance of the smile or the fancy verbalization.

☐ Expecting others to be as candid in analyzing your ideas as you are with their opinions; assuming the role of critic to test the truth of beliefs.

☐ Following a step-by-step, reasoned discussion process in search of truth; urging examination through an investigative method—enlisting, if necessary, the use of experts.

☐ Feeling safe within the confines of group thinking and consensus; negotiating with sincerity; finding it difficult, however, to stand up and be counted on an individual basis—particularly if there is conflict.

☐ Showing skills as a keen observer, as a part of a specialized team; using your ability to collect and analyze information.

☐ Planning and arranging for contingencies; recognizing the need to meet the unexpected—head on.

☐ Showing an imbalance when using the character **tension points** of *contention* and *consensus*.

You Intensify Your Contention-Consensus Imbalance by:

☐ Overpreparing yourself; overwhelming those who are primarily interested in a cursory or preliminary examination of an idea.

☐ Displaying a talent for absorbing, digesting, and solving difficult problems; making it difficult, at times, for others to follow the intricacies of ideas that have fascination only for you.

☐ Failing to win support for your critical issues; needing to confront those who are more assertive than you; appearing to lack strength in your conviction—or perhaps your desire for peace is greater.

☐ Displaying a single-minded determination that borders on stubbornness; withholding pertinent facts that may alter the course or direction.

☐ Refusing to admit to others that your proposal or solution is a bad fit; wasting energy trying to fit the wrong piece into the puzzle; hoping to save face.

☐ Reminding yourself **too infrequently** that others need to enlarge their frameworks in a way that is different. Being realistic about what to expect from others helps you to avoid shrinking your own world in the process of helping others.

PATTERN TWELVE
Leadership Interpretation

☐ Placing a greater emphasis on *individual* behavior than on *group* behavior. See chart 5A.

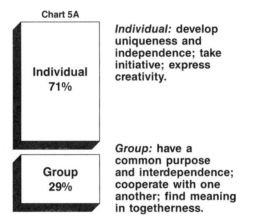

Chart 5A

Individual 71%

Individual: develop uniqueness and independence; take initiative; express creativity.

Group 29%

Group: have a common purpose and interdependence; cooperate with one another; find meaning in togetherness.

☐ Preferring *individual* behavior (71% of the time) over *group* behavior (29% of the time).

☐ Using language brilliantly—articulating phrases to encourage; devising slogans to unite effort; coining words that arouse the interest of others.

☐ Displaying self-confidence; bringing hope and opportunity to stagnant events; promising others that you will do bigger and better things than most people; placing pressure on yourself to fulfill the expectations.

☐ Demonstrating an uncanny sense of knowing what others need—when to provide incentives, when to allay anxieties, when to inject a sense of belonging.

☐ Visualizing beyond the present moment; being preoccupied with what will be—expansion, increased territory, authority, or power.

☐ Preferring to regard others as a faint extension of yourself; taking delight in the way they use your methods to solve their problems; observing that your form begins to take shape in their lives.

☐ Becoming inebriated with your success and victories over others; feeling omnipotent—sensing that you can do little wrong when you are on a hot streak; demanding that your importance be acknowledged.

☐ Being able to gain the loyalty of a wide range of people; identifying the needs of others; showing them that you have ideas—solutions to meet their needs.

☐ Demonstrating the ability to work with and through people; assigning tasks without hesitation to those who are anxious to be a part of your vision and success.

☐ Showing an imbalance when using the character **tension points** of *individual* and *group*.

You Intensify Your Individual-Group Imbalance by:

☐ Professing great faith in your ability to maneuver yourself into a good position; spurring others to greater efforts; forgetting to acknowledge that you need others to increase order and systematized planning.

☐ Believing that life will always be what it is now; giving too little thought to developing a support system for the future; failing to show appreciation to those who make it possible for you to stay in control.

☐ Being happy when things go your way; attributing success to your winsome mannerisms and appearance; assigning negative factors to those who cannot keep up with your pace.

☐ Losing contact with people down the line; forgetting that there is a need to replenish supplies and spirits; basing fewer of your decisions on the reality of first-hand experience.

☐ Reminding yourself **too infrequently** that you mask the potential aggressiveness of your actions. You encourage others to view competitive activities as a game, assuring them that they are in a privileged relationship within your circle. More than a few may be fully aware of the heights of your ambition and the potential effect on themselves and others.

PART II   You Deal With Right and Wrong by:

☐ Working toward equal emphasis on *justice* behavior and *caring* behavior. See chart 5B.

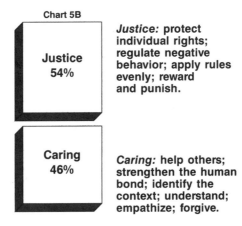

Chart 5B

Justice 54%

Justice: protect individual rights; regulate negative behavior; apply rules evenly; reward and punish.

Caring 46%

Caring: help others; strengthen the human bond; identify the context; understand; empathize; forgive.

☐ Preferring *justice* behavior (54% of the time) over *caring* behavior (46% of the time).

☐ Believing that your talent and abilities entitle you to special privileges under the law—tending to place your needs above others; assuming that you know what is best for them.

☐ Assuming a role as strategist; posing as an astute "general" who must know the terrain of handling good and bad; believing that, occasionally, the ends justify the means.

☐ Taking liberty occasionally in borrowing someone else's way of doing things; vowing to later reward the person you offend with part of your success.

☐ Projecting yourself as being concerned for law, order—and people; scrutinizing others to determine if their behavior is weaker than yours; discovering their points of vulnerability.

☐ Using the law and regulations when they directly benefit you in your opposition to flagrant offenders; advocating strong protective measures; being concerned that others are proportionately penalized for violating your rights.

☐ Providing yourself with incentives that often are on the fringes of acceptability and "legal" conduct; sensing when to assign "less clean" responsibility to others; washing your hands of actions when events go awry.

☐ Stating directly and openly what you contemplate; making known your intentions of how you will follow or attempt to use regulations to your advantage.

☐ Showing a balance when using the character **tension points** of *justice* and *caring*.

You Maintain Your Justice-Caring Balance by:

☐ Attracting others to your activities with the promise of fair and equitable rules; informing people that you will ensure them a good portion of the spoils.

☐ Fulfilling your commitment to treat others fairly; failing, however, to keep your word if the original estimates of success fall below the expectations; tending to take your full share before an equal distribution of the total purse.

☐ Surrounding yourself with a realistic influence, which provides for you a conscious attempt to maintain a sense of right and wrong; realizing that you are often caught up in a spirit of emotion, making careless, unintentional promises.

☐ Reveling in your good fortune when you get something for less than you were willing to pay; hoping that you did not take too great an advantage over the person who was less knowledgeable than you; consoling yourself with the thought that your actions, of course, were within the law.

☐ Reminding yourself **frequently** that you expect to be treated fairly and that you have an intuitive sense of when others are overly concerned with their own self-interests—at your expense. While you make attempts to stay within the legal boundaries, you, like others, have had thoughts of stepping outside the white line. You are equipped to identify and defend yourself against the unscrupulous.

PART III   You Pursue A Course Of Action by:

☐ Working toward equal emphasis on *contention* behavior and *consensus* behavior. See chart 5C.

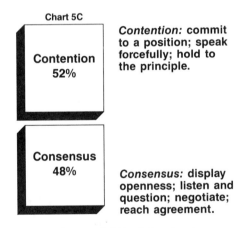

Chart 5C

Contention 52%

Contention: **commit to a position; speak forcefully; hold to the principle.**

Consensus 48%

Consensus: **display openness; listen and question; negotiate; reach agreement.**

☐ Preferring *contention* behavior (52% of the time) over *consensus* behavior (48% of the time).

☐ Visualizing what you desire; planning ways in which you will proceed; instilling confidence in those who are anxious to follow your leadership.

☐ Challenging others to share their concerns, doubts, and suspicions about your undertakings; respecting those who have greater expertise in areas that are unfamiliar to you.

☐ Revitalizing others with your thoughts and ideas; using your poise, cordiality, and social assertiveness to stimulate others to action.

☐ Believing in what you say as much as who you are. Your message is designed to reach people on all levels; your self-assurance is contagious.

☐ Giving credit for the profound effect that others have on your life; hoping to reflect the wide range of influences that have contributed to your philosophy.

☐ Showing versatility when necessary; adapting to a position when a cause can be better served; reflecting comfortableness in pursuing either direction—strong conviction or intense compromise.

☐ Being optimistic; experiencing the "wind at your back" when you throw off the shackles of self-doubt and give full range to your belief in yourself.

☐ Having a burning desire to communicate; sensing the build-up of momentum; feeling the air crackle with your unleashed energy; knowing that you give hope and raise the spirits of others; giving them the sensation of having the wind at their backs.

☐ Showing a balance when using the character **tension points** of *contention* and *consensus*.

You Maintain Your Contention-Consensus Balance by:

☐ Persuading, convincing, and contending effectively; making sure, however, to listen to others; providing them the opportunity to participate in decisions.

☐ Encouraging others with both a sense of reasoning and emotion; gaining acceptance for your belief by influencing the motivation of others; urging them to "throw wide the window to a larger world"; gathering them under your banner as they see the possibility of wider options for themselves.

☐ Putting your power over others into perspective; knowing that your actions create excitement and involvement; employing methods, however, that will deliberately provide people with an opportunity to examine your objectives; inviting them to decide with you on the meaningfulness of your programs and proposals.

☐ Recognizing the need for realistic communication with others; rising to specific occasions with a masterful persuasion that embodies your singleness of purpose; projecting yourself as a person of destiny; thinking of yourself as someone who can do no wrong.

☐ Reminding yourself **frequently** that you have limitations that affect others as sharply as your achievements. You stabilize yourself when your head is bent toward others—receiving and giving sound advice. Through this vital process you begin to realize the importance of attending to the needs of those who provide support for your efforts. You hope to leave a legacy for the future.

PATTERN THIRTEEN

Leadership Interpretation

PART I   You Seek A Sense Of Self-Importance by:

☐ Working toward equal emphasis on *individual* behavior and *group* behavior. See chart 6A.

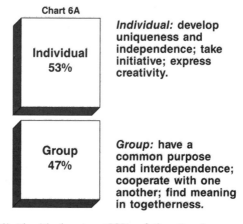

Chart 6A

Individual 53%

Individual: develop uniqueness and independence; take initiative; express creativity.

Group 47%

Group: have a common purpose and interdependence; cooperate with one another; find meaning in togetherness.

☐ Preferring *individual* behavior (53% of the time) over *group* behavior (47% of the time).

☐ Standing out in the crowd; doing the unusual; criticizing those whose work is substandard; urging others to be faithful to their calling.

☐ Identifying yourself with what you do rather than with who you are; making things work for you and, at the same time, providing a service to others.

☐ Responding to a system of reward and reinforcement; expecting to receive fair compensation for your efforts; becoming quiet and appearing troubled when you feel mistreated by others.

☐ Developing long-term involvements; demonstrating repeated efforts in successive stages to achieve the goal; acquiring a reputation for taking on bold ventures from start to finish.

☐ Shedding your stern, critical, and investigative manner on occasion; permitting others to express their appreciation to you; feeling warmed by their gentleness.

☐ Building relationships; avoiding walking in lock-step with the group, but using others as listening posts; hearing only what you want to hear.

☐ Expressing a callousness once you gain deep insights into others; examining the intentions of those who seek closeness; making them uneasy by your scrutiny; rejecting those who appear untrustworthy.

☐ Profiting from past experiences; demonstrating an unusual ability to learn from mistakes; retaining the best of what has been done; avoiding a repetition of previous errors.

☐ Showing a balance when using the character **tension points** of *individual* and *group*.

You Maintain Your Individual-Group Balance by:

☐ Recognizing that your individual achievements are more appreciated when accomplished within a group or team environment; finding it gratifying to compare your efforts to those of others.

☐ Appreciating the differences in people—skills, aptitudes, appearance; identifying the relationship between the "right mix" of people and increasing performance and compatibility; accepting the challenge of selecting people for the task.

☐ Admitting dependency upon other people; gathering accurate information; making correct assessments of those who can be most responsive to your needs.

☐ Pressing for results that can be evaluated; positioning yourself to receive personal acclaim; ensuring the success of a total group accomplishment by including key people whom you credit as more pivotal than yourself.

☐ Reminding yourself **frequently** that you can be unpredictable; constantly looking for those who have skills and talents which soften your approach. You recognize the abruptness with which you discard people and things—but for a larger purpose than your own needs. Still, you realize that people need advance notice to plan and adjust to new circumstances.

PART II   You Deal With Right and Wrong by:

☐ Working toward an equal emphasis on *justice* behavior and *caring* behavior. See chart 6B.

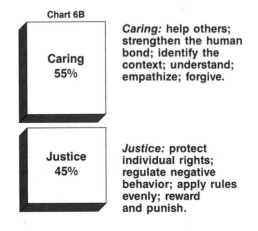

Chart 6B

Caring 55%

Caring: help others; strengthen the human bond; identify the context; understand; empathize; forgive.

Justice 45%

Justice: protect individual rights; regulate negative behavior; apply rules evenly; reward and punish.

☐ Preferring *caring* behavior (55% of the time) over *justice* behavior (45% of the time).

☐ Carefully weighing the choices available to you; struggling between your desire to accomplish and your need to consider the interests of others.

☐ Showing impatience when rules are disregarded by others; growing suspicious of those who gain by taking shortcuts and profiting beyond their contributions.

☐ Emphasizing the importance of the influential people in your life; recalling the challenge from them—to do just about anything that is necessary—to fulfill your obligations; recognizing, however, the need to respect laws and regulations.

☐ Struggling to put your life into perspective; acknowledging that people provide meaningfulness in your life on a regular basis; determining to place their interests over the controls—rules and regulations—that you believe are essential.

☐ Feeling guilty if you even think about infringing upon the possessions of others; disliking the priorities you've developed in your life that cause you restlessness and anxiety.

☐ Envying those who appear to be content in whatever they do; acknowledging your rambunctious nature, which exposes you to more temptations than others have; disliking the strictures on your behavior that result from those who fear your unorthodox way of handling pressure.

☐ Weighing the factors of law and your concern for people; deciding to work with the protection of both.

☐ Showing a balance when using the character **tension points** of *justice* and *caring.*

You Maintain Your Justice-Caring Balance by:

☐ Intensifying your efforts to be even-handed with others; evaluating the effects of your actions upon those around you; taking considerable pride in your efforts to be fair.

☐ Hoping to develop some flexibility in recognizing exceptions to the rules that you expect others to follow; increasing your insight about when to hold firm and when to show understanding; trying for greater comfort in this perpetual tug of war.

☐ Learning to recognize that sometimes the demands of others have more importance than your own, while at other times your own needs have priority; increasing your understanding of motivation—your own and that of others.

☐ Putting on a "tough and ready" appearance in tackling issues of unaccept-able behavior; sprinkling your approach with a willingness to listen; caus-ing others to recognize the seriousness of a problem when you are involved.

☐ Reminding yourself **frequently** that it is not always desirable to walk the tightrope that is based upon how you *think* others feel. In this significant struggle for maintaining your balance between *justice* and *caring,* it is helpful to come down from the tightrope—eliciting how people truly feel about the way in which you attempt to regulate their actions and empathize with their feelings.

PART III   You Pursue A Course Of Action by:

☐ Placing a greater emphasis on *contention* behavior than on *consensus* behavior. See chart 6C.

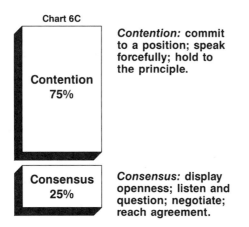

Chart 6C

Contention 75%

Contention: commit to a position; speak forcefully; hold to the principle.

Consensus 25%

Consensus: display openness; listen and question; negotiate; reach agreement.

☐ Preferring *contention* behavior (75% of the time) over *consensus* behavior (25% of the time).

☐ Being self-seeking; intending to get your own way; asserting that others lack your investigative skill and thoroughness. You tend to discount the contributions of others unless they have expert status.

☐ Stating your opinions with deep conviction; striking others as argumenta-tive; being driven by anger and frustration over delays.

☐ Preparing yourself against those who may attempt to impose their will on you; deciding to beat them to the punch.

☐ Projecting yourself as a formidable foe when upset; causing others to justify their actions to you in the hope of resolving differences in belief.

☐ Desiring, in the beginning, only to defend your beliefs against doubters; professing less interest in convincing others to change their position.

☐ Generating personal energy and a high level of excitement from your contending posture; welcoming new opportunities to engage others in verbal and thinking combat; displaying disappointment when others give in too easily.

☐ Knowing that opponents will surface; expecting attacks on both you and your ideas; running the risk of a self-fulfilling prophecy.

☐ Contending strongly for your opinions with friends and associates; being willing to risk the relationship; facing separation for crucial beliefs.

☐ Showing an imbalance when using the character **tension points** of *contention* and *consensus*.

You Intensify Your Contention-Consensus Imbalance by:

☐ Enjoying the strategy and the stakes—win–lose—in maintaining your position; relishing the maneuvering as you would a game of chess.

☐ Supporting your arguments with the most logical evidence, demonstrating little faith in the thinking of your opposition; disappointing those who desired a more human note in your arguments.

☐ Developing high expectations for yourself; projecting a defensiveness before others even attack; being evaluated as having a "chip on your shoulder."

☐ Showing little interest in giving lengthy and arduous speeches to state your opinions; keeping your contributions short, concise—sometimes using cutting remarks when others attempt to overwhelm people with long-winded explanations.

☐ Reminding yourself **too infrequently** that others will be more open to your opinions if you are willing to exchange and evaluate information. You know that an examination of critical issues can only take place when people are willing to forego preconceived ideas. You need to demonstrate a greater openness to new information with the goal of selecting the most workable solution.

PATTERN FOURTEEN
Leadership Interpretation

☐ Placing a greater emphasis on *individual* behavior than on *group* behavior. See chart 7A.

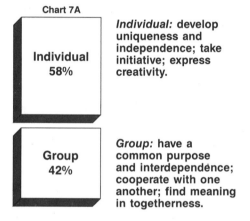

Chart 7A

Individual 58%

Individual: develop uniqueness and independence; take initiative; express creativity.

Group 42%

Group: have a common purpose and interdependence; cooperate with one another; find meaning in togetherness.

☐ Preferring *individual* behavior (58% of the time) over *group* behavior (42% of the time).

☐ Searching for creative ways to solve complicated problems; setting a chain of events in motion.

☐ Seeking control by keeping others curious; using carefully chosen words for their effect; adopting a formal manner.

☐ Getting others to accept your way as the best way; feeling pleased when others attempt to "clone" you; rejecting those who insist on an equal position in the area of your expertise.

☐ Driving yourself to succeed where others have failed; viewing yourself as a survivor; being willing to work hard to retain the present level—even to the point of taking on more than you can handle.

☐ Demonstrating a store of self-power that springs from an inner confidence; using energy appropriately; tackling rather than bypassing theoretical and practical issues; seeing them in a new light.

☐ Using new twists of thinking; protecting a secret idea; building a public image as an independent and unusual person.

☐ Approaching events with a studied quality; viewing your actions from the perspective of the future—how you will be judged.

☐ Preferring to be addressed by appropriate and special titles; seeking deference for your level of achievement.

☐ Showing an imbalance when using the character **tension points** of *individual* and *group*.

You Intensify Your Individual-Group Imbalance by:

☐ Striving for correctness; placing pressure on yourself to deal appropriately with crucial issues; tending to waver, however, at critical moments when the time for actual decision making arrives.

☐ Placing high importance on what you do; tending to be critical of others when they fall short of your expectations; paying a higher price than most people for any failure.

☐ Discussing alternative solutions within a small group setting; withholding the final solution from others; holding your cards close to your chest; arousing the resentment of others with this tactic.

☐ Refusing to be guided or restrained by deep loyalties that come with in-depth relationships; fearing to trust others.

☐ Retreating from group members or partner in a relationship when failure is imminent; hoping to disguise your inability to arrive at new and unusual solutions.

☐ Reminding yourself **too infrequently** that you tend to be ambivalent about taking others into your confidence; using a hidden agenda on too many occasions; failing to reveal to others the full story. Decision making would be less difficult for you if you had a support system of people from whom you could receive advice.

PART II   You Deal With Right and Wrong by:

☐ Placing a greater emphasis on *justice* behavior than on *caring* behavior. See chart 7B.

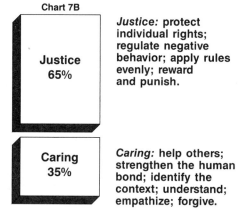

Chart 7B

Justice 65%

Justice: protect individual rights; regulate negative behavior; apply rules evenly; reward and punish.

Caring 35%

Caring: help others; strengthen the human bond; identify the context; understand; empathize; forgive.

☐ Preferring *justice* behavior (65% of the time) over *caring* behavior (35% of the time).

☐ Setting limits on yourself and others; reprimanding those who push behavior to the extremes; projecting a stern manner with those who merit public disapproval.

☐ Spending time in addressing the rules of the game; refusing to admit your own mistakes; diverting attention away from yourself by stressing the serious offenses of others.

☐ Demonstrating selectiveness for certain aspects of regulating behavior; being overly deferential to authority; complaining about the nuisances of rules and regulations; moving quickly, however, to enforce them on someone that you dislike.

☐ Finding ways to deflect blame from yourself to others; sharing blame only when it is necessary; tending toward a critical attitude with those close to you—friends, relatives, and associates; putting others on the defensive to avoid letting them entrap you in rules and regulations.

☐ Calculating the best way to get around irritating procedures; seeking special treatment for your rank, position, and achievement.

☐ Disarming people who generally view you as fairly traditional and conventional; surprising them with your activist side when law and order fail to protect your interests.

☐ Giving only average attention to the effects of your actions and decisions on others; rejecting complaints that you are uncaring; insisting that you do care about what people think of you.

☐ Showing an imbalance when using the character **tension points** of *justice* and *caring*.

You Intensify Your Justice-Caring Imbalance by:

☐ Demanding that people should live up to a standard; preferring that it have the weight of high authority; believing that an element of fear is a necessary deterrent to those who lack self-discipline.

☐ Setting yourself in a position where you can ascertain the effectiveness of procedures and regulations; indicating to others that your fairness is qualification for your role as enforcer.

☐ Judging those who lack your level of intensity; criticizing their efforts as unequal; penalizing them for falling short of what you expected of yourself.

☐ Finding it difficult to set yourself free from your own bondage of self-control—using excessive restraint to prove your worth; noting that physical ailments tend to accompany the internal conflicts and unresolved problems pertaining to your self-imposed overregulation.

☐ Reminding yourself **too infrequently** that you need more involvement with people; forgetting that you distance yourself from others; isolating yourself to build your feelings of self-righteousness; decreasing your need to gain approval from others.

PART III   You Pursue A Course Of Action by:

☐ Working toward equal emphasis on *contention* behavior and *consensus* behavior. See chart 7C.

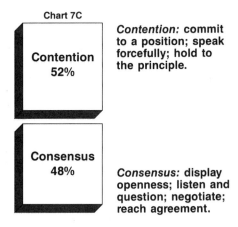

Chart 7C

Contention 52%

Contention: commit to a position; speak forcefully; hold to the principle.

Consensus 48%

Consensus: display openness; listen and question; negotiate; reach agreement.

☐ Preferring *contention* behavior (52% of the time) over *consensus* (48% of the time).

☐ Stating your intent to discover truth; encouraging others to identify and explore areas of knowledge and experience to document opinions and beliefs.

☐ Searching for ways in which to fill your thirst for increased knowledge; feeling that you never have enough; viewing the horn of plenty as half-empty rather than half-full.

☐ Trying out new thoughts with those who are curious; determining if they have a piece of the puzzle that you can use.

☐ Becoming inventive in your method of investigation; discovering ways to materially gain as a result of newly discovered knowledge.

☐ Reconciling yourself to the fact that you cannot control everything; trying to find some consolation in the realization that you can control your own reactions to events and situations.

☐ Incorporating a combination of persuasion and compromise in your methods; hoping to prove to others that your apparent bluntness in communicating indicates the urgent conviction of your beliefs.

☐ Developing well-thought-out approaches that will be acceptable to the powerful influences in your life; placing great confidence in your use of back-ups for people and things; defending yourself against those who judge such contingencies as acts of expediency.

☐ Showing a balance when using the character **tension points** of *contention* and *consensus.*

You Maintain Your Contention-Consensus Balance by:

☐ Preparing for future events; basing your advisements and assistance on your experience and the tested opinions of others; sharing a position that represents thinking on a broad spectrum.

☐ Using appropriate forcefulness; preferring that your approach be characterized as an "action-oriented conservatism"; resenting the criticism of others that you are assertive only when threatened by the opposition.

☐ Withholding comments until pivotal points and highlights of others' ideas have been stated; seizing the opportunities to aggressively question unsupported generalities.

☐ Viewing time and energy as limited; using these scarce resources wisely; avoiding the false moves and the pointless expenditure of forcefulness when it will not help.

☐ Reminding yourself **frequently** that you are slightly ahead of others—leading the way in creative systems, arousing the curiosity of others, paving the way for new thought. You recognize that the introduction of new ways must be accompanied by evaluation—anticipating and weighing the good and bad effects on others.

PATTERN TWENTY-THREE

Leadership Interpretation

PART I   You Seek A Sense Of Self-Importance by:

☐ Placing a greater emphasis on *group* behavior than on *individual* behavior. See chart 8A.

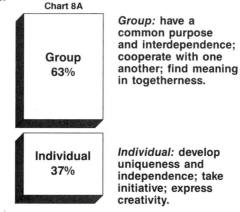

Chart 8A

Group **63%**	*Group:* have a common purpose and interdependence; cooperate with one another; find meaning in togetherness.
Individual **37%**	*Individual:* develop uniqueness and independence; take initiative; express creativity.

☐ Preferring *group* behavior (63% of the time) over *individual* behavior (37% of the time).

☐ Giving and receiving affection.

☐ Arousing support for those who are reluctant to seek assistance.

☐ Verbalizing well; being called upon as spokesperson to rally people to a common goal; injecting meaning into their lives. You emphasize the outcome of team effort.

☐ Defining yourself in relation to others; tending to attract those who have problems; encouraging people to express their difficulties.

☐ Projecting a good degree of independence; showing an assertive tendency when others choose to be selfish; calling up a righteous indignation when others are treated unfairly.

☐ Creating unusual opportunities for yourself; discovering that you have a need to forgive and to show tolerance for the mistakes of others; recognizing some of your own shortcomings in others; desiring to help them overcome their difficulties.

☐ Discussing your feelings and desires openly; creating an environment where others feel comfortable discussing personal information.

☐ Encouraging others to develop themselves; stimulating them by your excitement and ongoing attention to their activities.

☐ Showing an imbalance when using the character **tension points** of *individual* and *group*.

You Intensify Your Individual-Group Imbalance by:

☐ Trusting in the other person's good will in a relationship; hoping for kindness as you expose your vulnerability; risking rejection as you seek to satisfy your need for closeness to others.

☐ Being willing to give direction when pressed; trying to avoid arousing the opposition that often accompanies overt direction; seeking to retain the good will of others; running the risk of being viewed as soft by aggressive individuals.

☐ Discussing personal matters with others; encountering criticism for being too approachable; having your ease of intimacy misunderstood; searching for judgment as to when and where depth of interaction is appropriate.

☐ Making genuine attempts to satisfy others; placing their concerns above yours on many occasions; failing, at times, to be amply rewarded.

☐ Reminding yourself **too infrequently** of the need to set limits, with others, enforce the limits, and prevent others from imposing on your good nature. Some situations demand direct action—sometimes confrontation with those who would take advantage of you.

PART II   You Deal With Right and Wrong by:

☐ Placing a greater emphasis on *caring* behavior than on *justice* behavior. See chart 8B.

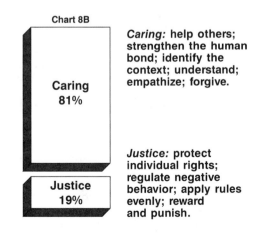

Chart 8B

Caring
81%

Caring: help others; strengthen the human bond; identify the context; understand; empathize; forgive.

Justice
19%

Justice: protect individual rights; regulate negative behavior; apply rules evenly; reward and punish.

☐ Preferring *caring* behavior (81% of the time) over *justice* behavior (19% of the time).

☐ Assuming a nonjudgmental stance in the face of those who fall short of society's expectations; accepting people where they are and helping them to deal with their problems in self-discipline.

☐ Searching for the common humanity in everyone; helping others to examine their problems in the warmth of your care and concern.

☐ Sensing the deep-seated problems that exist in people; helping them to identify their hostilities; making them comfortable with their true feelings; urging them to act on what they feel—not what they *should* feel.

☐ Supporting what people *want* to do; knowing that laws, rules, regulations cannot legislate the positive ways of relating—hugging and kissing, listening and responding, giving and receiving.

☐ Encouraging others to develop a guidance center that reflects their unique personality; urging inner regulation rather than depending upon direction from others.

☐ Dealing with right-wrong choices by accepting yourself as a person with both a light and a dark side; separating yourself from aggressive individuals who infringe on the rights of others; avoiding those who insist on extreme and unnecessary punishment.

☐ Claiming innocence for harm you inflict on others when you trespass on their rights; insisting that your actions, when they harm only yourself, are your business; maintaining your independence from authority; demanding to make your own appraisals.

☐ Finding it difficult to reconcile your feelings of belligerence with your show of good will—surprising yourself when you feel hostility toward those who have little or no regard for the concerns of others.

☐ Showing an imbalance when using the character **tension points** of *justice* and *caring*.

You Intensify Your Justice-Caring Imbalance by:

☐ Encouraging nonconformity; distinguishing between an unthinking compliance and an enlightened adherence to rules and regulations.

☐ Making excuses for law breakers; justifying a nonjudgmental attitude as essential for understanding; trying to help people get in touch with their feelings.

☐ Running the risk of having others mistake your concern for the individual as a flagrant disrespect for law and order; being too optimistic about your ability to change another's behavior.

☐ Being uncritical of those who resist regulations; neglecting to hold people responsible for the effects of their actions; overplaying the advocate role.

☐ Discovering that you tend to build an excessive number of relationships with people who resist complying with external standards, insisting that their internal norms are sufficient.

☐ Finding that people with "emerging independence" can drain you emotionally; concluding that your counseling manner keeps them emotionally dependent upon you.

☐ Reminding yourself **too infrequently** that encouraging others to share their problems is a way for you to receive acceptance and affection. You begin to recognize that, in defining the problems of others, you explore difficult areas in your own life as well.

PART III   You Pursue A Course Of Action by:

☐ Working toward equal emphasis on *contention* and *consensus* behavior. See chart 8C.

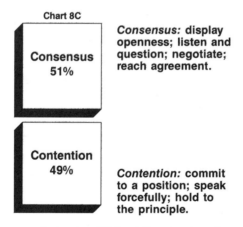

Chart 8C

Consensus 51%

Consensus: display openness; listen and question; negotiate; reach agreement.

Contention 49%

Contention: commit to a position; speak forcefully; hold to the principle.

☐ Preferring *consensus* behavior (51% of the time) and *contention* behavior (49% of the time).

☐ Evaluating your ideas and exchanging them with others; developing a set of conclusions that will be acceptable to all the interested parties.

☐ Trusting the information that is presented to you by others; responding to them by dealing in fairness.

☐ Committing yourself to a democratic process; advocating equality among people; using discussions to build personal relationships as a buffer that protects you in time of adversity.

☐ Demonstrating a willingness to compromise when there is a stalemate in the exchange of ideas; gaining future support for those times when you want a hearing and acceptance for your ideas.

☐ Offering moderate resistance to those who oppose your ideas; suffering at the hands of aggressive individuals who minimize your efforts as pollyannish; eventually giving in to others.

☐ Displaying simplicity, candor, and humility; setting an example for others in facing an unknown and sometimes hostile world; putting your cards on the table; startling others with your openness and honesty.

☐ Keeping firm-mindedness and a sharp tongue in reserve until the opportune time; revealing an independent spirit; becoming a worthy adversary for reckless and impulsive individuals; assuming the role of protector for others.

☐ Showing a balance when using the character **tension points** of *contention* and *consensus*.

You Maintain Your Contention-Consensus Balance by:

☐ Demonstrating an openness when others sincerely disagree with your opinions; refraining from being defensive; reserving your light artillery for those who try to dictate agreements.

☐ Supporting many different views; being criticized for not stating and defending a clear position; refusing to retaliate in kind.

☐ Respecting differing opinions when counseling; asking questions; reflecting the thinking of others; helping them to find their own answers.

☐ Seeking to maintain the balance of contending and negotiating behavior; fighting off the label of being too trusting and too forgiving; fearing the loss of respect and credibility if you are seen as gullible.

☐ Reminding yourself **frequently** that you favor a nondirective approach over the directive method; recognizing that some can benefit from your experience; acknowledging that some people seek "advice" not for direction but as another point of reference; seeking to apply the correct method for the situation.

PATTERN TWENTY-FOUR
Leadership Interpretation

PART I   You Seek A Sense Of Self-Importance by:

☐ Working toward an equal emphasis on *individual* behavior and *group* behavior. See chart 9A.

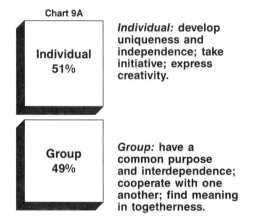

Chart 9A

Individual 51%

Individual: develop uniqueness and independence; take initiative; express creativity.

Group 49%

Group: have a common purpose and interdependence; cooperate with one another; find meaning in togetherness.

☐ Preferring *individual* behavior (51% of the time) and *group* behavior (49% of the time).

☐ Setting an example—active and vigorous; rising to the occasion when imagination is needed; demonstrating insight along with inventiveness.

☐ Desiring to be the best at what you do; creating opportunities to compete with yourself; evaluating your efforts; attempting to exceed your present limits.

☐ Stressing individual effort and performance because it is more easily recognized than group effort.

☐ Setting a visionary goal; viewing it as more challenging than a purpose or objective established by others.

☐ Competing successfully with others—particularly when you choose the contest; positioning yourself with those whose talents are equal to or greater than yours, providing you with the opportunity to compare your skill and ability to theirs.

☐ Making good choices in the selection of people; acknowledging that few things are accomplished in isolation; knowing that you need those who will recognize and appreciate your strengths.

☐ Finding effective ways to mesh your strong individual efforts into some kind of structure; believing that larger success can only come with a partnership or group identification.

☐ Taking advantage of situations that are viewed as "second rate"; adding your personal touch to bring it up to par; having others cite you as having made the difference.

☐ Showing a balance when using the character **tension points** of *individual* and *group*.

You Maintain Your Individual-Group Balance by:

☐ Combining your high opinion of yourself with your high expectations of the group or a relationship.

☐ Desiring close contact with those you respect; being selective in how you spend your time; welcoming competitiveness within the framework of the group.

☐ Viewing those who are more individualistic than you as being driven by greed; judging them as selfish, impatient, and exploitative. You seek to be seen in a different light.

☐ Developing the use of witticism and humor to soften your comments, which are often viewed as caustic, critical, and degrading to others; attempting to get others in line through the use of your evaluative communication and appraisal methods.

☐ Reminding yourself **frequently** that you desire independent thought and action within the group; desiring to avoid stilted behavior, recognizing, however, that you must guard against conflict or confrontation; finding it difficult to handle extreme behavior in others.

PART II   You Deal With Right and Wrong by:

☐ Placing a greater emphasis on *justice* behavior than on *caring* behavior. See chart 9B.

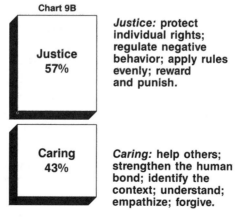

Chart 9B

Justice 57%

Justice: protect individual rights; regulate negative behavior; apply rules evenly; reward and punish.

Caring 43%

Caring: help others; strengthen the human bond; identify the context; understand; empathize; forgive.

☐ Preferring *justice* behavior (57% of the time) over *caring* behavior (43% of the time).

☐ Weighing the fun and good times that you desire with the need for order and discipline.

☐ Placing restrictions on yourself when you anticipate the fun results as too extreme.

☐ Encouraging others to enjoy themselves within the framework of your self-imposed rules.

☐ Viewing rules and regulations as necessary ways to protect the rights and privileges of others; expressing concern when it is apparent that one person is gaining at the expense of another.

☐ Fighting off the urge to overstep your prerogatives in order to have the competitive edge; fearing the possibility of losing. When the happiness of winning is tainted by unfair means, the urge to take a shortcut to victory diminishes.

☐ Complaining about the effects of a hierarchical system; arguing that it is designed to favor a few who are rewarded for pushing others to work hard for them.

☐ Using the existence of structured guidelines to get what is rightfully yours; insisting that these guidelines are to be closely followed.

☐ Giving ground on occasion by appealing to "the top"; seeking preferential treatment for generally obeying most of the regulations; believing that "special contacts" are built into any justice system.

☐ Showing an imbalance when using the character **tension points** of *justice* and *caring*.

You Intensify Your Justice-Caring Imbalance by:

☐ Desiring to make your competitive wins more satisfying; knowing that without rules others may overshadow your skill and talent with a disregard for fair play.

☐ Indicating a sense of self-importance when you show comprehension of regulations and guidelines; causing others to speculate that you do well because the rules are on your side—actually, it is because you know that the rules exist.

☐ Taking the side of people who have been harmed when others have disregarded the laws or rules; discovering possible solutions for yourself as you help them work through their problems.

☐ Insisting that at some point people must face penalties for neglecting their obligations to adhere to standards, law, and order. You decide to let them follow the normal course of events, withdrawing your active involvement in their rehabilitation.

☐ Reminding yourself **too infrequently** that you may be overly demanding in your expectations of others; reluctantly admitting that you tend to *label* those who defy regulations. You need to view each person within his or her context—as a unique individual with specific history and circumstances and a need for understanding.

PART III   You Pursue A Course Of Action by:

☐ Placing a greater emphasis on *consensus* behavior than on *contention* behavior. See chart 9C.

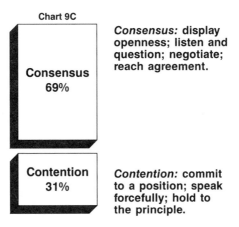

Chart 9C

Consensus 69%

Consensus: display openness; listen and question; negotiate; reach agreement.

Contention 31%

Contention: commit to a position; speak forcefully; hold to the principle.

☐ Preferring *consensus* behavior (69% of the time) over *contention* behavior (31% of the time).

☐ Sharing rather than imposing your opinions on others.

☐ Using others to convince people of the credibility of your ideas; feeling confident that your beliefs will be accepted on their merit.

☐ Comparing your ideas with the opinions of others; getting people to state their concerns and proposals; hoping to show the obvious differences in opinions between yours and theirs.

☐ Utilizing your expressive powers to get more people involved in an evaluation of issues; making attempts in the discussion to give comments equal weight and attention.

☐ Employing a "hit and retreat" approach in conveying ideas; falling back and regrouping when you encounter resistance; advancing with a different approach to handle objections.

☐ Seeking formal or studied appraisals of your ideas; keeping your ideas on target; gaining attention by stating your opinions a little differently each time you have an opportunity; gaining approval when others see your ideas as part of their thinking as well.

☐ Making attempts to overcome your impatience with the slowness of others; avoiding an appearance of being impulsive; withholding your usual demands for quick action; encouraging, instead, a cooling-off period that is followed by a serious attempt to reach conclusions.

☐ Showing an imbalance when using the character **tension points** of *contention* and *consensus*.

You Intensify Your Contention-Consensus Imbalance by:

☐ Removing yourself from possible attacks by those who disagree with your proposals; assigning others to voice the sentiments of your convictions.

☐ Believing that the appropriate time factor is crucial in securing acceptance for your belief; carefully scheduling the session with others when they will be most comfortable and relaxed.

☐ Being apologetic in taking another person's time to express a *deeply* held conviction, but knowing that you will express it regardless of whether that person is receptive or not.

☐ Saving your forcefulness for one-to-one situations; using public statements to build your "congenial image"—appearing confident and generally conciliatory in your remarks; injecting an occasional "biting" tone.

☐ Reminding yourself **too infrequently** that you have deep convictions that must be expressed. You forget that you forego doing so in order to gain praise for developing unity. You could also be admired for being true to yourself.

PATTERN THIRTY-FOUR

Leadership Interpretation

PART I   You Seek A Sense Of Self-Importance by:

☐ Placing a greater emphasis on *group* behavior than on *individual* behavior. See chart 10A.

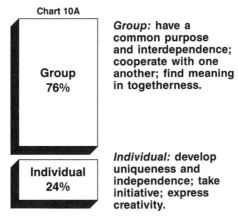

Chart 10A

Group 76%

Group: have a common purpose and interdependence; cooperate with one another; find meaning in togetherness.

Individual 24%

Individual: develop uniqueness and independence; take initiative; express creativity.

☐ Preferring *group* behavior (76% of the time) over *individual* behavior (24% of the time).

☐ Maintaining your integrity; doing those things which permit you to remain in control of yourself.

☐ Distinguishing yourself from those who tend to be aggressive and take unnecessary risk; resisting their enticements of reward and the power of their extravagant emotions.

☐ Demonstrating a predictable pattern of meals, work, leisure, and worship; knowing that people seek a sense of reliability in others.

☐ Identifying with disciplined figures from the past who had similar principles; attempting to build and to maintain a sense of continuity with those who came before.

☐ Showing discrimination in your selection of associates; scrutinizing those around you; attempting to discover if they are kindred souls—sharing a similar response to issues in life.

☐ Demonstrating unswerving loyalty and dedication to those who are of like mind; assuring them of your support in time of need.

☐ Displaying a well-studied approach to life; observing traditions and adhering to the daily rituals.

☐ Seeking satisfaction in the harmony of the ebb and flow of your daily life; building it into the rhyme and reason for being; gaining assurance that honored ways will endure after your time.

☐ Protecting yourself and those close to you; viewing the outside world as a dangerous and threatening force; acknowledging that it is frequently beyond your control; being motivated to keep the world at bay.

☐ Showing an imbalance when using the character **tension points** of *individual* and *group*.

You Intensify Your Individual-Group Imbalance by:

☐ Being heavily influenced by others' reactions and opinions, which make you rethink some of your positions; attempting to confirm the correctness of your actions.

☐ Relinquishing some of your decision-power to those who claim to have more skill than you; preferring that they bear the responsibility for unforeseen misfortune.

☐ Adhering faithfully to the etiquette and formalities that surround persons in authority; deepening your sense of powerlessness with each repetition.

☐ Concealing a great deal of your feelings; keeping a tight rein on the emotions that you allow yourself to feel; trusting your reactions only after seeing if they match those who think like you do.

☐ Reminding yourself **too infrequently** that there are dangers even in the safety and security of a close-knit group. Leaders can become demigods, seizing such opportunities to increase their power and advancing simplistic slogans around which you and others can rally.

PART II   You Deal With Right and Wrong by:

☐ Working toward an equal emphasis on *caring* behavior and *justice* behavior. See chart 10B.

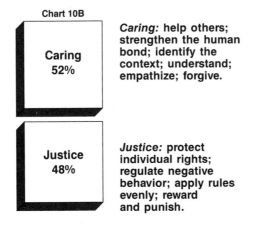

Chart 10B

Caring
52%

Caring: help others; strengthen the human bond; identify the context; understand; empathize; forgive.

Justice
48%

Justice: protect individual rights; regulate negative behavior; apply rules evenly; reward and punish.

☐ Preferring *caring* behavior (52% of the time) and *justice* behavior (48% of the time).

☐ Putting behind you those things that would tempt you; acknowledging, however, that you are capable of infringing on the rights and privileges of others if they overstep their prerogatives.

☐ Showing irritation and dissatisfaction with those who cannot discipline themselves; believing that small "sins" should be treated with gravity; concluding that minor offenses are the stepping stones to a major infraction.

☐ Supporting those who *acknowledge* their wrongdoing; viewing this action as a possible "conversion"; providing them with a listening ear when others, particularly aggressive people, reject their apologies.

☐ Remaining "obedient" to stringent regulation even though you find just cause to rebel; believing that you must work within the system to change rules rather than attack from the outside.

☐ Associating with those who share the same truths as you do; feeling uncomfortable with those who flaunt an extreme independence; fearing the effect of those who seem to be a "law unto themselves."

☐ Urging others to take pride in designing methods to govern their actions; stressing civilized ways to deal with appropriate behavior.

☐ Admitting that you have erred—reluctantly; showing little-used emotion to indicate the deep effect that your unacceptable behavior has upon you.

☐ Showing a balance when using the character **tension points** of *justice* and *caring*.

You Maintain Your Justice-Caring Balance by:

☐ Perceiving repentance as the basis of forgiveness for those who have failed to observe rules and regulations; reminding those who are unrepentant that it is more difficult for you to forget.

☐ Stressing the responsibility people have to themselves and to others—a belief in one another; concluding that rules exist because humans find it difficult to be consistently loyal, honest, and fair.

☐ Using your reasoning more than your emotional side to gain an appropriate perspective on when to show love and when to discipline—trying to do the logical thing.

☐ Accepting the fact that you eventually can make a difference in the lives of those who are more pliable than you; helping those who have more difficulty in conforming to standards.

☐ Criticizing situations that are unstructured and where "anything goes"; believing that occasions arise when people don't care enough about one another.

☐ Reminding yourself **frequently** that you are very human with tendencies to falter. Consequently, you impose restraints—often excessive—on yourself to ward off desires you find difficult to control.

PART III   You Pursue A Course Of Action by:

☐ Working toward an equal emphasis on *consensus* behavior and *contention* behavior. See chart 10C.

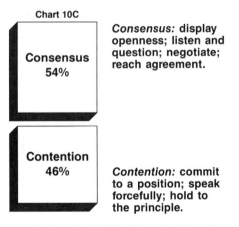

Chart 10C

Consensus 54%

Consensus: display openness; listen and question; negotiate; reach agreement.

Contention 46%

Contention: commit to a position; speak forcefully; hold to the principle.

☐ Preferring *consensus* behavior (54% of the time) and *contention* behavior (46% of the time).

☐ Trying your ideas on those who are most sympathetic to you; finding comfort, security, and fulfillment in what is familiar.

☐ Sharing conclusions about what ails your immediate world; believing that rituals—faith actions—provide a sense of predictability and stability; keeping some of the danger at a safe distance.

☐ Contending that there is a right and a wrong way for doing things; believing that keeping faith with the past is often the right way.

☐ Insisting that your best source of protection is in discussion—the give and take of question and answer; hoping for unity of opinion.

☐ Implying a sense of urgency; believing that there is a time to assert yourself in advancing an opinion; feeling, however, more comfortable in doing so within a small group of like-minded people.

☐ Viewing yourself as the guardian of knowledgeable resources—reading material, media messages; contending that these are better safeguarded through the support of people who consistently think like you do.

☐ Committing yourself to maintenance and stability rather than to unlimited progress.

☐ Rejecting popular appeals; waiting for evidence of promises; weighing the facts and opinions of others—preferring to "keep your feet on the ground"; taking the experience slowly; resisting those who would blow you off track with their inspiration.

☐ Showing a balance when using the character **tension points** of *contention* and *consensus*.

You Maintain Your Contention-Consensus Balance by:

☐ Attempting to manage the personal aspects of your life with tested practices; discussing your methods with those you trust.

☐ Preferring peace to confrontation; becoming argumentative only when your ideas are rejected for being outmoded or antiquated.

☐ Deciding to withdraw from heated conversation when you lack substantial facts to support your belief; protecting your image as one who develops principles based upon concrete data.

☐ Recognizing personal symptoms within yourself that reflect a desire to "punish" the other person for failure to support *all* that you believe; observing that you become uncommunicative with those who disappoint you. These are warning signals that you tend to be a grudge holder, becoming distressed if you are ignored.

☐ Reminding yourself **frequently** that, most often, you do not wish to alter your viewpoint; knowing that you become sensitive when others attack your ideas; desiring instead to consider opposing views and still be faithful to your deep convictions.

PATTERN ONE TWENTY-THREE
Leadership Interpretation

PART I   You Seek A Sense Of Self-Importance by:

☐ Working toward equal emphasis on *individual* behavior and *group* behavior. See chart 11A.

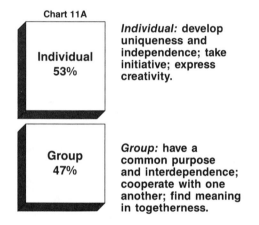

Chart 11A

Individual 53%

Individual: develop uniqueness and independence; take initiative; express creativity.

Group 47%

Group: have a common purpose and interdependence; cooperate with one another; find meaning in togetherness.

☐ Preferring *individual* behavior (53% of the time) and *group* behavior (47% of the time).

☐ Setting a course and refusing to deviate from it; giving warmth and helpfulness to those whom you permit close to you.

☐ Displaying confidence in your ability to enlarge your skills and to develop the talents of others.

☐ Challenging yourself to match or surpass the efforts of others in the performance of tasks; setting high personal goals.

☐ Desiring to prove your loyalty to the cause of others as well as your own; responding to both reasoning and inspiration; becoming involved with unproven adventures.

☐ Being preoccupied with gaining success by doing; tying your success into the larger whole; becoming concerned with the common good—something that has meaning beyond yourself.

☐ Demonstrating a willingness to provide direction when working with others; using subtle and effective suggestion to accelerate actions; employing methods of counseling and advisement to motivate people to act.

☐ Showing pleasure in the triumphs and good news of others even as you are concerned about their problems.

☐ Assuming a variety of responsibilities; preparing yourself to lead others; demonstrating flexibility and a willingness to move in and out of the leadership role according to circumstances; displaying multiple skills for such roles as critical thinker, data collector, problem solver, and back-up director.

☐ Showing a balance when using the character **tension points** of *individual* and *group*.

You Maintain Your Individual-Group Balance by:

☐ Stimulating people to become involved in your activities; keeping promises that you make; following the progress of people to the completion of the task.

☐ Developing friendships with others who desire an ongoing relationship with you; making them feel unsure, however, because of your need for independence—freedom to move in and out of a relationship or a group.

☐ Needing many people to whom you can express your universal ideas; making an impact on their private and public lives; desiring only a few associates for lasting and ongoing stimulation.

☐ Expecting support from friends and associates in your new ventures; showing disappointment when they are slow to respond; concealing your resentment over their failure to share your excitement.

☐ Reminding yourself **frequently** that you can be a strong, supportive arm to a recognized authority or a threatening presence who vies for power; becoming particularly troublesome to others if you are not privy to all information.

PART II   You Deal With Right and Wrong by:

☐ Working toward an equal emphasis on *caring* behavior and on *justice* behavior. See chart 11B.

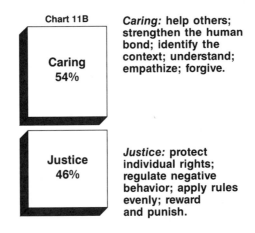

Chart 11B

Caring 54%

Caring: help others; strengthen the human bond; identify the context; understand; empathize; forgive.

Justice 46%

Justice: protect individual rights; regulate negative behavior; apply rules evenly; reward and punish.

☐ Preferring *caring* behavior (54% of the time) and *justice* behavior (46% of the time).

☐ Viewing your behavior and that of others within the context of the specific circumstances; asking the question: Why and in what way were the rules disregarded?

☐ Considering the many extenuating conditions that make breaking rules understandable.

☐ Judging a person's behavior according to public standards and norms; reacting to misconduct by quickly perceiving possible penalties; considering how all parties can gain from a bad experience.

☐ Expressing a need to identify factors that contribute to one's pattern of poor behavior; believing that ongoing appraisals of people are helpful; advocating a similar study and evaluation of standards and rules.

☐ Trusting that people have built-in character antennae that can be activated; believing in an inner system that can be roused from dormancy; knowing that helping people in this way can be more helpful than passing additional laws, rules, and regulations.

☐ Acknowledging that you, too, have thought of shortcuts—even though they run contrary to rules; discovering, however, that you prefer to honor the rights and privileges of others rather than coping with the guilt that you experience from a "quickie success."

☐ Showing a balance when using the character **tension points** of *justice* and *caring*.

You Maintain Your Justice-Caring Balance by:

☐ Attempting to give equal attention to what is good for the benefit of many and what is vital for the rights of the individual; knowing that new issues place intense pressure upon that balance.

☐ Having a high degree of affiliation with family and close friends; desiring to protect these individuals with the best laws possible; considering, as well, the need to assume responsibility for the best development of personality for each person.

☐ Struggling to lay aside your prejudices, particularly your dislike of a heavy-handed justice; realizing that you may be too easy on the offender if the offense has not directly affected your loved ones.

☐ Reminding yourself **frequently** that your slight favoritism toward *caring* behavior is tested by your ability to use "tough love" and by your intuitive judgment of people. You tend to be especially sensitive to needs—supplying reassurance to those who fear, providing attention to those who feel rejected, bringing release to those who feel tense. But, to maintain your balance on the *justice-caring* scale, you need to ask the question: What do you apply when you see gross injustice?

PART III   You Pursue A Course Of Action by:

☐ Placing a greater emphasis on *contention* behavior than on *consensus* behavior. See chart 11C.

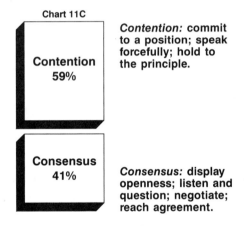

Chart 11C

Contention 59%

Contention: commit to a position; speak forcefully; hold to the principle.

Consensus 41%

Consensus: display openness; listen and question; negotiate; reach agreement.

☐ Preferring *contention* behavior (59% of the time) over *consensus* behavior (41% of the time).

☐ Using convincing arguments to clearly state your opinions; substantiating your conclusions with factual material.

☐ Demonstrating a provocative and persuasive style; immersing yourself in the credibility of your opinions; drawing upon your family and work experiences as illustrations; making believers of others because of your genuine sincerity.

☐ Appealing to people on a human interest level, showing more interest in them than in a desire to look good. The net effect is a demonstration of your ability to gain the respect and confidence of a variety of people.

☐ Assuming responsibility for conveying your beliefs from the strength of your convictions; refusing to accept just any answer; requiring an answer that is favorable to your position.

☐ Urging others to withhold judgment on your opinions; giving them ample time to reexamine their existing beliefs and to consider other options as well.

☐ Demonstrating an ability to carry through on a tough decision, even though it may cause temporary inconvenience to others.

☐ Asking people to trust you; placing your word on the line; expecting a great deal of yourself and a great deal of others.

☐ Showing an imbalance when using the character **tension points** of *contention* and *consensus.*

You Intensify Your Contention-Consensus Imbalance by:

☐ Being overly defensive when others react emotionally to your opinions; being especially sensitive to an oft-repeated charge that you tend to view problem situations too narrowly.

☐ Relying on consensus only when others fail to respond to your ideas; occasionally waiting too long before you begin negotiations in earnest; displaying reluctance to give in to others.

☐ Tending to manipulate others with the nudge of "having the best way for you"; causing some people to resist your proposals even when they know that you are right.

☐ Attempting to identify and control your tendency to lead others too far from the mainstream; appreciating that you have a fine-tuned ability to motivate and persuade; showing your independence from convention.

☐ Reminding yourself **too infrequently** that, while manipulation has a place in communicating beliefs, people do have a right to know and make decisions about what will affect them. Your firm direction can only be improved by input from others which diminishes the danger of manipulating, permits others occasional mistakes, and avoids antagonizing others, no matter how charming you are or how good your intentions.

PATTERN ONE TWENTY-FOUR

Leadership Interpretation

PART I   You Seek A Sense Of Self-Importance by:

☐ Placing a greater emphasis on *individual* behavior than on *group* behavior. See chart 12A.

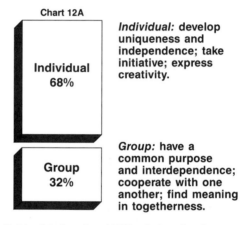

Chart 12A

Individual 68%

Individual: **develop uniqueness and independence; take initiative; express creativity.**

Group 32%

Group: **have a common purpose and interdependence; cooperate with one another; find meaning in togetherness.**

☐ Preferring *individual* behavior (68% of the time) over *group* behavior (32% of the time).

☐ Displaying enthusiasm; demonstrating personal strength and confidence.

☐ Deliberately creating some discomfort for others by deciphering hidden meanings; showing an ability to read between the lines.

☐ Spending time in anticipating questions; having answers at the tip of your tongue; making the experience of fielding difficult questions seem effortless.

☐ Being alert and conscious of timing; sensing when and how to orchestrate events and emotions; creating peaks and valleys that build toward a final culmination.

☐ Focusing your primary efforts on the rehearsal phase; achieving the sparkle of spontaneity only after repeated trial runs; passing off your achievement as "doing what comes naturally"; attempting to impress others.

☐ Being candid and direct; openly stating your dislike of routine activities; turning toward new and untried areas of life—either with people or situations.

☐ Projecting calmness in the face of unexpected news or information; believing that you can *choose* how you will react.

☐ Showing realism in your selection of other people; charming them while you appraise their attributes without sentimentality or idealism; disengaging yourself from those who tend to be overly dependent on you.

☐ Showing an imbalance when using the character **tension points** of *individual* and *group*.

You Intensify Your Individual-Group Imbalance by:

☐ Placing your welfare and personal interest above the concerns of others; hoping to accomplish your goals first.

☐ Avoiding long-term commitments; fearing possible monotony and sameness; agreeing to relationships in which others help you to develop an accelerated social life and many contacts with people.

☐ Placing excessive pressure on people to prove their individual worth; minimizing or taking for granted the most significant achievement of others—and yourself: working as a group member or moving a relationship forward.

☐ Failing to develop a sensitivity to people; emphasizing their need to get results on their own without a great deal of help from you; neglecting to place an equal value on their welfare.

☐ Reminding yourself **too infrequently** that you need to come to grips with the human factor question: What do you owe to others? In the work setting, is the responsibility fulfilled with the exchange of salary for work performance? In the personal setting, is the responsibility fulfilled with the completion of mutual roles or tasks?

PART II   You Deal With Right and Wrong by:

☐ Working toward an equal emphasis on *justice* behavior and on *caring* behavior. See chart 12B.

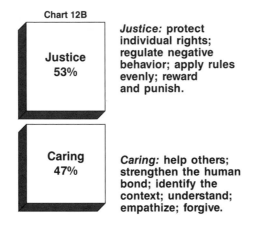

Chart 12B

Justice 53%

Justice: protect individual rights; regulate negative behavior; apply rules evenly; reward and punish.

Caring 47%

Caring: help others; strengthen the human bond; identify the context; understand; empathize; forgive.

☐ Preferring *justice* behavior (53% of the time) and *caring* behavior (47% of the time).

☐ Priding yourself on fair dealings with others; feeling that you can effectively direct activities to work with and gain from rules and regulations.

☐ Acknowledging your ability to find ways to get around regulations; deciding, instead, to use your ingenuity to get people to respect the rights of others.

☐ Setting an example of how people should respond to guidelines; showing promptness and adherence to requirements; demonstrating self-control.

☐ Keeping people in line through both attention to rules as well as counseling with people who tend to be careless; helping them view rules as necessary parameters for organizing time, space, and people.

☐ Emphasizing that everyone must carry a fair share; insisting that individuals be responsible for their actions; giving and withholding rewards to shape the motivation of people to get results.

☐ Re-examining the way in which your early experience with parents, teachers, and other moral instructors increased your awareness of being responsible for your actions; deciding that gaps existed because of differences in teaching. You depend upon inner convictions to assist in making choices.

☐ Showing a balance when using the character **tension points** of *justice* and *caring*.

You Maintain Your Justice-Caring Balance by:

☐ Holding yourself accountable for your actions; demanding that others do the same.

☐ Eliciting a favorable response for your insistence on fairness—matching rewards to results.

☐ Sensing that some people are concerned that you see them too clearly with your mind; failing, at times, to see them with your heart. You know that you are respected; you wonder to what extent you are feared.

☐ Admitting that your need for results often overshadows the concern you have for people and their struggles; believing that they don't always recognize the diligent effort you make in trying to be fair when assigning people to new positions or placing them in favored positions in your life.

☐ Reminding yourself **frequently** that, in fact, you do tend to judge people sternly and even harshly; recognizing that you sometimes fail to consider extenuating circumstances in your appraisals.

PART III   You Pursue A Course Of Action by:

☐ Placing a greater emphasis on *consensus* behavior than on *contention* behavior. See chart 12C.

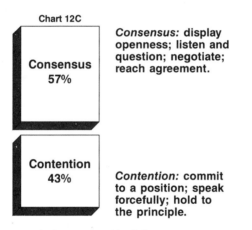

Chart 12C

Consensus 57%

Consensus: display openness; listen and question; negotiate; reach agreement.

Contention 43%

Contention: commit to a position; speak forcefully; hold to the principle.

☐ Preferring *consensus* behavior (57% of the time) over *contention* behavior (43% of the time).

☐ Engaging the interests of many people in your thinking and planning.

☐ Testing your credibility and acceptance; taking delight in revisiting, rethinking, and revising many and varied ideas into new shapes and alignments.

☐ Placing familiar objects or people in a new order with one another; creating a new dynamic and forcing a different perspective.

☐ Presenting an overview of your opinions; searching for new connections between the past and the present in the history of people and events.

☐ Enjoying a sixth sense—an intuitiveness—for creating new mixes and unions that will put your stamp on the future.

☐ Using an interchange of ideas; working toward solutions that are not etched in stone; permitting a degree of flexibility and openness.

☐ Demonstrating excellent reasoning ability and problem-solving techniques; scrutinizing others who consider themselves expert; upsetting those who are unprepared to deal with your matter-of-factness.

☐ Valuing consensus; showing an agreeableness to hard-nosed negotiation; desiring to have people involved and participating in the process.

☐ Showing an imbalance when using the character **tension points** of *contention* and *consensus*.

You Intensify Your Contention-Consensus Imbalance by:

☐ Using consensus as a method to make people believe that you are open to a variety of ideas; knowing that you have the ability to forcefully contend when your discussion efforts fail.

☐ Placing others on a stage, so to speak; orchestrating efforts; appearing to be part of a developing effort; providing some fanfare; moving the process toward consensus.

☐ Conveying a genuine excitement; promising rewards for results; brushing aside the concerns of those who fear that you see them primarily as means to the end.

☐ Tending to avoid sharing negative information with others; hoping to receive approval and agreement with your ideas.

☐ Reminding yourself **too infrequently** that others have the right to know what the potential dangers are; recognizing that you need to expose unfavorable as well as favorable data; sensing a character struggle within yourself if information is withheld.

PATTERN ONE THIRTY-FOUR
Leadership Interpretation

PART I   You Seek A Sense Of Self-Importance by:

☐ Working toward an equal balance on *individual* behavior and *group behavior.*
See Chart 13A.

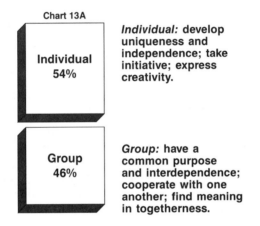

Chart 13A

**Individual
54%**

Individual: **develop uniqueness and independence; take initiative; express creativity.**

**Group
46%**

Group: **have a common purpose and interdependence; cooperate with one another; find meaning in togetherness.**

☐ Preferring *individual* behavior (54% of the time) and *group* behavior (46% of the time).

☐ Staking out a territory of knowledge and information in which you have few equals.

☐ Revealing an interest in the way things work, how they fit together; discovering meaning behind surface appearances.

☐ Using new twists of thinking; moving ahead with your inventive ideas; being persistent; showing efficiency and follow-through.

☐ Setting yourself apart from others; retreating from those who simply want to socialize.

☐ Conforming to the needs and desires of those you respect; building in-depth relationships with the same deliberateness that you employ in approaching a scientific project.

☐ Overcoming your critics' objections by working harder than most.

☐ Claiming ownership of the work that you have accomplished; showing reluctance to change any element of your plan; revealing an unwillingness to accept input that might force you to share ownership.

☐ Showing an inclination to work with respected key people in a group or relationship; admitting that you require time to feel comfortable with others.

☐ Accepting requests to tackle a problem with little or no idea of the solution; relying upon your self-confidence and discipline to meet the challenge.

☐ Showing a balance when using the character **tension points** of *individual* and *group*.

You Maintain Your Individual-Group Balance by:

☐ Building your sense of self-esteem on what you do; making the distinction between satisfaction in your work and simply "holding a job."

☐ Planning and completing tasks; developing appropriate skills or selecting those with needed talents; designing procedures that will facilitate the work task.

☐ Determining on first impression how others can serve your interests.

☐ Being obsessed with single-minded concentration on a vital project; placing aside other interests which interfere with your tasks.

☐ Criticizing those who have different interests than yours; believing that your observable and documented activities have a greater effect on others.

☐ Reminding yourself **frequently** of your need to increase social contact with others; recognizing that you need to build relationships with people outside of your immediate family; noting the narrowness in your appraisal of others, seeing them primarily as extensions of your work.

PART II   You Deal With Right and Wrong by:

☐ Working toward an equal emphasis on *justice* behavior and *caring* behavior. See chart 13B.

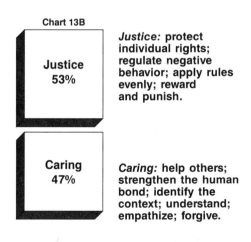

Chart 13B

Justice 53%

Justice: protect individual rights; regulate negative behavior; apply rules evenly; reward and punish.

Caring 47%

Caring: help others; strengthen the human bond; identify the context; understand; empathize; forgive.

☐ Preferring *justice* behavior (53% of the time) and *caring* behavior (47% of the time).

☐ Setting standards for how you believe others should conduct themselves.

☐ Placing strict requirements on those whom you permit close to you.

☐ Showing irritation with those who break rules and regulations; using nonverbalization—stern looks, cool manner; refusing to talk for periods of time.

☐ Criticizing people who trespass on your territory; refusing permission to those who request the use of your equipment and belongings.

☐ Holding personal achievement as inviolable; carefully scrutinizing people who wish to share credit with you when their demands are unjustified.

☐ Perceiving of yourself as an astute judge of people; assuming that most people operate from a motive of greed, leading you to be on-guard against the dishonesty of others.

☐ Demanding an outward manifestation of the worth of people; requiring them to do what they say they will do; showing little respect for those who excuse their behavior due to ignorance.

☐ Wrestling with your desire to gain at the expense of others' efforts; believing that, even though your work is original, you tend to blend the efforts of others into your overall effort; reconsidering how specific you should be in recognizing the contributions of others.

☐ Showing a balance when using the character **tension points** of *justice* and *caring*.

You Maintain Your Justice-Caring Balance by:

☐ Attending to the rights of others from a logical perspective; recognizing and applying principles that govern human relationships.

☐ Protecting family members and close associates from stern penalties and unfair procedures; showing more sentimentality than you care to admit.

☐ Withholding judgment and a decision to impose penalties until specific and accurate facts are available; incurring the anger of others for moving too cautiously and indecisively.

☐ Advocating the right of competent individuals to share in deciding the extent of the administration of rules; arguing that each situation tends to represent a different set of facts.

☐ Reminding yourself **frequently** that you enjoy solving complex problems—of any nature. Consequently, you willingly direct your attention to such regulatory issues. You recognize the need to resolve less complicated problems, as well, since they develop into time-consuming events that demand an inordinate amount of your time.

PART III   You Pursue A Course Of Action by:

☐ Placing a greater emphasis on *contention* behavior than on *consensus* behavior. See chart 13C.

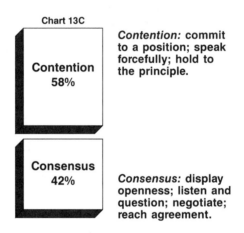

Chart 13C

Contention 58%

Contention: commit to a position; speak forcefully; hold to the principle.

Consensus 42%

Consensus: display openness; listen and question; negotiate; reach agreement.

☐ Preferring *contention* behavior (58% of the time) over *consensus* behavior (42% of the time).

☐ Documenting the reasons for your opinions with great care; being faithful to every detail.

☐ Presenting facts and figures that can be quantified; weaving them into an orderly picture with practical applications.

☐ Encouraging others to adapt to your plan rather than adapting to theirs.

☐ Demonstrating patience when explaining the purpose and the implementation of your ideas; becoming forceful and blunt with others if their questions reveal doubts or suggested alterations.

☐ Convincing others of the accuracy of your position; believing that only a few can suggest something that you have not already considered and rejected.

☐ Stating your ideas clearly; preferring that key thoughts be recorded—put in writing—to ensure that communication is direct and meaningful.

☐ Comparing your proposal and plans with those of others who have an inventiveness that is similar to your own; believing that your method of preparation is superior.

☐ Surprising those who perceive you as unassuming; catching their attention by your vigor and stubbornness in projecting your convictions; challenging others to be constructive in their criticism of your opinions.

☐ Showing an imbalance when using the character **tension points** of *contention* and *consensus*.

You Intensify Your Contention-Consensus Imbalance by:

☐ Keeping others in the dark about your decisions; encouraging others to talk while you listen; deciding in advance the direction that you will take, rendering input from others irrelevant.

☐ Showing irritation with those who intrude on your time and attempt to develop open communication with you; retreating psychologically into your own inner world when pressed.

☐ Withdrawing from those who show little or no interest in your opinions; being unwilling to involve them in your thinking by initiating discussion or drawing them out; feeling that your ideas have already spoken for you.

☐ Believing that you have as much skill in persuading others with your factual information as you do in researching and planning with hard data; claiming to communicate as well as you plan.

☐ Reminding yourself **too infrequently** that your tendency to retreat and withdraw into yourself is often seen by others as a rejection. Your attempt to protect your privacy may serve to intimidate others.

PATTERN TWO THIRTY-FOUR

Leadership Interpretation

PART I   You Seek A Sense of Self-Importance by:

☐ Placing a greater emphasis on *group* behavior than on *individual* behavior. See chart 14A.

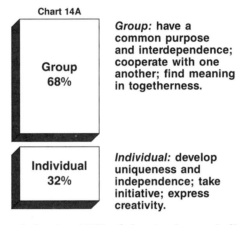

Chart 14A

| Group 68% | **Group:** have a common purpose and interdependence; cooperate with one another; find meaning in togetherness. |

| Individual 32% | **Individual:** develop uniqueness and independence; take initiative; express creativity. |

☐ Preferring *group* behavior (68% of the time) over *individual* behavior (32% of the time).

☐ Developing close ties with people; gaining their confidence; developing skills that require patience and repetition.

☐ Expressing your concerns in an articulate manner; preferring situations in which people have much in common.

☐ Demanding a great deal from yourself; often taking pressure off those who are easily rattled.

☐ Approaching tasks in a methodical way; dealing with critical issues in a conventional manner.

☐ Being predictable; minimizing personal risks to yourself and others.

☐ Inviting spirited cooperation; avoiding the intense rivalry of competitive combatants; preferring to compliment both sides; hoping to escape by being in the middle; striving for neutrality.

☐ Operating well within a relationship or a group.

☐ Avoiding mishaps and costly mistakes; projecting yourself as a valuable asset rather than a liability.

☐ Being singled out for your depth of knowledge or skill; learning to do one or two things well; avoiding the practice of spreading yourself too thinly.

☐ Showing an imbalance when using the character **tension points** of *individual* and *group*.

You Intensify Your Individual-Group Imbalance by:

☐ Assuming blame when others falter; becoming defensive and apologetic to those whom you wish to please.

☐ Using your specialized skills to maintain group or relationship functions, often at the expense of your own needs; finding it difficult, at times, to refuse the urgent requests of others.

☐ Showing ambivalence when acclaimed for performing extraordinary activities that also involve others; hoping that they do not feel left out; worrying about how they will perceive you.

☐ Being constrained by an overly strong emphasis on tradition; desiring freedom to question the need to observe rituals that stifle you; recognizing that ritual no longer serves the function for you that it does for others.

☐ Reminding yourself **too infrequently** that you need to resolve your struggle between individual and group accomplishment; needing to openly face your feeling that you can rise above the "leveling" effect of a group or relationship; needing to recognize your talents and respond to the need to develop them and to be recognized for them.

PART II   You Deal With Right and Wrong by:

☐ Working toward an equal emphasis on *justice* behavior and *caring* behavior. See chart 14B.

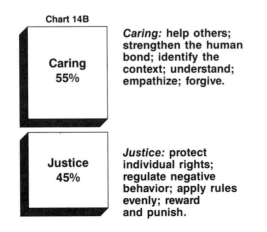

Chart 14B

Caring 55% — *Caring:* help others; strengthen the human bond; identify the context; understand; empathize; forgive.

Justice 45% — *Justice:* protect individual rights; regulate negative behavior; apply rules evenly; reward and punish.

☐ Preferring *caring* behavior (55% of the time) and *justice* behavior (45% of the time).

☐ Giving others the benefit of the doubt; tending to give them another chance.

☐ Refraining from intense competition, preferring to use friendly overtures rather than invoking severe rules and regulations; believing that pitting one person against another minimizes mutual respect.

☐ Stressing the importance of observing problems and offering corrective measures in the early stages; believing that people deviate from appropriate behavior over time—a gradual process that worsens and becomes ingrained.

☐ Approaching issues of conduct in a calm and methodical fashion; displaying a manner that conveys confidence; believing that a solution can be developed by working together.

☐ Viewing your temptations as natural; questioning those rules and regulations that cause anxiety because they have not been developed with the input of people they affect.

☐ Finding ways to screen yourself and those close to you in a protective cocoon; feeling that what you don't know can't hurt you; attempting to place self-responsibility ahead of the motivation that is aroused by the threat of punishment.

☐ Showing a balance when using the character **tension points** of *justice* and *caring*.

You Maintain Your Justice-Caring Balance by:

☐ Leading with your heart rather than with your head on occasions; failing at times to consider that the action of breaking rules is harmful to others, depriving people of their rights and privileges.

☐ Tending to be supportive and loyal to those who "fall short of the mark"; finding it difficult to use "tough love" with those who are close to you.

☐ Making others feel obligated because of your forgiving attitude; hoping in your mind that, if you broke rules, others would do the same for you.

☐ Looking for direction in your thinking; checking sources you trust before rendering an opinion on the rightness or wrongness of an act; hoping to gather support for your decision.

☐ Reminding yourself **frequently** that your view of justice is reflected by your participation as an enforcer; believing that you can be strict in certain circumstances, but in actuality leaning toward an empathetic response. You are less good at being forceful or exceling at judging, preferring to have "professionals" decide on the nature of punishment.

PART III   You Pursue A Course Of Action by:

☐ Placing a greater emphasis on *consensus* behavior than on *contention* behavior. See chart 14C.

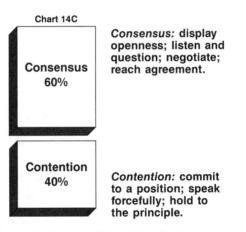

Chart 14C

Consensus 60%

Consensus: display openness; listen and question; negotiate; reach agreement.

Contention 40%

Contention: commit to a position; speak forcefully; hold to the principle.

☐ Preferring *consensus* behavior (60% of the time) over *contention* behavior (40% of the time).

☐ Being resilient; holding steadfast; bouncing back when others show opposition.

☐ Convincing others that your opinions are based on logic as well as on personal experience; willingly accepting the function of advisor on practical procedures as well as on theoretical issues.

☐ Pressing for high standards; putting your reputation on the line by hinting at change; depending upon others to initiate major shifts of direction.

☐ Using the strength of well-known experts to gain support for your ideas.

☐ Demonstrating conscientiousness in your efforts; receiving support from those who have trusted you in previous situations; using your credibility.

☐ Giving people the opportunity to think through to the conclusion that you draw; gaining respect for your thoughtfulness for those who are directly affected by your ideas.

☐ Identifying points of agreement; striving for a pleasing harmony; recognizing the importance of visible symbols that provide a continuity between past and future.

☐ Showing an imbalance when using the character **tension points** of *contention* and *consensus*.

You Intensify Your Contention-Consensus Imbalance by:

☐ Waiting for the more forceful people to raise their voices to introduce new ways of doing things.

☐ Developing expertise in an area before you are willing to express strong opinions one way or the other, with the result that others often consult individuals who are less qualified than you; feeling passed over.

☐ Becoming too strict and exacting when faced with critical decisions; tending to constrict your thought and action; narrowing your vision.

☐ Going by the "book"; feeling more comfortable with reliable and tested sources; being unwilling to trust your own capabilities.

☐ Reminding yourself **too infrequently** that change can bring benefits even though new ideas and practices raise conflict and disrupt the pleasing togetherness you build. Some problems cannot wait for consensus; delay is dangerous.

Appendix A

Glossary of Response Words/Phrases

A

accept circumstances — true to life, objective; down to earth; inclined to literal truth, practical.

accept others — cooperative, giving assent; going along with others; taking what others give.

accommodating — helpful, unselfish; showing consideration to others.

accurate — correct, exacting; meticulous in efforts.

activate others — start, stimulate others to new thought and action; motivate.

adaptable — adjustable, willing to compromise; demonstrating ease in changing situations.

adhere to custom — conform to established practice or accepted standards; develop habitual response.

adventurous — thrill seeking, rash; seeking excitement, eager for new experience.

aggressive — hostile, quarrelsome, pushy, assertive, bold.

agreeable — approving, concurring with others, pleasing; ready to agree or consent.

ambitious — goal oriented, hard working; eager to succeed.

approachable — open, friendly, favorably disposed.

argumentative — quarrelsome, scrappy, belligerent; disagreeing with others' opinions; apt to argue or debate.

arrogant — vain, overbearing, snobbish; high-and-mighty.

assertive	bold, positive, decided, emphatic, insistent.
attractive	inviting, appealing, alluring, well-favored, engaging.

B

bold	unafraid, fearless; willing to try new experiences; forward-looking.
brave	unflinching, heroic, confrontive with others; displaying courage.

C

calm	cool-headed, relaxed, unshaken, restful, collected.
captivating	seductive, irresistible, fascinating; turning the heads of others.
cautious	discreet, wary of others, guarded; on the "red alert."
charming	enchanting, winsome, charismatic; having a magnetic personality; delightful and agreeable.
cheerful	jolly, gleeful, elated; in high humor; of sunny disposition.
combative	warlike, aggressive, scrappy, offensive, making a stand against.
companionable	friendly, sociable, congenial; compatible with others.
compassionate	charitable, sympathetic, tenderhearted; showing love for others.
competitive	contending, opposing, fighting; in rivalry with others; trying to outdo others.
complacent	smug, self-satisfied, unconcerned; appearing to be at ease.
conceited	boasting, bragging, vain; puffed up, self-important.

confident	self-assured, certain, convinced, sure of oneself; having assurance or certainty of success.
confrontive	opposing face-to-face, challenging others eyeball-to-eyeball.
considerate	kind, serious, sensitive, mindful; attentive to others; observant of the rights and feelings of others.
contented	fulfilled, happy, pleased, joyful; comfortable and at ease, with no desire to experience anything different.
controlled	dominated by others, guided, managed, or governed.
convincing	persuading; bringing by argument and evidence to belief; influencing others with powerful appeal.
cooperative	united, joining forces; working side by side; pulling together.
cordial	warm, sincere, amiable, gracious; receptive and outgoing.
correct and exact	willing to remove the errors or mistakes; admonish or punish for the purpose of improving.
courageous	strong-hearted, showing fortitude, spunk, grit; dogged, gallant.
courteous	well-mannered, respectful and polite, thoughtful, kind.
creative	imaginative, resourceful, fruitful, gifted; acting in an individual way.
cultured	refined, enlightened, accomplished, well-read; artistically knowledgeable.

D

daring	venturesome, reckless, gutsy, game; willing to take a chance.
decided	having a fixed purpose; certain, definite, resolute, emphatic.

decisive	absolute, firm; final and convincing in decision making.
desire to please	adaptable to the needs of others; willing to do a favor or service for, oblige.
determined	unwavering, firm, purposeful, dedicated, persevering, showing stick-to-it-iveness.
diplomatic	artful, tactful; polite and cautious; smoothly skillful in handling others.
do favors for others	gratify the wishes of others; do a service; perform a courtesy.
do what others ask	aware of what others need and compliant to their requests or demands.
driven to succeed	motivated by possibilities of prosperity, good fortune; obsessed to make good; dedicated to conquest.

E

eager	enthusiastic, intense, fervent, greedy; impatient to get on with it; zealous.
easily influenced	easily persuaded; willing to change because of the force of another.
easily led	pliable; capable of being easily persuaded, taught, or controlled.
easygoing	casual, unexcitable, unworried, uncritical.
easy mark	soft touch, pushover; victim to those who are greedy; scapegoat for others.
easy to be with	congenial, harmonious, agreeable, suitable, like-minded.
enterprising	keen, innovative; up-and-coming; venturesome; wide-awake.
even-tempered	calm, steady, balanced, fair, dispassionate, equitable; not quickly angered or excited.
expect trouble	attentive, observant, watchful, on guard, apprehensive.

F

factual	true, proven, actual, certain, sure.
fast-paced	swift, highly mobile; moved quickly to action; accelerated in thought and action.
fearful	afraid, scared, worried, uneasy, nervous.
firm	determined, unwavering, resolute, tough, hard-nosed, inflexible.
fond of talking	having an inclination to talk; sociable.
forceful	strong, powerful, robust; full of energy; sometimes overpowering.
full of life	stirring, fervent, easily affected by emotions; desirous of excitement.
fun-loving	laughs easily, humorous, gay, enjoyable, looking for a good time.
fussy	picky, particular, agitated, hard to please.

G

generous	unselfish, considerate, big-hearted, willing to give.
gentle	kind, tender, humane; thoughtful and peaceful; refined in manner.
get along with others	helpful, kindly, loving, chummy, folksy.
God-fearing	devoutly righteous, devotional, worshipful.
go-getter	live wire, doer, hustler, dynamo, eager beaver.
good mixer	pleasant, cheery, talkative, genial; backslapping.
good-natured	agreeable, kindly, obliging.

H

harmonious	cordial, congenial, like-minded, in agreement; able to share similar feelings, ideas, or interests with others.
hesitate to act	slow to act or decide; holding back in uncertainty.
high-spirited	enthusiastic, spunky, feisty, dashing, fun-loving.
hold back words	hesitant in the expression of thought and action, losing a degree of freedom to state feelings.
hospitable	receptive, welcoming, open-handed, friendly, warm.
humble	modest, shy, unpretending, unassuming; without arrogance.

I

influence others	affect another person or a course of events, using power to sway; exercising power.
inspiring	encouraging, stirring, moving, promoting, exciting.
invent new things	originate, create, put together; adept or skillful in developing a new device or process from study and experimentation.

J

jovial	merry, laughing, gleeful, happy.
joyful	jubilant, full of joy, ecstatic, delighted; causing or bringing happiness.

K

kind	helpful, considerate, compassionate, understanding, well-meaning.

L

laugh easily

merry, joyful, bringing good feeling, able to get others to enter into a happy environment.

lenient

forgiving, permissive, gentle and understanding; not harsh or severe in judging or disciplining others.

life of the party

zestful, vigorous, glad, joyous; able to help others to enjoy.

lighthearted

carefree, lively, sunny; free and easy.

like to outdo others

striving to win, vying with another for profit, prize, or position.

lively

active, spirited, peppy, bouncy, full of life.

loyal

devoted, dependable, true, constant, unswerving.

M

meek and mild

gentle, kind, submissive, long-suffering, unassertive.

moderate

balanced, reasonable, toned down, middle-of-the-road.

N

naive

innocence, unsuspecting, inexperienced, unworldly, childlike.

neighborly

helpful, caring, kindly, polite, easy to get along with.

nervy

bold, cocky, brash, determined, brassy.

O

obedient	compliant, conforming, law-abiding, faithful, loyal; willing to do as told.
obey the rules	comply with, abide by, conform to, succumb to, bow to authority.
obliging	gracious, agreeable, cooperative, feeling a debt of gratitude; ready to do favors.
opinionated	inflexible, unyielding, bullheaded, uncompromising.
opportunistic	showing good timing, taking advantage; gaining an upper hand, sometimes at the expense of others.
optimistic	confident of exceeding the best possible outcome; forward-looking.
orderly	neat, proper, peaceful, organized, well-behaved.
outgoing	friendly, warm, informal, demonstrative.
outspoken	frank, direct, blunt, candid, honest, artless at times.

P

patient	steadfast, persistent, persevering, uncomplaining.
peaceful	quiet, calm, peace-loving, harmonious; not easily disturbed or excited.
persistent	immovable, unchangeable, tireless, unshakable.
personable	attractive, graceful, pleasing, winning; pleasing in person or personality.
persuasive	convincing, assuring, compelling; logical and moving.
pioneering	originating, discovering, establishing; being a forerunner.
playful	frisky, humorous, amusing, joking.

pleasant	pleasing, enjoyable, gratifying, agreeable, delectable.
poised	self-assured, calm, showing presence of mind and self-command.
polished	tasteful, well-bred, elegant, well-mannered, cultivated, refined.
popular	esteemed, approved by others, honored, well-liked; in demand.
positive	genuine, useful, assured, admitting no doubt; definite in beliefs.
possessive	grasping, overprotective, clinging; tenacious to own.
praised by others	deserving admiration; excellent, praiseworthy.
prayerful	worshipful, solemn, spiritual, devout, pious.
precise	exact, strict, specific; clearly expressive.
predictable	known, expected; showing a definite pattern of behavior and habit.
put up with things	regulated by others; restrained; placing a self-imposed check on one's actions.

Q

quiet and shy	bashful, self-conscious, timid, modest, reserved.
quiet-mannered	peaceful, restful, mild, unboasting.

R

ready to help	useful, supportive; providing service; beneficial.
relaxed	loose, free, easy; making less tense.
resigned	uncomplaining, submissive, meek, patient; put-upon.

respectful	obedient, accommodating, courteous; attentive to others, showing esteem.
restless	uneasy, excitable, agitated; on the go; driven, seeking change.
restrained	restricted, held back; suppressing feeling.
risk-taking	adventuresome, unprotected; willing to take a chance even when there is hazard in proceeding.

S

satisfied	reassured, comforting, free of doubt, being fulfilled.
say the right thing	appropriate; able to look at all sides of life; aware of what others need; warm, friendly, awake.
seek excitement	thrill-seeking, easily stirred up, looking for the unusual event.
self-reliant	assured, dependent upon one's own capabilities, judgment, or resources; self-governed.
sell an idea	persuade or satisfy by evidence or argument; make believable.
sense of humor	witty, amusing, enjoying laughter; able to look at all sides of life.
show excitement	spirited, fervent, avid, eager, passionate.
sincere in beliefs	credible, firm in faith, trusting, having conviction; free from pretense.
slow to anger	unhurried, deliberate, able to take things in stride.
sociable	congenial, providing occasion for conversation; enjoying the company of others.
softhearted	humane, charitable, forgiving, kind, sentimental.
soft-spoken	quiet, noncombative, mild-mannered, calming in speech.

spontaneous — natural, self-generated, unplanned, free and unrehearsed.

strong-willed — unyielding, self-assertive, determined, stubborn, fixed.

stubborn — unbending, dogmatic, opinionated, obstinate; not easily persuaded.

submissive — easily subjugated; willing to surrender to the will or authority of another; subordinated.

sure of self — showing self-esteem; cool, without doubt; confident.

sweet — attractive, nice, dear, kind, lovable.

sympathetic — compassionate, tenderhearted; generous, understanding.

T

tactful — polite, diplomatic, sensitive to the needs of others; discreet.

take charge — directive toward others, responsible, willing to give orders and instruct.

take the initiative — drive, push, assume leadership.

talkative — gabby, talky, effusive; showing a need for oral expression.

teachable — capable of or receptive to being taught; ready to receive knowledge and instruction.

tender-minded — intimate, personal, loving, softhearted.

thoughtful of others — attentive, helpful, kind; showing concern for the well-being of others.

timid — nervous, bashful, shy, retiring, apprehensive.

tolerant — permissive, patient; respecting the beliefs and practices of others.

tough-minded	firm and challenging when opposing others; strong, formidable; hard-nosed.
traditional	desiring to use beliefs handed down from generation to generation; habitual, established.
true to others	trustworthy, loyal, true-blue; steady in performance and promises to others.
trusting	believing, unsuspecting, accepting; confidence in what others say or do.

U

| upbeat | confident, enthusiastic, believing in the future, rousing. |

V

| vigorous | energetic, zealous, robust, red-blooded. |

W

well-disciplined	diligent, self-controlled; showing self-restraint.
well-liked	widely appreciated; sought after for company, well-received.
willing	accommodating, compliant; eager and prompt; ready to act.
willpower	firmness; drive and strength; resoluteness, insistence.

Y

| yield to authority | give in, submit to those with power; surrender. |

Appendix B

What Can Individuals Change About Themselves?			
	Impossible To Change	Possible To Change Partially	Possible To Change Substantially
(1) color of eyes	X		
(2) ability to verbalize		X	
(3) shyness		X	
(4) body weight		X	
(5) laziness			X
(6) manual dexterity		X	
(7) reliability			X
(8) feeling of inferiority			X
(9) skin color	X		
(10) tone of voice		X	
(11) tendency to lie			X
(12) response to authority			X
(13) habit of daydreaming			X
(14) perfectionism			X
(15) body coordination		X	
(16) concern for others			X
(17) tendency to blame others			X
(18) color perception	X		
(19) sexual attractiveness		X	
(20) superstitiousness			X
(21) artistic ability		X	
(22) like or dislike for others			X
(23) tendency to gossip			X
(24) fear of machinery			X
(25) meanness			X
(26) temper		X	
(27) sloppiness			X
(28) intellectual capacity		X	

Appendix C
The Behavior Indicator

(1) **Responding**

| Part I | What Are You The Most? |

Procedure:

- Note the first group of words* on panel A, row 1 (opposite page).

- Write an "M" in the symbol after *one* word that is *most* descriptive of your general behavior (see Example A).

- Follow the same procedure for each group of words on panels A, B, and C (pages 547, 548, and 549).

Response Time:
5-6 minutes

Most Descriptive of My Behavior:

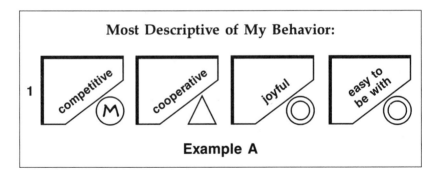

Example A

---

*See Appendix A, Glossary of Response Words/Phrases, for definitions. Complete your selections in those groups in which the meanings of the words are clear. Then return to those groups in which you need clarification.

Descriptive root words for Part I are adapted from *Varieties of Temperament*, by W. H. Sheldon, *Emotions of Normal People*, by W.M. Marston, and *Man for Himself* by E. Fromm.

PANEL A

Most Descriptive of My Behavior:

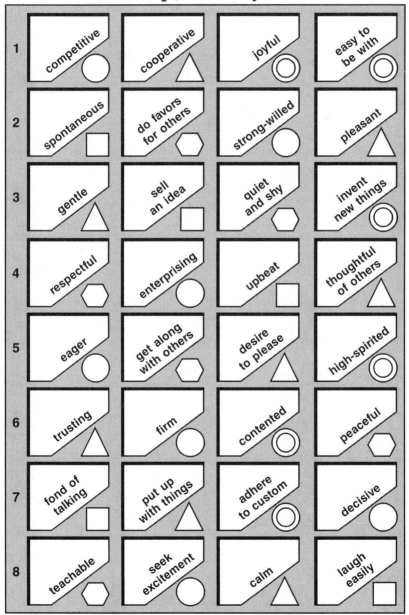

PANEL B

Most Descriptive of My Behavior:

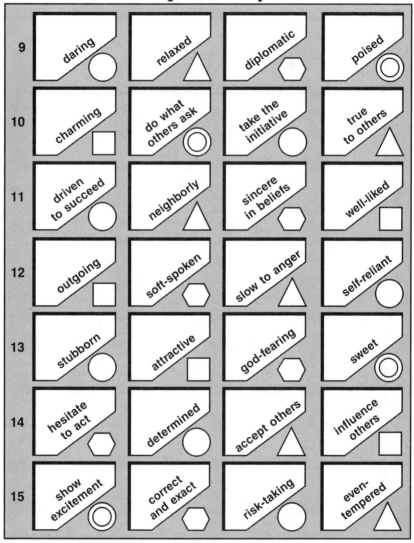

PANEL C

Most Descriptive of My Behavior:

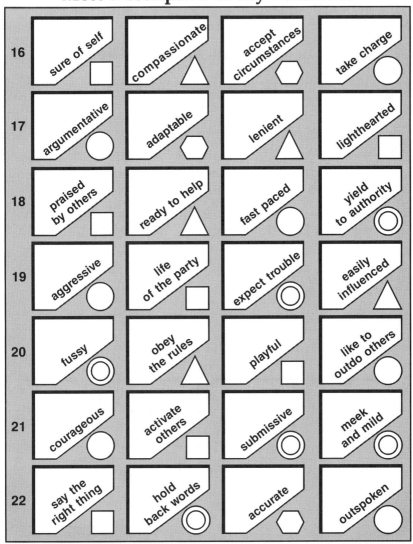

Responding (Con't.)

Part II   What Are You The Least?

Procedure:

• Note the first group of words on panel D, row 1 (opposite page).

• Write an "L" in the symbol after *one* word that is *least* descriptive of how you *feel* (see Example B).

• Follow the same procedure for each group of words on panels D, E, and F (pages 551, 552, and 553).

Response Time:
5-6 minutes

Least Descriptive of How I Feel:

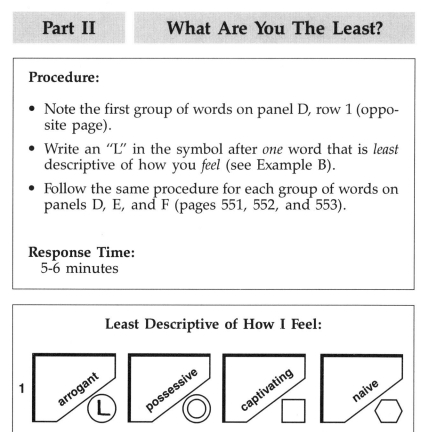

Example B

Descriptive root words for Part II adapted from *Man for Himself* by E. Fromm and *Emotions of Normal People* by W.M. Marston.

PANEL D

Least Descriptive of How I Feel:

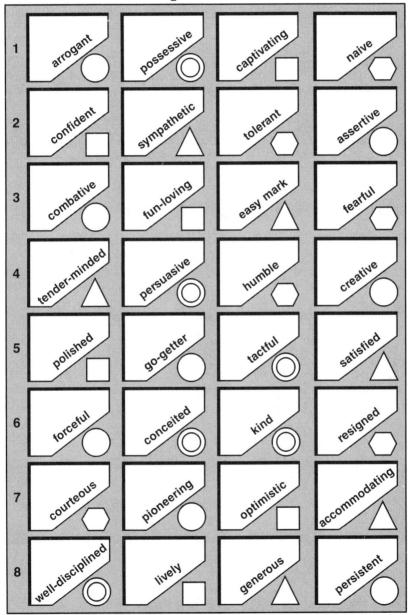

PANEL E

Least Descriptive of How I Feel:

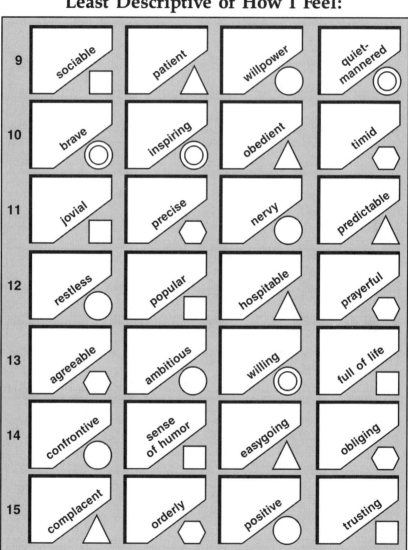

PANEL F

Least Descriptive of How I Feel:

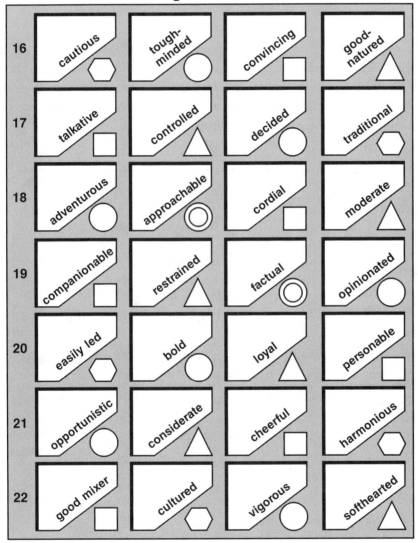

(2) Counting and. . . .

Step I	Count the Most
Refer to Part I, panels A, B, C **Pages 547, 548, 549**	• Count the number of M's in the circles. • Record the total in the circle, *Most* row on the opposite page. • Follow the procedure for the remaining symbols. **RECORD THE MOST** ➡

Step II	Count the Least
Refer to Part II, panels D, E, F **Pages 551, 552, 553**	• Count the number of L's in the circles. • Record the total in the circle, *Least* row on the opposite page. • Follow the procedure for the remaining symbols. **RECORD THE LEAST** ➡

Step III	Determine the Difference
Most (4) **Least** (7) **Difference** (-3) Example	• Find the difference between the numbers in the Most and Least circles on the opposite page. • Record the number in the difference row. • Follow the procedure for the remaining symbols. • Add a plus (+) or minus (−). See Example. *If* Most symbol is greater than Least = + Most symbol is less than Least = − Most symbol is same as Least = 0 **RECORD THE DIFFERENCE** ➡

....Recording

The Tally Page

Most: *Graph I,* page 558

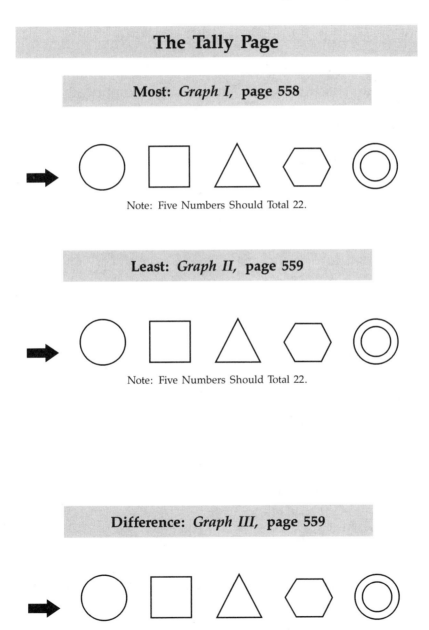

Note: Five Numbers Should Total 22.

Least: *Graph II,* page 559

Note: Five Numbers Should Total 22.

Difference: *Graph III,* page 559

Note: Use (+) or (−) where necessary.

③ Transferring. . . .

Transferring Numbers to Graphs

- Transfer the numbers in the symbols from the Tally page (555) to the symbols above each of the three graphs on pages 558 and 559.

  Note the example below:

Most — **Graph I**

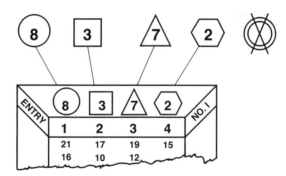

- Transfer:

  Most to Graph I

  Least to Graph II

  Difference to Graph III

Note: The ◯'s numbers are *not* transferred.

....Plotting and Graphing

Plotting: Use X's

- Begin with Graph I, page 558.

- Locate and place an X over the number in each column of the graph that corresponds to the number in the symbol.

  Note the example below.

- Estimate the X if the precise number is not shown.

- Plot Graphs II and III on page 559.

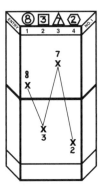

Graph I *Most*

Graphing: Connect the X's

- Begin with Graph I, page 558.

- Draw a line connecting the X's. See example above.

- Complete Graphs II and III on page 559.

④ Preparing....

Finding Your Entry Numbers

- Note the entry <u>bar</u> at the top of Graph I.

- Circle number 1 if the X in that column is above the midline (see Example below).

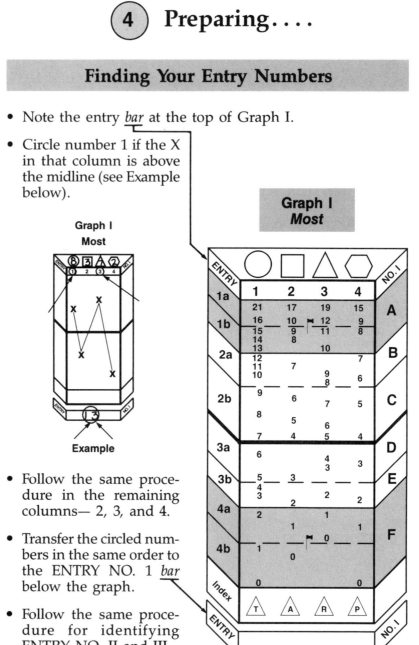

Graph I
Most

Example

- Follow the same procedure in the remaining columns— 2, 3, and 4.

- Transfer the circled numbers in the same order to the ENTRY NO. 1 <u>bar</u> below the graph.

- Follow the same procedure for identifying ENTRY NO. II and III.

....for Your Interpretation

Graph II
Least

Graph III
Difference

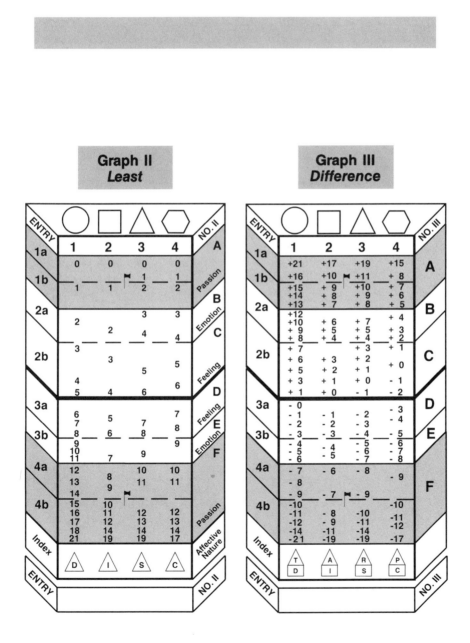

Bibliography

Aamodt, M. and Kimbrough, W. 1982. "Effect of Group Heterogeneity on Quality of Groups Task Solutions." *Psychological Reports*, Vol. 50.

Adler, Alfred. 1959. *Understanding Human Nature*. New York: Fawcett Books.

_____. 1956. *The Individual Psychology of Alfred Adler*, Heinz & Rowena Ausbacker (Eds). New York: Basic Books.

Brain/Mind Bulletin (1977) "'New Nervous System' May Effect Behavior Illness," *Brain/Mind Bulletin* 2, No. 15.

_____ (1977) "'Mind Mirror' EEG Identifies States of Awareness," *Brain/Mind Bulletin* 2, No. 20.

Capra, Fritjof. 1982. *The Turning Point*. New York: Bantam Books, Inc.

Dreikurs, Rudolf. 1967. *Psychodynamics, Psychotherapy, and Counselling*. Chicago: Alfred Adler Institute.

_____. 1953. *Fundamentals of Adlerian Psychology*. Chicago: Alfred Adler Institute.

Freud, Sigmund. 1920. *Introductory Lectures to Psychoanalysis*. New York: Boni & Liveright.

_____. 1955. Standard Edition. London: Hogarth Press. Figures refer to volume and page number in this edition.
Studies in Hysteria. 1893-95. 2:1.
Inhibitions, Symptoms and Anxieties, 1926. 20:77.

Fromm, Erich. 1973. *The Anatomy of Human Destructiveness*. New York: Holt, Rinehart and Winston.

_____. 1947. *Man For Himself*. New York: Rinehart and Company.

_____. 1941. *Escape From Freedom*. New York: Farrar and Rinehart, Inc.

Geier, John G. 1967. "A Trait Approach to the Study of Leadership in Small Groups." *The Journal of Communication*, December.

——————— . 1970. "Small Group Discussion Versus the Lecture Method: Experimental Study in Individual Decision-Making with Hypertensive Patients." *Western Speech,* Winter.

——————— . 1979. *The Personal Profile System.* Minneapolis: Performax Systems International, Inc.

Gilligan, Carol. 1982. *In A Different Voice.* Cambridge, Massachusetts: Harvard University Press.

Havice, Doris Webster. 1977. *Personality Typing: Uses and Misuses,* Washington D.C.: University Press of America.™

James, W. 1890. *The Principles of Psychology.* New York: Henry Holt & Co.

——————— , and Lange, C.G. 1922. *The Emotions.* Baltimore: Williams & Wilkins.

Jantsch, Erich. 1980. *The Self-Organizing Universe.* New York: Pergamon.

Jourard, Sidney M. 1963. *Personal Adjustment.* New York: MacMillan Co.

Jung, Carl Gustav. 1928. "On Psychic Energy." Read, Herbert, Fordham, Michael, and Adler, Gerhard, eds. *The Collected Works of Carl G. Jung,* Vol. 8. Princeton: Princeton University Press.

——————— . 1923. "Psychological Types." CW, Vol. 6.

——————— . 1929. "Problems of Modern Psychotherapy." CW, Vol. 16.

——————— . 1936. "The Concept of the Collective Unconscious." CW, Vol. 9.

——————— . 1951. "On Synchronicity." CW, Vol. 8.

Kohlberg, Lawrence. 1964. *Development of Moral Character and Moral Ideology, Review of Child Development Research,* Vol. I, eds. M.S. Hoffman and L.W. Hoffman. New York: Russell Sage Foundation.

Kretschmer, E. 1925. *Physique and Character.* New York: Harcourt Brace.

Kroenke, K., Wood, D., Mangelsdorff, A., Meier, N., Powell, J. 1988. "Chronic Fatigue in Primary Care, Prevalence, Patient Characteristics, and Outcome." *Journal of American Medical Association.* Vol. 260.

LeShan, Lawrence L. 1977. *You Can Fight For Your Life.* New York: Evans.

Lessing, Doris. 1980. *The Marriages Between Zones Three, Four, and Five.* New York: Alfred A. Knopf.

MacLean, Paul D. 1973. "A Triune Concept of the Brain and Behavior." T. Boag and D. Campbell, eds., *The Hincks Memorial Lectures*. Toronto: University of Toronto Press.

Marston, William Moulton. 1928. *Emotions of Normal People*. London: Harcourt, Brace & Co.

Moyers, Bill. 1988. "Interview with Northrup Frye," *Bill Moyers' World of Ideas*. Public Broadcasting System.

Pavlov, Ivan. 1960. *Conditioned Reflexes*. New York: Dover Publications, Inc.

Reich, Wilhelm. 1949. *Character Analysis*. New York: Orgone Institute Press.

Sheldon, W.H. and Stevens, S.S. 1942. *The Varieties of Temperament*. New York: Harper.

Simonton, O. Carl, Matthews-Simonton, Stephanie, and Creighton, James. 1978. *Getting Well Again*. Los Angeles: Tarcher.

Skinner, B.F. 1953. *Science and Human Behavior*. New York: MacMillan.

Sullivan, Harry S. 1953. *The Interpersonal Theory of Psychiatry*. New York: Norton & Co., Inc.

Titchner, E.B. 1912. *Text Book of Psychology*. New York.

Wundt, W. 1893. *Physiologische Psychologie*. Vol. 3.

Index

About The Authors

Dr. John Geier's career has encompassed many roles: scientific research, education and business and university administration. His research efforts in personality theory began with his doctoral studies in psychology at the University of Minnesota. His research into individuals' perceptions of tasks and interpersonal relationships provided models of health team compatibility and productiveness in clinics throughout the world. Later, these models were transferred to business and industry, resulting in the founding of John Geier and Associates, Inc. This organization evolved into the premier training and publishing company, Performax Systems International, Inc. One of Geier's works, *The Personal Profile System*, has sold in excess of five million copies.

Following the acquisition of Performax by the Carlson Companies, Geier headed the Division of Continuing Education at the University of Arizona for three years. More recently, in collaboration with Ms. Dorothy Downey, he has founded Aristos Publishing House and developed this first volume of the Aristos trilogy.

Ms. Dorothy Downey holds masters degrees in Public Health and Psychiatric Nursing from the University of Minnesota. During her tenure at the University of Minnesota, she developed and applied models of preventive health to families in all strata of society. She also developed practical models of interpersonal relationships, such as the contractual agreement between patient and professional that would safeguard patients' rights.

Downey's contact with Geier at the University of Minnesota in 1968 provided the impetus for utilizing her therapeutic models in business and industry as well as in nonprofit organizations. She assumed the administrative role of senior vice president for Geier and Associates and later for Performax Systems. With responsibilities that included the directing of research and development of materials, she was one of the pioneers, along with Geier, in introducing self-responding, self-scoring, and self-interpreting behavioral instruments. Since 1983, her time and effort have been exclusively devoted to the development of materials that are now available through Aristos Publishing House.

Aristos Publishing House is dedicated to the research, development, and distribution of materials that energize both young and old in living constructive and responsible lives.

The authors' works include the following Performax materials. They are in use by over 25,000 consultants throughout the United States and abroad.

- *The Personal Profile System* (translated into five languages)—Geier
- *The Action Projection System*—Geier
- *The Library of Classical Profile Patterns* (15 volumes)—Geier and Downey
- *Climate Impact Profile*—Geier, Downey, and M. Johnson
- *Persona Matrix with Workbook*—Geier
- *The Child's Profile*—Geier and Downey
- *Child's Library Set* (15 volumes)—Geier and Downey
- *Attitudinal Listening Profile*—Geier and Downey
- *Job Factor Analysis*—Geier
- *Activity Perception System*—Geier
- *Leadership Role Perception*—Geier